Applications of Rasch Measurement in Learning Environments Research

D0745416

ADVANCES IN LEARNING ENVIRONMENTS RESEARCH
Volume 2

Scope

The historical beginnings of the field of learning environments go back approximately 40 years. A milestone in the development of this field was the establishment in 1984 of the American Educational Research Association (AERA) Special Interest Group (SIG) on Learning Environments, which continues to thrive today as one of AERA's most international and successful SIGs. A second milestone in the learning environments field was the birth in 1998 of *Learning Environments Research: An International Journal* (LER), which fills an important and unique niche.

The next logical step in the evolution of the field of learning environments is the initiation of this book series, *Advances in Learning Environments Research,* to complement the work of the AERA SIG and LER. This book series provides a forum for the publication of book-length manuscripts that enable topics to be covered at a depth and breadth not permitted within the scope of either a conference paper or a journal article.

The *Advances in Learning Environments Research* series is intended to be broad, covering either authored books or edited volumes, and either original research reports or reviews of bodies of past research. A diversity of theoretical frameworks and research methods, including use of multimethods, is encouraged. In addition to school and university learning environments, the scope of this book series encompasses lifelong learning environments, information technology learning environments, and various out-of-school 'informal' learning environments (museums, environmental centres, etc.).

Applications of Rasch Measurement in Learning Environments Research

Edited by

Robert F. Cavanagh
Curtin University of Technology, Australia

Russell F. Waugh
Edith Cowan University, Australia

SENSE PUBLISHERS
ROTTERDAM/BOSTON/TAIPEI

A C.I.P. record for this book is available from the Library of Congress.

ISBN: 978-94-6091-491-1 (paperback)
ISBN: 978-94-6091-492-8 (hardback)
ISBN: 978-94-6091-493-5 (e-book)

Published by: Sense Publishers,
P.O. Box 21858,
3001 AW Rotterdam,
The Netherlands
www.sensepublishers.com

Printed on acid-free paper

CONTENTS

CONTENTS

AUTHOR BIOGRAPHIES

Yuko ASANO-CAVANAGH, BA (Tokyo Woman's Christian University), MEd (Tokyo Gakugei University), MA (ANU), PhD (ANU), specialises in semantics and pragmatics of Japanese and cross-cultural communication. She currently teaches Japanese and Japanese studies in the Department of Asian languages at Curtin University of Technology. Her research projects include semantic analyses of Japanese epistemic expressions, using the framework of the Natural Semantic Metalanguage Theory. The research approach she applies is scientific and strongly theoretically grounded. Recently, her research interests have expanded to include study of the pedagogy in Language other than English classrooms. She is a member of the Australian Linguistic Society, the Society for Teaching Japanese as a Foreign Language and the Australian Association for Research in Education.

Asrijanty ASRIL is a PhD student in the Graduate School of Education, University of Western Australia. Her PhD thesis examines the Indonesian Scholastic Aptitude Test which has been developed in Indonesian especially for Tertiary Entrance purposes by using Rasch analysis. She holds the degrees of B.Psych., M.SocResEval (MU).

Trevor BOND is currently Professor at James Cook University, having recently been Head of Department and Professor at the Hong Kong Institute of Education since 2005. He holds the degrees of Cert.Teaching, Dip.Phys.Ed, BEd (Hons.) and PhD. He is a widely published developmental psychologist and specialist Rasch researcher who has book chapters and articles in refereed journals around the world. He is co-author (with Christine Fox) of the widely used and acclaimed book: *Applying the Rasch Model: Fundamental Measurement in the Human Sciences*. Professor Bond has been instrumental in organizing and promoting Rasch measurement in Asia, particularly through his instigation of the Pacific Rim Objective Measurement Symposia.

Robert F. CAVANAGH is Professor in the Faculty of Education at Curtin University. He holds the degrees of BEd, MSc (Sc.Ed.), PhD. He is currently Director of Postgraduate Research in the Faculty of Education. Professor Cavanagh has many years experience in supervising postgraduate research students, including those researching primary and secondary education. He is coordinator of postgraduate studies at Curtin University where he teaches units in educational leadership, educational change and research methods. He has supervised many postgraduate students in Australia as well as overseas postgraduate students from countries such as Korea and Brunei and he is an expert in Rasch measurement as applied to education. Rob can be contacted at R.Cavanagh@curtin.edu.au

Jessica ELDERFIELD holds the degrees of B.Psych, MEd and has worked with the researchers at Edith Cowan University in relation to literacy and numeracy standards for some time. Her Master's Degree Thesis, Comparing Single-Level and Multilevel Regression Models in Analysing Rasch Measures of Numeracy, won the Western Australian Institute of Educational Research Prize in Education for 2008.

Sarah HOPKINS is Assistant Professor in the Graduate School of Education, University of Western Australia. She holds the degrees of PhD (Flinders), MEdStudies (Flinders), BEd (Melbourne). Dr Hopkins coordinates curriculum units for preparing graduate students to teach Mathematics in primary and secondary schools. Her research activities focus on mathematical learning difficulties, and the assessment of teaching quality and teaching effectiveness.

Stephen HOUGHTON is Winthrop Professor of Special Education and a registered psychologist in the Graduate School of Education, University of Western Australia, where he is Director of the Centre for Child and Adolescent Related Disorders. The developmental trajectories related to psychopathy and other forms of antisocial behaviour have been a major focus of Winthrop Professor Houghton's research since he arrived at UWA. The calibre of his research is reflected in 20 grants he has received from the Australian Research Council, The National Health and Medical Research Council, Healthway and the Commonwealth Department of Human Services and Health. To date, he has published over 100 articles in peer-reviewed journals, in addition to three books and seven book chapters. He is an editor of the British Journal of Educational Psychology and an editorial board member of three other international journals.

Stephen HUMPHRY is an Associate Professor with the Graduate School of Education at the University of Western Australia. He teaches masters units in Educational Assessment, Measurement and Evaluation and is involved in a number of research projects. He currently holds an Australian Research Council grant entitled *Maintaining a Precise Invariant Unit in State, National and International Assessment* with Professor David Andrich of UWA. He is a member of the Curriculum Council's Expert Measurement and Assessment Advisory Group and is involved in research on assessment and measurement, more broadly in Western Australia and Australia. He has presented at international conferences and has visited and worked with international organisations and institutions, including MetaMetrics and the Oxford University Centre for Educational Assessment. He holds the degrees of BPsych, PhD.

Penelope KENNISH graduated with honours from the University of Northumbria, England and has worked as a commercial and social researcher for the last 20 years. Currently employed by the Department of Education in Western Australia, she works in the Evaluation Branch. Penelope is in the third year of her PhD in Education at Curtin University of Technology, investigating factors that impact upon senior student engagement in classroom learning.

Deslea KONZA is Associate Professor in the Faculty of Education and Arts at Edith Cowan University and a specialist in language education. She holds the degrees of BA, Dip.Ed., Dip. Special Ed., MEd, and PhD. Deslea has had wide experience teaching students of all ages with a range of special needs, including those associated with blindness, profound hearing impairment, intellectual disabilities, physical disabilities and multiple disabilities. She also has wide experience in language development and she has published widely in books and journal articles throughout her university career.

Claire MALEY is an early childhood teacher employed with the Catholic Education Office in Townsville. She has recently completed her PhD which applied the Rasch model to the widely used Goodenough-Harris Drawing Test. Claire graduated with first class honours in the School of Education at James Cook University and was awarded an Australian Postgraduate Award scholarship to support her doctoral studies. Claire has presented in conferences in Australia as well as in Hong Kong, Tokyo and Taiwan.

Ida MARAIS is Assistant Professor in the Graduate School of Education, University of Western Australia. She holds the degrees of BSc Hons (1st Class), MSC Hons (1st Class) and PhD. Ida worked as computer analyst/programmer before being awarded a University of Auckland Doctoral Scholarship and studying cognitive psychology. Since then she has worked in the fields of Pyschology and Education in New Zealand and Australia. Currently, she is a research Fellow at the Psycho-metrics laboratory at the Graduate School of Education, University of Western Australia. Her research activities focus on psychological and educational measure-ment, especially the measurement of change over time, quantitative research methods and data simulation.

Roslyn NEILSON lectures in the Faculty of Education at the University of Wollongong, NSW, and also works as a Speech-Language Pathologist, specialising in language and literacy difficulties. She holds the degrees of B.A. (Hons.), M.Sc. (Applied), and Ph.D. (Psychology). Her doctoral dissertation was on phonological awareness in normally-developing readers and children with reading difficulties. She has developed several phonological awareness assessment tools, including the widely-used Astronaut Invented Spelling Test. rneilson@ozemail.com.au

Paul NEWHOUSE (Ph.D) is an Associate Professor in educational computing at Edith Cowan University in Perth, Western Australia. He is currently the director of the Centre for Schooling and Learning Technologies (CSaLT) in the School of Education. He has always considered himself to be both an educator and learner starting in an innovative state secondary school in Western Australia where he had the opportunity to implement a range of programmes and strategies across the curriculum based on emerging pedagogical philosophies. Since then he has had the privilege of conducting research in schools, developing curriculum, and sharing his experiences with pre-service and practicing teachers for over seventeen years at two universities. His focus is on implementation strategies for using computers to support learning in schools, particularly as applied to portable computing, and curriculum development in technology education.

Pey-Tee OON is currently a Research Scholar at the National Institute of Education in Nanyang Technological University in Singapore. Her PhD research focuses on the declining enrolment in physics at the university level. She holds the degrees of BSc (Hons) in Physics and MEd in Science. She has wide experience in the teaching of physics at the secondary level. She has also experience in the tutoring of students in research methodology at the university level. oonpeytee@yahoo.com

Sivanes PHILLIPSON is an Assistant Professor at the Department of Education Studies, Hong Kong Baptist University, with a PhD in developmental psychology. Dr Phillipson teaches a number of developmental psychology and teacher education courses including Human Development and The Professional Teacher. Her research interests include context of achievement in relation to Chinese learners and their parents, and the context of innovative learning and assessment. Sivanes has a special interest in Rasch Measurement, Structural Equation Modeling and Mediation Analysis, and widely uses these methods in her own research. She has published internationally in books and journals in the wider field of education and specifically in educational and developmental psychology. sivanes@hkbu.edu.hk

R SUBRAMANIAM is an Associate Professor in the Natural Sciences & Science Education Academic Group at the National Institute of Education in Nanyang Technological University. From July 2006 to Nov 2007, he was Associate Dean (Educational Research), and from Nov 2007 to Dec 2008, he was Associate Dean (Graduate Academic Programs). He has diverse research interests: physics education, chemistry education, primary science education, assessment and evaluation, ICT in science education, informal science education, science teacher education, and science communication. He has 55 research papers to his credit in international refereed journals, 25 refereed chapters in edited books of international publishers, and five books published by major international publishers. subramaniam.r@nie.edu.sg

Emma TOMKINSON is a specialist teacher of the Gifted and Talented. She holds the degrees of BA, Dip. Ed., MEd and has worked in Perth (Western Australia) and Sydney (New South Wales) helping gifted and talented students.

Rebecca WALKER is a PhD student in the Graduate School of Education, University of Western Australia. She holds the degrees of MEd (ECU), Grad Dip (ECU), B App Sc (ECU). She has extensive experience teaching in secondary schools and is regarded as a specialist teacher. Rebecca can be contacted at rebw2003@yahoo.co.au

Russell F. WAUGH works at two universities in Perth, Western Australia. He is a Professor in the Faculty of Education and Arts at Edith Cowan University and a Senior Research Fellow in the Graduate School of Education at the University of Western Australia, and he supervises doctoral students at both. He holds the degrees of BSc, MSc, BEd, MEd, and PhD (UWA). Russell is a former Fulbright Scholar and specializes in Rasch measurement using the Rasch Unidimensional Measurement Models (RUMM) computer program developed by Professors David Andrich, Barry Sheridan and Guanzhong Luo, mainly applied to psychological and educational variables in the human sciences. Russell has published widely through journals and books, nearly all with Rasch measures. Russell can be contacted at r.waugh@ecu.edu.au

Adrian YOUNG holds the degrees of BSc, MSc and Grad.Dip.Ed. and is currently completing a PhD thesis. He has been a special education teacher, university lecturer, Education Department manager and Military Psychologist in various countries such as New Zealand, Australia and the United Kingdom.

PREFACE

Since 1960, when Georg Rasch (1901–1981) produced his now well-accepted measurement model published as the "Probabilistic Models for Some Intelligence and Attainment Tests" (Rasch, 1960), there has been a quiet revolution in measuring variables in education, psychology, business and medicine. Rasch's initial measurement model, now called the Simple Logistic Model of Rasch, only applied to items in a dichotomous format, such as no/yes, disagree/agree, wrong/right. That measurement model has now been extended to more than two scoring categories and is called the Partial Credit Model of Rasch or the Polytomous Logistic Model or the Rating Scale Model. Rasch measurement has also been extended to include a judges model (Many Facets Rasch Measurement Computer Program by J.M. Linacre) and the Rasch Pair-Wise Comparison Model (where many people compare many essays, projects or assignments in pairs as worse/better).

Rasch measurement and the associated computer programs offer advantages over Classical Test Theory (sometimes called True Score Theory) which had been the dominant measurement model in schools and universities up until recent years. Rasch computer programs like RUMM and WINSTEPS: (1) produce linear, unidimensional scales; (2) require that data must fit the measurement model; (3) produce scale-free person measures; (4) produce sample-free item difficulties; (5) calculate standard errors; (6) estimate person measures and item difficulties on the same linear scale in standard units (logits); and (7) check that the scoring system is being used logically and consistently. These are major advantages over Classical Test Theory. Rasch measurement is now being widely used in 'high-stakes' testing in many developed nations and by many Year 12 Certification and Assessment bodies, sometimes also incorporating university entrance measures. The reasons for this are mainly advances in computer power and the widespread use of personal computers that can handle large data sets, together with the creation of powerful Rasch measurement computer programs like Rasch Unidimensional Measurement Models (RUMM2030) and WINSTEPS.

An additional reason for the increased use of Rasch measurement is that Rasch measures have been shown to be better than 'measures' based on Classical Test Theory (just using the total score as the 'measure' on a set of items after, and most often not even with, Confirmatory Factor Analysis). Rasch measurement requires the researcher to design the items in a scale from easy to hard, but with certain conditions in mind. The conditions mean that the probability of answering positively must be related to the difference between the person measure (technically the person parameter) and the item difficulty (technically the item parameter). Using a simple example, this means that persons with low measures are expected to answer the easy items positively (but not the medium or hard items); persons with medium measures are expected to answer the easy and medium items positively (but not the hard items); and persons with high measures are expected to answer the easy, medium and hard items positively. Items which do not fit this pattern are discarded as not part of the measure. It also should be noted the Rasch measurement model is based on probabilities and so it allows for the view that a person with a high measure will not answer a medium or easy item positively, sometimes.

While all education and psychological variables are in one sense multi-dimensional, because they involve complex brain, attitude, self-efficacy and sometimes behaviours, Rasch measures allow person responses to be predicted accurately on all items that fit the measurement model using only a person parameter (as the person measure), and an item parameter on the same scale (as the difficulty measure). In this sense, the measure is said to be unidimensional and this is very useful in research. If there are useful 'mathematical laws' that can be created or found in the field of education (teaching and learning), then it seems likely that they will be found using linear, unidimensional scales based on Rasch measurement models. This is one area that needs special attention from educational researchers.

The research papers in this book have been produced by highly competent people working with Rasch measures to understand and interpret issues at the forefront of variables related to Learning Environments Research. The research papers cover a variety of issues relating to the Educational Learning Environment. We thank all the contributors for their input and for their efforts, and we hope that their work inspires you to improve your research by using Rasch measurement and the two current best Rasch computer programs in the world today, RUMM 2030 and WINSTEPS.

Robert F. Cavanagh (Curtin University of Technology) and
Russell F. Waugh (Edith Cowan University and the University of Western Australia)
March 2011

SECTION ONE: THE UTILITY OF RASCH MEASUREMENT FOR THE LEARNING ENVIRONMENT

ROBERT F. CAVANAGH AND RUSSELL F. WAUGH

1. THE UTILITY OF RASCH MEASUREMENT FOR LEARNING ENVIRONMENTS RESEARCH

The purpose of this introductory chapter is to show in simple ways, how using a Rasch model can benefit learning environments research. As such, it is deliberately non-technical and written for readers who do not wish to pursue complex mathematical matters either now, or perhaps not even later. There are many established instructional courses and texts on applying the Rasch model and we assume that researchers requiring a more formal and theoretical understanding will consult these (for example, Bond & Fox, 2007). The chapter is structured into a series of sections each dealing with a particular aspect of the model or its application. The first section is about measurement in the human sciences.

MEASUREMENT IN THE HUMAN SCIENCES

According to quantity calculus (de Boer, 1994), measuring quantities in the physical sciences requires the assignment of a numerical value and a unit of measurement. For example, if my weight is 90 kilograms, the numerical value is 90 and the unit is the kilogram. When the metric system was first developed, standard one kilogram masses were available and my weight should be the same as the weight of 90 of these masses. We could concatenate 90 of these masses to measure my weight. Similarly, other fundamental units such as the metre are available in the physical sciences and measurement using these is also possible using concatenation. When a system of units is used to measure a quantity, the numerical value is 'sufficient' for comparing different objects in different places and at different times. The challenge for social science metricians is to develop measures that are 'invariant' in the same way as physical science measures. This has been done for reading ability. The Lexile Reading Framework is used to measure an individual's reading ability and this ability is reported as a number of Lexiles.

The obvious difficulty in constructing such measures in the human sciences is the unclear nature of the qualities of persons and phenomena to be quantified. Attitudes towards the teacher, beliefs about collaborative learning, reading ability and so on, are latent traits not directly observable or physically manifest. Does this mean we cannot measure these qualities of persons? The answer is 'no' and the part of the solution to this problem lies in the theory of conjoint measurement (Luce & Tukey, 1964).

R.F. Cavanagh and R.F. Waugh (eds.), Applications of Rasch Measurement
in Learning Environments Research, 3–15.

Consider the density of objects which we know is defined as the ratio of the mass of an object to its volume. Mass and volume are observable qualities of objects. We can feel mass by picking up an object and can see its volume and feel its size. But unless we examine objects of either the same volume or the same mass, the differences in density are not apparent. And, when we constrain observations by fixing either mass or volume, we limit the objects whose density is being described to objects of either similar mass or of similar volume. Conjoint measurement theory requires concurrent consideration and testing of multiple attributes of a quantity. For example, observing the mass and volume of many objects of differing density and recording these in a table such as Table 1 below. In this table, the observations of mass and volume have been ordered from small to large. The table has additive scales for mass and volume.

Table 1. Conjoint measurement of density

Mass (kilograms)	0.2	0.4	0.6	0.8	1.0
Volume (litres)					
0.5	0.40	0.80	1.20	1.60	2.00
1	0.20	0.40	0.60	0.80	1.00
1.5	0.13	0.27	0.40	0.53	0.67
2	0.10	0.20	0.30	0.40	0.50
2.5	0.05	0.16	0.24	0.32	0.40

The diagonal relation between cells (the dotted line) shows that as mass increases and volume decreases, density increases. The matrix provides a representation of density that is generalisable to objects of different masses and sizes. The crucial aspect of this representation is the ordering within the matrix. Knowing the ordering (greater than/less than) of masses and volumes enables us to predict with a high degree of certainty, the ordering of density (more dense/less dense). Although density cannot be physically concatenated, it can be ordered by knowing the order of quantities that can be physically concatenated.

Measuring a latent trait in persons, for example, the ability to perform simple arithmetic operations, requires the abilities of different persons to be ordered from less ability to more ability. Because the ability is latent, we cannot observe it directly. Instead we need to make observations that can be ordered and then these will enable ordering of the abilities of different persons. Recording the completion or non-completion of tasks can provide the observational data we require.

4

Of course, the tasks must test the ability under examination which necessitates us having a very clear understanding of the nature of that ability. To assess this ability, we can observe the proportion of tasks that each person can complete and we can also observe the proportion of persons that can complete each task. A set of such observations for ten persons attempting six tasks is presented in Table 2 below. The data has been aggregated for persons and for items to show the proportion of tasks completed by each person and also the proportion of persons completing each task. It has then been sorted by person ability (number of tasks completed) and task difficulty (difficult tasks had a low level of completion).

Table 2. Data matrix with persons ordered by ability and items ordered by difficulty

Task Persons	A	B	C	D	E	F	Proportion correct (Person ability)
George	☺	☺	☺	☺	☺	☺	100%
Avril	☺	☺	☺	☺	☺		83%
Edward	☺	☺	☺		☺		66%
June	☺	☺	☺	☺			66%
Ben	☺	☺	☺	☺			66%
Hannibal	☺		☺	☺			50%
Claudette	☺	☺		☺			50%
Francis	☺	☺					33%
Ivor	☺	☺					33%
Desmond	☺						17%
Proportion correct (Item difficulty)	100%	80%	60%	60%	30%	10%	

As was the case with the table of density data, the two scales are additive and thus person performance and item difficulty data are ordered. Similar to the diagonal relation in the density matrix, the values of person ability and item difficulty increase with the level of a third attribute. In this instance the attribute is the probability of task completion.

In conclusion, when data from tests, attitude scales or other instruments demonstrate the properties shown in Tables 1 and 2, this is evidence of additive conjoint measurement. Measures of latent traits in the human sciences can be constructed provided there is an additive measurement structure within data produced by the measure. These measures are invariant because although they are sensitive to differing levels of the trait in different persons, the scale against which the persons are measured does not vary. The physical analogy is a thermometer that is sensitive to different temperatures but the scale is fixed. We believe additive conjoint measurement is an important requirement for human science research because in its absence, comparisons between groups and individuals cannot be made with a high degree of surety. Additive conjoint measurement is a requirement for data to fit the Rasch model (Rasch, 1960).

DIMENSIONALITY

A Rasch model analysis conducted with computer programs such as RUMM2020 (RUMMLab, 2007) and WINSTEPS (Linacre, 2009) tests how well data fits the Rasch model with the requirement that items are indicating a common construct. This commonality between items is not manifest as high inter-item correlation in data. Indeed low or negative correlations are to be expected. The Rasch model requires the trait of interest to be unidimensional with the majority of variance within the data accounted for by a single factor. Consequently, unidimensionality is not tested by a factor analysis of raw scores. Alternatively, when using a Rasch model computer program an item-trait interaction chi-square test is applied. Take the lowest total score r. Each person with total score r answers each item and records a response. The program compares the person response for Item 1 (for those that have total score r), the person response for Item 2 (for those that have total score r), the person response for Item 3 (for those that have total score r), and so on. It then repeats this procedure for those persons who have total score $r + 1$, and so on, over all items along the scale. The idea is that there should be good agreement about which items are easy and which are hard all along the scale and this occurs when there is a good fit to the Rasch measurement model. The item-trait interaction chi-square provides a summary statistic for dimensionality. The probability should be p > 0.05 and preferably much higher. This would indicate that there is no significant statistical interaction between the responses to the items and the person measures along the scale. That is, there is good agreement between all persons about the difficulties of the items along the scale and that a single measure (technically the person parameter) can accurately predict each person's response to each item. It is in this sense, in Rasch measurement, that the measure is unidimensional. The total score is not a unidimensional measure, unless the data fit a Rasch measurement model.

   Unidimensionality can also be assessed by Principal Components Factor Analysis of the residual data after the Rasch measure has been extracted. If the data are unidimensional, there should be minimal structure within the residuals. Table 3 shows the Principal Component factor loadings for nine items. Although one of the nine factors accounted to 18% of the variance, the higher loadings (bolded type) are distributed across different factors suggesting mainly noise is left after the measure was extracted.

Table 3. PC loadings for course experience survey (N=194 secondary school students)

PC1	PC2	PC3	PC4	PC5	PC6	PC7	PC8	PC9
−0.44	−0.43	−0.31	0.03	−0.49	0.49	−0.17	0.10	0.04
−0.16	**0.71**	−0.29	−0.21	−0.15	−0.14	−0.36	−0.42	0.03
0.44	−0.32	0.31	−0.57	0.07	−0.17	−0.43	0.23	0.04
−0.27	−0.52	−0.53	0.01	0.31	−0.47	0.20	−0.11	0.04
0.33	0.39	−0.43	0.11	**0.56**	**0.39**	0.01	0.27	0.03
−0.42	−0.06	**0.63**	−0.19	0.38	0.32	0.20	−0.32	0.04
−0.56	0.49	0.23	−0.05	−0.18	−0.27	0.23	0.48	0.03
0.19	−0.04	0.36	**0.86**	−0.02	−0.15	−0.26	−0.04	0.04
0.72	0.07	0.01	−0.10	−0.43	0.03	0.51	−0.14	0.04

Many of the instruments developed for learning environment research are based on multi-dimensional construct models and multi-dimensionality in the data is confirmed by Confirmatory Factor Analysis. For these instruments, multiple Rasch analyses are recommended – one for each dimension. One benefit of the multiple analyses is provision of detailed diagnostic information on each of what would originally have been sub-scales. Another is that the unidimensionality of the sub-scale data is confirmed independently of the other sub-scales. When sub-scale data are to be subject to multi-variate analyses such as multi-level modeling, scale testing and refinement using the Rasch model negates the need for sample splitting when multiple parametric analyses are performed (for example, when proceeding from Exploratory to Confirmatory Factor Analysis).

NOTE: Strictly, no variable in education is probably unidimensional since they all involve complex interactions between 'something' in the brain, attitudes, self-efficacy and behaviour (hand movements, hand/eye coordination and so on). But, we can use a single measure to predict accurately a person's response to an item.

TREATMENT OF ERRORS

The traditional treatment of measurement errors applies to Classical Test Theory and True Score Theory. According to these theories, a person's score is comprised of two additive components. One component is the 'true' level (for example, true ability) and the other is an error component (random error). The smaller the error component, the greater the test reliability. Traditionally, reliability is a property of the test and assumes that precision is the same across all the test scores irrespective of where the score is situated on the scale. However, scores at the extremities of a scale are less precise than those in the centre due to differences in the comparative amounts of information available about the respective scores. These differences in the precision of scores are estimated in a Rasch model analysis. Each person's score has an associated error of measurement – the standard error of measurement. Similarly, the errors of measurement in item difficulty are also estimated. Notwithstanding the desirability of having maximum information on persons and items, the availability of standard errors enables a more accurate comparison of data from different instruments or from different groups of people from the same instrument. Alternatively, correlational techniques for comparing instruments and groups are less accurate.

GENERALISABILITY

Measures that are invariant do not show bias or function differently as a result of person factors such as gender. A Rasch analysis estimates an expected value for an item for persons with the same ability level. These predicted values can then be compared with observed values for different groups of person (for example, males and females). RUMM2020 generates Item Characteristic Curves (ICC) and overlays the observed values for groups of persons. Figure 1 below is the ICC for Item Four in the *Course Experience Survey* with inclusion of observed scores for females and males. The observed scores for three class intervals of males and females are plotted. When male and female affirmativeness levels (the 'person location logit' on the horizontal axis), were the same for the respective class intervals, the observed female scores were higher than those of the males. This item is favourably biased towards female students.

In contrast, for Item Seven in the *Course Experience Survey*, the observed scores for females and males with the same affirmativeness level do not differ significantly. This item does not display differential functioning.

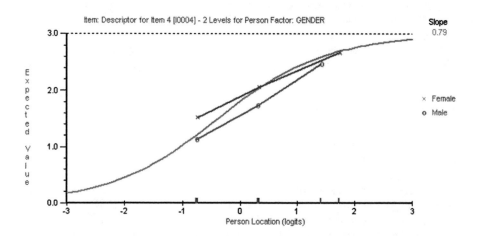

Figure 1. Differential item functioning – course experience survey (N=194).

Identification of differential item functioning (DIF) in learning environment research is particularly important. We expect the constituent items in instruments to perform the same for females and males (see Figure 2), for children of different ages, for children of different cultural backgrounds, for different class groups and for different subject areas. If there is bias at the item level due to DIF, between-group comparisons become unreliable. Interestingly, the absence of DIF does not reduce instrument discrimination. This issue is examined in the next section.

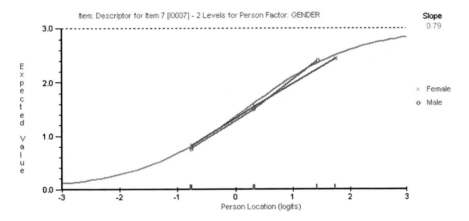

Figure 2. No differential item functioning – course experience survey (N=194).

DISCRIMINATION

The scores estimated for persons or groups need to reflect their ability level (affirmativeness in the case of attitude scales). Persons who have more of the trait of interest should be scored higher. The Rasch model estimates person ability on a logit scale. A logit is the logarithmic odds of a person completing a task or affirming a statement in an attitude scale. Figure 3 shows the distributions of *Course Experience Survey* scores for students reporting on either their favourite or non-favourite school subject. Students reporting on their favourite subject (mean score 0.70 logits) were more affirmative than those reporting on a non-favourite subject (mean score -0.38 logits).

Often in quantitative learning environment research, the research objectives concern differences between groups of persons or differences over time. In both cases, the Rash technique is to plot different data sets on the same scale so that all scores are conjointly calibrated. The person scores have been calibrated against the same item difficulty measures. Then the distributions of scores are compared by graphical (Person-Item Distribution) or statistical (Analysis of Variance) methods. For the data displayed in Figure 3, One-way Analysis of Variance estimated the F-statistic as 51.3 ($p < 0.01$).

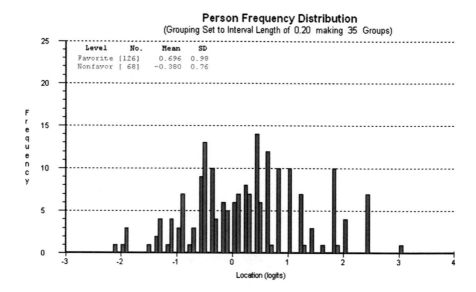

Figure 3. Person frequency distributions – course experience survey (N=194).

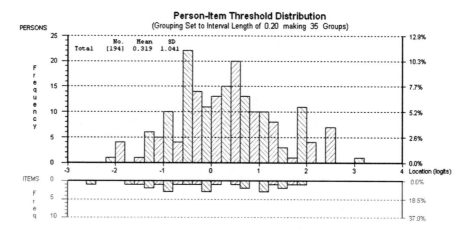

Figure 4. Person-item threshold distribution – course experience survey (N=194).

TARGETING

In order to accurately and equitably measure attributes of persons, the measure needs to provide the subjects with tasks of varying difficulty that are commensurate with their level of ability. Estimating the ability level of a high performing student requires that a task of high difficulty is provided for that student. Similarly, low ability students should be provided with the opportunity to display competence at a much lower level. The additive aspect of measurement referred to in the first section also requires that the easier tasks are attained by the higher ability persons. Application of the Rasch model allows both person ability scores (person location) and item difficulty scores to be plotted on a common logit scale. Person scores are plotted against item difficulty estimates for *Course Experience Survey* data in Figure 4. The 27 data points for the item difficulty plot are the result of items being responded to on a four category response scale.

RESPONSE SCALE CATEGORIES

Many of the learning environment instruments utilise an ordinal response scale that allows respondents to express varying degrees of agreement with a stem statement. The response categories whether numbered or not, are usually converted into scores for data analysis. For example, a four point scale could have 'none of the time' scored as 1, 'some of the time' scored as 2, 'most of the time' scored as 3, 'all of the time' scored as 4. The fundamental issue in the scoring process is whether the numbers allocated to the respective response categories denote categorical/nominal data or ordinal data. Irrespective of the scoring intentions, assumptions of ordinality should be tested before statistical or even arithmetic operations are performed with the data. The Rasch Rating Scale model (Andrich, 1978a, 1978b &1978c) estimates item thresholds that show the response patterns for each item in relation to the level of affirmativeness. A threshold is the person location (logit) at which there is an equal probability of persons with the same affirmativeness selecting either of two adjacent response categories. On either side of the threshold we would expect the choice of response category to be related to the level of affirmativeness. More affirmative persons are expected to select a more affirmative category. A Rasch analysis estimates the thresholds allowing the order to be scrutinised. Figure 5 below shows the Category Probability Curves for Item Seven in the *Course Experience Survey*. Students responded on a five-point scale. The Rasch model has been applied to generate curves for each response category that show the probability of how students with differing levels of affirmativeness (horizontal person location logit scale) will choose that category. Students with an affirmatives level of -0.5 logits have an almost equal probability of selecting categories 0, 1 or 2. Alternatively, choices between Categories 2 and 3 are more related to the student's position on the person location axis. We assumed that students of lower affirmativeness were not able to make a logical choice between the lower categories so data on two categories (0 and 1) were combined into a single category. The Category Probability Curves for Item Seven using a four point scoring model are presented in Figure 6. In this display, the thresholds are ordered according to level of student affirmativeness.

The collapsing of categories that was applied to logically order the response categories necessitates a rescoring of data if raw data are analysed. The Rasch estimations of student affirmativeness take this into account.

I0007 Descriptor for Item 7   Locn = 0.433   Spread = 0.409   FitRes = -1.677   ChiSq[Pr] = 0.400   SampleN = 195

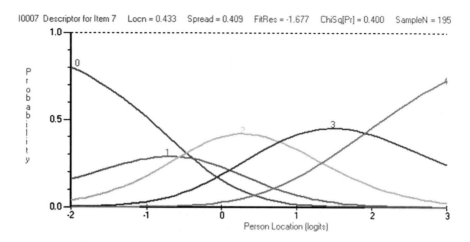

Figure 5. Five category probability curves for item seven - courses experience survey (N=194).

I0007 Descriptor for Item 7   Locn = 0.185   Spread = 0.499   FitRes = -1.030   ChiSq[Pr] = 0.415   SampleN = 194

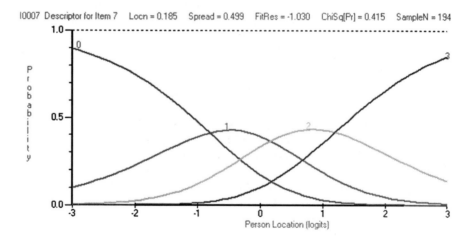

Figure 6. Four category probability curves for item seven - courses experience survey (N=194).

LINEAR SCALES AND INTERVAL DATA

Data which are interval are ordinal, but in addition, there needs to be constant equal-sized intervals which can be expressed numerically. The application of additive conjoint measurement discussed in the first section ensures ordinality in the measure of the latent trait of interest but not necessarily intervality. Rasch model computer programs (for example RUMM202020 and WINSTEPS) compute success-to-failure odds for persons and then calculate the natural logarithm of these odds (a logit). When the odds are 50:50, the logit is zero. Persons more likely to succeed at a task or affirm an attitude have a positive logit location and those less likely a negative logit location. The graphic display of person scores in Figure 4 illustrates person scores plotted on an interval scale.

The establishment of ordinality followed by conversion of ordinal data into interval data is viewed by us as an important precursor to the application of statistical tests that were developed for interval or ratio data. While there is always the possibility of a monotonic relation between raw scores and ordinal and interval data, the presence of such a relation is not guaranteed. We have reservations about parametric statistical tests being applied to data that has not been shown to be ordinal. For example, estimating correlation coefficients, multiple regression analysis, structural equation modeling and hierarchical linear modeling.

DATA-TO-MODEL FIT AND MODEL TO-DATA FIT

Rasch models are mathematical models that are applicable for ascertaining certain properties in data. The Rasch model expresses the relation between the probability of completing a task, the ability of persons and the difficulty of the task. Such a measurement model should not be confused with a model of the construct of interest – a construct model. When the data fit the Rasch model, an interval measure of the construct of interest has been created. The starting point for the measurement process is careful specification of the construct model including operation definitions, internal structure (sub-constructs, elements or facets). Following instrument development and administration, the data is then tested for fit to the measurement model which in turn enables confirmation of the hypotheses incumbent in the construct model.

This process can be contrasted with an exploration of properties of data. For example an Exploratory Factor Analysis informing the specification of a construct model. In this case, the model of the construct of interest is modified to fit the empirical data. In qualitative research, this is analogous to a grounded theory approach.

MOVING INTO THE MODERN MEASUREMENT PARADIGM

Traditional approaches to measuring attributes of persons, True Score Theory and Classical Test Theory assume that the raw score (X) obtained by any one individual is made up of a true component (T) and a random error (E) component: $X = T + E$. This basic assumption has the following consequences:

a. adding the item scores on a test to obtain the 'measure' means that almost any total score from a set of items will fit this model;

b. the total score as the 'measure' is not linear because equal differences between parts of the 'measure' do not represent equal amounts of the 'measure'. That is, the difference between 40% and 50%, for example, does not equal the same amount of knowledge (or ability) as the difference between 70% and 80%;

c. the total score does not represent any unit of the 'measure';
d. the items are NOT designed on a scale from easy to hard as would normally be expected in a' ruler' measuring ability or knowledge, for example. In contrast in a ruler measuring length, for example, the cm units are ordered linearly from low to high (1cm, 2cm, 3cm, 4cm and so on);
e. where partial scores are given for partially correct answers, no tests are done to ensure that the marking of each item is consistent and logical; and
f. the total score as the 'measure' depends on the sample used and is NOT independent as would normally be required of a linear measuring instrument. For example, a cm ruler measures length or height irrespective of who or what is being measured. It is an independent measure.

Proponents of Modern Measurement Theory such as Item response Theory and the Rasch Model often make comparisons between the properties of these theories. For example, see Table 4.

Table 4. Comparison of classical theory and item response theory features

Classical test theory	Item response theory
Measures of precision fixed for all scores	Precision measures vary across scores and items
Longer scales increase reliability	Shorter, targeted scales can be equally reliable
Test properties are sample dependent	Test properties are sample free
Mixed item formats leads to unbalanced impact on total test scores	Easily handles mixed item formats
Comparing respondents requires parallel scales	Different scales can be placed on a common metric
Summed scores are on ordinal scale	Scores are on an interval scale
Missing data is problematic	Missing data is expected
Graphical tools for item and scale analysis	

(Adapted from Reece, 2009)

We believe there are tangible benefits for learning environments research that applies the methods of Modern Measurement Theory. These methods are not new and have been used in human science research for 50 years.

CONCLUSION

In this introductory chapter, we have attempted to provide an overview of principles and techniques associated with application of the Rasch model and worthy of consideration by learning environment researchers. This is not exhaustive nor is it in-depth. The chapters which follow build upon this introduction. They also reflect the inclusive and diverse interpretations of the Rasch model and why we are convinced it is one of the ways forward for quantitative learning environments research.

REFERENCES

Andrich, D. (1978a). Application of a psychometric rating model to ordered categories which are scored with successive integers. *Applied Psychological Measurement, 2*(4), 581–594.

Andrich, D. (1978b). Rating formulation for ordered response categories. *Psychometrika, 43*(4), 561–573.

Andrich, D. (1978c). Scaling attitude items constructed and scores in the Likert tradition. *Educational and Psychological Measurement, 38*(3), 665–680.

Bond, T. G., & Fox, C. F. (2007). *Applying the Rasch model: Fundamental measurement in the human sciences* (2nd ed.). Lawrence Erlbaum Associates, Inc.

deBoer, J. (1994). On the history of quantity calculus and the international system. *Metrologia, 31*, 405–429.

Linacre, J. M. (2009). *WINSTEPS.* Retrieved from www.winsteps.com/winsteps.htm

Luce, R. D., & Tukey, J. W. (1964). Simultaneous conjoint measurement. *Journal of Mathematical Psychology, 1*, 1–27.

Rasch, G. (1960). *Probabilistic models for some intelligence and attainment tests.* Chicago: MESA Press.

Reeve, B. B. (2009). *An introduction to modern measurement theory.* Retrieved November 21, 2009, from http://appliedresearch.cancer.gov/areas/cognitive/immt.pdf

RUMMLab. (2007). *RUMM2020 Rasch unidimensional measurement models.* RUMM Laboratory Pty Ltd.

Robert F. Cavanagh (Curtin University of Technology)
and
Russell F. Waugh (Graduate School of Education, University of Western Australia)

SECTION TWO: ASSESSMENT AND DEVELOPMENT IN THE LEARNING ENVIRONMENT

JESSICA M. ELDERFIELD AND RUSSELL F. WAUGH

2. HIGH STAKES STATE-WIDE TESTING OF THE LEARNING ENVIRONMENT OUTCOMES

The Case of Numeracy

Key words: numeracy, value-added performance, school effectiveness, monitoring standards, school effects, teacher effects, primary, secondary, Rasch measurement.

ABSTRACT

This study investigated the differences between two competing regression methods (single-level Means-on-Means regression and Multilevel Modelling) used to produce value-added performance-indicator information for the monitoring of school effectiveness. Data from 24 government secondary schools with a total of 2862 students in 132 Year 8 classes in Western Australia were used. The dependent variable was a Rasch-created linear measure of Year 8 Numeracy. The five independent variables were: (1) a Rasch-created, linear measure of Year 7 Numeracy; (2) gender; (3) ethnic group (Aboriginal and Torres Strait Islander, or non-Aboriginal and Torres Strait Islander status); (4) language background (English or other than English); and the school-level variable (5) school socioeconomic status. The findings of this study suggest that residual-based performance indicators calculated using the Multilevel model are more accurate and fair than those produced using the single-level Means-on-Means regression model, and would enable both schools and teachers to report on accountability and investigate a greater range of school effectiveness issues with more confidence.

INTRODUCTION

This study investigated the differences between two competing regression methods (single-level Means-on-Means regression and Multilevel Modelling) used to produce value-added performance-indicator information for the monitoring of school effectiveness. Data from 24 government secondary schools with a total of 2862 students in 132 Year 8 classes in Western Australia were used. The dependent variable was a Rasch-created linear measure of Year 8 Numeracy. The five independent variables were: (1) a Rasch-created, linear measure of Year 7 Numeracy; (2) gender; (3) ethnic group (Aboriginal and Torres Strait Islander, or non-Aboriginal

R.F. Cavanagh and R.F. Waugh (eds.), Applications of Rasch Measurement
in Learning Environments Research, 19–43.

and Torres Strait Islander status); (4) language background (English or other than English); and the school-level variable (5) school socioeconomic status. The findings of this study suggest that residual-based performance indicators calculated using the Multilevel model are more accurate and fair than those produced using the single-level Means-on-Means regression model, and would enable both schools and teachers to report on accountability and investigate a greater range of school effectiveness issues with more confidence.

EDUCATIONAL ACCOUNTABILITY IN AUSTRALIA

In 1998, all Year 3 primary school students in Australia were required to participate in the first ever national population assessment of literacy, the leading step in the Australian Commonwealth's National Literacy and Numeracy Plan (DEETYA 1998). This Plan is still in place today (2009) and measures the educational outcomes of Year 3, Year 5, Year 7 and Year 9 students in literacy and numeracy against agreed national minimum standards (benchmarks). The underlying logic of the Plan was outlined by then Minister Kemp in the following words, "Australia will go a long way toward countering other forms of educational and social disadvantage if strong foundational literacy and numeracy skills are successfully taught to all children" (DEETYA 1998, p. 7). Thus, literacy and numeracy are seen in this plan as most important for success in school and later learning. The assessment instruments used by the government are deemed objective in that they are constructed using Rasch Measurement. All of the assessments are calibrated on a linear scale on which both the difficulty of assessment items and the abilities of students can be mapped (Curriculum Corporation, 2007; Louden & Wildy, 2001). Such scale creation makes it possible to track the achievement progress of children over time. Having linear data also allows the researcher to apply further parametric statistical methods, such as the single-level means-on-means and multilevel models used in this thesis. This is in stark contrast to the assessment instruments used in England.

Until 2008, under the Australian Commonwealth's National Literacy and Numeracy Plan, each State and Territory had its own assessment instrument to measure literacy and numeracy outcomes. In May 2008, as part of the National Assessment Program – Literacy and Numeracy (NAPLAN), these State and Territory-based assessments were replaced by National tests (MCEETYA, 2007). Despite the change in assessment coordination, school administrators are still required to use data from these assessments as a basis for their State or Territory school reports. In these reports, school administrators are required to use their own contextual information, and thorough examination of the National assessment data, to report on how they plan to ensure students will meet the minimum standards (benchmarks) set by the Australian Commonwealth government. These are then used for the allocation of funds from both the State and Commonwealth governments (DET, 2002).

All Australian States and Territories have released policies to manage both the schools' accountability reporting requirements to the State or Territory, and the State or Territory's accountability reporting requirements to the Australian Government. In 2002, under legislative authority, the Western Australian government released the School Accountability Framework (DET, 2002). The Framework makes clear the link between accountability and outcomes as it requires all schools to report at both the district and school levels on the educational outcomes of the students, as measured by the government's Literacy and Numeracy assessments.

The Education Department of Western Australia (now the Department of Education and Training) launched the local Data Club program in 1999 (Louden & Wildy, 2001), followed by the Assessment for Improvement program (Cook, 2005). The aim of the Data Club was to support schools in making performance judgements based on their assessment data for both: (1) accountability; and, (2) school improvement purposes (Louden & Wildy, 2001). The Data Club program analyses the schools' National assessment data and provides every government primary school in Western Australia with an analysis of their student outcomes in the form of a series of descriptive graphs, as well as like-school comparisons and value-added analyses (DET, 2007c). The aim of the Assessment for Improvement program was to, "...build teachers' ability to blend their classroom monitoring with WALNA results to judge student achievement and plan for future teaching and learning" (Cook, 2005, p. 4). Prior to 2008 the data used in both programs was the state-based Western Australian Literacy and Numeracy Assessment data. Both programs will continue to support schools in their analysis and interpretation of the new National Literacy and Numeracy Assessment measures (DET, 2008).

Value-added analysis, such as that provided by the Data Club, tracks the same group of students and measures their progress in terms of residuals (Fitz-Gibbon, 1996). Unlike the multilevel value-added analyses being implemented throughout England and in some parts of the United States of America, the Data Club Program applies the Single-Level Means-on-Means regression method for their value-added analyses (Louden & Wildy, 2001). This method uses a school's mean prior performance and relevant socioeconomic data as the predicting variables to calculate their value-added residual. Residual indices indicate how much better (or worse) than expected a group has performed after accounting for prior performance and socioeconomic factors. In other words, the residual represents the effect that a school has on student performance, after accounting for prior performance and student context. Schools in Western Australia are able to use these school level residuals to track the performance of their students over time (Louden & Wildy, 2001).

Given the continuing interest in school improvement and accountability, and the increasingly high public stakes placed on student outcomes there is a need to investigate the methods used to analyse student outcome data and the validity of value-added residuals as indicators of school performance in Western Australia. It appears that means-on-means value-added residuals are being used for accountability purposes both in Western Australia and in other countries in spite of some expressed doubt about the advisability of their use for this purpose.

AIMS AND RESEARCH QUESTIONS

The general aim was to compare the results from these two competing methods of analysing school performance data for the monitoring of numeracy with Western Australian data. Based on the current literature and rationale for comparison of methods, four separate research questions are posed in order to explore this aim for the purpose of providing accurate, reliable and useful performance feedback to schools in Western Australia.

Research Question 1

Research Question 1 investigates the phenomenon of '*aggregation bias*' using the single-level Means-on-Means regression method. Three separate single-level linear regressions were used to determine the amount of variance in students' numeracy data that can be explained by the independent variable of prior performance at three increasing levels of aggregation: the individual student, class and school-levels.

Research Question 2

Research Question 2 investigates how much of the variability in student outcomes can be explained at the student, class and school levels? To investigate this question, the individual student level numeracy data were analysed using a Multilevel regression model, to separate out, and estimate variation at the student, class and school-levels.

Research Question 3

Research Question 3 investigates whether the value-added performance indicators of both classes and schools are ranked differently when analysed using the means-on-means regression method as opposed to the Multilevel method. To do this the positional ranks of the class and school level residuals under each regression model were compared and differences noted. A Spearman's rho correlation for rank ordered data was then employed to investigate whether the ranks of the class and school level value-added residuals differed significantly under each method. Classes and schools that fell outside 95% statistical confidence boundaries under each method were also identified.

Research Question 4

Examination of the class level residuals from both regression models was undertaken to investigate Research Question 4: to what extent are different classes within a particular school identified as 'more' or 'less' than effective according to the residual score under both the single-level means-on-means, and multilevel modelling methods?

RESEARCH DESIGN AND ADMINISTRATIVE PROCEDURES

The data were collected as part of the Teaching for Growth study at the University of Western Australia (Louden, Rohl & Hopkins, 2008). Permission to conduct this present research study was obtained from the Human Research Ethics Committee of Edith Cowan University. The Teaching for Growth study's original approval was gained on the basis of the ethics application made by the University of Western Australia which contained: (1) an information letter, for all children, parents or guardians, teachers and school leaders, explaining the purpose of the research; (2) an invitation to participate in the research; and, (3) a letter of informed consent to participate, and approval from the Education department of Western Australia (Louden, Rohl & Hopkins, 2008). No student, teacher or school names were given to the researchers as the data were all de-identified. All student names and dates of birth were permanently removed from the data base. No student addresses were ever asked for or collected. All teacher names were permanently removed from the data base. No teacher addresses were ever asked for, or collected. All school names, addresses and school codes were permanently removed from the data base. All students, teachers and schools were referred to by a sequential case code (1, 2, 3, 4...) for analysis purposes. This was not linked in any way to any personal information. In addition, the chief investigator of the Teaching for Growth study at the University of Western Australia gave written permission to the Human Research Ethics Committee of Edith Cowan University for the previously collected numeracy data to be used in this research project.

Sample Characteristics

The data gathered were from 24 secondary schools with a total of 2862 students in 132 Year 8 classes. Overall the sample had more metropolitan schools (71%) than rural (29%). This differs in comparison to all Government schools containing Year 8 classes as there are conversely more rural schools (67%) than metropolitan (33%). The sample also had more large schools (83%) than small (17%). This again differs from all Government schools containing Year 8 classes where there are approximately equal numbers of small (51%) and large (49%) schools (Personal database communication, 2007). A comparison of the resultant sample against all Government schools containing Year 8 classes, stratified across size, sector and socioeconomic status, is provided in Table 1. The sample did not manage to recruit schools from small rural school in bands 0 and 1, and from large rural schools in band 2.

Table 1. Number and percentage of state and sample schools stratified across: size, sector and socioeconomic status

Size	Sector	Socioeconomic band	0	1	2	3
Small	Rural	All schools	42	18	22	3
			(24.0)%	(10.3%)	(12.6%)	(1.7%)
		Sample	0	0	2	1
			(0.0%)	(0.0%)	(8.3%)	(4.2%)
	Metropolitan	All schools	1	0	0	3
			(0.6%)	(0.0%)	(0.0%)	(1.7%)

Size	Sector	Socioeconomic band	0	1	2	3
		Sample	1	0	0	0
			(4.2%)	(0.0%)	(0.0%)	(0.0%)
Large	Rural	All schools	5	14	13	0
			(2.9%)	(8.0%)	(7.4%)	(0.0%)
		Sample	1	3	0	0
			(4.2%)	(12.5%)	(0.0%)	(0.0%)
	Metropolitan	All schools	9	14	12	20
			(5.1%)	(8.0%)	(6.9%)	(11.4%)
		Sample	2	5	2	7
			(8.3%)	(20.8%)	(8.3%)	(29.2%)

Note
1. 'Metropolitan' means metropolitan area of Perth
2. 'Rural' means rural area of Western Australia
   Source: All schools data comes from the Department of Education and Training
   (Personal database communication, 2007).

COMPUTER SOFTWARE USED FOR ANALYSIS

Two statistical packages were used in the analysis of data in this thesis. SPSS (Statistical Program for the Social Sciences) v.13.0. SPSS was the program used for data merging, data transformation, data screening and general descriptive analysis, as well as for the Multiple Regression used in the single-level Means-on-Means analysis. It was used as it is one of the most widely used programs for analysis within the social sciences, and has the advantage of a wide range of supporting documentation available to guide the user.

Multilevel modelling analysis remains less widespread within the social sciences, although the literature contains increasing references to it. It is only recently available as an application within SPSS, and so a more specialised and dedicated statistical program was chosen to undertake this analysis, namely MLwiN. MLwiN was created by the Centre for Multilevel Modelling team at the University of Bristol and is referenced via the Internet from http://www.cmm. bristol.ac.uk/MLwiN. The use of this software has been used in a number of recent studies (Browne, Subramanian, Jones, & Goldstein, 2005; Louden et.al. 2005; Rowe, 2004). In addition, in an investigation into the use of software packages for linear multilevel models, five software packages used for such analyses were compared on their performance analysing simulated databases and reviewed on four features: data input and data management; statistical capabilities; output; and, user friendliness including documentation (Zhou, Perkins & Hui, 1999). The investigation concluded that MLwiN provided the most user-friendly interface to generate random effects analyses and analysis of residuals, both of which were used in this thesis.

The Variables

There were three levels of data used in this study in the application of the multilevel regression model: (1) Level 1 - Student (*i*); (2) Level 2 - Class (*j*); and (3) Level 3 - School (*k*). In other words, a student belongs to a class, which in turn belongs to a school. The variables used in the analyses included variables from the student numeracy assessment, student background variables, and a school level socio-economic indicator. The dependent or outcome variable in all the analyses was 'Year 8 Numeracy'. The independent or explanatory variables used to account for variance in the outcome variable in the analyses included the following level 1 student variables: (1) prior achievement (Year 7 numeracy), (2) gender (male or female), (3) ethnic group (Aboriginal and Torres Strait Islander, or non-Aboriginal or Torres Strait Islander status), (4) language background other than English; and the following level 3 school variable, (5) school socioeconomic status. Only those explanatory variables that contributed significantly to each of the analyses were retained.

Residual Estimates

One of the terms in a regression model, single-level or multilevel, is the residual. Strictly speaking, a residual estimate is the error term in a regression equation which represents the unexplained variance left over after all other possible relevant factors have been included in the equation (Fitz-Gibbon, 1996). Residual estimates are termed 'value-added' when prior performance is included as an independent variable. Value-added refers to the relative effect of the school on outcome performance, after adjusting for prior performance and other contextual variables (Strand, 1998; Rowe, 2004).

Positive value-added residuals occur when a school's achieved measure is higher than its expected measure, given its prior performance and other contextual factors. Negative value-added residuals occur when a school's achieved measure is lower than its expected measure, given its prior performance and other contextual factors. When used as performance indicators, value-added residuals are often categorised in three categories indicating: (1) 'higher than expected performance'; (2) 'as expected performance'; and, (3) 'lower than expected performance'.

RESULTS

Three single-level value-added linear regression models were applied to investigate Research Question 1 which looked at the relationship between the outcome variable (Year 8 Numeracy measures) with the predictor variable (prior performance, Year 7 Numeracy measures) at increasing levels of aggregation: the individual, aggregated-class, and aggregated-school levels. Year 8 Numeracy measures were regressed on Year 7 Numeracy measures (see Table 2). The regression was significant at each of the three levels; individual, aggregated-class, and aggregated-school. *F*-test statistics showed that Year 7 Numeracy measures significantly accounted for variance in Year 8 Numeracy measures at each of the three levels. Furthermore, the R^2 statistic increased considerably at each level, with prior performance accounting for just half of the variance in Year 8 Numeracy measures ($R^2 = .50$) at the individual-level, 84% of the variance at the aggregated class-level, and over 90% at the aggregated-school level.

Table 2. Regression analysis summary for Year 7 numeracy performance predicting Year 8 numeracy performance at the individual, aggregated class, and aggregated school levels

	β	t	R^2	F
Individual-level	.758	58.231**	.575	3390.898**
Aggregated Class-level	.924	27.544**	.854	758.684**
Aggregated School-level	.957	15.508**	.916	240.491**

Note. β =standardised slope, t = t-test, R^2 = percentage of variance explained· F = F-test, *$p < 0.05$ (one tailed), ** $p<0.01$ (one tailed).

The increasing R^2 statistic at each level indicates the presence of aggregation bias. This phenomenon influences the interpretation of school effectiveness data. For example, data aggregated at the school-level attributes more of the variance in student performance to prior performance, leaving less room to investigate or question the effects of student backgrounds, teachers, classrooms and schools on student outcome. With this understanding, the single-level means-on-means regression method on aggregated data creates incomplete and upwardly biased estimates.

Figure 1 shows scatter plots that demonstrate the relationship between Year 8 Numeracy measures and prior performance at each of the three levels. These plots graphically represent the value-added regressions at each of the levels, and how increasingly aggregating information lead to a loss of information and an extreme reduction in variance. It can be noted that as the data were increasingly aggregated, less of it fell outside the 95% confidence limits for the regression equation. That is, aggregating the data meant only the mean-point estimates at the class and school levels were available for analysis. This analysis ignored student-level information. Ignoring variance at the student-level averaged out the measurement error at higher levels, and therefore left the aggregated class and school data to be analysed with reduced measurement-error. In addition, the aggregation of data concealed any irregular results. That is, irregular results from only one or two students could lead to misleadingly high or low average results for a class or school. Once data have been aggregated, the variance of individual performance is lost and it is difficult to determine to what extent outlying results may have contributed to the extreme school residuals.

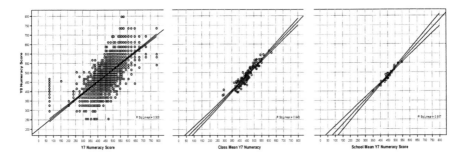

Figure 1. Scatter plots demonstrating the relationship between Year 8 Numeracy measures and Year 7 Numeracy measures (prior performance) at the individual-level (N_i=2507), aggregated class-level (N_j=132), and aggregated school-level (N_k=24), showing lines of 'best fit' and 95% confidence levels.

Summary of Results for Research Question 1

In total, these results indicated that the amount of variance in students' numeracy data that could be explained by the independent variable of prior performance considerably increased at three escalating levels of aggregation, thus highlighting the presence of aggregation bias. The analyses highlighted that by aggregating student outcome data, the means-on-means method did not account for: (1) the inherent hierarchical structure of student outcome data; (2) unaccounted error due to aggregation with the means-on-means method; and, (3) the upwardly biased estimates produced by aggregating student-level data. The loss of vital within-school variance leads to the likelihood of higher correlations being reported and the risk of Type 1 errors, reporting a relationship between variables when none exists.

In order to investigate Research Questions 2, 3 and 4 both single-level and multilevel regression models were employed. Unconditional, value-added and student background multilevel regression models were applied to the individual student outcome data; and, a single-level student background linear regression model was applied to the student outcome data aggregated at the class and school-level. Each regression model used the Year 7 Numeracy measures (prior performance), and other significant student background information, to estimate the variance in Year 8 Numeracy measures.

The multilevel regression analyses were formulated, in part, to partition the total variability in Year 8 numeracy performance into its three components: students within classes, classes within schools, and between schools. The results of this analysis inform Research Question 2, which asks, how much of the variability in student outcomes can be explained at the student, class and school levels. Class and school level residual estimates from the single-level means-on-means and the multilevel regression models were saved for comparison to investigate Research Questions 3 and 4. Research Question 3 was investigated by comparing the stability of residual ranks under each regression model. Positional changes in the class and school ranks under each model were compared, then a Spearman's rho correlation for rank-ordered data was employed to investigate whether these ranks differed significantly under each model at either the class or school level. Research Question 4 investigated the extent to which different classes within a particular school had been identified as 'more' or 'less' than effective according to the student background residual score under the single-level means-on-means, and multilevel modelling methods.

Summary of Results for Research Question 2

The results of the Unconditional Multilevel Model, with no independent variables, show that a majority of variation in student performance is found at the student or class-level, and less at the school level. This model was extended to a Value-added multilevel regression model by adding each student's prior achievement (Year 7 Numeracy) as a predictor. The results again show that a majority of variation in student performance is found at the student or class-level, both significant at the one percent level. School-level variation is minimal and significant at the five percent level.

The value-added multilevel model was again extended to the final Student Background by including the following student level 1 predictors, all significant at five percent or lower: (1) gender (male or female); (2) ethnic group (Aboriginal and Torres Strait Islander, or non-Aboriginal or Torres Strait Islander status); and, a school level 3 predictor (3) school socioeconomic status. Variation due to clustering between schools is no longer found to be significant. Variation at the student and class-level remain significant at the 1 percent level. In summary, regardless of the model employed, a majority of variation in student performance is found at the student or class-level, not at the school-level.

Summary of Results for Research Question 3

Research Question 3 was investigated by comparing the stability of residual ranks saved from the application of each regression model. Firstly, positional changes in class and school ranks under each model were compared, then, a Spearman's rho correlation for rank-ordered data was employed to investigate whether these ranks differed significantly under each model at either the class or school level. Schools that fell outside 95% statistical confidence boundaries under each method were also identified. Table 3 presents positional changes to the top and bottom ten class residuals under each model. The top and bottom ten classes are shown, as those were the ranks that estimated significantly higher or lower performance under each model, and thus were more likely to have consequences for schools in regards to using performance indicators for school effectiveness reporting. Those classes that were estimated to have higher than expected performance under each model are highlighted in green. Those classes that were estimated to have lower than expected performance under each model are highlighted in red. The results for all 132 classes show that only seven of the classes remained stable in rank, including the lowest ranked class. None of the highest ranked classes remained stable in their ranking under both models. Sixty-three of the 132 classes improved their ranking under the multilevel model, whilst 62 of the 132 classes went down in rank under the multilevel model, compared to the single-level model.

There were some marked differences for some classes in regards to the effectiveness category that they were labelled with under each regression method. Under the single-level means-on-means model as compared to the multilevel model: (1) two classes went from being labelled with 'as expected performance' to 'lower than expected performance'; (2) one class went from being labelled with 'higher than expected performance' to 'as expected performance'; (3) one class went from being labelled with 'lower than expected performance' to 'as expected performance'; and most notably, (4) seven classes went from being labelled with 'as expected performance' to 'higher than expected performance'.

Table 4 presents positional changes to all the 24 of the school residuals under each model. The results show that only 2 of the 24 schools remained stable in rank, including the lowest ranked schools. Eleven of the 24 schools improved their ranking under the multilevel model, whilst eleven of the 24 schools went down in rank under the multilevel model.

These results show that the ranking of class and school residuals, as indicators of numeracy performance, are sensitive to variations in the type of regression analysis employed in their estimation. This finding has implications for schools when using residuals as indicators of performance for school effectiveness and accountability purposes, as they may find themselves to be significantly more effective under one model and not in another.

Spearman's rho correlations for rank-ordered data were then employed to further investigate whether these ranks differed significantly under each model, at both the class and school-levels. The results, shown in Table 5, indicate that the ranks of class-level residuals and the ranks of school-level residuals, under both the single-level and multi-level models are significantly correlated, and are therefore not significantly different.

These results all contributed to answering Research Question 3, which investigated whether the value-added performance indicators of both classes and schools are ranked differently when compared using the means-on-means regression method and the multilevel method. Class and school level residuals from the single-level means-on-means regression model and the multilevel regression model were saved in order to compare their positional ranks. Although the Spearman's rho correlation for rank ordered data showed that the ranks of the class and school level value-added residuals did not differ significantly under each method, a vast majority of residual ranks changed position under each model. Furthermore, some classes and schools were identified as performing significantly higher, or lower, under each model.

Table 3. Positional changes to the top and bottom ten class residuals under the single-level and multilevel student background models

Class	Position under single-level	Position under multilevel	Change under multilevel
57	1	37	down 36
18	2	3	down 1
39	3	5	down 2
30	4	32	down 28
107	5	1	up 4
122	6	16	down 10
13	7	12	down 5
114	8	2	up 6
95	9	11	down 2
54	10	4	up 6
76	11	8	up 3
62	24	9	up 15
66	30	7	up 23
24	36	10	up 26
46	45	6	up 39
118	106	125	down 19
78	111	127	down 16
29	115	124	down 9
51	119	122	down 3
130	120	130	down 10
75	122	114	up 8
73	123	120	up 3
111	124	128	down 4
20	125	118	up 7
128	126	86	up 40
23	127	123	up 4
36	128	131	down 3
60	129	129	stable rank
67	130	106	up 24
83	131	126	up 5
108	132	132	stable rank

Table 4. Positional changes in school residuals under the single-level and multilevel student background models

School	Position under single-level	Position under multilevel	Change under multilevel
8	1	5	down 4
10	2	8	down 6
22	3	1	up 2
18	4	3	up 1
3	5	2	up 3
20	6	7	down 1
2	7	4	up 3
16	8	6	up 2
13	9	12	down 3
15	10	11	down 1
6	11	14	down 3
11	12	9	up 3
5	13	10	up 3
1	14	15	down 1
24	15	20	down 5
12	16	19	down 3
19	17	17	stable rank
17	18	16	up 2
21	19	18	up 1
9	20	13	up 7
4	21	22	down 1
7	22	23	down 1
14	23	21	up 2
23	24	24	stable rank

Table 5. Spearman's rho correlation coefficients for class and school residual ranks under the single-level and multilevel models

Model	1.	2.	3.	4.
1. Single-level Class residual	1.000	0.916**	–	–
2. Multilevel Class residual	–	–	–	–
3. Single-level School residual	–	–	1.000	0.908**
4. Multilevel School residual	–	–	–	–

Note. *$p < 0.05$ (two tailed), ** $p < 0.01$(two tailed)

Summary of Results for Research Question 4

Table 6 investigates research question 4, to what extent are different classes within a particular school identified as 'more' or 'less' than effective according to the residual score under: (1) both the single-level means-on-means; and, (2) the multilevel modelling methods? Eleven of the 24 sample schools had classes that were identified as achieving significantly 'higher than' or 'lower than' expected Year 8 Numeracy performance under either the single-level or multilevel regression models. Those classes that were estimated to have higher than expected performance under each model are highlighted in green. Those classes that were estimated to have lower than expected performance under each model are highlighted in red. 'Discrepancy A' signifies that a class within a school was identified as having either significantly 'higher than' or 'lower than' expected Year 8 Numeracy performance, where all other classes within the school did not. 'Discrepancy B' signifies that a school contained classes that were identified as achieving both significantly 'higher than' and 'lower than' expected Year 8 Numeracy performance.

Results show that all of the eleven schools containing classes with 'higher than' or 'lower than' expected performance by either regression model, also contained classes identified as having 'as expected' performance (Discrepancy A). Furthermore, one of the eleven schools contained classes identified as having both 'higher than' and 'lower than' expected performance (Discrepancy B). It is expected that schools contain classes with varying residuals, both positive and negative, as the residual estimates are components of the random part of the regression equation and are thus assumed to be independent. However, these results show that the aggregation of data to the school-level under the single-level model, or analysis of only the school-level residuals under the multilevel model, fails to identify individual classes that may be achieving significantly 'higher than' or 'lower than' expected performance as opposed to other classes within their school. Again, this has possible implications for schools, such as those in Western Australia, whose value-added performance indicators are produced using school-level data to estimate their residuals.

Table 6. Class-level residuals within those schools containing significantly 'higher than' or 'lower than' expected performance

School	Class	Single-level residual rank	Multilevel residual rank	Discrepancy A	Discrepancy B
3	11	63	53		
3	12	76	110		
3	13	7	12		
3	14	82	119	*	
3	15	41	66		
3	16	67	43		
3	17	19	17		
3	18	2	3		
7	33	66	85		
7	34	64	61		
7	35	80	95		
7	36	128	131	*	
7	37	73	71		
7	38	57	42		
8	39	3	5		
8	40	46	73	*	
8	41	32	65		
11	44	84	87		
11	45	65	72		
11	46	45	6	*	
11	47	21	36		
11	48	117	117		
11	49	98	92		
12	50	86	80		
12	51	119	122		
12	52	100	91		
12	53	89	89	*	
12	54	10	4		

School	Class	Single-level residual rank	Multilevel residual rank	Discrepancy A	Discrepancy B
12	55	110	90		
12	56	72	83		
13	57	1	37		
13	58	49	40		
13	59	94	97	*	
13	60	129	129		
13	61	93	100		
13	62	24	9		
16	75	122	114		
16	76	11	8		
16	77	38	35		
16	78	111	127		
16	79	59	57	*	
16	80	33	14		
16	81	42	59		
16	82	77	29		
17	83	131	126		
17	84	102	93		
17	85	105	56		
17	86	47	33		
17	87	121	121	*	
17	88	116	94		
17	89	26	22		
17	90	29	19		
21	107	5	1		
21	108	132	132		
21	109	56	45	*	*
21	110	78	82		
21	111	124	128		
22	112	43	70		
22	113	13	44		

School	Class	Single-level residual rank	Multilevel residual rank	Discrepancy A	Discrepancy B
22	114	8	2		
22	115	27	60		
22	116	31	54		
22	117	91	112	*	
22	118	106	125		
22	119	28	52		
22	120	14	31		
22	121	16	28		
22	122	6	16		
24	130	120	130		
24	131	71	58	*	
24	132	70	68		

In summary, different classes within a particular school were identified as 'more', 'as', or 'less' than effective, according to the residual score under both the single-level means-on-means, and multilevel modelling methods.

DISCUSSION

Schools in Australia have been functioning under a structured accountability system with a focus on student outcomes since 1998 (DET, 2007a; Louden & Wildy, 2001). Under the National Literacy and Numeracy Plan, the literacy and numeracy outcomes of all Year 3, Year 5, Year 7, and Year 9 students are measured and reported against agreed national benchmarks (DEETYA, 1998). The Plan ties State and Commonwealth funding to student achievement. Western Australian education policy dictates that schools must use a self-appraisal of their literacy and numeracy assessment measures to summarise their performance in producing quality student outcomes for their school and District reports (DET, 2002). Following this, schools must make a judgement of their performance to their respective district authority as either: performing 'effectively'; or conversely, 'in need of intervention or help' (DET, 2007a, p. 4).

Under these relatively new accountability requirements, Western Australian schools found the State and National accountability and reporting requirements a complex task. Firstly, schools were finding it difficult to analyse and present the information needed to inform school improvement. Secondly, schools were battling to make fair judgements of their relative effectiveness in relation to others whilst accounting for student background factors, such as: socioeconomic status; prior performance; Aboriginal and Torres Strait Islander status; language background other than English; and, gender (Louden & Wildy, 2001). In other words, schools were finding it difficult to represent the 'value' they were adding to student outcomes whilst accounting for student and school contextual factors.

In response, the Education Department of Western Australia (now the Department of Education and Training, DET) launched the local Data Club program to support school leaders in making performance judgements based on their student outcome data for school improvement and accountability purposes (Louden & Wildy, 2001). The Data Club program uses the single-level means-on-means regression model to analyse student outcome data in order to calculate value-added residuals, amongst other analyses (DET, 2007c). Value-added residuals are used as indicators of a school's relative performance.

The political aim for Governments monitoring the relative effectiveness of schools, knowing how schools are performing in relation to others, is to develop quality in education to increase the effectiveness of schools (DET, 2002; Earl, 1995; Fitz-Gibbon, 1996; Rowe, 2004). This implies that schools must be able to use performance indicator information for school improvement, as well as for the mandatory accountability reporting requirements. Much research has been completed on the development of quality performance indicators as a way to fairly and reliably evaluate and report the effectiveness of schools in producing quality student outcomes (Aitkin & Longford, 1986; Fitz-Gibbon, 1996; Raudenbush & Willms, 1995; Woodhouse & Goldstein, 1988; Rowe, 2004). Much of this research has shown that the single-level means-on-means and multilevel methods differ in terms of interpretive validity (Goldstein, 1997) and statistical efficiency (Rowe, 2004, 2005).

The present study applied what is considered to be best practice in the analysis of student outcome data, Multilevel modelling, with linear Rasch measures, in order to estimate the variance in student outcomes at the individual, class and school-levels, and to calculate value-added performance indicators of school effectiveness with Western Australian numeracy data. It compared these indicators with those created under the current method of analysis in Western Australia, the single-level means-on-means method. This has not previously been calculated with linked numeracy data from Western Australian Primary and Secondary Schools.

The present study used valid sources of data for analysis, collected from 2862 students, in 132 Year 8 classes, in 24 secondary schools, and created linear measures of numeracy. There were two main sets of data used in this study: (1) the outcome or dependent variable made up of individual student data from a Mathematics assessment specially designed by the Department of Education for Year 8 students for the current and ongoing Student Growth Study at the University of Western Australia (Louden, Rohl & Hopkins, 2008); and, (2) prior performance, or the main independent variable, individual student data from the Numeracy strand of the Year 7 Western Australian Literacy and Numeracy Assessment. Student's scored responses on items from both assessments were calibrated on a common Western Australian Monitoring Standards in Education scale by fitting the student response data to Rasch measurement models (Rasch,1960/1980) using the RUMM computer program (Andrich, Sheridan & Luo, 2005). The Rasch measurement model is currently the only known way to create a linear scale in the human sciences and is currently world's best practice in measurement (Waugh, 2006; Wright, 1999). Scales created by Rasch measurement are universal, meaning that the movement of a student or school's performance on an assessment is measurable. For example, for the purposes of this study, a student's Year 7 score for numeracy can be compared with the same student's numeracy score one year later in Year 8. The resulting difference would indicate measurable growth or decline in performance for that student.

Four other independent variables used to account for variance in the outcome variable in the analyses were collected from the class teacher at the time of student assessment. These included the following student-level variables: (1) gender (male or female), (2) ethnic group (Aboriginal and Torres Strait Islander, or non-Aboriginal or Torres Strait Islander status), (3) language background other than English; and the school-level variable, (4) school socioeconomic status.

Answering Research Question 1

Research Question 1 investigated the phenomenon of '*aggregation bias*' using the Means-on-Means method. Three separate single-level linear regressions were used to determine the amount of variance in students' numeracy data that was explained by the independent variable of prior performance at three increasing levels of aggregation: the individual student, class and school-levels. The present study found that the R^2 statistic from the three Single-Level regression analyses, carried out to estimate the amount of variation in Year 8 Numeracy performance accounted for by prior performance (Year 7 Numeracy), increased notably at the individual-level ($R^2 = 0.575$), aggregated class-level ($R^2 = 0.854$), and aggregated school-level ($R^2 = 0.916$). Therefore, when aggregated to the highest level, a reported 91.6% of variance in Year 8 numeracy measures could be attributed to the prior performance of the school. These findings are in line with the comments, criticisms and findings from social researchers and statistical experts, as reported below.

Social researchers have warned against the use of using aggregated data in single-level regression methods for the creation of residual estimates for over seventy years (Goldstein, 1997; Robinson, 1950; Rowe, 2004; Thorndike, 1939). Previous research findings in school effectiveness studies showed that, as data are aggregated at higher levels, the regression estimates of the impact of independent variables, such as socioeconomic status and prior performance, are biased upwards (Fitz-Gibbon, 1996; Robinson, 1950; Rowe, 2004). Robinson labelled this problem as the 'ecological fallacy' (Robinson, 1950). The Data Club program reports that the lowest correlation between average school performance for Year 3, and socio-economic status is reported to be approximately $r = 0.6$ (DET, 2007c). Therefore, approximately 36% of the variance in average Year 3 school performance is purported to being explained by the schools' socio-economic context. The 'fallacy' lies in the interpretation of results. In the case of student performance and home-background, increasing amounts of variance in student performance are attributed to the home-background of the student at higher levels of aggregation.

In the present study, Figure 1 showed scatter plots demonstrating the relationship between Year 8 Numeracy scores and prior Year 7 numeracy performance at each of the three levels. These plots graphically represented the value-added regressions at each of the levels, and showed how increasingly aggregating information leads to a loss of information and an extreme reduction in variance. As the data were increasingly aggregated, less of it fell outside the 95% confidence limits for the regression equation. That is, aggregating the data meant that only the mean-point estimates at the class and school levels were available for analysis. Class and school-level analyses ignored student-level information. Ignoring variance at the student-level averaged out the measurement error at higher levels, and therefore left the aggregated class and school data to be analysed with reduced measurement-error. These findings are in line with comments and research that indicated that aggregation leads to the loss of vital between-student and within-class variance which results in the calculation of less efficient estimates (Raudenbush & Willms, 1995) and the risk of Type 1 errors Hill and Rowe (1996).

Answering Research Question 2

Research Question 2 investigated how much of the variability in student outcomes can be explained at the student, class and school-levels. To investigate this question, the individual student-level Year 8 numeracy data were analysed using a Multilevel regression model, to separate out and estimate variation at the student, class and school-levels.

The first set of estimates presented in Table 4 are the results of the Unconditional Multilevel Model with no independent variables. These show that a majority of variation in student performance is found at the student-level (68.309%), followed by the class-level (18.012%), and school level (13.679%). This model was extended to a Value-added Multilevel regression model by adding each student's prior achievement (Year 7 Numeracy) as a predictor. The results show a majority of variation in student performance was found at the student-level. However, the parameter estimates for variation at the school-level were those that decreased most dramatically. Variation at the student and/or class-levels remained significant at the 1 percent level. School-level variation reduced its significance to the 5 percent level.

The value-added Multilevel model in the present study was again extended to a Student Background model by including the following student level 1 predictors, all significant at 5 percent or lower: (1) gender (male or female); (2) ethnic group (Aboriginal and Torres Strait Islander, or non-Aboriginal or Torres Strait Islander status); and, a school level 3 predictor (3) school socioeconomic status. Variation due to clustering between schools was no longer found to be significant. These findings could be explained by the mediating effect that a teacher has on the student group, above and beyond the effect of the school (Hill & Rowe, 1998). However, as found by Hill and Rowe's multilevel models (1998), the lack of independent variables at the class level could have also attributed to this finding.

The results from the present study are in line with other research into school effectiveness showing that the amount of variance in student outcomes accounted for at the school-level is less than what is accounted for at the student and class-levels, as demonstrated in studies such as those by Hattie (2003), Hill and Rowe (1996, 1998). What was found in studies such as these was that once the effects of prior performance and other student background information were taken into account by the regression model, the effects of the school reduced in their significance.

Answering Research Question 3

Research Question 3 investigated whether the value-added performance indicators of both classes and schools were ranked differently when analysed using the means-on-means regression method as opposed to the multilevel method. To do this, the positional ranks of the class and school level residuals under each regression model were compared and differences noted. A Spearman's rho correlation for rank ordered data was then employed to investigate whether the ranks of the class and school level value-added residuals differed significantly under each method. Classes and schools that fell outside 95% statistical confidence boundaries under each method were also identified.

The present study found that there were marked positional differences between the ranks of value-added performance indicators for both classes and schools when analysed using the single-level Means-on-Means regression method as opposed to the multilevel regression method. Of the 132 classes in this study, only seven of the classes remained stable in rank, including the lowest ranked class. None of the highest ranked classes remained stable in their ranking under both models. Sixty-three of the 132 classes improved their ranking under the multilevel model, whilst 62 of the 132 classes went down in rank under the multilevel model, compared to the single-level model. Table 6 presented positional changes for 24 of the school residuals under each model. The results showed that only two of the 24 schools remained stable in rank, again, including the lowest ranked schools. Eleven of the 24 schools improved their ranking under the multilevel model, whilst eleven of the 24 schools went down in rank under the multilevel model. These results are in line with the following comments and research findings.

Governments in other countries, such as England, commonly use residuals calculated by the Means-on-Means and Multilevel modelling methods to compare the effectiveness of schools in producing quality student outcomes by ranking them and their standard errors in the form of league tables (Rowe, 2004). Studies such as those by Woodhouse and Goldstein (1988), and Aitkin and Longford (1986), have compared several regression models in order to uncover the variability in the ranking of schools using residual estimates. Aitkin and Longford's study (1986) investigated the ranking of residuals under a Means-on-Means model and four alternate Multilevel models. Their results indicated that the Means-on-Means model gave notably different results to those results created using the Multilevel models (Aitkin & Longford, 1986).

Classes and schools were also labelled as having either: (1) 'higher than expected performance'; (2) 'as expected performance'; and, (3) 'lower than expected performance', under each regression method. As mentioned, categorisation was dependent not only on the regression method applied, but also on how the confidence intervals were calculated. Only one school was categorised as achieving higher than expected performance under the single-level means-on-means model, while under the multi-level model, all schools were seen to have achieved as expected performance. On the other hand, the results showed that there were marked differences for some classes in regards to the effectiveness category that they were labelled with under each regression method. Under the single-level means-on-means model as com-pared to the multilevel model: (1) two classes went from being labelled with 'as expected performance' to 'lower than expected performance'; (2) one class went from being labelled with 'higher than expected performance' to 'as expected performance'; (3) one class went from being labelled with 'lower than expected performance' to 'as expected performance'; and most notably, (4) seven classes went from being labelled with 'as expected performance' to 'higher than expected performance'.

Despite these differences in rankings, the results of the spearman's rho correlations for rank-ordered data showed that the differences were not statistically significant. However, the difference in positional ranking raises possible impli-cations for schools when presenting their performance indicator information for accountability and school improvement purposes. This is discussed further under implications later in this chapter.

Answering Research Question 4

Examination of the class level residuals from both regression models was under-taken to investigate Research Question 4: to what extent are different classes within a particular school identified as 'more' or 'less' than effective according to the residual score under both the single-level means-on-means, and multilevel modelling methods? This question originated from the research that also underpins Research Question 2, that more variation in student outcomes can be explained at the student and class levels (Hattie, 2003; Hill & Rowe, 1998).

The results of the present study showed that 11 of the 24 schools contained classes with significantly 'higher than' or 'lower than' expected performance under both the single-level and the multilevel regression model. All 11 of these schools were identified as having classes with either significantly 'higher than' or 'lower than' expected Year 8 Numeracy performance, where all other classes within the school did not (Discrepancy A). Furthermore, one of the eleven schools contained classes identified as having both 'higher than' and 'lower than' expected perfor-mance (Discrepancy B). These results showed that the aggregation of data to the school-level under the single-level model, or analysis of only the school-level residuals under the multilevel model, failed to identify individual classes that could be achieving significantly 'higher than' or 'lower than' expected performance as opposed to other classes within their school.

On the one hand, it was expected for schools to contain classes with varying residual values, both positive and negative, as the residual estimates are components of the random part of the regression equation and are thus assumed to be independent.

However, the inability of aggregated school regression models to partition variance at the class level was considered noteworthy and worth investigating. Identifying differential class effectiveness has possible implications for schools, such as those in Western Australia, whose value-added performance indicators are produced using school-level data to estimate their residuals.

SUMMARY AND CONCLUSIONS

If the previous State and current National assessments, and their associated performance indicator analyses, aim to identify areas in which learning environments can be improved, then it is imperative that reliable and valid information is provided to school communities. The logic of "...countering other forms of educational and social disadvantage if strong foundational literacy and numeracy skills are successfully taught to all children" (DEETYA 1998, p. 7) will be unattainable if information provided to school communities is not transparent, and cannot be trusted. Students will obviously be disadvantaged if school administrators, their teachers and school community have predetermined expectations of their performance which are based on flawed or unfair estimates. The results of the multilevel analyses applied in this study show that if educators have access to more accurate and reliable indicators of student performance, based on individual student-level data, they would be more likely to: (1) better inform investigations into the effects of individual learning environments (classrooms); and, (2) reduce the predetermined expectations resultant from biased estimates of school effectiveness.

Moreover, as Australia moves to a national testing system it is necessary to investigate how reliable and replicable the results of the present study are. Further research is needed that includes data: (1) from all Australian States and Territories, including independent school data; (2) in other strands of student outcomes, such as literacy; and, (3) in other year levels.

REFERENCES

Aitkin, M., & Longford, N. (1986). Statistical modelling issues in school effectiveness studies. *Journal of the Royal Statistical Society. Series A (General)*, *149*(1), 1–43.

Andrich, D., Sheridan, B., & Luo, G. (2005). *RUMM: A windows-based item analysis program employing Rasch unidimensional models*. Perth, WA: RUMM Laboratory.

Browne, W. J., Subramanian, S. V., Jones, K., & Goldstein, H. (2005). Variance partitioning in multilevel logistic models that exhibit overdispersion. *Journal of the Royal Statistical Society: Series A (Statistics in Society)*, *168*(3), 599–613.

Cook, J. (2005). *Reporting to systems and schools*. Paper presented at Curriculum Corporation Conference, Brisbane, Australia. Retrieved June 20, 2007, from http://cmslive.curriculum.edu.au/verve/_resources/Cook_edited.pdf

Curriculum Corporation. (2007). *National literacy and numeracy testing 2008*. Curriculum Corporation. Retrieved November 6, 2007, from http://www.curriculum.edu.au/ccsite/nap,19875.html

Department of Employment, Education, Training and Youth Affairs (DEETYA). (1998). *Literacy for all: The challenge for Australian schools. Commonwealth literacy programs for Australian schools.* Australian Schooling Monograph series, 1/1998. Canberra: AGPS.

Department of Education and Training (DET). (2002). *School accountability framework*. Perth: Government of Western Australia.

Department of Education and Training (DET). (2007a). *National and international perspectives and approaches to school accountability: Executive summary*. Perth: Government of Western Australia. Retrieved March 31, 2007, from http://www.det.wa.edu.au/education/accountability/Docs/ National%20and%20International%20Perspectives%20and%20Approaches%20-%20Exec%20Summary.pdf

Department of Education and Training (DET). (2007b). *Western Australian literacy and numeracy assessment (website)*. Perth: Government of Western Australia. Retrieved August 3, 2007, from http://www.det.wa.gov.au/education/walna/index.html

Department of Education and Training (DET). (2007c). *DataClub 2007*. Perth: Government of Western Australia. Retrieved June 20, 2008, from http://www.det.wa.edu.au/education/accountability/ Docs/DataClub.ppt

Department of Education and Training (DET). (2007d). *Guidelines for analysis of WALNA: Years 3, 5 and 7*. Perth: Government of Western Australia. Retrieved June 20, 2008, from http:// www.det.wa.edu.au/mse/pdfs/walna.pdf

Fitz-Gibbon, C. T. (1996). *Monitoring eduction: Indicators quality and effectiveness*. London: Continuum.

Goldstein, H. (1997). Methods in school effectiveness research. *School Effectiveness and School Improvement, 8*(4), 369–395.

Goldstein, H. (2001). Using pupil performance data for judging schools and teachers: Scope and limitations. *British Education Research Journal, 27*(4), 433–442.

Hattie, J. A. C. (2003). *Teachers make a difference: What is the research evidence?* Keynote paper presented at the ACER Annual Conference, Melbourne, Australia. Retrieved April 24, 2008, from http://www.acer.edu.au/documents/RC2003_Hattie_TeachersMakeADifference.pdf

Hill, P. W., & Rowe, K. J. (1996). Multilevel modelling in school effectiveness research. *School Effectiveness and School Improvement, 7*(1), 1–34.

Hill, P. W., & Rowe, K. J. (1998). Modelling student progress in studies of educational effectiveness. *School Effectiveness and School Improvement, 9*(3), 310–333.

Louden, W., Rohl, M., Barratt-Pugh, C., Brown, C., Cairney, T., Elderfield, J., et al. (2005). *In teachers' hands: Effective literacy teaching practices in the early years of schooling*. Final Report for Department of Education Science and Training. Perth: Edith Cowan University.

Louden, W., Rohl, M., & Hopkins, S. (2008). *Teaching for growth: Effective teaching of literacy and numeracy*. Final Report for the Department of Education and Training, Western Australia. Perth: The University of Western Australia.

Louden, W., & Wildy, H. (2001). *Developing schools' capacity to make performance judgements*. Final Report. Report prepared for Australian Commonwealth Department of Education, Employment, Training and Youth Affairs (DETYA). Perth, Western Australia: Edith Cowan University.

Ministerial Council on Education, Employment, Training and Youth Affairs (MCEETYA). (1995). *National report on schooling in Australia 1995*. Carlton: Curriculum Corporation.

Rasch, G. (1960/1980). *Probabilistic models for some intelligence and achievement tests*. Copenhagen: Danish Institute for Educational Research. (Expanded edition, 1980. Chicago: University of Chicago Press)

Raudenbush, S. W., & Willms, J. D. (1995). The estimation of school effects. *Journal of Educational and Behavioural Statistics, 20*(4), 307–335.

Robinson, W. S. (1950). Ecological correlations and the behaviour of individuals. *American Sociological Review, 15*, 351–357.

Rowe, K. (2004, April 19–22). *Analysing and reporting performance indicator data: 'Caress' the data and user beware!* Background paper to invited address presented at the 2004 Public Sector Performance conference, under the auspices of the International Institute for Research, Sydney. Retrieved February 2, 2008, from http://www.acer.edu.au/documents/Rowe-IIR_Conf_2004_ Paper.pdf

Rowe, K. (2005). *Practical multilevel analysis with MlwiN & LISREL: An integrated course* (4th Rev. ed.). Camberwell: Australian Council for Educational Research.

Strand, S. (1998). A 'value added' analysis of the 1996 primary school performance tables. *Educational Research, 40*(2), 123–137.

Thorndike, E. L. (1939). On the fallacy of imputing correlations found for groups to the individuals and in smaller groups composing them. *American Journal of Psychology, 52*, 122–124.

Waugh, R. F. (2006). Rasch measurement. In N. J. Salkind (Ed.), *Encyclopedia of measurement and statistics* (Vol. 3., pp. 820–825). Thousand Oaks, CA: Sage Publications.

Woodhouse, G., & Goldstein, H. (1988). Educational performance indicators and LEA tables. *Oxford Review of Education, 14*(3), 301–320.

Wright, B. D. (1999). Fundamental measurement. In S. E. Embretson & S. C. Hersberger (Ed.), *The new rules of measurement* (pp. 65–104). Mahwah, NJ: Lawrence Erlbaum Associates, Publishers.

Zhou, X.-H., Perkins, A. J., & Hui, S. L. (1999). Comparisons of software packages for generalized linear multilevel models. *The American Statistician, 53*(3), 282–290.

Jessica M. Elderfield and Russell F. Waugh
(Faculty of Education and Arts, Edith Cowan University)

ROSLYN NEILSON, RUSSELL F. WAUGH AND DESLEA KONZA

3. A RASCH ANALYSIS OF THE ASTRONAUT INVENTED SPELLING TEST

The Early Literacy Learning Environment for Young Children

Key words: invented spelling, Rasch measurement, phonemic awareness, orthographic awareness, literacy assessment, early childhood literacy, early primary literacy.

ABSTRACT

The Astronaut Invented Spelling Test (AIST) was designed as an assessment tool for monitoring the literacy progress of students in the early years of schooling. The test uses an invented spelling format, in which children are encouraged to try to write words that they have probably not been taught how to spell. In the initial development phase of the test, AIST spelling responses were scored to give credit to all reasonable representations of all the phonemes in the test words, with bonus points awarded for use of specific conventional patterns of English orthography. A Rasch analysis was subsequently used to explore the psychometric properties of the test, based on data from two large samples of Australian schoolchildren in their first four years of schooling (N=654 and N=533). Of the original 48 AIST items, 28 were found to provide an excellent fit to the Rasch measurement model. These 28 items, ordered from easy to hard, were calibrated in terms of item difficulty on the same scale as the student measures. The scales for both samples were unidimensional and reliable, with Person Separation Indices of 0.96. The order of item difficulty that emerged from the Rasch analysis provided strong evidence about the early development of phonemic and orthographic awareness. By combining the item difficulty scale and the student measures, the Rasch analysis of the AIST provides early literacy teachers with a classroom-based assessment tool that is not only psychometrically robust for screening purposes, but that also supports the choice of specific instructional targets in the classroom.

INTRODUCTION

Young children vary greatly in the speed and efficiency with which they respond to formal reading and writing instruction in their first few years at school. Teachers are faced with the rather difficult task of keeping a careful check on individual differences in early literacy progress within their classrooms, so that those learners

*R.F. Cavanagh and R.F. Waugh (eds.), Applications of Rasch Measurement
in Learning Environments Research, 45–75.*
© 2011 Sense Publishers. All rights reserved.

who need extra support can be identified before they have experienced sustained failure (Stanovich, 1986; Torgeson, 1992; Wolf, 2008), and so that teaching programs can be adapted to the needs of students in particular learning environments (Foorman, Francis, Fletcher & Schatschneider, 1988). It is an important challenge for educators to ensure that the assessment tools used for the ongoing assessment of children's early literacy progress are as valid, reliable, efficient and diagnostically useful as possible.

Many onventional standardised tests of reading and spelling are not entirely suitable as assessment tools in the very early stages of learning to read and write, due to the problems of 'floor effects'. When new literacy skills are just starting to emerge in a population, it takes a substantial amount of exposure and learning time for children's test scores to spread out so that the bottom tail of the distribution can be clearly identified. Standardised reading and spelling test scores achieved by children who are in fact at risk, therefore, may not register as being within the critically low range for several crucial months in the schooling process.

One way to try to circumvent the problem of floor effects when assessing very early literacy progress is to assess variables other than reading and spelling – variables that typically emerge before formal schooling commences, and that are correlated with later reading and spelling success. The DIBELS screening project (Good & Kaminski, 2002) has pioneered important work in this area, and has included in its test battery well-established precursor skills such as phonemic awareness and alphabet letter knowledge. There are, however, some concerns that even the early DIBELS measures are subject to floor effects (Catts, Petscher, Schatschneider, Bridges & Mendoza, 2009). Clay's (1985) *Concepts about Print* test is another example of an endeavour to evaluate pre-reading or emergent literacy skills, but evidence about its predictive strength is not strong (National Early Literacy Panel, 2008).

It is often the case that a simpler form of ongoing assessment is used by busy classroom teachers: children's progress is documented with reference to sets of 'levelled' books in their schools' purchased reading schemes (Clay, 1985). While the 'levelled book' method of assessing children does provide a fairly valid measure of literacy progress (Center, Wheldall & Freeman, 1992), there are obvious questions to be asked about the standardisation of levels across different commercial reading schemes. More importantly, however, there are also questions to be asked about the range of skills that may underlie successful oral reading of the kinds of books that tend to be included in early reading programs. This is an issue that is particularly critical in the beginning stages of learning to read, where children may provide a successful oral rendition of the relevant books through rote memory, prediction of repetitive text, or use of contextual and picture cues, in the absence of independent word attack skills. Given that early phonological and code-breaking abilities are so important in predicting how well students will succeed in literacy (National Early Literacy Panel, 2008), it is unfortunate that these might be the skills that are overlooked when levelled books are used as a sole criterion of progress.

A recent meta-analysis carried out by the USA National Early Literacy Panel (NELP, 2008) has formally evaluated the efficiency of a range of variables that have been used for predicting later progress in decoding, reading comprehension, and spelling. One variable in the research literature that was reported by the NELP (p. 59) to yield consistently strong predictions was invented spelling. It will be argued in this paper that invented spelling has the potential to provide useful new avenues for research, both in terms of its potential as a classroom-based assessment strategy that might circumvent some of the practical problems that tend to be associated with the tracking of early literacy progress, and in terms of its diagnostic usefulness.

Invented spelling is a term used to refer to what individuals do when they try to write down a word that they do not already know how to spell. It has long been recognised (Bissex, 1980; Chomsky, 1979; Read, 1971) that when young children experiment with writing words they have not been taught, they draw on whatever knowledge they have of the alphabet, and they also draw on their own ability to analyse the sounds in the spoken words – that is, their phonemic awareness. Indeed, errors made during invented spelling have provided a rich source of information about the development of phonemic awareness (Ehri 1989; Treiman 1993). Invented spelling tests of various forms have been used extensively in research studies (e.g. Mann, Tobin & Wilson, 1997; Morris & Perney, 1984; Richgels, 1995; Tangel & Blachman, 1995), and in clinical analyses of literacy development (e.g. Snowling & Stackhouse, 1996; Gillon, 2004).

There are several reasons why invented spelling may be of particular interest in the search for efficient classroom-based assessments of early literacy progress (Richgels, 2001; Ukrainetz, 2006). In terms of task analysis, invented spelling is particularly relevant as an early literacy predictor because it is a complex phenomenon, reflecting several underlying skills that are well established as correlates of literacy success. In order to invent spelling at any level more sophisticated than a mere scribble-like modelling of the writing process, children need to be able to write some letters of the alphabet and know that the alphabet letters somehow map onto sounds in words (Byrne, 1988), and they need to have at least some phonemic awareness – that is, the ability to attend to and identify sounds in words. Alphabet knowledge is itself a very robust early predictor of how well children are likely to progress in the early years of school (Foulin, 2005; Share, Jorm, Mclean & Matthews, 1984), and phonemic awareness has been the subject of decades of research in its role as an enabling factor in learning to read and spell (e.g. Adams, 1990; Byrne, 1998; Gillon, 2004; Torgeson & Mathes, 2000).

There are also practical reasons to consider the use of invented spelling tests as early literacy assessments. When invented spelling attempts are scored, testers assign marks to partially correct attempts, rather than marking spelling responses as either correct or incorrect. This flexibility allows floor effects to be minimised when children's spelling skills are still very limited. In addition, tests of invented spelling can be administered as group tasks rather than requiring individual administration, since testers can score children's written responses after the test has been administered, rather than having to record spoken responses in real time as is required by conventional phonemic awareness and oral reading assessments. This means that invented spelling has the potential to be an efficient assessment tool for busy classroom teachers.

One potential problem with respect to using invented spelling for classroom-based assessment is that only limited information can be gained about a child's underlying literacy skills if he or she spells a word correctly. A conventional spelling may reflect robust linguistic mastery, but it may also merely reflect a kind of logographic 'drawing' of the word, in the way that children often learn to write their names. It may also possibly reflect a shallow and possibly very transient rote-learned response (the kind of spelling that is learned for the Friday classroom test but forgotten by Monday). As Ehri (1989) has pointed out, it is only spelling mistakes that provide testers with insight into the processing strategies by which a word was spelled. In order to circumvent the problem of invented spelling tests using words that children are likely to have learned by rote, several researchers have used non-words for spelling tests, both in research settings (Stage & Wagner, 1992) and in published individually administered tests (e.g. Neilson, 2003a). It is difficult, however, to imagine a classroom full of very young children making sense of a test that required them to write nonsense; the dangers of increased error variance attributable to sheer confusion seem unacceptably high. There is, there-fore, an arguable need for practical, effective and standardised classroom-based assessments that involve the invented spelling of real words.

AIMS

This discussion paper reports on the development and subsequent statistical analysis of an assessment tool that attempts to contribute to the available battery of tests for monitoring early literacy progress: a group-administered test of invented spelling that can be used for the purpose of tracking the development of early literacy skills.

The *Astronaut Invented Spelling Test*, or *AIST*, was originally developed by the first author for her own clinical use. Subsequent clinical experience and small-scale research indicated that the test was proving to be useful, with data collected being valid and reliable, and it was informally self-published for local distribution in Australia 2003. A large database of children's performance on the test has been collected by the first author and her colleagues since 2003, documenting the responses of children in a range of New South Wales and Victorian metropolitan and rural schools from the first to the fourth years of schooling. In order to evaluate the test more rigorously and to explore its psychometric properties, the database of available *AIST* scores was analysed by the second author using a Rasch analysis technique in late 2008.

This discussion paper will first describe the *AIST* and report on initial data that was collected and analysed using conventional psychometrics based on a quanti-tative Total Score system, with all test items included in the total. A 'diagnostic' breakdown of the Total Score will also be described, based on a priori assumptions about the development of phonemic and orthographic awareness. The results of a Rasch analysis carried out on the large data set will then be presented, along with an analysis of the items that proved to be the strongest in terms of Rasch scoring. Finally, the resultant Rasch item difficulty scale will be discussed in the light of what it can contribute to a practical, teaching-based model of the development of phonemic and orthographic awareness.

THE ASTRONAUT INVENTED SPELLING TEST (AIST)

The AIST is a simple written test that can be administered to groups of children (or to individual children) in about five to ten minutes. Students are provided with a response sheet that contains four slightly offbeat illustrations of astronauts with nametags attached to their sleeves. The tester begins by announcing that the astronauts got lost on a space walk, and states that if the children can write the names into the tags, the astronauts might be found again. Younger children are reassured that they are not expected to know how to spell the names, but the astronauts will be saved if they simply try to write down some of the sounds they can hear in the words. The astronaut names are then dictated in a simple guessing game format. The names are contextually appropriate to the illustrations, and are also humorous and slightly politically incorrect (a feature of the test which children tend to enjoy): Bobby Blockhead, Tubby Twinkle, Fred Fixit and Smiley Sam. Experience shows that children are generally able to make substantial spelling efforts on the task after a few months of formal schooling, or once they have mastered at least a few alphabet letters. Children continue to find the task challenging and entertaining up to about Grade 3.

The very colloquial quality of the astronaut names means that the words are likely to be familiar to young children (indeed, the word *twinkle* will have been sung countless times by many of the students), but are also unlikely to have been encountered in spelling lists. The spelling of at least some of the names, therefore, really does have to be invented, thereby reflecting phonemic awareness rather than rote learning. Each astronaut has a first and a second name, but the names are dictated to the children as whole phrases that are three or four syllables long. The length of the phrases to be written down introduces an additional working memory component into the task.

The astronaut names contain 39 phonemes, sampling a range of consonants and consonant clusters and some long and short vowels. The words also include nine examples of orthographic patterns (Bear et al., 2004) or spelling conventions that are not immediately obvious from a simple sounding-out perspective, such as the doubling of consonants to signal a short vowel in *Tubby*, and the use of the common –le pattern for the syllabic /l/ at the end of the name *Twinkle*.

The AIST scoring system in its original form – a traditional psychometric form – involves firstly allocating one point to what is defined as a reasonable representation of each of the 39 phonemes in the names. For example, if *Smiley* is spelled SMILE, full marks are awarded for the representation of the five phonemes in the word. It has been found that some phonemes in the set of names present consistent problems to young children because of their inherent allophonic variations; this problem particularly affects the short vowels (e.g. u/a; i/e) and the voicing feature of stop consonants in post-vocalic position (e.g. block/blog; fret/Fred). The original scoring system allows a half point to be allocated to spelling attempts that are affected by allophonic variation, in order to reflect the fact that a spelling attempt that marks the presence of a phoneme, even if somewhat inaccurately, is stronger than a response that does not mark the phoneme at all. The second step involves allocating a possible nine additional bonus points for the use of the specified orthographic conventions. The original AIST scoring system, therefore, allows for the calculation of a Total Score (maximum = 48) derived by summing up the phonemes correctly and the orthographic bonus.

The AIST also specifies a system for breaking down the Total Score into four Diagnostic Subscores, in order to yield separate percentage correct scores for three different categories of phonemes and the orthographic bonus. The categories of phonemes are defined on the basis of their position within the syllabic structure of the words, rather than in terms of the qualities of the phonemes themselves. The three phonemic Diagnostic Subscores are:

a. Consonants (1): the consonants on the external boundaries of syllables - e.g. /s/ and/m/in *Sam*, and /f/ and /d/ in *Fred* (n = 20);
b. Vowels: 8 short vowels and 5 long vowels or diphthongs (n = 13); and
c. Consonants (2): the consonants that occur in internal-syllable position in clusters - e.g. /r/ in *Fred*; /w/ and the pre-consonantal nasal phoneme /ng/ in Twinkle (n = 6).

The rationale underlying the three phonemic components of the AIST Diagnostic Subscores reflects well-establish evidence (Read, Bissex, Chomsky, Gentry, Richgels, Treiman) that when children first use letters and sounds in their analysis of the speech stream, their representations of the sounds in words are partial, reflecting only the salient phonemes, with salience being characterised largely by the position of the phoneme within the syllable and its phonetic context. Children then move on to show fuller phonetic analysis, at which point their spelling attempts show that they can identify all the phonemes in words.

There is some disagreement amongst spelling researchers as to the nature of the development of orthographic awareness in young children. 'Stage' theorists have been characterised as arguing that orthographic spelling strategies represent a new strategy that emerges only after the phonemic stage has consolidated. At that point, spelling becomes a matter of using visually-based pattern knowledge rather than phonemic analysis. This may not be an entirely accurate account of the stage theory approach, as perhaps the most influential of the stage theorists, Ehri (e.g. Ehri 1989) has always stressed the continuity between phonemic and orthographic strategies, in the sense that the former necessarily underpins and informs the latter. Orthographic knowledge, in Ehri's terms, becomes 'bonded' in the lexicon with awareness of phonemes.

It has been argued by 'repertoire' theorists (e.g. Apel & Masterton, 2001; Apel, Masterton & Neissen, 2004; Bourassa & Treiman, 2001), that it is misleading to suggest that one source of spelling knowledge is left behind as another source develops; mature spellers draw on a range of strategies in different contexts and for different purposes, including phonemic analysis when this is necessary. There is, moreover, clear evidence that there are several forms of orthographic knowledge that appear very early in children's spelling strategies, such as the ability to judge whether or not sequences of letters form patterns that look like English words (Treiman).

When the AIST was originally designed, it was hypothesised that the three phonemic subscores would show clear developmental trends; the relationship of these trends to the orthographic components of the test, as reflected in the fourth Diagnostic Subscore, was left open.

AIST DATA COLLECTION

By the time Rasch analysis was carried out in 2008, scored AIST responses were available for a sample of 1308 Australian children, collected over several years from six separate schools in NSW and Victoria. In all cases, the AIST was administered by the first author or students under her supervision, or by a trained speech pathologist, as part of a consultative service to the schools who had requested benchmarking of the children in specific grades. When a school requested that the test be re-administered to the same class in later grades (as often occurred), the results of the second testing were not included in the data set to be presented here.

Testing took place at whatever time of year the school chose to organise the assessments, and involved whichever grades the school wanted to be benchmarked. In all cases whole cohorts in a grade level were tested, with the proviso that written parental consent was obtained for children to participate in the testing. The consent forms explained the procedure and the rationale for testing, specified that children could withdraw from the assessment if they wished to do so, and also stated that the *AIST* data might be used as part of a norming study, with the stipulation that no schools and no children would be identified individually. It was found in practice that teachers kept encouraging parents to return the signed consent forms, and only a negligible number of children failed to return permission notes during the data collection process.

Participating schools ranged from middle class through to working class and economically disadvantaged. None of the schools represented a high socio-economic status. Children came from the mix of cultural backgrounds that is typical of Australia in the early 21st century, although in the grades tested there were no newly-arrived immigrant children who were not fluent in English. Two children with profound hearing loss participated in the testing, but their results were not included in the reported norms. All other mainstreamed children with special needs, such as mild cognitive impairment, mild hearing loss and specific language disorders, partici-pated in the data collection.

The first year of formal schooling has various labels in different educational districts, including Prep, Pre-Primary, Kindergarten and Reception. NSW refers to this year as 'Kindergarten', but this is an ambiguous term that is to refer to a preschool year in some districts, so for convenience the more generally accepted term 'Reception' will be used here. The fourth year of schooling is called Year 3 or Grade 3 in most school districts.

A small number of children participated in the data collection but were completely unable to attempt the invented spelling task. Up to 15 percent of Reception early attempts had to be discarded for this reason, with a much smaller percentage in the latter part of the Reception year. The issue of children whose spelling attempts cannot be scored will be discussed again below.

It was immediately apparent in the course of data collection that not only were there very dramatic increases on the AIST Total Score over the first four years of schooling, but there was also a strong effect of time of testing within the first two years. The Reception and Grade 1 data sets were therefore further subdivided into 'Early', Middle' and 'Late' for the purposes of data analysis. Figure 1 illustrates the mean AIST Total Score (max = 48, with all items equally weighted) for the original Australian sample for each grade level. An ANOVA showed a highly significant effect of grade level, with $F(3, 1300) = 253.77$, $p < .0000$ (Cohen effect size $d = 5.1$).

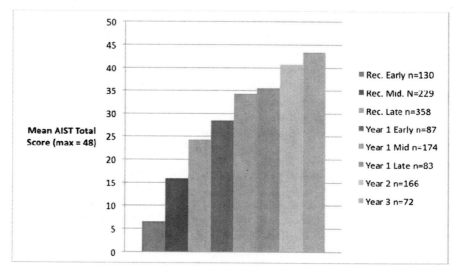

Figure 1. Mean AIST total score, reception to year 3, Australian sample (N = 1308).

RELIABILITY AND VALIDITY OF DATA FROM THE AIST
(ORIGINAL SCORING SYSTEM)

Inter-rater reliability for AIST scoring has been checked in several informal and formal studies (e.g. Bryant, 2003). About 96 or 97 percent agreement between scorers has been consistently achieved. Less competent spelling responses produced by children – that is, attempts that include difficult-to-decipher letters and/or randomly guessed letters – are much more likely to generate inter-rater disagreements on individual items than stronger spelling attempts are. It has been found, however, that the scoring disagreements seldom make a difference to the rank of a child's score within a given group, since children who write in this way are consistently ranked low in their class.

Immediate test-retest reliability for the *AIST* has been demonstrated to be extremely high. The study that demonstrated this feature of the test occurred when a class of 28 children had completed the whole test for the purposes of filming a demonstration DVD, and the cameraman then asked for a full re-shoot of exactly the same process. New response sheets were handed out, and the testing was repeated exactly as it had been done before. The correlation between the class *AIST* scores on the first and second filming was r = 0.98, with a slight but non-significant shift upwards for the mean Total Score.

Somewhat lower test-retest reliability statistics have been obtained when sets of students have been re-assessed in subsequent years, as might be expected when the skills being monitored are ones that change rapidly during the early developmental years. In all cases of data collection, moreover, the first data collection in a school has been followed up by a period of remedial phonemic awareness intervention offered to the lowest-performing children. Despite the interventions and the time lags, however, the underlying skills measured by the *AIST* have proved to be stable, with test-retest correlations in three separate schools ranging from r = 0.63 to r = 0.75 over periods of six to 12 months.

Concurrent validity has been examined in several small-scale research studies involving the correlation of *AIST* scores with other literacy variables, including phonemic awareness and word recognition. The *AIST* has shown correlations of between 0.81 and 0.89 with the *Sutherland Phonological Awareness Test-Revised*, which is itself a well-established Australian test of phonological awareness (Bryant, 2002; Neilson 1999; Neilson 2003a; Neilson 2009); a correlation of 0.78 with the Word Identification subtest of the *Woodcock Reading Mastery Scales* (Neilson, 2003a; Woodcock, 1987); and a correlation of .84 with the *Burt Test of Word Reading* (Clay, 1985).

PATTERNS EMERGING FROM THE DIAGNOSTIC SUBSCORES

The four Diagnostic Subscores of the *AIST* – that is, the subsets of items involving three different aspects of phonemic skills and the one orthographic measure – have shown a distinctive pattern of development over the first years of schooling. This pattern has been replicated in several different cross-sectional data sets or school cohort studies. The pattern is documented in Figure 2, which shows the mean percentage correct for each the four AIST Diagnostic Subscores over the first four years of schooling for the entire Australian data set. Clearly, the items included in the Consonants (1) Subscore items are the most accessible for children as they start school. The Vowel phonemes are represented soon after that. The items that comprise the Consonants (2) Subscore require a good deal more schooling experience to be mastered. By Grade 3, however, it is only the Orthographic Bonus that seems to separate out strong and weak spellers. These patterns of development suggest that although the developing skills of phonemic and orthographic awareness do show some overlap in the early years, they tend to develop at different rates; orthographic awareness (at least insofar as it is measured by the *AIST*) is established considerably later than phonemic analysis.

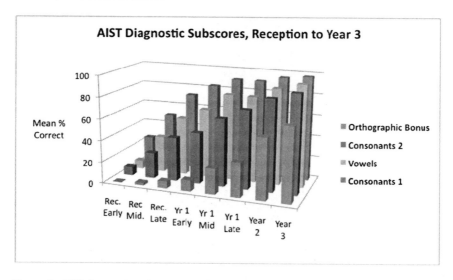

Figure 2. AIST diagnostic subscores: mean percentage correct over four years of schooling.

RASCH ANALYSIS OF THE AIST

After several years of clinical use of the *AIST*, it was clear that the test provided the basis for a useful, practical, and stable assessment of early literacy skills, and that subsets of the items seemed to document stable and potentially useful patterns of information about the development of phonemic and orthographic awareness. Questions remained, however, about the test's psychometric features, which at that point relied on summing the individual items and calculating conventional descriptive statistics based on the Total Scores and Diagnostic Subscore components. There were particular reasons to be concerned about this traditional psychometric practice because of the nature of the *AIST* items themselves. The problem was that the original choice of items was based on the inclusion of specific words that would hopefully generate useful information about young children's developing spelling skills, from relatively simple words like *Fred* to phonemically and orthographically complex words like *Twinkle*. The words, however, were presented in the context of meaningful names, and this meant that not all of the sounds in all the words were expected to be useful or unambiguous in terms of generating information about phonemic and orthographic awareness. Each phoneme or orthographic feature was, however, given the status of an 'item', with each item carrying the same weight in the construction of the *AIST* Total Score. More careful calibration of the items was clearly needed.

The *AIST* data was therefore submitted to the second author for a Rasch measurement analysis with the RUMM 2020 computer program (Andrich, Sheridan & Luo, 2005). This program is used to create a linear scale, in standard units (logits), where the items are calibrated on the same scale as the student measures. The items are ordered from easy to hard on this scale and the student measures are ordered from low to high. In simple terms, students with low measures can only answer the easy items positively; students with medium measures can only answer the medium and easy items positively; and students with high measures can answer the easy, medium and hard items positively. The RUMM program checks that the item data and the student measures fit this measurement model. Items not fitting are discarded.

The size of the available data set, over 1300 cases, meant that there was a risk that the Rasch analysis would generate statistically significant, rather than psycho-metrically significant, chi-square results at several stages. The data set was therefore divided at random into two separate sets within each of the grade levels. This division into two data sets then allowed for a replication of the results of the Rasch analysis itself. The two data sets are referred to below as Sample A and Sample B. Note that although the two samples represent different groups of students, they are not entirely independent, since results in the two samples were collected from the same classes in the same schools.

One major change had to be made to the original scoring system of the AIST for the purposes of the Rasch analysis. All half-point scores allocated for partially accurate identification of phonemically ambiguous items had to be changed to zero, because the Rasch program required items to be scored 1/0. This meant that no scoring distinction was made between, for example, the spelling FEX/*fix* and the obviously less mature FX/*fix*, or the very immature B for *Block* and the somewhat stronger BG for the same syllable. The alternative compromise would have been to award all semi-accurate responses one full point; this decision, however, would have created other problems, such as making a difficult item such as the short /u/ in *Tubby* to appear to be much easier than it was (this word generated a very large number of examples of a/u confusion). It was recognised that the unavoidable loss of the half-point options might have introduced some confounding between the responses of stronger and weaker spellers on specific items.

RESULTS

An initial Rasch analysis was performed on the original 48 items, separately by sample. It was found that 20 items did not fit the measurement model, and they were discarded due to misfit statistics. The reason for the misfits was that the difficulty levels of the items did not relate consistently to the abilities of the students. That is, some generally high-scoring students found the particular items easy while some found them difficult, and the same discrepancies held for lower-scoring students. The twenty discarded items included six whose half-point allocations had been disallowed (e.g. e/i in *fix*, t/d in *head*). This was a predictable outcome, given the concerns discussed above. One discarded item involved a case where a scoring rule had to be followed in the interests of overall consistency, although it actually led to a counter-intuitive scoring practice: that is, when children wrote only the letters SM for *Smiley Sam*, the AIST scoring criterion of allocating points to letters in phonemic sequence meant that the /m/ had to be scored as if it belonged within the relatively difficult consonant cluster in the first word *Smiley*, even if there was a good chance that it really represented the much easier /m/ in *Sam*. Four discarded items were probably problematic within the Rasch analysis because they were too easy, in that virtually all the students got them correct; these were the beginning sounds in each of the astronaut names. The reasons why the remaining items did not fit the measurement model were not immediately obvious, but some suggestions will be made in the course of the discussion below.

The results below relate to the 28 items that were finally included in the Rasch analysis.

Sample A and Sample B were used to create two unidimensional, linear scales using the Rasch Unidimensional Measurement Models (RUMM2020) program (Andrich, Sheridan & Luo, 2005). Rasch measures for the two samples are shown in Table 1.

Table 1. Ordered AIST measures by stage progression in the samples A and B

	Early R	Mid R	Late R	Early Y1	Mid Y1	LateY 1	Year 2	Year 3	Total
Number SA	89	91	50	81	57	145	99	42	654
Number SB	50	88	165	30	92	20	67	30	542
Mean Measure SA	−3.59	−2.20	−1.62	−0.12	+0.60	+1.88	+3.00	+4.02	
Mean Measure SB	−4.07	−1.97	−0.63	−0.14	+1.29	+1.39	+3.56	+3.92	
Standard Deviation SA	1.33	1.85	1.96	2.08	1.64	1.80	1.99	1.67	
Standard Deviation SB	1.25	2.06	2.13	1.81	1.87	1.33	1.77	1.70	

Note: (1) EarlyR means early reception pre-school students, MidR means middle reception pre-school students, LateR means late reception pre-school students, EarlyY1 means early Year 1 students (aged 6), MidY1 means middle Year 1 students, LateY1 means late Year 1 students, Year 2 means Year 2 students (aged 7) and Year 3 means Year 3 students (aged 8); (2) SA means sample A and SB means sample B; (3) Measures are in standard, linear Rasch measurement units called logits; (3) The mean Rasch measures show an orderly progression from pre-school to Year 3 in both samples, as expected.

DIMENSIONALITY

There was an item-trait interaction chi-square $\chi^2 = 268.26$ (df = 252, p = 0.12 for Sample A and chi-square $\chi^2 = 294.64$ (df =274, p = 0.0001) for Sample B. This means that a single parameter for each student (the student measure) and a single parameter for each item (the difficulty) could be used to predict, with reasonable accuracy, each student's responses to all the items, to create a unidimensional scale. The unidimensionality of the scale was clearly valid for Sample A, but there was some significant interaction with Sample B. The interaction was mainly due to three items, Item 15, the phonemic representation of the /i/y/ in *Tubby*, Item 38, the phonemic representation of /a/ in *Sam* and Item 45, the orthographic bonus allocated to the use of the letter Y for the second vowel phoneme in *Tubby*. There are several possible reasons why the name *Tubby* might have generated some instability in the test. Some children clearly interpreted the word as *tummy* rather than *tubby*, for reasons probably relating to the humorous illustration of the astronaut. It is also possible that exposure to the TV program '*Teletubbies*' generated some extraneous interference in the data (that is, evidence of spelling knowledge not related to invented spelling). In addition, the orthographic pattern involving Y at the ends of words may have been subject to unpredictable interference due to children's exposure to the particular spellings of common names (e.g. Toni/Tony); note that the equivalent orthographic point for the Y in the name *Bobby*, Item 41, was one of the twenty items discarded from the Rasch item scale for reasons of misfit.

SUMMARY OF FIT RESIDUAL STATISTICS

The RUMM2020 program estimates the overall fit residual statistics that are the differences between the actual values and the estimated values from the measurement model. When the data do fit the measurement model, the standardised fit residual statistics have a distribution with a mean near zero and a standard deviation near one. Table 2 shows that this is clearly the case for the two AIST data sets, Sample A and Sample B. Consistent with a Rasch measurement model, too, there is a good pattern of person and item responses for the two scales of 28 items.

Table 2. Global item and standardised student fit residual statistics

	Item mean	Item SD	Student mean	Student SD
Sample A	-0.47	0.72	-0.35	0.70
Sample B	-0.44	0.74	-0.32	0.62

Note: These are standardised fit residuals. When the data fit the measurement model, the standardised fit residuals have a mean near zero and a standard deviation (SD) near one, as is the case here.

Person Separation Index

In the RUMM program, the Person Separation Index is an estimate of the true score variance among the students and the estimated observed score variance, using estimates of their ability measures and the standard errors of these measures (Andrich & van Schoubroeck, 1989). Persons Separation Indices are interpreted like a Cronbach Alpha (Cronbach, 1951), which is an estimate of a test's internal consistency. For a good measure, it is desirable that this index should be 0.9 or greater, as it is an indicator that the student measures are separated by more than their standard errors. The Person Separation Indices and the Cronbach Alphas for both Sample A and Sample B are 0.96. This indicates that there is very good separation of the measures in comparison to the standard errors, and the power of the tests-of-fit is excellent for both data sets.

Individual Item Fit

The location of each item on the scale is the item difficulty in standard units, called logits (a term referring to 'log odds of answering successfully'). All the items fit the measurement model with probabilities greater than p=0.01 for both Sample A and Sample B (except for the three items mentioned). The residuals represent the difference between the observed responses and the expected responses, calculated from the Rasch measurement parameters. Standardised residuals should fall within the range of –2 and +2 standardised logits, and this was the case for both Sample A and Sample B.

Targeting

The RUMM2020 program produces a student-measure item-difficulty, or targeting graph, on which the student measures are placed on the same scale as the item

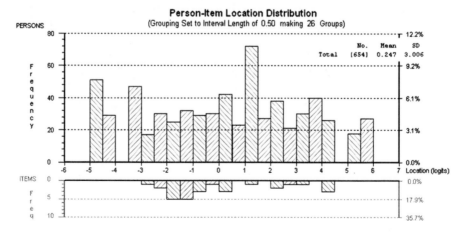

Figure 3. Targeting graph for AIST (Sample A).

Note: The student measures are on the top side from low (–4.6 logits) to high (+5.6 logits). The item difficulties are on the bottom side from easy (–3 logits) to hard (+4.3 logits).

difficulties in standard units or logits. Figure 3 shows the targeting graph for Sample A; Sample B was very similar. Figure 3 shows that the student measures cover a range of about –5 to +6 logits, and the item difficulties cover a range of about –2.48 to +4.3 logits. The test, as a whole might therefore, be improved by the addition of some more difficult items to 'cover' the students with higher measures and some easier items to 'cover' the students with lower measures.

DISCRIMINATION

The RUMM2020 program produces Item Characteristic Curves that can be used to examine the relationship between the expected response and the mean group student measures. The curves display how well the item discriminates between groups of students. An example of one Item Characteristic Curve is given in Figure 4, for Item 5 in Sample A (the /b/ in *Blockhead*). This curve shows that the item discriminates well for students with different measures. The Item Characteristic Curves for all the other 28 items were checked for both samples, and were found to be satisfactory; they are not reported here to avoid unnecessary repetition.

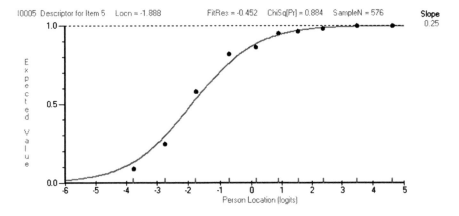

Figure 4. Item characteristic curve for item 5 (Sample A).

CONSISTENCY OF USE OF SCORING CATEGORIES

The RUMM2020 program produces graphs of the scoring categories for each item. The Scoring Category Curves show the relationship between the probabilities of scoring in each category (zero for incorrect, one for correct) on each item. Figure 5 is the Scoring Category Curve for Item 3 in Sample A, the second /b/ phoneme in *Bobby*. This figure shows that the scoring was done logically and consistently. When students have a low measure on Item 3, they have a high probability of obtaining a zero score, and when they have a high measure, they have a high probability of scoring one. The Scoring Category Curves for all the other items for both samples were checked, and they were also found to be satisfactory.

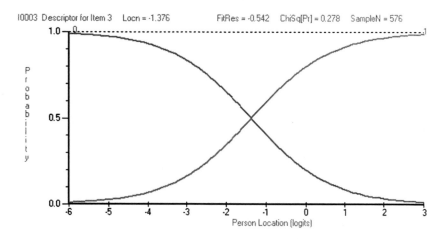

Figure 5. Scoring category curve for item 3 (Sample A).

Note

1. The blue curve is the probability of scoring zero by student measure. As the student measure increases, the probability of scoring zero decreases, as required for logical scoring.
2. The red curve is the probability of scoring one by student measure. As the student measure increases, the probability of scoring one increases, as required for logical scoring.

CHARACTERISTICS OF THE SAMPLE

The RUMM2020 program displays the measures in a graphical format separated by any situation variable, in this case gender (see Figure 6). The gender difference was not statistically significant in Sample A (a one-way ANOVA showed F (1, 652) = 0.59, p = 0.44) (Cohen's effect size d = 0.06). In Sample B, measures for females were statistically significantly higher than for males (a one-way ANOVA showed F (1, 532) = 5.34, p = 0.005 (Cohen's effect size d = 0.28). The mean measures increased statistically significantly by grade level from Early Reception (pre-primary) to Year 3 in both samples (see Table 3), as was expected. A one-way ANOVA showed F (7, 646) = 164.9, p < 0.000 for Sample A (Cohen's effect size d = 5.04), and F (7, 391) = 108.7, p<0.000 for Sample B (Cohen's effect size d = 5.36).

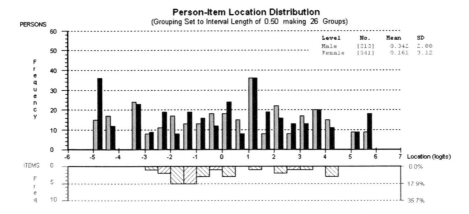

Figure 6. Target graph by Gender (Sample A).

Note: There is a colour error in the RUMM program. Maroon in the graph is blue in the right hand side data (males). Green in the graph is red in the data (females).

Table 3. Mean Rasch measures in logits by stage (Samples A and B)

Stage	Number	Sample A	Sample B	Mean SD	Number	Mean SD
1	89	−3.59	1.33	50	−4.07	1.25
2	91	−2,20	1.85	88	−1.97	2.06
3	50	−1.61	1.96	165	−0.63	2.13
4	81	−0.12	2.08	30	−0.14	1.81
5	57	+0.61	1.64	92	+1.29	1.87
6	145	+1.58	1.80	20	+1.39	1.33
7	99	+3.00	1.99	67	+3.56	1.77
8	42	+4.02	1.67	30	+3.92	1.70

Table 4. Difficulties in logits for the 28 final items in Sample A and Sample B (ordered from easiest to hardest), and diagnostic subscore categories corresponding to each item

| | | | | Original | AIST | Diagnostic | |
| | | | | Subscores | | | |
Item No.	Item Difficulty Sample 1	Order of difficulty (easiest to hardest), and description of item	Item Difficulty Sample 2	Cons. (1)	Vowels	Cons . (2)	Orth. Bonus
37	−2.64	1 /s/ in **S**am	−3.13	√			
26	−2.25	2 /f/ in **F**ixit	−2.39	√			
16	−2.09	3 /t/ in **T**winkle	−2.60	√			
14	−1.96	4 /b/ in **T**ubby	−2.00	√			
5	−1.89	5 /b/ in **B**lockhead	−1.92	√			

39	−1.68	6 /m/ in Sam	−1.97	√			
35	−1.65	7 /l/ in Smiley	−1.32	√			
25	−1.56	8 /d/ in Fred	−2.08	√			
3	−1.38	9 /b/ (2nd) in Bobby	−1.01	√			
36	−1.31	10 /i/ (y, etc.) in Smiley	−1.06		√		
15	−1.27	11 /i/ (y, etc.) in Tubby	−1.41		√		
29	−1.23	12 /s/ (part of x) in Fixit	−1.34	√			
7	−1.03	13 /o/ in Blockhead	−0.91		√		
9	−0.94	14 /h/ in Blockhead	−1.10	√			
34	−0.91	15 /ai/ in Smiley	−0.80		√		
8	−0.71	16 /k/ in Blockhead	−0.48	√			
18	−0.04	17 /I/ in Twinkle	+0.04		√		
10	+0.11	18 /e/ in Blockhead	−0.13		√		
38	+0.16	19 /a/ in Sam	−0.11		√		
28	+0.16	20 /k/ (part of x) in Fixit	+3.60			√	
17	+1.21	21 /w/ in Twinkle	+0.90			√	
47	+2.21	22 **Orth.**: X in Fix	+2.21				√
45	+2.31	23 **Orth.**: Y in Tubby	+2.56				√
19	+2.61	24 /ng/ (n) in Twinkle	+2.74			√	
48	+3.21	25 **Orth.**: SMILEY	+3.60				√
44	+4.04	26 **Orth.**: BB in Tubby	+4.46				√
40	+4.21	27 **Orth.**: BB in Bobby	+4.62				√
46	+4.31	28 **Orth.**: LE in Twinkle	+4.54				√

FINAL ITEMS AND ITEM DIFFICULTIES FOR THE TWO SAMPLES

The final 28 items selected by the Rasch analysis, together with their difficulties expressed in Logits, are presented in order from easiest to hardest in Table 4 for the two samples. There is reasonable agreement about the item difficulties in the two samples, but this is not perfect.

Table 4 also provides an annotation of each item according to the Diagnostic Subscore categories that were originally proposed as part of the AIST scoring system. It is clear that the order of item difficulty on the Rasch linear scale strongly supports the proposed categorisation of items in terms of stages of spelling development. Firstly, the separation of the phonemic and the orthographic skills seems clear-cut; the first 21 of the 28 items refer to phonemic skills, with only one phonemic item overlapping with the later-developing orthographic skills. There is fairly clear separation within the phonemic categories, too; the easiest nine of the 21 phoneme items correspond to Consonants (1), with only three Consonants (1) items overlapping with the emergence of the vowels. The three Consonants (2) items are all more difficult than the vowels.

STUDENT MEASURES SCALE

The RMM2020 program produces a list of student measures with their corresponding Raw Scores (out of 28), listed from lowest to highest and indicating the weakest to strongest students in terms of invented spelling skills. Table 5, for example, shows a partial list of students with the lowest Student Measures, with their corresponding Raw Scores (out of 28) on the Rasch Scale.

Table 5. Partial list of students with lowest measures and raw scores

ID	Raw score	Maximum score	Rasch measure	SE
26	0	28	−4.878	1.25
29	0	28	−4.878	1.25
28	0	28	−4.878	1.25
21	0	28	−4.878	1.25
215	0	28	−4.878	1.25
303	0	28	−4.878	1.25
116	0	28	−4.878	1.25
165	1	28	−4.047	0.89
74	1	28	−4.047	0.89
77	1	28	−4.047	0.89
154	1	28	−4.047	0.89
151	1	28	−4.047	0.89
40	1	28	−4.047	0.89
167	2	28	−3.457	0.71
175	2	28	−3.457	0.71
42	2	28	−3.457	0.71
41	2	28	−3.457	0.71
183	2	28	−3.457	0.71
216	2	28	−3.457	0.71
110	2	28	−3.457	0.71

INFERENCES FROM THE MEASURES OF THE TWO LINEAR RASCH SCALES

Since both the data show a good fit to the measurement model for the test and a linear unidimensional scale has been created, it follows that valid inferences about teaching goals can be made on the basis of the two scales. That is, information about the student measures can be combined with the item difficulties, allowing teachers to modulate the difficulty of what they are teaching to suit the ability levels of the students.

Given the nature of the AIST items, however, mere inspection of the item difficulty scale does not make it clear what the specific teaching implications are at each item difficulty level. This is obviously the case with respect to the 22 phoneme items (although it will be argued below that this problem to some extent applies to the orthographic items as well). The problem is that although each item may be 'tagged' as a phoneme within a word, the actual difficulty of the item relates not to the identity of the phoneme itself but to its position within the syllabic structure of the speech stream. The /k/ in *Blockhead*, for example, which is at the boundary of a syllable, is considerably easier than the /k/ in /fiks/ (*Fix*), which is located within a syllable. This is the case even though both /k/ phonemes are followed by another consonant. What the Rasch analysis of the *AIST* ultimately shows is that teachers need at least an intuitive understanding of basic phonetics, as well as a clear conceptualisation of the developmental nature of phonemic awareness, if they are to make reasonable interpretations of the *AIST* results.

The *AIST* item difficulty scale provided by the Rasch analysis does yield many interesting clues as to the nature of the development of phonemic and orthographic awareness, as well as hints to areas where further research is needed. All these issues will be addressed below.

DISCUSSION

Levels of Phonemic Awareness

As mentioned above, the teaching implications of each *AIST* item are not self-evident, and it is important for teachers to be able to interpret *AIST* results in terms of an understanding of the nature of the development of phonemic awareness and spelling if they are to make efficient use of the linear Item Difficulty scale generated by the Rasch analysis. In order to facilitate this kind of interpretation, a model of the developmental process will be presented here. The model aims to relate the invented spelling skills and/or weaknesses involved in each item to the actual phonemic processing skills that children are able to use at given stages in their development.

The Rasch analysis largely supported the model underlying the original *AIST* Diagnostic Subscore breakdown of items – that is, a model of spelling development which specifies that children progress through a semi-phonemic through to a fully phonemic analysis of the speech stream. The later development of orthographic knowledge observed in the original *AIST* scoring system was also supported in the Rasch analysis. Table 3, above, showed that the items included in the three phonemic Subscores and the Orthographic Bonus could be juxtaposed against the Item Difficulty scale, with groups of Diagnostic Subscore items being fairly clearly clustered within sections defined by the linear Rasch Scale itself.

Table 6. Summary: Model of seven levels of invented spelling skills and strategies, with levels super-imposed on the linear Rasch AIST Item difficulty scale

Level	Strategies	Features of invented spelling skills	AIST-2 marker items
Zero	Non-phonemic	No relationship between letters/shapes and sounds.	(Unable to be scored)
One	Entry into Semi-Phonemic	Letters represent sounds only at the beginning of utterances.	Only first consonants of first names; not included in Rasch Scale
Two	Early Semi-Phonemic	Consonants at the beginning of syllables within words. Some vowels. Letter names represent whole syllables.	37 /s/ in Sam 26 /f/ in Fixit 16 /t/ in Twinkle 14 /b/ in Tubby 5 /b/ in Blockhead
Three	Semi-Phonemic	CVC syllables represented - some vowels, and consonants at the end as well as at the beginning. Vowels may not be accurate.	39 /m/ in Sam 35 /l/ in Smiley 25 /d/ in Fred 3 /b/ (2nd) in Bobby 36 /i/ (y, e, etc.) in Smiley 15 /i/ (y, e, etc.) in Tubby
Four	Early Phonemic	Almost all phonemes represented, including a few consonants in clusters.	29 /s/ (part of x) in Fixit 7 /o/ in Blockhead 9 /h/ in Blockhead 34 /ai/ in Smiley 8 /k/ in Blockhead 18 /i/ in Twinkle (NOT e) 10 /e/ in Blockhead
Five	Phonemic and Emerging Orthographic	Most consonants in clusters represented, and some simple spelling conventions used.	38 /a/ (NOT e) in Sam 28 /k/ (part of x) in Fix 17 /w/ (NOT r) in Twinkle 47 Orth: x in Fix 45 Orth: y in Tubby
Six	Late Phonemic and Early Orthographic	All phonemes represented. A range of spelling conventions emerging.	19 /ng/ (n) in Twinkle 48 Orth: Smiley 44 Orth: bb in Tubby 40 Orth: bb in Bobby 46 Orth: le in Twinkle

65

Careful analysis of the Rasch Item Difficulty scale, though, provides much more information about the development of phonemic and orthographic awareness than is encompassed in the original definitions of the Diagnostic Subscores. This section of the discussion will use the Item Difficulty scale as the basis for proposing a more detailed developmental model of the role of phonemic awareness in invented spelling. The model will be specified in terms of 'levels', with the levels super-imposed upon the linear Rasch scale in order to act, in a sense, as milestones. The milestones are needed in order to characterise and summarise sets of strategies that children are progressively able to bring to the task of invented spelling as their skills mature. Each level will have groups of AIST Rasch items assigned to it, serving as typical marker items – items that are, of course, adjacent on the Item Difficulty scale.

It is acknowledged that no matter how linear and reliable the scale data are in terms of group statistics, children's developing skills emerge gradually and take a while to consolidate, and children's performance on any given assessment occasion will be affected by extraneous factors. Overlaps between the superimposed 'levels', and inconsistencies involving specific items, will therefore be expected when the scale is being used to interpret individual students' invented spelling levels.

The model, which aims to provide a meaningful way of understanding the progression of item difficulties, is summarised in Table 6. Seven developmental 'milestones', or groups of skills and strategies, are specified in the model. Levels Zero and One are too low in terms of phonemic awareness to involve items that are included in the Rasch Item Difficulty scale. Levels Two to Six are associated with specific AIST items that cluster together and jointly provide examples of the relevant skills, weaknesses and related strategies.

The above model will be discussed more fully in the following section, and associated inferences will be drawn at each level with respect to teaching implications.

DISCUSSION OF THE MODEL: TEACHING IMPLICATIONS

Level Zero: Non-Phonemic Strategies

Non-phonemic strategies are evidenced by children whose invented spelling attempts cannot be scored because their responses show no correspondence at all to the sounds in the astronaut names. As was mentioned above, this phenomenon is quite often encountered in groups of children who have just entered school; about 15% of AIST responses from Early Reception classes had to be discarded in the analysis of the AIST data. Children at this level may fulfil the task requirements as best they can by scribbling, or simply colouring in the astronauts, or filling up the name tags with letters and letter-like shapes. When letters have been used, it is important for testers to remember that the child has learned alphabet shapes as visual patterns rather than as symbols that relate to sounds.

The presence of non-phonemic strategies in a writing task at school is in an important sense an atypical developmental pattern – it is the product of an extreme mismatch between the child's school readiness and the demands of formal schooling.

Children responding at this level to the AIST are possibly experiencing bewilderment and stress within the formal school setting, even if they are only in Early Reception. It is suggested that children in this predicament should be provided with urgent remedial attention in the form of pre-literacy phonological awareness games, systematic exposure to the alphabet where both letter names and letter sounds are taught, and very explicit introduction to the concept of phonemes in words.

Level One: Entry into Semi-Phonemic Strategies

This level of responding represents children's very first realisation that words have sounds that can be represented with letters of the alphabet. The only sounds that are salient for the child, however, are those in onset position at the beginning of an utterance – in this case, at the beginning of the whole astronaut name. Children at this level will often represent the initial letters in all four of the astronaut names, but after that they may fill the name tags with random letters from their own names and possibly some copied fragments from other children in the class. Other less adventurous children will simply write the first letter and give up.

The strategy of attending to and identifying only initial sounds is not atypical in preschool children, but it represents a level of skill that puts schoolchildren at serious risk of misunderstanding what is being taught in early literacy classes. The strategy betrays a very imprecise understanding of what is meant in the classroom by the term 'sounds'. It is possible that some children take alphabet instruction quite literally when they learn, for example, that 'B' is for 'ball'. It should become apparent to children very early in their school career, however, that the word 'sound' actually refers to more than just the beginning of the speech stream. Like Level Zero children, they are at risk of feeling bewildered; if they do use random letters beyond the first sound, rather than just leaving the rest of the nametags blank, it suggests that they have reached an entirely unprofitable conclusion about the mysterious letters beyond the beginnings of words.

Children functioning at this level are not yet ready to benefit from systematic phonics programs. Early phonological awareness programming is necessary; part of the program should involve alerting children to sound features of words and phonemes beyond the first sound, and clarifying the role of alphabet letters.

Level Two: Early Semi-Phonemic Strategies

AIST items that are useful markers at Level Two (Early Semi-Phonemic Strategies):
    37   s in Sam
    26   f in Fixit
    16   t in Twinkle
    14   b in Tubby
     5   b in Blockhead

At Level Two, children are able to explore sounds beyond the onset of an utterance and identify consonants at the beginnings of syllables within the speech stream, rather than attending only to the very first sound in the speech stream. They demonstrate this skill by writing the first letters in the astronauts' second names as well as their first names, and sometimes by representing the consonant at the beginning of the second syllable in a word.

It is important to emphasise that, according to this model, true phonemic (or rather, semi-phonemic) awareness starts to emerge only at Level Two. That is, awareness of the role of alphabet letters in mapping onto sounds in words only starts to become productive when a consonant other than the first one in a word or phrase can be identified. This means, therefore, that the traditional early drilling of 'letters' and 'sounds' (B says /b/ for *ball*) does not ensure that children are ready to move forward in terms of phonemic awareness and spelling strategies. Some separate vowels may possibly be represented at Level 2, although not necessarily accurately. More frequently, however, instead of representing vowels as such, children commonly use alphabet letter names to represent whole syllables, including the vowel – e.g. using the letter B to represent the whole second syllable in Tubby.

This very early level of phonemic awareness is commonly observed at the time when young children are introduced to systematic phonics programs in formal literacy education. Phonics programs often (wrongly) assume that once children have been taught a particular phoneme in initial position, they will be able to attend to that phonemes in all positions in syllables, and will therefore be able to segment and blend short words once they have been exposed to a small set of phonemes. It is therefore very important for teachers in Reception classes to remember that they will normally have to be very careful to extend children's phonemic awareness to encompass sounds beyond the consonants at the beginning of syllables as the early phonics activities are introduced.

Level Three: Semi-Phonemic Strategies

AIST items that are useful markers at Level Three (Semi-Phonemic Strategies):

39 /m/ in Sam
35 /l/ in Smiley
25 /d/ in Fred
3 /b/ (2nd phoneme) in Bobby
36 /i/ (last vowel) in Smiley
15 /i/ (last vowel) in Tubby

Children at Level Three can often represent consonants at the ends of syllables as well as at the beginning. At this level, vowels are starting to emerge as phonemes that are represented separately rather than as part of the letter names. The presence of vowels is more likely to be marked when they end a syllable than when the syllable is closed with a consonant – for example, the second vowels in Smiley and Tubby appear well before the /o/ and /e/ vowels in Blockhead.

It is clear that at this stage children will need extensive support as they con-solidate their awareness of phonemes in all positions in consonant-vowel-consonant syllables. Children also still show little or no awareness of the less accessible consonants in words, such as the internal consonants in clusters. Teachers must remember, therefore, that even if a phoneme such as /l/ can easily be identified in words like *Smiley*, it may not yet be apparent to children in words like *slime*.

While this level of 'semi-phonemic' performance would be within the average range in Reception classes, this level reflects delayed progress in Year 1, where children are expected to know their short vowels (that is, vowels in closed syllables), and already working with consonant blends and more difficult vowel digraphs. Year 1 children who are delayed enough in their literacy skills to be referred to the classic Reading Recovery program (Clay, 1975), are also unlikely to have progressed beyond Level 3 in terms of their phonemic awareness. They may not, therefore, have the phonemic awareness skills to benefit from the kind of 'making and breaking' Reading Recovery activity that assumes full mastery of phonemes in all positions within short words. Careful exploration of children's phonemic awareness is absolutely essential at this stage in literacy development.

Level Four: Early Phonemic Strategies

Children who are able to draw on early phonemic strategies are relatively consistent about identifying all the easier consonants in words – that is, the consonants at the boundaries of syllables. They also show greater accuracy in the identification of the short vowels in closed syllables, such as the short /i/ in Twinkle.

AIST-2 items that are useful markers at Level 4 (Early Phonemic Strategies):

29 /s/ (part of the x) in Fix
 7 /o/ in Blockhead
 9 /h/ in Blockhead
34 /l/ in smiley
 8 /k/ in Blockhead
18 /i/ in Twinkle (NOT e)
10 /e/ in Blockhead

It is only at this stage of phonemic awareness development that children are really ready to benefit from systematic spelling instruction, in the sense that they will be able to map the sounds they hear in words onto the letters with which the words are spelled. Indeed, at this 'early phonemic' stage, systematic spelling instruction can provide an important boost to further development in phonemic awareness, provided that sufficient support is given in terms of identifying the inaccessible consonants in clusters and classifying the ambiguous short vowels. This kind of support may be all that is needed to move children towards Level 5 in terms of their spelling strategies. It is essential, however, that spelling is seen as more than the rote learning of visual patterns, but instead is treated as an opportunity for children to explore sound-letter mappings in words in precise detail.

Level Five: Phonemic and Emerging Orthographic Strategies

AIST items that are useful markers at Level Five (Phonemic and Emerging Orthographic Strategies):

28 /k/ (part of the x) in Fix
38 /a/ (NOT e) in Sam
17 /w/ (NOT r) in Twinkle
47 Orthographic Bonus: x in Fix
45 Orthographic Bonus: y in Tubby

Children at this level of development can identify almost all the phonemes in words, including some fairly difficult consonants in clusters such as the /w/ in Twinkle and the /k/ phoneme that is part of the x in Fix. Their representation of short vowels is starting to respect letter-choice conventions that are somewhat ambiguous phonetically, such as the short 'a' in Sam, which is very close to an allophone of short 'e'. Some simple spelling conventions are also starting to emerge.

The careful exploration of sound-letter mapping patterns discussed with respect to Level 4 skills can now be used by teachers to help children to notice spelling patterns that are less regular, or spelling choices that depend on positional rules. This is the point at which a pattern-detection form of learning can come into play during children's reading and spelling activities, allowing children to detect statistical regularities in the alphabetic code, and thereby allowing orthographic patterns to be mastered.

Level Six: Late Phonemic and Early Orthographic Strategies

AIST items that are useful markers at Level 6 (Late Phonemic and Early Orthographic Strategies):

19 /ng/ (N) in Twinkle
48 Orthographic Bonus: Smiley
44 Orthographic Bonus: bb in Tubby
40 Orthographic Bonus: bb in Bobby
46 Orthographic Bonus: le in Twinkle

Children at Level Six can identify all the phonemes in words, including the notoriously difficult pre-consonantal nasal phoneme in *Twinkle* (Treiman, 1993). Children are consolidating their use of spelling conventions that are not predictable from simple sounding out of the words. Level Six therefore represents the point at which phonemic awareness can to some extent be taken for granted in children's literacy development. Future progress will involve the development of fluency and automaticity in decoding and encoding, and more sophisticated use of the spelling conventions and morphemic patterns of the English alphabetic code.

STAGE AND REPERTOIRE MODELS OF SPELLING

The model of the development of phonemic awareness in spelling described above is superimposed along a linear scale of item difficulty, with the labelled 'levels' in the model intended to serve as developmental milestones. The strong linearity of the Rasch scale supports the position that the milestones relevant to the phonemic skills are sequential; once a certain level of refinement of phonemic analysis has been achieved, less mature strategies are no longer used. Indeed, there is a good deal of evidence (e.g. Ehri 1989) to suggest that mature spellers find it very difficult to go back in time, as it were, and attend to phonetic aspects of the speech stream in order to 'hear' sounds in words in the way that immature spellers do. Adults consequently find it difficult to understand why young children who have not yet been influenced by the orthographic system find many phoneme categories ambiguous or confusing (Ehri, 1989; Read, 1971); teachers are very often surprised, for example, when children spell *train* as CHRAN.

It was interesting that the orthographic skills tapped by the *AIST* grouped together strongly in the Rasch analysis, falling clearly at the high end of the linear scale. The set of items covering orthographic strategies appeared in a cluster, emerging only after virtually all phonemic awareness skills were consolidated. This at first glance seems to provide support for the position commonly held in the literature that alphabetic or letter-name skills precede the development of orthographic strategies (e.g. Bear et al., 2004) – the position that has been questioned by Treiman and others. It is, however, quite possible that this evidence about the emergence of orthographic strategies is an artefact of the items included in the *AIST*, and also a function of the *AIST* items that were discarded by the Rasch analysis. This possibility will be explored in some detail in the following section.

ORTHOGRAPHIC AWARENESS AND THE AIST RASCH ANALYSIS

Orthographic awareness is a complex phenomenon. One of the simpler aspects of orthographic awareness involves 'mental orthographic images' (Bear et al., 2004), or simple visual memory representations, for whole words or for specific grapheme choices in specific words. This kind of knowledge may well be dependent on sheer exposure, and may not involve any phonemic underpinning or linguistic sophistication at all; the ubiquitous correct spelling of the whole word *the* in the writing of very immature spellers is a testimony to this. An example of this aspect of the use of orthographic strategies in otherwise immature spellers may have emerged from the Rasch analysis itself, in terms of an explanation of why Item 43 had to be discarded. This was the item that awarded an orthographic bonus point for the use of EA, rather than merely E, in the word *head* – a spelling convention based simply on a particular grapheme choice in the language. Clearly, Rasch misfit statistics showed that some strong spellers found this item difficult and some weak spellers found it easy. It is indeed very plausible that *head* might be one of those words that some students knew how to spell correctly, without this knowledge necessarily relating one way or the other to their phonemic awareness. In this case, that is, the orthographic item clearly did not belong on a linear scale that tapped into the emergence of phonemic awareness.

Another aspect of orthographic awareness involves sensitivity to spelling patterns that reflect morphemic consistencies rather than representing the phonemes in words. It is well established (Treiman, 1993) that morphemic information carried by spelling, such as plural and past tense endings, is established relatively early in the development of orthographic skills (compare the words *duct* and *ducked*). The AIST did not include any items involving plurals or past tense endings, and this may be one reason why orthographic skills were not in evidence amongst the easier items on the Rasch Item Difficulty scale.

Amongst the orthographic items that were included in the Rasch analysis, however, there is an interesting hint of evidence about orthographic skill development that merits further exploration with respect to morphemic knowledge. Item 47 represented the orthographic bonus point for the use of the letter X for a post-vocalic /ks/ cluster (the X in *Fix*). The use of the letter X is traditionally introduced to children not as a phonemic cluster but as one of the 26 letters of the alphabet; it is typically taught rather late in the first year of schooling, well after both C/K and S. In terms of sheer awareness of sounds, therefore, it is not surprising that the X in *Fix* was treated often phonemically rather than orthographically by younger children. When young children were attending closely to the phonemes in the word *fix*, they tended to notice the /s/ component of the cluster at the boundary of the syllable more easily than the /k/ component buried within the syllable; this was confirmed by the relative positions of Items 29 and 28 on the Rasch Item Difficulty scale in Table 3 above (Logits -1.23 for /s/ and +0.16 for /k/, respectively, for Sample A). The orthographic bonus for X, Item 47, was, unsurprisingly much more difficult than both the phonemic items (Logits +2.21). The interesting question to ask, however, is why Item 47 was the easiest of the orthographic items on the scale. It may be significant that this orthographic bonus item involves a spelling choice that can depend largely on morphemic sensitivity. The spelling choice of the letter X (rather than –cks) for *fix* may be based merely on knowledge of the conventional spelling of the word, but it may also reflect sensitivity to a consistent orthographic pattern in the language: the X versus –cks choice tends to reflect whether or not the /s/ component of a syllable-final /ks/ cluster is a plural (compare the words *dux* and *ducks*).

Other aspects of orthographic awareness reflect sensitivity to conditional and positional grapheme-phoneme relationship patterns. These context-sensitive patterns include the doubling of consonants at syllable junctures to signal short or long vowels in the preceding syllable (doubling occurs in *Bobby* and *Tubby* but not in *Smiley*), and the very difficult spelling representation of the post-consonantal syllabic /l/ (the LE in *Twinkle*). Significantly, the remaining orthographic items that were included in the hardest set of AIST items in the Rasch analysis all involved these quite difficult context-sensitive rules. The clear-cut inclusion of these items on the linear unidimensional Rasch scale, however, raises the very interesting question of the extent to which their emergence is dependent on the prior establishment of mature phonemic awareness.

In general, therefore, if different orthographic items had been included in the AIST, orthographic skills might not have appeared as a separate cluster of difficult items on the Rasch linear scale. If simpler items had been included in the test, they might possibly have appeared scattered amongst the easier items of the Item Difficulty scale; this in turn would have supported a concurrent repertoire approach, rather than a sequential stage approach, to the conceptualisation of spelling development. On the other hand, the simpler orthographic items might have been discarded in the way that the EA in head was discarded, due to misfit characteristics in terms of the linear Rasch scale. It is possible, that is, that only the difficult context-sensitive orthographic patterns, and not the simpler mental orthographic images and morphemic patterns, are dependent on the establishment of mature phonological processing.

These ideas are, of course, merely speculations, and there is clearly place for further research into the development in orthographic awareness. It is hoped that further Rasch analyses might help to clarify the question of how teachers can best manage the complex inter-twining of phonemic and orthographic awareness, as they help their students to learn to read and spell.

SUMMARY AND CONCLUSIONS

The Rasch analysis of the psychometric properties of the AIST has shown that it is indeed possible to use a simple, classroom-based assessment of invented spelling to yield a reliable scoring scale of data that is characterised by good global item fit as well as person-item fit to the Rasch measurement model, good Person Separation Indices, good item-trait interaction chi-squares (indicating the measurement of a unidimensional trait), and good targeting of items against person measures (although there was indication of a need for some easier and more difficult items in the scales.)

Not only does the AIST provide a useful measurement tool in an area of education where there is a strong need for reliable and efficient monitoring of early literacy progress, but the patterns of item difficulty observed on the AIST can also lead teachers into useful insights into how to support young children in the development of phonemic awareness.

The Rasch analysis of the AIST in its present form supported the concept of orthographic awareness developing as a somewhat separate stage after the establishment of strong phonemic skills, but further research needs to be carried out exploring in more detail the possible interactive relationship between developing phonemic awareness and different aspects of orthographic skills.

REFERENCES

Adams, M. J. (1990). *Beginning to read: Thinking and learning about print*. Cambridge, MA: MIT Press.

Andrich, D., Sheridan, B., & Lou, G. (2005). *Rasch unidimensional measurement models (RUMM 2020): A windows based computer program employing Rasch unidimensional measurement models*. Perth, WA: RUMM Laboratory.

Andrich, D. A., & van Schoubroeck, L. (1989). The general health questionnaire: A psychometric analysis using latent trait theory. *Psychological Medicine, 19*, 469–485.

Apel, K., & Masterton, J. J. (2001). Theory-guided spelling assessment and intervention: A case study. *Language, Speech and Hearing Services in Schools, 32*, 182–194.

Apel, K., Masterton, J. J., & Niessen, N. J. (2004). Spelling assessment frameworks. In C. A. Stone, E. R. Silliman, B. J. Ehren, & K. Apel (Eds.), *Handbook of language and literacy* (pp. 644–660). New York: Guildford Press.

Bear, D. R., Invernizzi, M., Templeton, S., & Johnston, F. (2004). *Words their way: Word study for phonics, vocabulary and spelling instruction* (3rd ed.). Upper Saddle River, NJ: Pearson: Education Inc.

Bissex, G. L. (1980). *Gnys at Wrk: A child learns to read and write*. Cambridge, MA: Harvard University Press.

Bourassa, D. C., & Treiman, R. (2001). Spelling development and disability: The importance of linguistic factors. *Language, Speech and Hearing Services in Schools, 32*, 172–181.

Bryant, D. (2002). *The astronaut invented spelling test: A validation study*. Unpublished Honours thesis, Faculty of Education, University of Wollongong.

Byrne, B. (1998). *The foundation of literacy: The child's acquisition of the alphabetic principle*. Hove, UK: Psychology Press.

Castles, A., & Coltheart, M. (2004). Is there a causal link from phonological awareness to learning to read? *Cognition, 91*, 77–111.

Catts, H. W., Petscher, Y., Schatschneider, C., Bridges, M. S., & Mendoza, K. (2009). Floor effects associated with universal screening and their impact on the early identification of reading disabilities. *Journal of Learning Disabilities* (published Online December 19 2008).

Center, Y., Wheldall, K., Freeman, L., Outhred, L., & McNaught, M. (1992). Evaluating the effectiveness of reading recovery. *Educational Psychology: An International Journal of Experimental Educational Psychology, 12*, 263–274.

Chomsky, C. (1979). Approaching reading through invented spelling. In L. Resnick & P. Weaver (Eds.), *Theory and practice of early reading* (Vol. 2, pp. 43–65). Hillsdale, NJ: Lawrence Erlbaum Associates.

Clay, M. (1975). *The early detection of reading difficulties* (3rd ed.). Auckland, NZ: Heinemann.

Cronbach, L. J. (1951). Coefficient alpha and the internal structure of tests. *Psychometrika, 16*, 297–333.

Ehri, L. (1989). The development of spelling knowledge and its role in reading acquisition and reading disability. *Journal of Learning Disabilities, 22*(6), 356–265.

Ehri, L. (1992). Review and commentary: Stages of spelling development. In S. Templeton & D. R. Bear (Eds.), *Development of orthographic knowledge and the foundations of literacy* (pp. 307–332). Hillsdale, NJ: Lawrence Erlbaum Associates.

Ehri, L., & Wilce, L. S. (1980). The influence of orthography on readers' conceptualisation of the phonemic structure of words. *Applied Psycholinguistics, 1*(4), 371–385.

Foorman, B. R., Francis, D. J., Fletcher, J. M., & Schatschneider, C. (1988). The role of instruction in learning to read: Preventing reading failure in at-risk children. *Journal of Educational Psychology, 90*(1), 37–55.

Foulin, J. P. (2005). Why is letter-name knowledge such a good predictor of learning to read? *Reading and Writing, 18*, 129–155.

Gillon, G. T. (2004). *Phonological awareness: From research to practice*. New York: The Guilford Press.

Good, R. H., & Kaminski, R. A. (Eds.). (2002). *Dynamic indicators of basic early literacy skills* (6th ed.). Eugene, OR: Institute for Development of Educational Achievement.

Juel, C. (1988). Learning to read and write: A longitudinal study of 54 children from first through fourth grades. *Journal of Educational Psychology, 80*, 437–447.

Mann, V. A., Tobin, P., & Wilson, R. (1997). Measuring phonological awareness through the invented spellings of kindergarten children. *Merrill Palmer Quarterly, 33*, 364–392.

Morris, D., & Perney, J. (1984). Developmental spelling as a predictor of first grade reading achievement. *Elementary School Journal, 84*, 441–457.

National Early Literacy Panel. (2008). *Developing early literacy*. National Institute for Literacy, Ed Pubs, PO Box 1398, Jessup, Maryland 20794-1398. Retrieved from www.nifl.gov

Neilson, R. (1999). A discussion on approaches to phonological awareness. *Australian Journal of Language and Literacy, 22*(2), 88–102.

Neilson, R. (2003a). *The Sutherland phonological awareness test – Revised*. Jamberoo, NSW: Language, Speech and Literacy Services.

Neilson, R. (2003b). *The astronaut invented spelling test*. Jamberoo, NSW: Language, Speech and Literacy Services.

Neilson, R. (2009). Assessment of phonological awareness in low-progress readers. *Australian Journal of Learning Difficulties, 14*(1), 53–66.

Read, C. (1971). Pre-school children's knowledge of English phonology. *Harvard Educational Review, 41*, 1–34.

Richgels, D. J. (1995). Invented spelling ability and printed word learning in kindergarten. *Reading Research Quarterly, 30*, 96–109.

Richgels, D. J. (2001). Invented spelling, phonemic awareness, and reading and writing instruction. In S. B. Neuman & D. K. Dickinson (Eds.), *Handbook of early literacy research* (pp. 142–155). New York: Guilford Press.

Share, D., Jorm, A., Maclean, R., & Matthews, R. (1984). Sources of individual differences n reading achievement. *Journal of Educational Psychology, 76*, 95–129.

Snowling, M., & Stackhouse, J. (1996). *Dyslexia, speech and language: A practitioner's handbook.* London: Whurr Publishers.

Stage, S. A., & Wagner, R. K. (1992). Development of young children's phonological and orthographic knowledge as revealed by their spellings. *Developmental Psychology, 28*(2), 287–296.

Stanovich, K. E. (1986). Matthew effects in reading: Some consequences of individual differences in the acquisition of literacy. *Reading Research Quarterly, 21*, 360–407.

Stanovich, K. E. (1992). Speculations on the causes and consequences of individual differences in early reading acquisition. In P. B. Gough, L. C. Ehri, & R. Treiman (Eds.), *Reading acquisition* (pp. 307–342). Hillsdale, NJ: Erlbaum.

Tangel, D., & Blachman, B. (1995). Effect of phoneme awareness instruction on the invented spelling of first grade children: A one-year follow-up. *Journal of Reading Behavior, 27*, 153–185.

Torgeson, J., & Mathes, P. (2000). *A basic guide to understanding, assessing, and teaching phonological awareness.* Austin, TX: Pre-Ed.

Treiman, R. (1993). *Beginning to spell: A study of first-grade children.* New York: Oxford University Press.

Ukrainetz, T. A. (2006). Using emergent writing to develop phonemic awareness. In L. M. Justice (Ed.), *Clinical approaches to literacy intervention.* San Diego, CA: Plural Publishing.

Woodcock, R. W. (1987). *Woodcock reading mastery test-revised.* Circle Pines, MN: American Guidance Service.

Wolf, M. (2008). *Proust and the squid: The story and science of the reading brain.* New York: Harper Collins Publishers.

Roslyn Neilson
(University of Wollongong)

Russell F. Waugh and Deslea Konza
(Faculty of Education and Arts, Edith Cowan University)

ASRIJANTY ASRIL AND IDA MARAIS

4. APPLYING A RASCH MODEL DISTRACTOR ANALYSIS

Implications for Teaching and Learning

ABSTRACT

An analysis of distractors in measuring achievement provides information about students' understanding of the variable being measured in the classroom environment. To be able to provide information, a distractor should contain some aspect of the correct answer. Also, the proficiency required to choose the distractor with information should be less than the proficiency required to get a correct answer but greater than the proficiency required to choose an incorrect answer. An item which works in three categories can provide greater potential diagnostic information for teaching and learning than an item in which alternatives are all simply incorrect. An analysis of distractors is especially important for teaching and learning because it can provide information about misunderstandings and misconceptions, especially for lower proficiency groups. It has been noted that constructing multiple choice items with the intention to better capture students' understanding would be beneficial. The many advantages of multiple choice items, which already include ease of scoring, reliability and applicability to large scale assessment, will be extended. By applying a distractor analysis, the performance of students in different ranges of proficiency on various distractors can be shown.

Rasch analysis provides a method to detect whether distractors have information, especially if there is some ordering implied. In inferring whether distractors have information, distractors should meet content and statistical criteria, that is, a distractor should contain some aspect of the correct answer and scoring polytomously should yield a better fit, including thresholds that are ordered.

INTRODUCTION

Multiple choice tests are used widely because of their objective scoring and efficiency. Tests using this format, however, have been criticised, especially for their impact on learning. One criticism is that multiple choice testing leads to multiple choice learning, that is, learning emphasising facts rather than concepts and learning that encourages a lower level of thinking (Frederiksen, 1984; Shepard, 2000). Others have argued that multiple choice tests are neutral tools, and do not necessarily encourage one type of learning over another (Haladyna, 2004).

R.F. Cavanagh and R.F. Waugh (eds.), Applications of Rasch Measurement
in Learning Environments Research, 77–100.

Aiken (1982) and Green (1981) showed that multiple choice tests can measure higher levels as well as lower levels of cognitive ability, depending on how the items are constructed. Multiple choice tests may not be suitable for all purposes, but some argue that they have a place in both the classroom and in large-scale assessments of student learning (Haladyna, 2004).

In multiple choice formats, each item consists of a stem or stimulus and a number of response options including the correct response and some distractors. Items in this format are commonly scored dichotomously, that is, 1 for a correct answer and 0 for all distractors, and then analysed according to the dichotomous Rasch model. Since all distractors are scored 0, usually no information regarding student proficiency is obtained from responses to distractors. However, distractors may not all work in the same way (Andrich & Styles, 2009). Certain distractors may distract some persons more than others. An implausible distractor may not be chosen by persons in the middle range of proficiency but may still be chosen by persons of low proficiency. This is potentially important for teaching and learning because the choice of distractor could provide information on the misunderstandings and misconceptions of lower proficiency students and could provide possible reasons for their poor performance.

Several Item Response Theory models have been proposed to obtain such information from distractors (Bock, 1972; DeMars, 2008; Penfield & de la Torre, 2008; Thissen, Steinberg, & Fitzpatrick, 1989). However, all these models are based on the traditional paradigm with its focus on finding models that explain the data better, models "that better characterise the responses of the alternatives that might have information" (Andrich & Styles, 2009, p. 3). In the Rasch paradigm, in contrast to the traditional paradigm, a model that defines measurement according to the criterion of invariance is chosen a priori (Andrich, 2004).

This chapter demonstrates how a distractor analysis based on the Rasch model is applied to provide more information of students' proficiency in the construct being measured, in this case quantitative reasoning. The method applied in this chapter is based on the work of Andrich and Styles (2009) and involves rescoring responses and using the polytomous Rasch model in addition to the dichotomous Rasch model to analyze multiple choice responses. It is an effort to optimize the information available from multiple choice item distractors.

The polytomous Rasch model can be expressed in the form

$$\Pr\{x_{ni}\} = [\exp(x_{ni}(B_{nk} - \delta_i) - \sum_{k=1}^{x} \tau_{ki})]/ \sum_{x=0}^{m_i}[\exp(x_{ni}(B_{nk} - \delta_i) - \sum_{k=1}^{x} \tau_{ki})] \qquad (1)$$

where $x \in \{0,1,2...m_i\}$ is the integer response variable for person n with ability B_{nk} responding to item i with difficulty δ_i, and $\tau_{1i}, \tau_{2i,...} \tau_{mi}$, $\sum_{x=0}^{m_i} \tau_{xi} = 0$ are thresholds between $m_i + 1$ ordered categories where m_i is the maximum score of item i, $\tau_0 \equiv 0$ ((Andrich, 1978, 2005; Wright & Masters, 1982)

The dichotomous Rasch model is a special case of Eq. (1) and is expressed as

$$\Pr\{ X_{ni} = x\} = [\exp(x(\beta_n - \delta_i))] /[1 + \exp(\beta_n - \delta_i)] \tag{2}$$

where $x \in \{0,1\}$ and there is only one threshold, δ_i.

ANALYSIS OF DISTRACTORS

Andrich and Styles (2009) argued that multiple choice item distractors with infor-mation about person performance can be identified by applying the polytomous Rasch model. In fact, it is the case that, "if data fit the polytomous model for more than two categories, then dichotomisation of these responses to just two categories post hoc is contradictory to the model" (Andrich & Styles, 2009, p. 5). That is, if there is enough evidence that a certain distractor deserves partial credit then this distractor needs to be scored as 1 instead of 0, while the correct answer is scored 2. All other distractors (assuming there is no information in them) are still scored 0. If the data fit this model better than the dichotomous model, then the polytomous method of scoring should be used.

A distractor with potential information can be identified by examining the distractor plot, which shows the relationship between each response option and the trait being measured. A correct response is expected to display a monotonic increasing pattern, that is, as person proficiency increases the observed proportion of correct responses increases, and follows the Item Characteristic Curve (ICC) closely. The ICC displays the probability of getting an item correct within the range of proficiency, based on Eq. (2). A distractor with no information in the range of proficiency being measured is expected to show a monotonic decreasing pattern, that is, the observed proportion is expected to decrease as the proficiency of persons increases (Andrich & Styles, 2009).

A distractor with potential information shows a single peak in the ICC. The peak can be manifested in the middle or at the lower end of the continuum. The latter occurs when the item is relatively easy for the persons so that most persons' locations are at the higher end of the continuum and the plot for the distractor shows mainly a decreasing pattern. Figure 1 shows examples of distractors potentially having information. The peak in the ICC is indicated with a circle. In the plot at the top of Figure 1, distractor 4 has a single peak in the middle of continuum. In the plot at the bottom distractor 2 has a peak at the lower end of the continuum. In this plot the ICC mainly decreases, but not monotonically. It shows a very small increase at the lower end of the continuum and then decreases, forming a slight peak. If more persons with lower proficiency were added the peak should be more pronounced and in the middle range of the continuum.

It is important to note that 'no information' distractors may also potentially have information if the proficiency range were extended to include less proficient persons. That is, sometimes with the range of persons measured, only the right hand side of a curve that is monotonically decreasing rather than peaked, is observed.

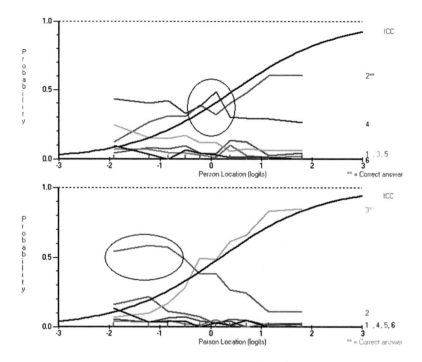

Figure 1. Plots of distractors with potential information.

Plots like the ones above indicate distractors potentially deserving partial credit. However, more evidence is needed to determine whether the distractor really deserves partial credit or not. According to Andrich and Styles (2009), in order to get partial credit a distractor should meet both content and statistical criteria. With regard to content, the distractor deserving partial credit should contain some aspect of the correct answer. Also, the proficiency needed to solve this distractor should be less than the proficiency needed for a correct response and greater than the proficiency associated with the other distractors. In terms of statistical criteria, polytomous scoring of the item should result in better fit than dichotomous scoring.

To see whether polytomous rescoring results in better fit, a comparison of item fit before and after rescoring should be made. Polytomous rescoring is considered successful when there is some evidence of an improvement in fit after rescoring. Both graphical and statistical indicators of fit should be considered. The chi-square (χ^2) test is used as a statistical test of item fit in this chapter. The χ^2 test is based on the difference between the observed scores of all persons and their expected values based on the model. The smaller the value of χ^2, the greater the probability that the item fits the model.

A graphical indicator of fit is the ICC. A comparison of fit between dichotomous and polytomous scoring can also be made by examining the respective ICCs (Item

Characteristic Curve). Other graphical fit indicators for polytomous items are the Category Characteristic Curve (CCC) and Threshold Characteristic Curve (TCC). The CCC shows the probability of each response category across the whole continuum. For fit of responses to the model it is expected that, across the continuum, successive categories would successively show the highest probability. The estimates of the thresholds, which define these categories, would be in their hypothesised order on the continuum. This means that, when a person is of very low proficiency relative to the item location, the probability of a response of 0 is most likely; when a person has a moderate proficiency relative to the item location, a score of 1 is most likely, and when a person's proficiency is high relative to the item location, the most likely score is 2.

The TCC shows the conditional probability of success at each latent threshold. It also shows the distances between thresholds. For fit of responses to the model it is expected that thresholds not be reversed and that there is a reasonable distance between thresholds. When the thresholds are very close to each other it means the ordered categories may not be working as intended. The software used for analysis in this chapter, RUMM2030 (Andrich, Sheridan, & Luo, 2010) provides the half-distance between thresholds as the θ parameter. For an item, i, with two thresholds, τ_{1i} and τ_{2i}, from Eq.(1), $\theta = \frac{1}{2}(\tau_{2i} - \tau_{1i})$. We use this parameter later in the chapter to test whether the distance between the thresholds of an item is significantly greater than 0.

The CCC and TCC of an item in which the thresholds are in the correct order and have good fit are shown in Figure 2 (top). For this item the response categories are working as intended. The dots, which represent the observed values, are close to each curve, indicating a good fit. Figure 2 (bottom) shows an example of an item in which the response categories are not working as intended. It is clear from the CCC that category 1 never has the highest probability. The TCC shows that there is systematic misfit at threshold 1. It under-discriminates and the dots are quite far from the curve. In addition, it shows that the thresholds are reversed. Threshold 2 has a lower location on the continuum than threshold 1 with its curve to the left of threshold 1.

Further steps to check whether distractors have information are described in Andrich and Styles (2009). These steps are described in the next section in conjunction with an application to real data.

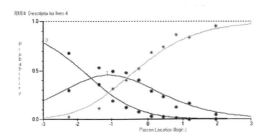

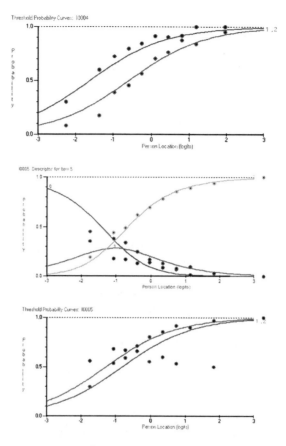

Figure 2. CCC (left) and TCC (right) of an item showing categories working as intended (top) and not working as intended (bottom).

APPLICATION

In this section, an analysis of distractors in the Quantitative subtest of the Indonesian Scholastic Aptitude Test (ISAT) is described. The ISAT consists of three subtests: Verbal, Quantitative and Reasoning, but only the Quantitative subtest analysis is described here. The data were obtained from the Center for Educational Assessment, Indonesia, and are from students who were applicants to an undergraduate program in one university in Indonesia in 2005. There were 833 students, including 339 males and 494 females. The 30 multiple choice items in the test all have five response options, that is, one correct response and four distractors. The data were initially scored dichotomously and missing responses were scored as incorrect. That is why the distractor plots shown later have six instead of five response options. The sixth option indicates missing responses.

Identifying Items with Potential for Rescoring

Even though distractor plots can be used to identify distractors potentially having information, Andrich and Styles (2009) recommended an earlier, preliminary step to screen distractors. This involves dividing the sample into three class intervals, based on the total score. For each item, the proportion of persons who chose each distractor is calculated. Of particular interest is the proportion in the middle class interval. When this proportion is higher than chance, the item should be considered for potential rescoring. The rationale behind this step is that the probability will be higher than chance if there is some aspect of the distractor that is partially correct. The reason for choosing three class intervals is that it may show clearly a single peak in the middle class interval of the ICC on the continuum of proficiency.

Table 1 shows the proportion of persons who chose each response option for each of the three class intervals for two items in the ISAT Quantitative subtest. Because there are five response options for each item in this test, each option has a 0.2 probability of being chosen by chance. For item 51, the proportions in the middle class interval for each distractor is very low with a maximum of 0.03. Item 51 is a very easy item so most of the persons chose the correct answer, leaving all the distractors with a below chance probability of being chosen. In contrast, for item 56 the proportion in the middle class interval is 0.39 for option B, which is higher than the chance probability of 0.2. Hence item 56 is an item that could potentially be rescored as a polytomous item in which the correct answer, option C, is scored 2, option B is scored 1 and the other options are scored 0.

Table 1. Proportions for each response option for items 51 and 56

Item 51

Class Interval	Mean	A	B	C (Key)	D	E	F (Missing)
1	−1.164	0.12	0.10	0.69	0.04	0.02	0.03
2	−0.044	0.01	0.02	0.91	0.02	0.01	0.03
3	1.031	0.00	0.00	0.95	0.03	0.01	0.00

Item 56

Class Interval	Mean	A	B	C (Key)	D	E	F (Missing)
1	−1.164	0.14	0.55	0.14	0.06	0.04	0.07
2	−0.044	0.06	0.39	0.47	0.04	0.03	0.02
3	1.031	0.03	0.16	0.76	0.02	0.01	0.02

When the above procedure was applied to all 30 items, 16 items showed potential to be rescored as polytomous items. They were items 55–60, 62, 64, 68, 70, 71, 72, 75, 77, and 79.

Analysis of Distractor Plots and Wording of Items

The next step was an analysis of the distractor plots and wording of these 16 items. Due to space restrictions the distractor plots and wording of only four items are shown in Figures 3 and 4 respectively. It is clear from Figure 3 that not all distractors show the single peak structure as described earlier. A clear single peak is observed in item 56 for distractor 2 and item 62 for distractor 4. For item 55, a single peak is not really evident: distractor 3 for this item shows that the observed proportion is highest in the lowest group and lowest in the highest groups, but the decreasing trend is not apparent in the middle range. For item 70, distractor 3 shows that a decreasing pattern is observed only at a location of approximately 0.5; in the lowest range the curve is flat and it increases in the middle range. Also, unlike the other three items in which the curve of the correct answer is relatively close to the ICC, in item 70 the curve for the correct answer does not follow the ICC (Item Characteristic Curve).

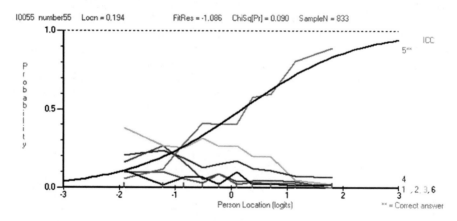

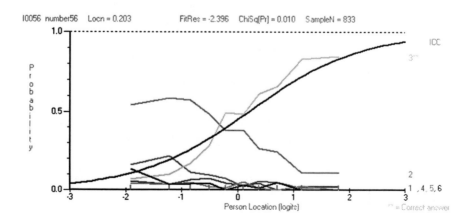

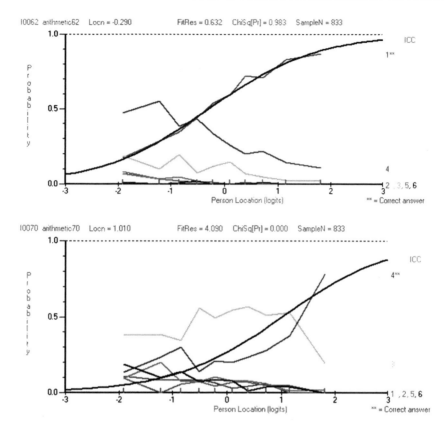

Figure 3. Distractor plot items 55, 56, 62, 70.

To understand the items better, the content was examined. The wording of items 55, 56, 62 and 70 is presented in Figure 4.

Item 55 is a number sequence item. The item requires students to identify the sequence pattern and use the pattern to complete the next sequence. The correct answer for item 55 is option e. The pattern of the sequence is $2^1\ 3^1\ 2^2\ 3^2\ 2^4$, so the next number is 81 or 3^4. There are about 20–30 % of students in each class interval, especially below 1 logit, who chose option c. Students who chose option c apparently used the last three numbers in the sequence to build a pattern, resulting in an answer of 25, which is option c (distractor 3 in Figure 3).

Item 56 is also a number sequence item. In this item the sequence pattern is adding the prime numbers to each number presented. The correct answer is 30 (option c) resulting from 19 + 11 (the next prime number). Apparently option b (distractor 2 in Figure 3) was chosen by test takers who may not know about prime numbers and who thought that the pattern is odd numbers, that is 3 5 7 with the next number being 9, which makes the answer 28 (option b). These test takers ignored the first number in the sequence, which is 2.

For item 62, there was a considerable proportion of persons, especially of lower proficiency, who chose option d (distractor 4). In examining the content, it appears that persons who chose this option may not have understood the concept of operation order, that is that multiplication and/or division should be performed first before addition and/or subtraction. The students who chose option d performed the operation directly from left to right without consideration of the operation order.

Instruction: Find a correct number to complete the sequence

55.   2   3   4   9   16   ...
a. 17
b. 21
c. 25
d. 27
e. 81*

56.   2   4   7   12   19   ...
a. 27
b. 28   potential for partial credit
c. 30*
d. 31
e. 32

Instruction: Find the correct answer.

62. $6 \times 45 \times \dfrac{1}{9} + 33 - 3 \times 12 = ...$
a. 27*
b. 31
c. 390
d. 720   potential for partial credit
e. 3.600

70.   The average Mathematics score of grade 5 students in one class is 6.5. Of 48 students in the class, there are 28 boys and 20 girls. If the average score of girls is 6.8. What is the average score of boys?
a. 6.0
b. 6.1
c. 6.2
d. 6.3 *
e. 6.4

Figure 4. Items 55, 56, 62, 70.

Item 70 is an arithmetic problem. The item requires students to calculate the average score for boys with all the information provided. The analysis showed that this was one of the most difficult items and also the worst fitting item. The item under-discriminated. The correct answer for this item is 6.2857 which is then rounded to 6.3 (option d, distractor 4 in Figure 3). A significant number of students in each class interval chose option c which is 6.2. A possible explanation for this is that there is a considerable proportion of students who may not know how to round a number or they may know how to round a number but did not pay attention after the first digit. Rounding is perhaps less significant in quantitative reasoning, the variable being measured, resulting in an item that discriminated poorly between students.

RESCORING AND ASSESSING FIT BEFORE AND AFTER RESCORING

All 16 items identified earlier were rescored to polytomous items with the correct answer scored 2, the distractor with potential information scored 1 and all other

Table 2. Fit of the 16 items before and after rescoring

Item	χ^2 Probability dichotomous	χ^2 Probability polytomous	Threshold difference polytomous	$\theta > 0$ polytomous
55	0.090	0.869	disordered	
56	0.010	0.258	1.08	yes
57	0.000	0.000	0.34	yes
58	0.114	0.025	1.55	yes
59	0.000	0.000	0.51	yes
60	0.025	0.038	1.28	yes
62	0.983	0.636	0.58	yes
64	0.000	0.006	disordered	
66	0.742	0.158	disordered	
68	0.183	0.003	disordered	
70	0.000	0.000	1.37	yes
71	0.155	0.017	disordered	
72	0.313	0.181	disordered	
75	0.000	0.001	0.14	no
77	0.313	0.548	disordered	
79	0.000	0.000	disordered	

distractors scored 0. Table 2 shows the fit of the items before and after re-scoring, more specifically the probability value of the chi-square test of fit before and after rescoring. It also shows whether the thresholds of the new poly-tomous items were disordered and if not, it shows the distance between the thresholds. In the last column it shows whether θ, the half-distance between thresholds, is significantly greater than 0 ($p < 0.05$). Disordered thresholds indicate that the item did not work as a polytomous item. Ideally thresholds should be ordered, with the half-distance between thresholds significantly greater than 0.

It is clear from Table 2 that only half of the items had thresholds that were in order. Of the eight items that had ordered thresholds θ was significantly greater than 0 for all except item 75. Of the items that had ordered thresholds, three items showed an improvement in fit (items 56, 60, 75). However, the fit improvement for items 60 and 75 were marginal, whereas for item 56 there was a noticeable improvement. For item 56, when scored dichotomously the χ^2 probability was 0.010 and after rescoring it increased to 0.258.

Of the other items discussed earlier (items 55, 62 and 70), item 55 showed an improvement in fit after rescoring, with a χ^2 probability of 0.090 before rescoring, and 0.869 after rescoring. The thresholds, however, were not in order. Item 62 fitted well when scored dichotomously with a χ^2 probability of 0.983. After rescoring the probability reduced to 0.636. The thresholds were in order although the difference between thresholds, 0.58, was relatively small. Item 70 did not fit with either scoring system, having a χ^2 probability of 0.000 in both. However, when scored polytomously, the thresholds were in order.

A graphical analysis of fit is also very informative, so for items 55, 56, 62 and 70 the ICCs before and after rescoring, as well as the CCCs and TCCs after rescoring, are presented in Figures 5 to 8. Consistent with the χ^2 probability in Table 2, the ICC for item 55 in Figure 5 shows that the item fitted better after rescoring. Before rescoring it over-discriminated. However, the CCC shows that there is no region in the continuum that the middle category, a score of 1 for the distractor with potential information, has the highest probability. This is manifested in disordered thresholds. As shown in the TCC, the location of threshold 1 is greater than threshold 2 while it is expected that threshold 1, which is the intersection of the curves of a probability of 0 and a probability of 1, would be lower than threshold 2, which is the intersection of the curves of a probability of 1 and a probability of 2. Thus there is no evidence to support assigning partial credit to distractor 3 of item 55. This is also consistent with the distractor plot of item 55 in Figure 3, in that it does not show a single peak.

The graphical fit of item 70 is shown in Figure 6. Item 70 was an under-discriminating item. In terms of χ^2 probability as indicated earlier, it was under-discriminating both before and after rescoring. However, examining the ICC it is apparent that it discriminated better after rescoring although it still showed relatively poor discrimination. The CCC and TCC show that the thresholds were in order. However, examining the observed proportions in the CCC and TCC it appears that threshold 2 did not discriminate. Except for the highest group, in all class intervals the observed proportion was relatively similar. This indicates that the categories were not working as intended. Considering this evidence, rescoring was not justified for item 70. In fact the distractor plot shown earlier for this item showed that none of the distractors showed potential to get partial credit.

In the case of item 62, shown in Figure 7, the ICC shows that, although the fit is acceptable after rescoring it did not fit as well as when it was scored dichotomously. The CCC shows that the middle category (score 1) as well as the other categories (scores 0 and 2) have regions of the continuum where their probability was the highest. The TCC shows that threshold 1 was lower than threshold 2, which is as expected. However, examining the observed proportion it appears that there is some misfit at threshold 1, that is, the observed proportion in some class intervals does not follow the ICC closely, although in general the trend is in line with the ICC. Except for threshold 1, which shows some misfit, the other statistical criteria indicated support for rescoring item 62 as polytomous. The distractor plot shown in Figure 3 also indicates that distractor 4 of item 62 had potential to get partial credit.

Andrich and Styles (2009) suggested that a distractor can be given partial credit if it contains some aspect of the correct answer and if it requires more proficiency than the other distractors. As described earlier, item 62 was about operation order (see Figure 4). Choosing option d (distractor 4) may indicate that the students could calculate correctly but did not understand the concept of operation order. To get the correct answer, option a, students needed to calculate correctly *and* know the operation order. The students who chose other distractors apparently did not calculate correctly *and* did not get the concept of operation order. This indicates there is some aspect of the correct answer in distractor 4 which requires more proficiency than the other distractors. Thus, in terms of content, distractor 4 of item 62 may deserve partial credit. Considering that there was some misfit at threshold 1, it can be argued that it is not justified to score item 62 polytomously. However, the misfit was not systematic and evident only on some class intervals. The trend in general was in line with the ICC. Therefore we considered the evidence sufficient to rescore item 62 polytomously.

As stated earlier, only item 56 met all the criteria of fit improvement and threshold order. The χ^2 fit probability increased from 0.01 to 0.258. The ICC of item 56, shown in Figure 8, confirmed a better fit after rescoring. Before rescoring, it over discriminated and after rescoring, it discriminated well. The CCC and TCC show that the thresholds are in order with threshold 1 lower than threshold 2, as expected. However, at threshold 1 some misfit was observed, that is, the observed proportion correct for the three highest class intervals was lower than expected. In contrast, threshold 2 over discriminated somewhat. Again, as in item 62, despite some misfit at the thresholds, we considered that item 56 could be rescored as polytomous because, in general, the thresholds still followed the ICC and all other statistical criteria were met.

In terms of content, as described earlier, item 56 was a sequence number item. In order to get the correct answer (option c) the students needed to know the concept of a prime number. Students who chose option b (distractor 2) may not have understood the concept of a prime number and created a pattern based on odd numbers. The persons who chose the other distractors apparently did not deduce a reasonable pattern. Therefore, it seems that distractor 2 required more proficiency than the other distractors and contained some aspect of the correct answer. We considered item 56 justified to be rescored as polytomous.

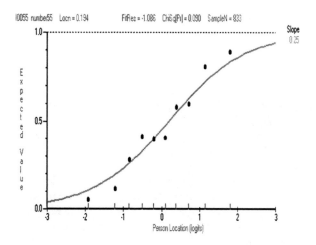

Figure 5a. ICC item 55 before rescoring.

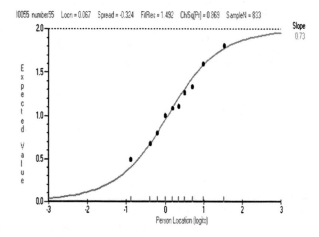

Figure 5b. ICC item 55 after rescoring.

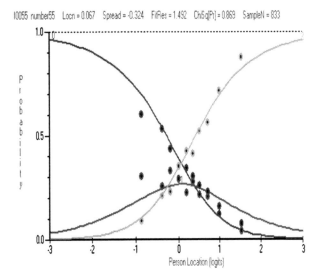

Figure 5c. CCC item 55.

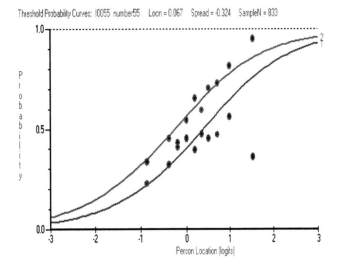

Figure 5d. TCC item 55.

Figure 5. Graphical fit item 55.

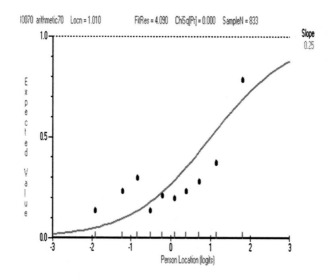

Figure 6a. ICC item 70 before rescoring.

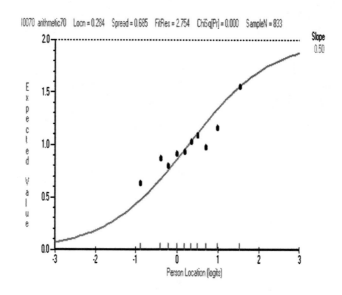

Figure 6b. ICC item 70 after rescoring.

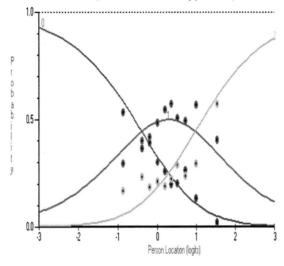

I0070 arithmetic70 Locn = 0.284 Spread = 0.685 FitRes = 2.754 ChiSq[Pr] = 0.000 SampleN = 833
1.0
0.5
0.0
Probability
0
1
2
-3
-2
-1
0
1
2
3
Person Location (logits)

Figure 6c. CCC item 70.

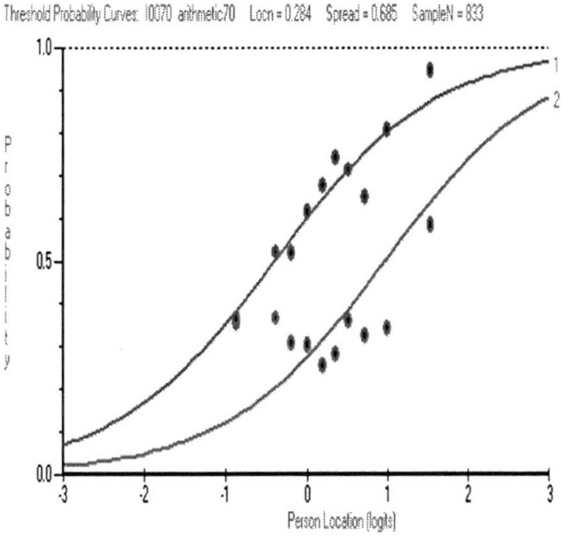

Threshold Probability Curves: I0070 arithmetic70 Locn = 0.284 Spread = 0.685 SampleN = 833
1.0
0.5
0.0
Probability
1
2
-3
-2
-1
0
1
2
3
Person Location (logits)

Figure 6d. TCC item 70.

Figure 6. Graphical fit item 70.

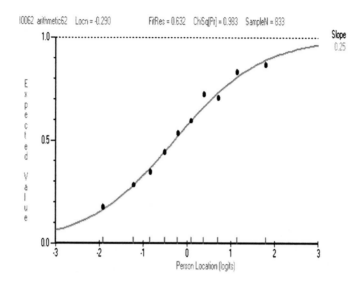

Figure 7a. ICC item 62 before rescoring.

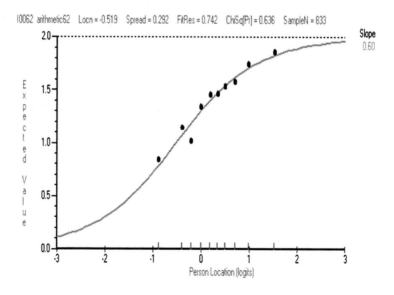

Figure 7b. ICC item 62 after rescoring.

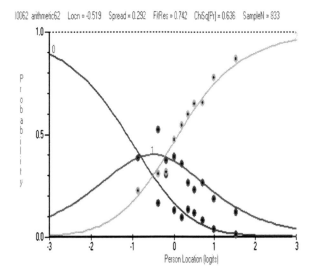

Figure 7c. CCC item 62.

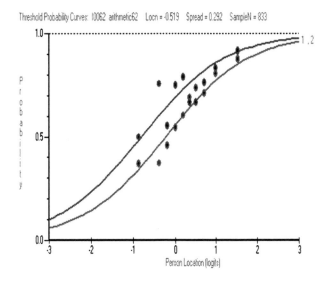

Figure 7d. TCC item 62.

Figure 7. Graphical fit item 62.

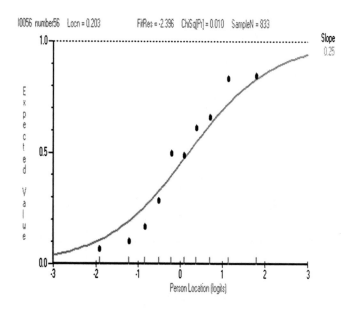

Figure 8a. ICC item 56 before rescoring.

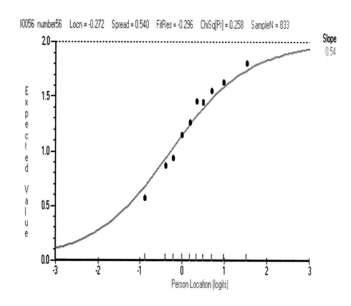

Figure 8b. ICC item 56 after rescoring.

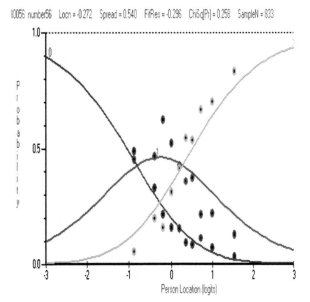

Figure 8c. CCC item 56.

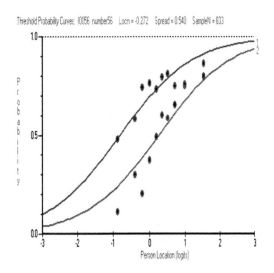

Figure 8d. TCC item 56.

Figure 8. Graphical fit item 56.

97

IMPLICATIONS FOR TEACHING AND LEARNING

In this chapter, we showed how an analysis of distractors provides information about students' understanding of the variable being measured. Only a few items, two out of the 30, could be rescored polytomously. This is consistent with previous findings (for example Bock, 1972; Andrich and Styles, 2009) that very few items could justifiably be rescored polytomously. The most likely reason for this is that the distractors were not constructed purposely to provide information. The ISAT distractors, although constructed with some consideration for plausibility, were not specifically designed to reflect order on the proficiency continuum. To be able to provide information, a distractor should contain some aspect of the correct answer. Also, the proficiency required to choose the distractor with information should be less than the proficiency required to get a correct answer but greater than the proficiency required to choose an incorrect answer.

Because multiple choice tests are expected to be useful diagnostic tools which provide information about students' understandings (Frederiksen, 1984; Sadler, 1998; Shepard, 2000), constructing multiple choice items with distractors reflecting some order of understanding will serve this purpose. Furthermore, applying the polytomous Rasch model to multiple choice items can provide some additional advantages. An item which works in three categories can provide greater potential diagnostic information for teaching and learning than an item in which alternatives are all simply incorrect. For example, if a multiple choice item requires two operations to get the correct answer, distractor analysis will show whether students did not get the correct answer because they could not do *either* of the operations or because they could do only one but not the other. When the item is scored dichotomously, this information is not obtained as it only shows whether students could perform *both* operations (got the correct answer) or *none* (got an incorrect answer). In this way multiple choice items approximate the diagnostic opportunity of extended response items.

Secondly, by applying the Rasch model, fit to the model can be checked. In the case of the polytomous model, this means that the ordering of the thresholds is not assumed but needs to be checked. Analysis according to the model will show whether the intended order as presented in the distractors works empirically in the same way. It may be the case that the order, as represented in the distractors, is not observed empirically. Disordered thresholds show that a higher threshold is not more difficult than a lower threshold. This means that the distractor assigned a higher score does not require more proficiency than a distractor assigned a lower score. This provides the opportunity to study the content and order of distractors in detail before assigning partial credit for certain distractors. If there is no evidence that scoring polytomously yields a better fit, then scoring polytomously is not justified and the item needs to be scored dichotomously.

SUMMARY

An analysis of distractors is especially important for teaching and learning because it can provide information about misunderstandings and misconceptions, especially for lower proficiency groups. It has been noted that constructing multiple choice items with the intention to better capture students' understanding will be beneficial (Sadler, 1998). The many advantages of multiple choice items, which already include ease of scoring, reliability and applicability to large scale assessment, will be extended. By applying a distractor analysis, the performance of students in different ranges of proficiency on various distractors can be shown.

Rasch analysis provides a method to detect whether distractors have information, especially if there is some ordering implied. The Rasch model as a frame of reference provides a tool to examine data. In inferring whether distractors have information, distractors should meet content and statistical criteria, that is, a distractor should contain some aspect of the correct answer and scoring polytomously should yield a better fit, including thresholds that are ordered.

ACKNOWLEDGEMENTS

Data in this study were provided by the Center for Educational Assessment, Indonesian Ministry of Education, Jakarta. The first author gratefully acknowledges the financial support during her study at the University of Western Australia. The support was received from the Department of Education, Employment, and Work place Relations (DEEWR) of Australia through the Endeavour Postgraduate Awards. Both authors gratefully acknowledge David Andrich and Irene Styles who read an earlier manuscript and provided expert advice.

REFERENCES

Aiken, L. R. (1982). Writing multiple-choice items to measure higher-order educational objectives. *Educational and Psychological Measurement, 42*(3), 803–806. doi:10.1177/001316448204200312.

Andrich, D. (1978). A rating formulation for ordered response categories. *Psychometrika, 43,* 357–374.

Andrich, D. (2004). Controversy and the rasch model: A characteristic of incompatible paradigm. *Medical Care, 42*(1), I-7-I-16.

Andrich, D. (2005). The rasch model explained. In S. Alagumalai, D. D. Curtis, & N. Hungi (Eds.), *Applied Rasch measurement: A book exemplars* (pp. 27–59). Dordrecht, The Netherlands: Springer.

Andrich, D., Sheridan, B. E., & Luo, G. (2010). *Rumm2030: A window program for Rasch unidimensional models for measurement.* Perth, Australia: RUMM Laboratory.

Andrich, D., & Styles, I. (2009). Distractors with information in multiple choice items: A rationale based on the Rasch model. In E. V. Smith, Jr. & G. E. Stone (Eds.), *Criterion referenced testing: Practice analysis to score reporting using Rasch measurement models* (pp. 24–70). Maple Grove, MN: JAM Press.

Bock, D. (1972). Estimating item parameters and latent proficiency when the responses are scored in two or more nominal categories. *Psychometrika, 37,* 29–51.

DeMars, C. E. (2008). *Scoring multiple choice items: A comparison of irt and classical polytomous and dichotomous methods.* Paper presented at the annual meeting of the National Council of Measurement in Education, New York.

Frederiksen, N. (1984). The real test bias: Influences of testing on teaching and learning. *American Psychologist, 39*(3), 193–202.

Green, B. F. (1981). A primer of testing. *American Psychologist, 36*(10), 1001–1011.

Haladyna, T. M. (2004). *Developing and validating multiple-choice test items.* Mahwah, NJ: Lawrence Erlbaum.

Penfield, R. D., & de la Torre, J. (2008). *A new response model for multiple-choice items*. Paper presented at the annual meeting of the National Council on Measurement in Education, New York.

Sadler, P. M. (1998). Psychometric model of student conceptions in science: Reconciling qualitative studies and distractor-driven assessment instruments. *Journal of Research in Science Teaching, 35*(3), 265–296.

Shepard, L. A. (2000). The role of assessment in a learning culture. *Educational Researcher, 29*(7), 4–14.

Thissen, D., Steinberg, L., & Fitzpatrick, A. R. (1989). Multiple-choice models: The distractors are also part of the item. *Journal of Educational Measurement, 26*(2), 161–176.

Wright, B. D., & Masters, G. N. (1982). *Rating scale analysis: Rasch measurement*. Chicago: MESA Press.

Asrijanty Asril
(Center for Educational Assessment, Indonesian Ministry of Education and Graduate School of Education, University of Western Australia)

Ida Marais
(Graduate School of Education, University of Western Australia)

ROB F. CAVANAGH

5. ESTABLISHING THE VALIDITY OF RATING SCALE INSTRUMENTATION IN LEARNING ENVIRONMENT INVESTIGATIONS

ABSTRACT

Rating scale instruments have been widely used in learning environment research for many decades. Arguments for their sustained use require provision of evidence commensurate with contemporary validity theory. The multiple-type conception of validity (e.g. content, criterion and construct), that persisted until the 1980s was subsumed into a unified view by Messick. He re-conceptualised types of validity as aspects of evidence for an overall judgment about construct validity. A validity argument relies on multiple forms of evidence. For example, the *content, substantive, structural, generalisability* aspect, *external,* and *consequential* aspects of validity evidence. The theoretical framework for the current study comprised these aspects of validity evidence with the addition of *interpretability*. The utility of this framework as a tool for examining validity issues in rating scale development and application was tested. An investigation into student engagement in classroom learning was examined to identify and assess aspects of validity evidence. The engagement investigation utilised a researcher-completed rating scale instrument comprising eleven items and a six-point scoring model. The Rasch Rating Scale model was used for scaling of data from 195 Western Australian secondary school students. Examples of most aspects of validity evidence were found, particularly in the statistical estimations and graphical displays generated by the Rasch model analysis. These are explained in relation to the unified theory of validity. The study is significant. It exemplifies contemporary validity theory in conjunction with modern measurement theory. It will be of interest to learning environment researchers using or considering using rating scale instruments.

INTRODUCTION

This paper commences with a brief discussion of how the notion of validity has evolved from an accuracy-oriented approach to a unified theory (Messick, 1989). Next is an explanation of how the multiple types of validity evidence proposed by Messick (1989) were incorporated by Wolfe and Smith (2007a & b) into a seven-element framework of instrument development activities.

R.F. Cavanagh and R.F. Waugh (eds.), Applications of Rasch Measurement in Learning Environments Research, 101–117.

The examples of validity evidence used in this paper were drawn from reports of an investigation into student engagement in classroom learning. For background, the design and outcomes of this investigation are explained. The research objectives follow. Then the Wolfe and Smith (2007a & b) framework and examples from the engagement study framework are used to explain and illustrate aspects of validity evidence, in particular, evidence obtained through application of the Rasch Model (Rasch, 1960).

BACKGROUND

Validity

Early in the last century, a realist philosophy of science underpinned discussions about validity in educational and psychological measurement (Kane, 2001). Validity was viewed as the degree of accuracy attained in estimating the variable of interest. More accuracy in the measure was assumed to indicate greater validity. Applying this 'criterion-based' model of validity assumed the criterion measure was the value of the attribute of interest and "the test was considered valid for any criterion for which it provided accurate estimates" (Kane, 2001, p. 319). Hence validity was demonstrated by the performance on the test being commensurate with the task or ability it was designed to estimate. However, this approach requires the task or ability to be clearly defined in order for validity of the estimation to be assessable. In some instances, a suitable 'criterion measure' may not be available; for example, when an ability is latent and not directly observable or operationally definable. Kane (2001, p. 320) recounted that one solution to this predicament lay in using "a criterion measure involving some desired performance (or some desired outcome) and interpret[ing] the scores in terms of that kind of performance". For example, a panel of experts making subjective judgements about the content domain covered by the test in consideration of the attribute of interest (see Angoff, 1988). This content-based approach is limited by potential circularity – the process could be self-fulfilling.

The criterion-based and content-based definitions of validity were extended in the middle of the last century in cognizance of a view that measures should be observable indicators of theoretical constructs or of a theoretical framework. The proposed notion of construct validity concerned the need for test performance to be understood in terms of the construct or psychological quality of interest (see Cronbach & Meehl, 1955). Up until the late 1980s, this perspective was seen as additional to previous conceptions and not as a replacement - the three models were selectively applied with no requirement for application of all models or for the development of an overarching protocol. However, three methodological principles were developed from the construct-based model - "the need for extended analysis in validation, the need for an explicit statement of the proposed interpretation, and the need to consider alternate interpretations" (Kane, 2001, p. 234). The principles were subsequently applied to the other approaches as well as transcending the theory-based context from which they were derived. This led to unification of validity models. According to Wolfe and Smith (2007a):

Messick (1989) summarised the philosophical basis of and historical trends in the concept of validity, and that summary emphasises the shift in considering multiple types of validity to viewing validity as a unified concept for which multiple types of evidence are appropriate, depending on the nature of the interpretations and uses of the measures (p. 98). Indeed, Messick (1998) elucidated: What is singular in the unified theory is the kind of validity: All validity is of one kind, namely, construct validity. Other so-called separate types of validity – whether labelled content validity, criterion-related validity, consequential validity, or whatever – cannot stand alone in validity arguments. Rather, these so-called validity types refer to complementary forms of evidence to be integrated into an overall judgment of construct validity (p. 37).

Messick's (1995) validation framework posited six aspects of validity evidence. Wolf and Smith (2007b) applied this framework to identify instrument development activities that underpin validity arguments. These were: (1) evidence of the content aspect; (2) evidence of the substantive aspect; (3) evidence of the structural aspect; (4) evidence of the generalisability aspect; (5) evidence of the external aspect; and (6) evidence of the consequential aspect. Wolf and Smith (2007b) added an additional aspect from the Medical Outcomes Trust Scientific Advisory Committee (1995): (7) Evidence of the interpretability aspect. These seven aspects provided the model of validity evidence that was applied to evaluate the methodology and outcomes of a study into student engagement in classroom learning. Prior to explaining the methodology applied in this evaluative process, the research design of the student engagement study is explained.

DESIGN OF THE STUDENT ENGAGEMENT RESEARCH

The design was informed by the principles of integrated mixed-methodology research and applied a combination of iterative methods (Caracelli & Greene, 1997).

Phase One commenced with an extensive review of literature on participation and engagement in schooling research. An examination of Bio-ecological models of intellectual development and engagement (see Bronfenbrenner & Ceci, 1994) suggested Bio-ecological concepts would be useful in developing theory (Marjoribanks, 2002a & b). Similarly, Flow Theory concepts (Csikszentmihalyi, 1990) were also found to be useful for conceptualising engagement (Shernoff, Csikszentmihalyi, Schneider & Shernoff, 2003). Defining the *domain* of the construct was based on these two theories. A *construct map* was developed that specified the eleven *facets* of the construct based on theories of learning and a curriculum model. A *construct model* of engagement was proposed. Five hierarchically ordered statements of student proficiency levels were postulated for each facet. The processes and outcomes of this phase were reported in Cavanagh, Kennish and Sturgess (2008a). The construct model for the facets and proficiency levels is presented in Tables 1 and 2.

Phase Two comprised pilot studies designed to test the features of the construct map. In the first pilot test, *Phase 2(a)*, the ordinality of the proficiency levels in the facets was evaluated with the assistance of eight experienced teachers. They were provided with lists of the proficiency level statements that had been disordered and were asked to rate the un-ordered statements as describing low, medium or high engagement.

This generated 24 data points for analysis. The scores were processed to identify patterns in the ranking of the statements. Generally, the proficiency levels postulated to be higher were identified as characteristic of the students with the higher engagement scores (Cavanagh, Kennish & Sturgess, 2008b).

In *Phase 2(b)*, the second pilot test, 12 secondary school students were interviewed using an interview schedule and rating protocol developed from the construct map. The student's responses to questions about the 11 facets and five levels were used by the researchers to rate the students on a six-point scale for each facet. Student and facet scores were conjointly processed and sorted to ascertain whether the students with the higher overall scores were characterised by the higher proficiency levels. The higher proficiency levels were consistently identified in the students with the higher engagement scores (Cavanagh, Kennish & Sturgess, 2008b) (see Figure 1). In addition to providing evidence about the ordering of the proficiency levels, this phase collected data on the performance of the researcher-completed rating scale instrument.

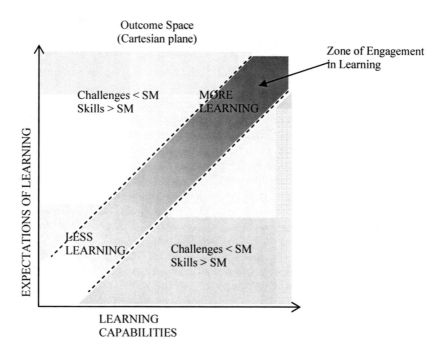

Figure 1. Zone of engagement in learning.

Table 1. Construct model A

	1. Self-esteem	2. Self-concept	3. Resilience	4. Self-regulation	5. Self-efficacy
More capability	Has positive self image	Strives to be perfect	Unqualified expectations of coping	Responsible for learning	Perseveres in the face of adversity
	Confident to make decisions	Motivated by self reflection	Can deal with failure	Improves own learning	Has deter-mination
	Has pride in self	Self reflecting	Expects success	Understands own learning	Recognises contextual influences
	Trusts self to act	At ease comparing self with others	Overcomes small setbacks	Assesses own learning	Has expectations of self
Less capability	Sees worth in self	Compares self with others	Is aware of problems	Aware of learning	Makes effort

Table 2. Construct model B

	6. Explanation	7. Inter-pretion	8. Application	9. Perspective	10. Empathy	11. Self-knowledge
More demanding	Sophisticated	Profound	Masterful	Insightful	Mature	Wise
	In-depth	Revealing	Skilled	Thorough	Sensitive	Circumspect
	Developed	Perceptive	Able	Considered	Aware	Innocent
	Intuitive	Interpreted	Apprentice	Aware	Developing	Thoughtful
Less demanding	Naive	Literal	Novice	Uncritical	Egocentric	Unreflective

Phase Three was the major study. 195 Year Eight to 12 Western Australian secondary school students were interviewed. Each student was rated by two researchers on a zero (minimal evidence) to five (much evidence) scale for each of the 11 facets in English, Mathematics, Science or Society and Environment (see Tables 1 and 2). RUMM2020 was used to estimate statistics and generate displays. For example, summary test-of-fit statistics, category probability curves and threshold locations, individual item fit statistics, item characteristic curves - differential item functioning, person-item threshold distributions and Varimax location loadings (factor analysis of residuals). The results showed the data fitted the Rasch rating Scale Model very well. At the conclusion of the interview, each interviewee completed the Classroom Experience Survey (CES). The CES is a self-report instrument and students answer on a six point rating scale. Student rate their classroom learning experiences with boredom (reverse scored), engagement and flow. The construct of interest is still engagement but an alternative construct map was applied in construction of the CES. The CES asks directly about student experiences associated with engagement/disengagement whereas the interview instrument elicits multi-faceted data about classroom learning and expectations of learning.

Research Objectives

The study sought to show how evidence in accounts of rating-scale application can support an argument for research validity. The subject of the validity argument was an investigation into student engagement in classroom learning. The instrumentation applied in the study included a rating scale instrument and Rasch Rating Scale model data analysis (Andrich, 1978a, b & c). The research questions were:

What aspects of validity evidence in the Wolf and Smith (2007) validity framework can be identified? and

How well do the statistics and graphical displays produced by a Rasch Rating Scale model analysis provide evidence of validity?

METHODOLOGY

The methodology was basically an audit in which a series of indicators or standards were specified and an object of evaluation was assessed against the indicators. The indicators were the seven instrument development activities in the Wolf and Smith (2007b) framework. The object of the evaluation was the intentions, processes and outcomes that constituted an investigation of student engagement in classroom learning. Data on the empirical investigation were contained in published materials, presentations, and materials submitted for publication. Some of these had been subject to formal peer review while others were reports for clients and meeting presentations.

The analytic procedure initially identified particular activities and outcomes that could exemplify validity evidence. Then these potential evidences were more carefully examined in relation to the Wolf and Smith (2007b) framework. Examples of written statements, tables and graphical displays were chosen as both evidence of an aspect of evidence as well as for illustrating the meaning of that aspect.

The following section of the report is organised according to the seven aspects. It commences with evidence of the content aspect.

RESULTS

1. Evidence of the Content Aspect

(a) Evidence of the content aspect of validity includes clear statements of the intent of a study or instrument development process. For example, the *purpose* of the investigation of student engagement in classroom learning was defined as the objective measurement of this construct (Cavanagh, Kennish & Sturgess, 2008a). This goal was made more explicit through specification of two research questions: "Can a linear scale that measures student learning capabilities be constructed? And, Can a linear scale that measures expectations of student learning be constructed?" (Cavanagh & Kennish, 2009, p. 4). The 2008 and 2009 reports on *Phase One* were written early in the investigation. Both were subject to blind peer review prior to acceptance by the Australian Association for Research in Education and the American Educational Research Association.

Stating the *domain of inference* also assists specification of the *purpose*. For example, *Phase One* applied cognitive theories – Bio-ecological theory of development and Flow Theory. The *domain of inference* was also criterion-based since it concerned student engagement attitudes and behaviours. The *type of inferences* to be drawn from applying the instrument, another specification of *purpose*, concerned both individual students and groups of students. Potential *constraints* that could have arisen from data collection mediums and formats, funding availability and time availability can limit the realisation of the *purpose*. Careful attention to the research design can pre-empt potential limitations and this attention needs to continue throughout instrument development.

(b) The *test specifications* centre on the processes used to specify the construct model. The construct of student engagement in classroom learning was assumed to be latent in that it was not directly observable. A theory-based model was developed which identified the *internal structure* of the model (e.g. facets) and *external relationships* with other constructs (e.g. motivation, participation and disengagement). The internal structure of the construct model was explicated in the construct map developed in *Phase 1*. The *test specifications* also explain the chosen instrument item formats, scoring models and scaling models. For example, researcher-rating of subjects during student interviews and student self-report ratings were used in *Phase 3*. Additionally, a polytomous scoring model was applied and the Rasch Rating Scale Model (Andrich, 1978 a, b & c) was used for scaling.

(c) *Item development* requires decisions to be made about the type of scale, the number of response categories and the labeling of response categories. In the engagement study, these differed between the researcher-completed instrument and the student self-report instrument. The *Phase 3* researcher-completed instrument required two researchers to rate each student on a six-point scale for 11 aspects of engagement.

(d) The content of the theoretical frames can be subject to *expert review*. In *Phase 2(a)*, the experts were eight experienced teachers. The re-ordering of the proficiency level statements in line with the construct map structure was taken as evidence of the teachers affirming the structure of the *construct map*.

(e) Evidence of *item technical quality* can be gained from pilot studies and field tests. For example, in *Phase 2*. Quality can be more rigorously assessed by estimation of statistics to show how well the distribution of observed values fits with values predicted by a measurement model. RUMM2020 estimates residuals for each item. These are the difference between the raw score and the score predicted by the Rasch Rating Scale Model. RUMM2020 also generates an Item Characteristic Curve (ICC).

The ogive shows the relation between the expected value for an item and person locations measured in logits. The observed scores for class intervals are then plotted over the ICC. For example, Figure 2 shows the ICC for an item eliciting data on student 'empathy' in the classroom (n=194 students) from *Phase 3*.

The logits on the horizontal axis are the logarithmic odds of 'empathy' being identified in the students. When the observed scores for three class intervals of students were plotted, these were close to the respective values predicted by the model. The fit residual was 0.96 (<±2.5) due to the observed scores being close to the predicted scores – RUMM2020 identifies fit residuals as extreme when they exceed ±2.5.

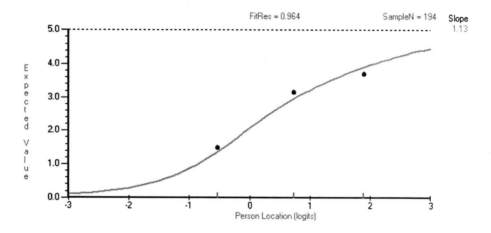

Figure 2. Item characteristic curve for item 10.

2. Evidence of the Substantive Aspect

The substantive aspect of validity concerns observed consistencies among item responses being explained by the theory or hypotheses informing an investigation. The literature on student engagement identifies differences in engagement between females and males. For example, Fullerton (2002, p. 39) had previously shown for Australian students that gender was a strong influence on: "… students' engagement, with females showing significantly higher levels of engagement than males". RUMM2020 generates a Person Frequency Distribution that plots the distribution of calibrated person scores for different groups of persons. In Figure 3 from *Phase 3* data, the frequencies of calibrated engagement scores from the researcher-completed instrument are plotted for females and males. The distributions show higher scores for the females - their mean score was 0.89 logits in comparison to a mean score of 0.49 for the males. This concurrence between theory-based expectations and person scores is evidence of the substantive aspect of validity.

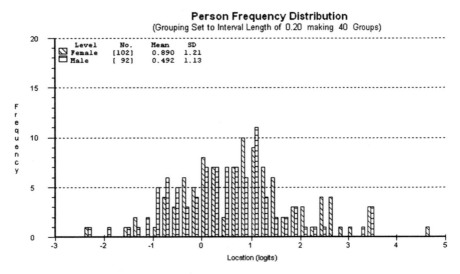

Figure 3. Person frequency distribution – females and males.

Implicit in the construct of engagement are motivational concepts such as satisfaction, enjoyment and favour or preference for particular experiences. Another theory-based expectation is that students rated on their favourite subject would have higher engagement scores than those rated on non-favourite subjects. In Figure 4 from *Phase 3* data, the frequencies of calibrated engagement scores from the researcher-completed instrument are plotted for favourite and non-favourite subjects. The distributions show higher scores when favourite subjects were rated - the mean score was 1.01 logits in comparison to a mean score of -0.03 for non-favourite subjects.

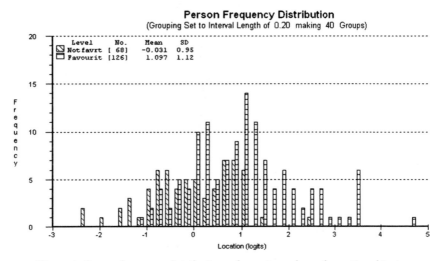

Figure 4. Person frequency distribution – favourite and non-favourite subjects.

The construct map contained hierarchically organised proficiency levels for each sub-construct and statements of these levels were used by the researchers to rate each student. The statements were used to score students on a six-point rating scale. A score of zero was assigned for minimal evidence of the student attribute under examination and scores increased to a maximum of five when there was much evidence of the student attribute. The functioning of this polytomous scale for each sub-construct/item in *Phase 3* was examined by RUMM2020 generating Category Probability Curves for each item. The Category Probability Curves for Item 7 ('interpreting' what has been learned) are presented in Figure 5. The probability of a category being selected is plotted on the vertical axis and student location (engagement score measured in logits) is plotted on the horizontal axis.

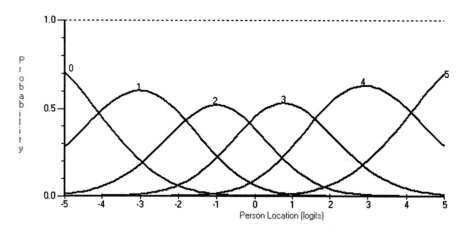

Figure 5. Category probability curve for item 7.

The probability of selecting Category 0 (minimal evidence) decreases from a value of 0.7 for students located at -5.0 logits (low engagement score) to a value of zero for students located at -1.0 logits (higher engagement score). The distribution of probability values for Category 1 shows students with higher engagement scores were generally more likely to select this category. Similarly, students with even higher engagement scores were generally more likely to select Category 2, and so on for the other three categories. The shape and ordering of curves confirms the theorised order of the proficiency levels and also shows the ratings were not made in an idiosyncratic manner. This concurrence between theory-based expectations and item functioning is further evidence of the substantive aspect of validity.

3. Evidence of the Structural Aspect

The structural aspect of validity concerns the construct *domain* and the adopted *scoring* model. For example, by ascertaining if the requirements of a unidimensional measurement model are met when a unidimensional trait is measured. In the case of unidimensionality, this can be gauged by extracting the linear Rasch measure from data set, and then conducting a Principal Components Factor Analysis of the residuals after the initial Rasch scaling. This process was applied to *Phase 3* data. Table 3 shows the percentage of the total variance accounted for by each of the principal components. This variance is not evenly distributed across the 11 principal components suggesting a structure within the residuals that likely indicates there is some multi-dimensionality in the data. Further evidence for multi-dimensionality is presented in Table 4. Four items (Items 2–5) load strongly on the first factor.

Table 3. Principal components summary

PC	Eigenvalue	Percentage	Cumulative Percent	Std Err
PC001	3.174	28.85%	28.85%	0.438
PC002	1.491	13.55%	42.41%	0.198
PC003	1.266	11.50%	53.91%	0.17
PC004	1.063	9.67%	63.58%	0.134
PC005	0.981	8.92%	72.50%	0.127
PC006	0.949	8.63%	81.13%	0.119
PC007	0.711	6.46%	87.59%	0.092
PC008	0.631	5.74%	93.32%	0.087
PC009	0.603	5.49%	98.81%	0.087
PC010	0.215	1.96%	100.76%	0.094
PC011	-0.084	-0.76%	100.00%	0.055

Table 4. Principal components loadings

Item	Fact1	Fact2	Fact3	Fact4	Fact5	Fact6	Fact7	Fact8	Fact9	Fact10	Fact11
I01	0.31	−0.56	0.33	−0.29	−0.45	−0.34	−0.09	−0.12	−0.25	0.03	0.00
I02	0.47	0.05	0.44	0.60	0.22	−0.22	0.12	−0.24	0.25	0.01	0.00
I03	0.70	0.04	−0.08	0.13	0.26	−0.02	−0.36	0.53	−0.12	0.03	0.00
I04	0.57	0.40	−0.27	−0.06	−0.22	0.13	0.59	0.09	−0.15	0.02	0.00
I05	0.55	0.21	−0.19	−0.53	0.17	0.26	−0.26	−0.34	0.25	0.03	0.00
I06	−0.38	−0.32	0.50	−0.07	0.22	0.63	0.12	0.07	−0.11	−0.14	0.00
I07	−0.50	−0.16	−0.46	0.08	0.52	−0.19	0.04	−0.25	−0.39	0.03	0.00
I08	−0.54	−0.53	−0.28	−0.15	0.05	−0.15	0.21	0.25	0.45	0.09	0.00
I09	−0.69	0.49	0.40	−0.08	−0.04	0.04	−0.06	0.05	−0.07	0.33	0.00
I10	−0.63	0.57	0.13	−0.21	−0.02	−0.38	−0.06	0.09	0.06	−0.27	0.00
I11	−0.43	0.02	−0.39	0.48	−0.51	0.30	−0.28	−0.09	0.03	−0.03	0.00

4. Evidence of the Generalisability Aspect

Wolfe and Smith (2007b, p. 215) explained that "the generalisability aspect of validity addresses the degree to which measures maintain their meaning across measurement contexts". The maintenance of meaning could be interpreted as part of the specific objectivity requirement of the Rasch Model. That is, comparison of two items' difficulty parameters are assumed independent of any group of subjects studied. For example, in terms of group independence, an item for which the success rate does not differ between males and females. For an item, a lack of group independence (dependency on groups of subjects) is referred to as differential item functioning (DIF). In *Phase 3*, RUMM2020 showed whether data from any items displayed DIF due to student gender. The Item Characteristic Curve presented in Figure 6 shows the observed scores for three class intervals of girls and boys for Item 5. The differences in observed scores between the genders for the three class intervals were not significant.

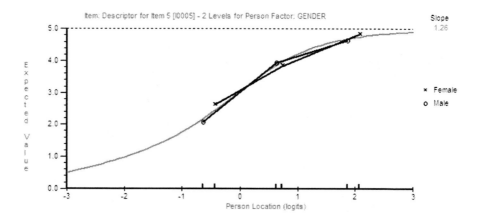

Figure 6. Item characteristic curve for item 5.

Another issue in generalisability is the consistency of measures across items. For example estimating the person separation reliability index (internal consistency reliability coefficient) which is the proportion of variance considered true in the calibrated person scores. The internal reliability index estimated by RUMM2020 is termed the Person Separation Index and this was 0.90 for data from *Phase 3*.

5. Evidence of the External Aspect

The external aspect of validity can be shown by the relation between a measure and an external measure of a similar construct. For example, data obtained by applying two different methods of data collection (e.g. self-report questionnaire versus behavioural observations). In *Phase 3*, the Classroom Experience Survey (CES) was administered to all the students in addition to the primary instrument. Evidence of the external aspect of validity was confirmed by using RUMM2020 to plot data from both instruments onto a common scale. The data fitted the Rasch Rating Scale Model well suggesting data from both instruments were measures of a similar latent trait.

6. Evidence of the Consequential Aspect

The consequential aspect of validity centres on judgments about how the score interpretations might be of consequence. For example, the consequences of specifying cut scores using either normative or absolute standard-setting methods. Reporting on *Phase 3* findings to a client used interview transcript textual data to qualify the attributes of students who were scored in the bottom 10% of the sample. This classification was used to illustrate the qualities of students with low engagement. It was not used to identify groups or individual students, a procedure which was considered to have ethical consequences due to the terms of reference of the evaluation.

7. Evidence of the Interpretability Aspect

The interpretability aspect of validity concerns the qualitative interpretation of a measure in terms of how well its meaning was communicated. One form of communication is through use of graphical displays such as the RUMM2020 Item Map. The Item Map for students and items is presented in Figure 7.

```
---------------------------------------------------------------
LOCATION         PERSONS           ITEMS
[uncentralised thresholds in logits]
---------------------------------------------------------------
                         O     |
                               | I0006.5
4.0                            |  I0007.5
                               |
                               | I0008.5
                   oooooo      | I0009.5
                         O     |
3.0                            |  o  |
                         O     |
                      oooo     | I0011.5 I0010.5
                     ooooo     |
                        oo     | I0002.5 I0001.5
2.0                    oooo     |
                    oooooo     | I0004.5 I0006.4
                      oooo     | I0007.4 I0003.5
                  oooooooo     | I0008.4
               oooooooooooo    |
1.0  oooooooooooooooooooooooo            | I0010.4
        Ooooooooooooooooooo             | I0011.4 I0009.4
         ooooooooooooooooo              | I0005.5 I0003.4
```

```
              Oooooooooo  |  I0004.4
           Ooooooooooooooo   |I0006.3I0001.4              I0008.3
I0002.4
0.0       ooooooooooooooo  |I0011.3I0001.3 I0010.3 I0005.4
           Ooooooooo     |I0005.3I0002.3              I0007.3
I0004.3
                          I0009.3
           Oooooooooo  |  I0003.3
           Ooooooooo   |  I0002.2 I0010.2
              Ooooooooooo  |  I0008.2 I0011.2 I0001.2
                          I0009.2 I0010.1
-1.0          oooooo   |  I0005.2
                   Oo  |  I0006.2 I0004.2
                  Ooo  |  I0009.1
              Oo       |
                          I0002.1
-2.0              o    |  I0007.2 I0003.2
                          I0011.1 I0006.1
                 oo    |

                       |  I0005.1
-3.0                   |  I0004.1 I0008.1



-4.0                   |
                       |  I0007.1
                       |  I0001.1 I0003.1
--------------------------------------------------------------
```

Figure 7. Item map – 11-items (N= 195).

Both student affirmativeness locations and item difficulty locations are plotted on the logit scale (range -4.2 logits to +4.6 logits). The display enables comparison of the scores of individual students and also comparison of the difficulties of items and of affirming either of the six proficiency levels in the construct model. It shows how well the item difficulties 'matched' the students, abilities.

SUMMARY AND DISCUSSION

The Wolfe and Smith (2007a & b) aspects of validity evidence were exemplified by activities undertaken in the student engagement in classroom learning study. Also, a connection was established between research design principles and practices, data analyses using a measurement model (the Rasch Model), and a unified view of validity. Examples of all seven aspects of validity evidence were found in reports on the investigation of student engagement in classroom learning. Also the RUMM20220 outputs provided convincing evidence of validity. While the statistics were crucial, these were complemented by the graphical displays which assisted in interpreting the analysis and the results. However, restricting the available evidence of validity to one study is potentially limiting although drawing of examples from only one study could enable deeper scrutiny. With these matters in mind, readers are recommended to consult the two Wolfe and Smith (2007a& b) articles for a comprehensive explanation of measure validation.

The confluence of validity theory, measurement theory/measurement models, and an account of an empirical investigation (student engagement) highlights some intersections worthy of discussion. First, is the intersection between validity theory and research design. For example, using a structured perspective on validity as a vehicle for identifying validity evidence in an investigation The theory could be applied in post hoc evaluative processes such as seeking evidence of the purpose of the study, ascertaining whether theoretical rationales have been used to explain patterns in data, confirming that actions that might emanate from interpretation of results have been anticipated and documented, and finding out if the way results are communicated is appropriate for those who need to interpret the measure. Similarly, an a priori approach could be used in which a structured view of validity is used to inform research design decisions such as developing the construct map, selecting a measurement model and designing items.

Second is the intersection between validity theory and a measurement model. This is illustrated by Wolfe and Smith (2007a & b) showing how applying the Rasch Model in instrument development and validation activities strongly aligns with a unified view of validity and aspects of validity evidence. A measurement model that provides appropriate aspects of evidence will strengthen validity arguments. An obvious example is the Rasch Model and the generalisability aspect of validity. When data fit the Model, individual items are invariant across groups of respondents and time, and measures are stable across instrumentation and scoring designs. Another example is the Rasch Rating Scale Model and the structural aspect of validity. The Rating Scale Model requires the scoring structure to be unidimensional because it was designed for unidimensional construct domains.

Third is the intersection between research intentions and the measurement model. In the same way that validity arguments require evidence, demonstrating that research objectives have been achieved also requires evidence. A linear view of the research process suggests methodological decisions including instrumentation choices are a consequence of the research objectives and of the inferences required for these to be attained. From this perspective, the measurement model could be seen as a vehicle for making the inferences that show the research objectives were achieved. Also, the degree to which the inferences support achievement of the research objectives could be construed as an indication of validity. From a validity perspective, research objectives articulate the reason for constructing a measure and articulation of *purpose* is evidence of the content aspect of validity. Similarly specifying the measurement model in *test specification* also provides evidence of the content aspect of validity. Hence, decisions about research design processes including articulation of research objectives and choice of a measurement model should be informed by concurrent consideration of aspects of validity.

The above three intersections of the confluences between validity theory, measurement theory/measurement models and research design are due to application of a particular approach to research. The key elements in this approach are: first, the detailed and comprehensive specification of the construct of interest; second, attention to provision of aspects of validity evidence in research design and implementation; and third, selection of a measurement model that will test how the data conforms to theoretical expectations.

CONCLUSION

Ensuring the validity of an investigation requires attention to all aspects of the endeavour before, during and after the empirical work is undertaken. One way to monitor and present a strong argument for validity is to apply the Wolfe and Smith (2007) framework. This provides a theoretically defensible model (Messick's unified theory), that is particularly amenable to studies using rating scales. The current study has exemplified most aspects of validity evidence recommended by Wolfe and Smith (2007). The Rasch Rating Scale analysis provided convincing evidence of several of these aspects and these were complemented by the attention given to the development of construct models, instrument specification and selection of an appropriate measurement model.

REFERENCES

Andrich, D. (1978a). Application of a psychometric rating model to ordered categories which are scored with successive integers. *Applied Psychological Measurement, 2*(4), 581–594.

Andrich, D. (1978b). Rating formulation for ordered response categories. *Psychometrika, 43*(4), 561–573.

Andrich, D. (1978c). Scaling attitude items constructed and scores in the Likert tradition. *Educational and Psychological Measurement, 38*(3), 665–680.

Andrich, D., Sheridan, B., Lyne, A., & Luo, G. (2003). *RUMM: A windows-based item analysis program employing Rasch unidimensional measurement models*. Perth: Murdoch University.

Angoff, W. H. (1988). Validity: An evolving concept. In H. Wainer & H. Braun (Eds.), *Test validity* (pp. 9–13). Hillsdale, NJ: Lawrence Erlbaum.

Bronfenbrenner, U., & Ceci, S. J. (1994). Nature-nurture reconceptualised in developmental perspective: A bioecological model. *Psychological Review, 101*(4), 568–586.

Caracelli, V. J., & Greene, J. C. (1997). Crafting mixed-method designs. In J. C. Greene & V. J. Caracelli (Eds.), *New directions for evaluation* (pp. 19–33). San Francisco: Jossey-Bass Publishers.

Cavanagh, R. F., & Kennish, P. (2009). *Quantifying student engagement in classroom learning: Student learning capabilities and the expectations of their learning*. Paper submitted for presentation at the 2009 annual conference of the Australian Association for Research in Education, Canberra.

Cavanagh, R. F., Kennish, P., & Sturgess, K. (2008a). *Development of theoretical frameworks to inform measurement of secondary school student engagement with learning*. Paper presented at the 2008 Annual Conference of the Australian Association for Research in Education, Brisbane.

Cavanagh, R. F., Kennish, P., & Sturgess, K. (2008b). *Ordinality and intervality in pilot study data from instruments designed to measure student engagement in classroom learning*. Paper presented at the 2008 annual conference of the Australian Association for Research in Education, Brisbane.

Cronbach, L. J., & Meehl, P. E. (1955). Construct validity in psychological tests. *Psychological Bulletin, 52*, 281–302.

Csikszentmihalyi, M. (1990). *Flow: The psychology of optimal experience*. New York: Harper & Row.

Fullarton, S. (2002). *Student engagement with school: Individual and school-level influences*. Camberwell, Victoria: ACER.

Kane, M. T. (2001). Current concerns in validity theory. *Journal of Educational Measurement, 38*(4), 319–342.

Kennish, P., & Cavanagh, R. F. (2009). *How engaged are they? An inductive analysis of country student views of their engagement in classroom learning*. Paper submitted for presentation at the 2009 annual conference of the Australian Association for Research in Education, Canberra.

Marjoribanks, K. (2002a). Family background, individual and environmental influences on adolescent's aspirations. *Educational Studies, 28*(1), 33–46.

Marjoribanks, K. (2002b). Environmental and individual influences on Australian students' likelihood of staying in school. *Journal of Genetic Psychology, 163*(3), 368–381.

Messick, S. (1995). Validity of psychological assessment: Validation of inferences from persons' responses and performances as scientific inquiry into score meaning. *American Psychologist, 50,* 741–749.

Messick, S. (1998). Test validity: A matter of consequences. *Social Indicators Research, 45*(4), 35–44.

Rasch, G. (1960). *Probabilistic models for some intelligence and attainment tests.* Chicago: MESA Press.

Shernoff, D. J., Csikszentmihalyi, M., Schneider, B., & Shernoff, E. S. (2003). Student engagement in high school classrooms from the perspective of flow theory. *School Psychology Quarterly, 18*(2), 158–176.

Wolfe, E. W., & Smith, E. V. (2007a). Instrument development tools and activities for measure validation using Rasch models: Part 1 – instrument development tools. *Journal of Applied Measurement, 8*(1), 97–123.

Wolfe, E. W., & Smith, E. V. (2007b). Instrument development tools and activities for measure validation using Rasch models: Part 11 – validation activities. *Journal of Applied Measurement, 8*(2), 294–234.

Rob F. Cavanagh
(School of Education, Curtin University of Technology)

PEY-TEE OON AND R. SUBRAMANIAM

6. RASCH MODELLING OF A SCALE THAT EXPLORES THE TAKE-UP OF PHYSICS AMONG SCHOOL STUDENTS FROM THE PERSPECTIVE OF TEACHERS

ABSTRACT

Application of the Rasch measurement model to assess the psychometric properties of a scale relating to factors influencing the take-up of physics among school students, as seen from the lens of physics teachers, is reported in this chapter. It is among the very few studies in the science education literature that use Rasch analysis in the treatment of Likert scale survey data. A total of 190 teachers from 100 schools in Singapore participated in this study. Based on the evaluation of infit and outfit statistics of the survey data, a 29-item scale was finally obtained. Rating scale analysis, person-item mapping, principal component analysis using standardised residuals, differential item functioning, reliability/separation indices, and other Rasch measurements are reported for this reduced scale. The six-point rating scale was found to have been used adequately. No meaningful secondary dimension was found in the data. Invariant property of the scale holds to a reasonable extent, and the items constructed were appropriate for use in a physics teacher sample. The scale developed is useful for obtaining data about the physics teaching and learning environment in school. Implications of the study are discussed.

Key words: Physics enrolment, Rasch model, rating scale analysis, differential item functioning, unidimensionality, principal component analysis, standardised residuals, person-item map, category probability curves.

INTRODUCTION

Over the years, educational research in learning environments has greatly enhanced the teaching and learning of science. Many innovations and initiatives introduced into the school curriculum and learning environments draw support from such evidence-based research. Provision of valid and reliable data to stakeholders is, of course, imperative for promoting accountability in learning environments.

When conducting educational research, the survey method is among the most common approaches to collect data from a large sample. Especially where the format uses a Likert scale, the data obtained is amenable to sophisticated statistical analyses. This can provide rich insights into the data collected as well as permit the answering of various research questions. It needs no reiterating that the insights

R.F. Cavanagh and R.F. Waugh (eds.), Applications of Rasch Measurement in Learning Environments Research, 119–139.

provided are contingent on the robustness of the analytical approach used to treat the data. In the science education literature, where Likert scale survey approaches are used, the prevalent form of analysis is to assume that data obtained are interval in nature. This is, in fact, an erroneous assumption as the data obtained are ordinal in nature. The ordinal data needs, in fact, to be converted into interval level data using Rasch analysis before the usual statistical analyses can be done, but this is rarely the case. Indeed, in the science education literature, there are very few published works that use Rasch analysis in the treatment of survey data.

The principal objective of this chapter is to develop and validate a scale on factors influencing the take-up (FIT-UP) of physics among school students, as viewed from the perspective of physics teachers, using the Rasch model.

DECLINING INTEREST IN PHYSICS

Interest in physics, both at the school and university levels, has been decreasing over the years. Among the countries facing this problem include Germany (Tobias & Birrer, 1999), the United States (National Science Foundation, Division of Science Resource Statistics, 2004), Australia (Dobson, 2006; Lyons, 2006), England, Wales and Northern Ireland (Assessment and Qualifications Alliance, 2007; Institute of Physics, 2001), Ireland, South Korea, Mexico, Netherlands, and Spain (Organisation for Economic Co-operation and Development, 2005 as cited in Barmby and Defty, 2006). The severity of the issue can be seen from the fact that in the UK itself, physics departments in 24 universities have closed down (Smithers & Robinson, 2006) in recent years.

Stakeholders in industry and education are registering concerns about this state of affairs owing to their failure to recruit good physics graduates and qualified physics teachers (Institute of Physics, 2001; Roberts, 2002). Many have shown an increasing interest in knowing the reasons for this issue, especially in the context of how the current physics teaching and learning environment contributes towards it.

To address the trend of declining interest in physics in school as well as the declining enrolment in physics at the university level, significant effort needs to be made to understand the current teaching and learning environment in secondary schools, as it pertains to physics, since students' inclination to pursue interest in physics is formed at this stage. While there are several studies that have surveyed students' views of the issue, teachers' opinions have been given less attention. Physics teachers' views are crucial because their proximity to students is likely to endow them with more insights on this issue. Their views can provide an additional channel to gather information on why students shy away from physics and thus triangulate the data obtained from students. Information that cannot be drawn from students, owing to their limited experience, can possibly be captured from teachers since they are likely to look at the issue in a more pragmatic manner (Politis, Killeavy, and Mitchell (2007).

Politis, et al. (2007) designed a survey that encompasses several factors which influence the take-up of physics at the secondary level from the perspective of teachers:

a. Curriculum issues, laboratory issues, and teaching and learning resources.
b. Students' learning experience and attitudes towards physics (e.g. Students avoid physics because it is more difficult to achieve high grades in physics than in other subjects; Physics is perceived to be a difficult subject by students).
c. Issues related to teaching of physics (e.g. Physics requires considerable competence in the mathematical sciences).

However, a couple of limitations were found in their study. A number of factors that have been reported in the literature as being important are absent in their scale. These include the boring nature of physics (e.g. Spall, Stanisstreet, Dickson & Boyes, 2004); the irrelevance of physics (e.g. Angell, Guttersrud & Henriksen, 2004); and the heavy load of the physics curriculum (Woolnough, 1994). Also, like in most pertinent studies in the literature that use the survey approach to explore aspects of the physics teaching and learning environment, such as why physics is not appealing to students (e.g. Angell, *et al.*, 2003; Spall, Barrett, Stanisstreet, Dickson & Boyes, 2003), they used the classical test theory to interpret the results. The psychometric properties of the scale were indicated by their analyses of raw scores.

To better understand the ground realities of what motivates students to sign up or not sign up for physics in school, an instrument that includes various factors, as documented in the literature, is desirable as it can help to comprehensively survey the views of physics teachers. The present study aims to address this and to use Rasch analysis to assess the psychometric properties of the instrument. In fact, in the science education literature, there seems to be a general lack of awareness of the potential of Rasch analysis in treating survey data. Only a few studies have appeared, and that too, in more recent times.

MEASUREMENT PROBLEMS IN SCIENCE EDUCATION THAT USE SURVEY METHODS

Classical Test Theory (CTT) using raw scores is constrained by several limitations, the principal disadvantage being that it relies on sample statistics to derive scale estimates (Embretson & Reise, 2000) – the conclusions drawn regarding the scale properties are thus sample dependent. For example, estimates such as item-total correlations, Cronbach's alpha, etc. yield different results with different samples.

Another measurement flaw is the direct inference of the linearity of the Likert-scale. In science education, data related to students' attitudes are frequently needed (Liu & Boone, 2006). Reid (2006), in his critical review on science attitude measurement studies, reported that *"there is no way of knowing whether the scale in an individual attitude question is linear, equally spaced* (p. 12). *It is impossible to measure the spacing"* (p. 13). *Only* interval scales allow meaningful comparisons to be made with inferential statistics. An equal interval scale is crucial for any survey study but many test developers in science education seem to be unaware that its violation will lead to misleading results.

Furthermore, a number of studies reported on scale validity that is based on content validity, as judged by experts in the relevant domain in science education (e.g. Siorenta & Jimoyiannis, 2008). Content validity based solely on professional judgment is insufficient for establishing validity (Messick, 1981; 1989). As quoted by Fisher (1997): *"The conventional focus on content validity has misled us about what is important in educational measurement"*.

Moreover, test developers in science education are rarely concerned about whether respondents use the response categories in the intended manner. Respondents may react differently from the way that test developers intended (Andrich, 1996). The response categories need to be able to indicate how the various respondents selected a specific category (Stone & Wright, 1994) in order to obtain interpretable results. This, again, is rarely taken into account in science education research.

RASCH MEASUREMENT MODEL

The Rasch model is based on the assumption that the probability of any person being successful on any test item is governed by item difficulty (D) and person ability (B). Rasch (1960, 1980) expressed this relationship mathematically as:

$$P(x=1) = \frac{\exp(B_n - D_i)}{1 + \exp(B_n - D_i)};$$

where $P(x=1)$ is the probability of answering the item correctly, B_n is the ability of the person n, and D_i is the difficulty of the item i. For example, if the item difficulty is equal to person ability, the probability of a correct response is .50. This is the simplest form of the Rasch model, which is to analyse dichotomous data, where the prediction of probability is based on either a person answering the item correctly or incorrectly. Rasch demonstrated that in this form, the item and person parameters are separable (Wright & Mead, 1977). In short, Rasch measurement applies a statistical model to raw scores to produce item difficulty and ability data that are *measures* (Liu & Boone, 2006). Measures are linear, on a unit, and of unidimensional quantities (Wright, 1999). It thus allows for quantitative comparisons.

The dichotomous model can be generalised for polytomous data using the Rating Scale Model (RSM) (Andrich, 1978). This is usually used to examine the quality of response categories in Likert-type scales (Bond & Fox, 2007). This model describes the probability, P_{nij}, that a person n of ability B_n is observed in category j of a rating scale on a particular item i of difficulty D_i, as opposed to the probability $P_{ni(j-1)}$ of being observed in category $(j-1)$; F_j is the threshold assumed to be constant across all items. The mathematical expression for RSM is as follows (Linacre, 2009):

$$\log(P_{nij}/ P_{ni(j-1)}) = B_n - D_i - F_j$$

In short, the RSM expresses the probability of a person choosing a given category on an item as a function of the agreeability of that person and the endorsability of the entire item at the given threshold (Kyriakides, Kaloyirou, & Lindsay, 2006). It can thus place person and item estimates on an interval scale.

In the context of the foregoing, Rasch analysis is adopted in the present study because estimates generated by Rasch analysis are linear, instrument-free, sample-free, and robust to missing data (Wright and Masters, 1982).

OBJECTIVES

Specifically, the present study seeks to examine the psychometric properties of the 29-item scale that was obtained after a process of evaluation of infit and outfit MnSq (mean of the squared residuals) as well as Zstd (standardized Z values) fit statistics, of the original 65 item scale. The specific research questions are as follows:

1. Is the six-point rating scale used optimally?
2. Is the FIT-UP scale reliable?
3. Do the 29 items measure an underlying construct – factors influencing students' take-up of physics?
4. Do the items target the sample well?
5. Does the FIT-UP scale show the property of measurement invariance across relevant subsamples?

METHODOLOGY

DEVELOPMENT AND VALIDATION OF INSTRUMENT

Whilst taking into consideration the various factors reported in the literature that contribute to the declining interest in physics among school students, this study also builds on the basis of the study of Politis *et al.* (2007). Discussions were also held with physics educators in secondary schools, junior colleges, and universities in Singapore in order to get further insights on the issue.

Pursuant to the foregoing, 16 domains were identified. Items were crafted to represent these domains. Four academic staff from the National Institute of Education in Nanyang Technological University in Singapore helped to validate the first draft of the scale. Whilst they are largely in agreement that the scale is comprehensive and appropriate, they also provided useful feedback. This led us to revise the instrument.

To pilot the instrument, a study using 35 physics teachers was conducted. The aim was to check for appropriateness of items for the scale, ambiguity in item phrasing and effectiveness of use of response categories. Analysis of the results led to the rephrasing of 13 items, deletion of seven items and addition of two items. It was noted that 23.5% of the teachers selected the neutral stance on average across all items. We felt that teachers need to make a stand rather than stay ambivalent. A case was thus established for converting the original five response categories into six categories, with the neutral category giving way to Slightly Agree and Slightly Disagree categories. This led to the formulation of a 65-item instrument, with items being randomly distributed. It was administered to the main sample, which comprised 190 physics teachers.

Data Collection Procedure

Stratified random sampling was employed to identify 125 secondary schools and 10 junior colleges in the four district zones in Singapore. The school principals were requested to nominate two very experienced physics teachers to complete the survey form individually. Teachers were assured that their identities would be kept anonymous. To facilitate ease of mailing, two stamped envelopes addressed to the second author were enclosed. There were returns from 91 (73%) secondary schools and 9 (90%) junior colleges.

Participants

Participants were physics teachers (N = 190) teaching in secondary schools and junior colleges in Singapore. Of these, 151 (79.5%) were from coeducational schools, 23 (12.1%) were from girls' schools, and 16 (8.4%) were from boys' schools. There were 111 (58.4%) male and 66 (34.7%) female teachers, with 13 (6.9%) teachers who did not indicate their gender. Their number of years of experience in teaching physics spanned a spectrum: 0–5 (30%), 6–10 (23.2%), 11–15 (16.8%), and 15+ (28.9%). Most of them had Bachelor's degrees (87.9%) while some had Master's degrees (11.1%). With regard to specialisation at the university, 92 (48.4%) of them specialised in physics, 77 (40.5%) in engineering, and 19 (10%) in others (e.g. mathematics).

DATA ANALYSES

A literature search found that Rasch analysis could be performed using a sample size of around 200 (e.g. Lee, Fisher, 2005; Pomeranz, Byers, Moorhouse, Velozo, & Spitznagel, 2008). Linacre (2004) reports that it can be done on even fewer samples. The use of 190 teachers in this study is thus reasonable.

We examined the 65-item FIT-UP scale using Rasch analysis. Based on Infit and Outfit MnSq as well as Zstd statistics, the 65 item scale was reduced to a 29 item scale. An Infit/Outfit MnSq range from .60 to 1.40 and an Zstd range from -2 to 2 were used as criteria to evaluate if items conformed to the Rasch model.

In the present study, we examine the psychometric properties of the 29-item FIT-UP scale using the Rasch framework, with the intention of generating further analyses that could be used to assess the validity and reliability of the revised scale.

The data for the 29 items was subjected to Rasch analysis using WINSTEPS software, version 3.68.1 (Linacre, 2009). Rasch estimates were obtained after nine iterations.

Each analysis is tied to a particular research objective of the study. Generally, it entailed six analyses as follows: (1) Fit statistics; (2) Rating scale analysis; (3) Reliability indices; (4) Principal Component Analysis (PCA); (5) Person-item map; and (6) Differential Item Functioning (DIF).

Missing data accounted for a minuscule 0.36% of the data. As WINSTEPS is able to estimate incomplete data using the joint maximum likelihood estimation, no treatment for missing data is necessary.

RESULTS

Effectiveness of Response Categories

The RSM model was used to examine the optimal usage of response categories (Wright & Masters, 1982). In the RSM context, a set of criteria is used to verify the functioning of each response category (Linacre, 2004):

a. A minimum of 10 observations is needed for each category, $N > 10$.
b. Average category measures must increase monotonically with categories, $N(q)_{increase}$.
c. Outfit mean square statistics should be less than 2.00, $MS < 2$.
d. The category threshold should increase monotonically with categories, $\tau_{increase}$.
e. Category thresholds should be at least 1.4 to 5 logits apart, $\tau_{1.4\text{-}5\ logits}$.
f. The shape of the probability curves should peak for each category, $Curves_{peak}$

It was found that each category satisfied the criterion for minimum counts of 10 observations (Table 1).

Table 1. Summary of category structure of the 6-point rating scale

Category	Observed count (%)	Average measure	Outfit MnSq	Threshold calibration
1. Strongly disagree	454 (4)	−.73	1.18	none
2. Disagree	1724 (14)	−.40	1.11	−1.94
3. Slightly disagree	2402 (20)	−.16	.82	−.60
4. Slightly agree	3209 (26)	.26	.87	−.21
5. Agree	3651 (30)	.74	.97	.35
6. Strongly agree	865 (7)	1.17	1.11	2.39

The average measures were ordered and increased monotonically from -.73 (*Strongly disagree*) to 1.17 (*Strongly agree*). The Outfit MnSq statistic for each category was below 2.00, indicating expected category usage (Linacre, 2002). In addition, threshold calibrations increased monotonically. However, the distance between Categories 3 and 4 was only 0.39 logits apart while that between 4 and 5 was 0.56 logits apart. They did not meet the minimum range of 1.4 to 5 logits apart. Inspection of the category probability curves (Figure 1) revealed that each category emerged as a distinct peak, though Categories 3 and 4 showed low peaks.

Since one of Linacre's criteria was not met, an attempt was made to reorganise the six rating scale categories (123456) into five categories (123345). Categories 3 and 4 were collapsed as the category threshold between them was only .39 logits apart and also showed low peaks. Table 2 summarises the adequacy of the original and collapsed categories. Collapsing the categories did not improve the category threshold between Categories 3 and 4, and between Categories 4 and 5.

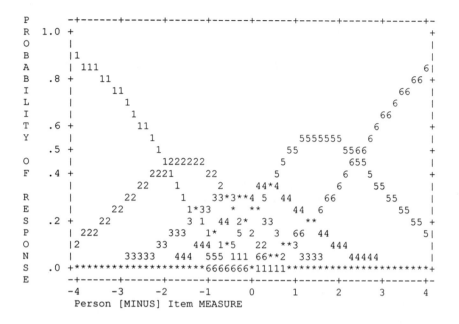

Figure 1. Category probability curves for the 6-point rating scale.

Table 2. Summary of rating scale analysis for original and collapsed scales

	Rating scale	
	Original	Revised
	123456	123345
Linacre's criteria		
N > 10	√	√
$M(q)_{increase}$	√	√
MS < 2	√	√
$\tau_{increase}$	√	√
$T_{1.4-5\ logits}$	X	X
curves$_{peak}$	√	√
Reliabilities		
Person	.84	.82
Item	.99	.99

Note. √ indicates satisfied; x indicates not satisfied

Reliability and Separation Indices

Item and person reliability indices were .99 and .84. Both had estimates above the threshold of .80 and are thus acceptable (Bond & Fox, 2007). The high item reliability infers that the items developed included both more endorsability as well as less endorsability items. The acceptable person reliability indicates that the instrument does include items where some teachers scored higher and some scored lower (Bond & Fox, 2007). The item separation index was 9.75 (SD = .75) and person separation index was 2.28 (SD = .31), with acceptable overall model root mean square error (RMSE): .07 and .12 respectively. These indices indicate the spread of items and persons along the measured variable. The commonly accepted criterion for the separation indices is 3.0 (Bond & Fox, 2007) or at least 2.0 (Lee, Grossman & Krishnan, 2008). The values obtained indicate excellent separation between the FIT-UP items and acceptable separation between the physics teachers.

Unidimensionality

The lower the measure, the higher is the endorsement (easier to be agreed with); the converse holds true for the higher measure. For example, items probing career prospects of physics graduates, recognition of physics education in today's society, ease of learning physics, and students' interest in learning physics are more difficult to endorse. On the other hand, items probing effect of grades in motivating students in learning physics and the importance of the laboratory in the learning of physics are easier to endorse.

Fit statistics assess the extent to which the data have been modeled by the strict mathematical expectations of the Rasch model (Gustafson, 1980; King & Bond, 2003). It examines the extent to which the items prompt an underlying construct satisfactorily. For items that do not fit the Rasch model, it means that they do not define a common construct – in the present study this would mean factors influencing the students' decision in physics. It is important to assess this because the items crafted in the instrument should *only* contribute to this aspect so that meaningful interpretations can be made. It is of interest to emphasise that this rigorous criterion exceeds the practice of traditional frameworks where this aspect is traditionally judged by experts (face validity), and the latter may give inconsistent results.

To measure the fit of the items, Infit and Outfit statistics were used. The Infit statistic (weighted) is sensitive to ratings on items located close to the teachers' ability. The Outfit statistic (unweighted) is sensitive to unexpected observations such as items that are much easier or harder than teachers' ability. The fit statistics are reported as the MnSq (Meansquare) and Zstd (Standaridised z values). Infit/ Outfit MnSq range of 0.6 to 1.4 and Zstd range from –2 to +2 are regarded as being acceptable in assessing if items measure an underlying unidimensional latent trait (Bond & Fox, 2007).

For the present data, the Infit MnSq ranges from .81 to 1.17 whereas the Outfit MnSq ranges from 0.82 to 1.21 (see Table 3). The means of 1.0 and .99 (ideal value is 1.0) are achieved for Infit and Outfit MnSq respectively. The Infit Zstd ranges from –2.0 to 1.90 while the Outfit Zstd ranges from –2.0 to 2.0. The means of -.10 are achieved for both Infit and Outfit Zstd (ideal value is .00). All items thus stayed within the range expected for fit statistics.

Table 3. Item statistics from Rasch analysis (N =190)

Items	Measure	Error	Infit		Outfit		PTMEA correla-tion
			MsSq	Zstd	MnSq	Zstd	
Recognition of physics education							
1. A career in physics is perceived to be of high status	.52	.07	.91	−1.0	.91	−1.0	.58
2. Physics education provides career opportunities which will bring wealth	.61	.07	.83	−2.0	.83	−2.0	.48
3. Studying physics is regarded highly in society	.45	.07	.84	−2.0	.84	−1.9	.55
Perceived difficulty of physics							
4. Students find physics to be difficult	−1.03	.07	.81	−2.0	.83	−1.8	.26
5. Students generally do not do well in physics	−.36	.07	.91	−1.0	.93	−.80	.31
6. The content in physics is generally abstract for students	−.73	.07	.83	−2.0	.84	−1.9	.27
The value of co-curricular activities							
7. Co-curricular activities (for example, collaboration between local physicists and teachers, talks by external speakers, visitations to relevant places like science centers, competitions, etc.) can make students realise how interesting physics is	−.83	.09	.90	−.80	.89	−1.0	.42
The value of physics in society							
8. People need to understand the nature of physics because it has an important effect on their lives	−.43	.08	1.09	.80	1.06	.60	.41
9. Physics is able to increase one's appreciation of nature	−.77	.08	1.17	1.4	1.13	1.10	.38
10. There is a need for the public to understand physics in order for technological progress to occur in a country	−.41	.08	1.15	1.4	1.11	1.0	.48
11. The knowledge from physics can help to eradicate poverty in the world	.20	.07	1.07	.80	1.08	.90	.35
12. The value of physics lies in its usefulness in solving practical problems	−.90	.09	1.05	.50	1.05	.50	.39
13. A country needs physicists to become developed	−.78	.08	1.02	.20	.97	−.30	.44
The grade effect							
14. Good examination results motivate students in learning physics	−1.54	.10	.92	−.70	.84	−1.4	.20
Heavy load of physics contents							
15. There is too much content to be mastered in physics	−.19	.07	1.12	1.3	1.14	1.5	.17

Items	Measure	Error	Infit		Outfit		PTMEA correla-tion
			MsSq	Zstd	MnSq	Zstd	
16. The syllabus in physics is heavily content-loaded	−.66	.07	1.06	.70	1.08	.90	.20
Mathematics puts students off							
17. The mathematics used in physics puts students off	−.52	.07	1.09	1.1	1.11	1.2	.23
18. Working with lots of formulae and mathematics in physics puts students off	−.57	.07	1.1	1.2	1.13	1.5	.19
19. Students require mathematics skills to do well in physics	−1.11	.09	1.13	1.1	1.06	.50	.15
20. Students encounter difficulties in solving quantitative problems in physics	−.57	.07	.95	−.50	.96	−.40	.27
The career prospects of physics graduates							
21. Physics education opens up greater opportunities for future careers	.17	.07	.96	−.50	.97	−.30	.55
22. Physics graduates have limited job choices	−.72	.07	1.17	1.9	1.18	2.0	.34
23. There is less emphasis on hiring physics graduates in industry	−1.16	.07	.91	−1.0	.90	−1.1	.31
The value of laboratory work							
24. Students understand the physics content better through laboratory work	−.52	.08	.82	−1.7	.82	−1.7	.36
25. The laboratory is a vital part for students to learn physics	−1.1	.09	1.09	.80	1.04	.40	.44
Relevance of studying physics							
26. Students like to study physics because using the knowledge gained they can explain physical phenomena to people	−.13	.07	.94	−.60	.93	−.70	.42
27. Students will choose to study physics in the future because it is relevant to their lives	.31	.07	1.03	.40	1.03	.40	.37
Interest in physics							
28. It is difficult to arouse the interest of students in physics	−.25	.07	.91	−1.0	.93	−.80	.34
29. Students favor other careers (e.g. Law and Finance) rather than physics-based careers (e.g. teaching physics)	−1.49	.08	1.16	1.50	1.21	1.9	.21
Mean	.07	.07	1.0	−.10	.99	−.10	

Note. "PTMEA correlation" means point measure correlation.

Point-measure (PTMEA) correlation was also examined. The PTMEA correlation should range from −1 to 1, with negative values indicating that items are improperly scored or do not function as intended (Linacre, 2009). All items in the scale show positive correlation coefficients. In general, 65.5% of them exhibited moderate to strong correlations (.31 to .58). However, a few items (4, 6, 14, 15, 16, 17, 18, 19, 20, 29) displayed low correlations (.15 to .27). This is a sign of the possible existence of sub-dimensions in the scale (Mok, Cheong, Moore, Kennedy, 2006). It can be confirmed by performing Principal Component Analysis (PCA).

PCA employs standardised residuals to identify possible dimensions existing in the FIT-UP (residuals are the differences between what the Rasch model predicts and what are observed). A variance greater than or equal to 50% for the Rasch dimension can be regarded as proof that the scale is unidimensional (Linacre, 2009). If a significant amount of variance is found in the second dimension (first contrast), the scale may be multidimensional. Generally, scale unidimensionality can be assumed if the first contrast has the strength of less than 3 items (in terms of eigenvalues) and the unexplained variance by the first contrast is less than 5% (Linacre, 2009).

For the FIT-UP scale, the Rasch dimension explained 39.3% of the variance, which is below the desired norm. The second dimension had an eigenvalue of 4.2 and accounted for 8.7% of the data that were not modeled. The residual scree plot in Figure 2 shows the factor structure of the FIT-UP. It can be seen that Items A, B, C, D (corresponding to Items 4, 17, 20, and 6) showed the largest contrast loadings (>.50). They are likely to correlate on an additional dimension.

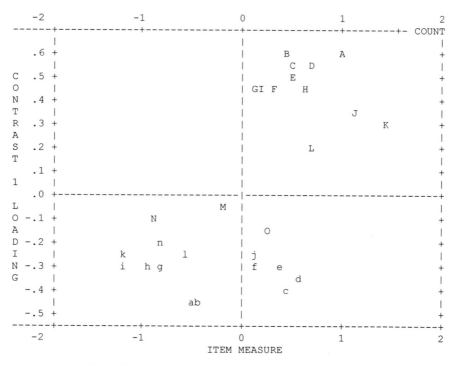

Figure 2. Plot of standardized residuals of the FIT-UP scale.

APPROPRIATENESS OF THE FIT-UP ITEMS FOR THE PHYSICS TEACHERS

Figure 3 shows the person-item map that places physics teachers and the FIT-UP items on an interval scale. Since measures of items and teachers are calibrated on the same scale, it can reveal the relationship between item endorsement and person agreement simultaneously (King & Bond, 2003). It can also determine if the item difficulties were appropriate for the targeted sample.

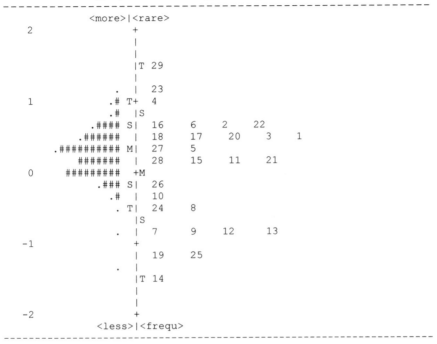

Figure 3. Person-item map of the 29 items with N=190 teachers.

Note. Each "#" represents four teachers and "." is one teacher.

In the figure, 'M' represents mean for person and item, 'S' represents one sample standard deviation away from the mean, and 'T' represents two sample standard deviations away from the mean. Teachers located closer to the lower end least agreed with the reasons being studied. On the contrary, those located at the upper end agreed most with the FIT-UP items.

The right side of the figure depicts the items arranged in endorsability order. Items at the bottom of the figure were less challenging while items at the top were more challenging to be agreed with by teachers. It means that items near the bottom are frequently endorsed while those near the top are less frequently endorsed.

An instrument that is well-targeted at the intended sample will show that the cluster of the persons is located opposite to the cluster of items (Bond & Fox, 2007). For the data in the present study, the item measures range from –1.54 to 1.49 logits while person measures range from –1.30 to 1.15. Persons and items clustered opposite to each other. In addition, the person mean estimate (.25) is centered around the item mean estimate (.00), with no wide divergence. The very good overlap of persons and items indicate that the 29 items are adequate to assess teachers with different views of the FIT-UP scale. That is, the items are reasonably well-targeted at the sample.

MEASUREMENT INVARIANCE

If the invariance principle holds, item estimates should remain stable across relevant subsamples (Bond & Fox, 2007). To investigate whether items function in the same way for subsamples, Rasch measures for male and female teachers were calculated (Table 4).

Table 4. Differential item functioning for male and female teachers

Item	Gender	Measure	S.E.	DIF contrast	Joint S.E.	t	df	p
1	Male	.56	.09	.03	.14	.23	150	.82
	Female	.52	.11					
2	Male	.61	.09	−.09	.14	−.63	150	.53
	Female	.70	.11					
3	Male	.52	.09	.13	.14	.90	150	.37
	Female	.39	.11					
4	Male	1.08	.09	.07	.15	.48	151	.63
	Female	1.01	.12					
5	Male	.36	.09	.00	.14	.00	150	1.00
	Female	.36	.11					
6	Male	.73	.09	.00	.14	.00	150	1.00
	Female	.73	.11					
7	Male	−.87	.11	−.07	.18	−.40	151	.69
	Female	−.80	.14					
8	Male	−.45	.10	−.06	.16	−.35	151	.73
	Female	−.40	.13					
9	Male	−.89	.11	−.24	.18	−1.36	154	.18
	Female	−.64	.14					
10	Male	−.32	.10	.27	.17	1.61	147	.11
	Female	−.59	.14					
11	Male	.20	.09	.04	.15	.27	150	.79
	Female	.16	.12					
12	Male	−.90	.11	.02	.19	.13	150	.90
	Female	−.93	.15					
13	Male	−.86	.11	−.16	.18	−.89	153	.37
	Female	−.70	.14					
14	Male	−1.49	.13	.14	.22	.63	149	.53
	Female	−1.63	.18					
15	Male	.19	.09	.08	.15	.52	147	.60
	Female	.11	.12					
16	Male	.64	.09	.01	.14	.05	150	.96
	Female	.63	.11					
17	Male	.52	.09	.00	.14	.00	150	1.00
	Female	.52	.11					
18	Male	.65	.09	.20	.14	1.44	150	.15
	Female	.44	.11					
19	Male	−1.17	.12	−.20	.19	−1.04	153	.30
	Female	−.97	.15					

Item	Gender	Measure	S.E.	DIF contrast	Joint S.E.	t	df	p
20	Male	.66	.09	.32	.14	2.25	150	.03
	Female	.34	.11					
21	Male	.08	.09	−.22	.14	−1.51	151	.14
	Female	.30	.11					
22	Male	.69	.09	−.13	.14	−.93	150	.35
	Female	.82	.11					
23	Male	1.13	.09	−.09	.15	−.58	149	.56
	Female	1.22	.12					
24	Male	−.48	.10	.28	.17	1.61	144	.11
	Female	−.76	.14					
25	Male	−1.06	.12	.13	.20	.64	149	.52
	Female	−1.19	.16					
26	Male	−.06	.09	.12	.15	.77	147	.44
	Female	−.18	.12					
27	Male	.34	.09	.00	.14	−.01	150	99
	Female	.34	.11					
28	Male	.27	.09	.02	.14	.17	150	.86
	Female	.25	.11					
29	Male	1.49	.10	−.09	.17	−.55	147	.58
	Female	1.59	.13					

The Differential Item Functioning (DIF) contrast is the difference in measure for an item between male and female teachers. It should be at least .50 logits for DIF to be noticeable (Linacre, 2009). The magnitude of the DIF contrast is depicted in Figure 4 for each item.

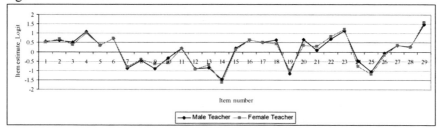

Figure 4. Plot of item estimate (measure) between male and female teachers.

Although some items are more difficult for females and some are more difficult for males to endorse, none of them showed a contrast of more than .50. Furthermore, except for item 20, none of the others displayed significant DIF (p > .05; −2 ≤ t ≤ 2). The DIF between male and female teachers for item 20 was, however, not significant as the contrast was merely .32 (< .50). This indicates the invariant structure of the FIT-UP scale for gender subsamples.

FURTHER ASSESSMENT OF THE FIT-UP SCALE

Items 4, 6, 17, and 20 were considered for deletion because they displayed high factor loadings (> .50) in the first contrast in PCA as well as low PTMEA correlations. After removing them, a total of 39.3% of the variance was accounted for by the Rasch model for the remaining items, which is still the same as that for the earlier 29-item scale. But, the first contrast had achieved a lower eigenvalue (3.0), which represented 7.4% (previously it was 4.2 or 8.7%) of the unexplained variance. This indicated that deletion of these four items did not significantly enhance the unidimensionality of the FIT-UP scale.

After deletion of the four items, the new 25-item scale was reassessed for its psychometric properties. Item and person reliabilities did not show any changes, which were .99 and .84, respectively. The same held true for item and person separation indices: 9.64 (SD = .75; model RMSE = .08) and 2.28 (SD = .31; model RMSE = .12), respectively. All the 25 items stayed within the acceptable range for Mnsq and Zstd. Person measures ranged from -1.30 to 1.15 while item measures ranged from -1.54 to 1.49. There was no noticeable wide gap between items and persons. Also, none of the 25 items reported significant DIF. All these results indicate that the new 25-item scale, although demonstrating good psychometric properties, did not show substantial improvement over the earlier 29-item scale. That is, the 29-item scale can be used in place of the 25-item scale.

DISCUSSION

The 29-item scale is reasonably well-targeted at the physics teacher sample. Items in the scale form a continuum from 'easy to endorse' to 'difficult to endorse'. All 29 items stayed within acceptable fit indices. Scores on the FIT-UP scale also showed high item and person reliabilities. The scores had acceptable to high, item and person separation indices. These findings suggest that items and persons are reliably calibrated on an interval scale.

The six point response categories can be kept as it is since it functions adequately, however, it failed to satisfy only one of Linacre's six criteria. Collapsing the 'Slightly Disagree' and 'Slightly Agree' categories did not improve the fit. Inclusion of the neutral category in place of the 'Slightly Disagree' and 'Slightly Agree' categories may encourage some respondents to not think deeply about the meaning of the items before responding. This may affect responses in other categories as well.

The DIF contrast between male and female teachers did not exceed .50. The difference between them can thus be attributed to chance. Therefore, item measures were invariant across gender subsamples.

It would appear that Items 4, 6, 17 and 20, based on the results of PCA, do not seem to be part of the underlying construct. Dropping them from the scale did not improve the scale substantially. Though a variance of about 40%, which is not far off from 50%, was accounted for by the Rasch dimension, inspection of the items did not reveal a meaningful secondary dimension. The four items pass the test of face validity in relation to the main construct. Indeed, they are widely recognised in the literature as being important for the FIT-UP (e.g. Angell, Guttersrud & Henriksen, 2004; Blenkinsop, McCrone, Wade & Morris, 2006; Gill, 1999; Kessels, Rau and Hannover, 2006; Smithers & Robinson, 2008; Williams, Stanisstreet, Spall, Boyes & Dickson, 2003; Woolnough, 1993). An interesting point to note is that these four items were negatively worded. It is possible that such negatively worded items could have correlated with the secondary dimension. Support for this point of view is provided by the work of Wolfe & Smith (2007), who reported on problems with negatively worded items when using Rasch analysis. In the final FIT-UP scale, it is recommended that these items be framed positively.

It is not uncommon in studies involving Rasch analysis for the Rasch dimension emerging from PCA to be less than 50% (Fischer, 2006; Higgins, 2002; Cervellione, Lee & Bonanno, 2008). Thus, the approximately 40% variance for the Rasch dimension accounted for in our study is not unreasonable, especially in the context of the explanations provided in the foregoing paragraph.

It is thus reasonable to assume that the FIT-UP scale is essentially unidimensional.

IMPLICATIONS

The present study is among very few studies in science education literature where the psychometric properties of a survey scale were examined comprehensively using the Rasch framework. A more recent study in the science education literature focused on the development of an instrument to assess students' metacognition, self-efficacy and constructivist science learning processes using the Rasch approach (Thomas, Anderson, Nashon, 2008). The present study is more comprehensive in that it uses Rasch analysis more rigorously. We took a few more steps than Thomas, *et al* (2008) so that more statistical parameters in relation to Rasch analyses (e.g. PCA on the residuals, DIF, etc) could be extracted. These allow the psychometric properties of the scale to be better investigated.

The differences in item endorsability allow us to capture a few aspects that deserve attention in the physics learning environment in schools. For example, teachers endorsed the point that students understand physics content better through laboratory work (Item 26). This suggests that the learning environment, which presently comprises classrooms for theory lessons and laboratories for practical work, may need to blend to some extent so that physics can be taught in a dynamic setting. Here we are not referring to the amalgamation of theory lessons and traditional practical work in a single venue but rather a setting where concepts covered in the theory lessons are reinforced through 'hands-on and minds-on' work in the laboratory. This may entail equipping the laboratory with a suite of supporting resources for teaching – for example, demonstration set-ups, materials for simple activities, etc, on top of the traditional experiments. Another endorsement by the teachers was not unexpected – the content in physics is generally abstract for students (Item 6). The challenge here is for teachers to present content in pedagogically interesting ways that can connect with students at the contextual level while scaffolding understanding at the conceptual level. This may entail more training for physics teachers - for example, sharing sessions on best practices to link content to everyday contexts, professional development programs to equip them with creative and innovative approaches to engage students, and so on.

It is clear that teachers need help to improve the learning environment in physics as otherwise they may persist in the conventional way of doing things. Self-directed initiatives to transform the learning environment are also possible but this has to be balanced against teaching workload and administrative commitments. All these can help to improve student interest in the subject, and promote a more salubrious classroom learning environment for learning physics.

It is suggested that the present study has implications for science education research, where awareness of Rasch analysis in treating survey data is rather low.

LIMITATIONS

The sample surveyed (N = 190) is a small fraction of the physics teacher population. It cannot thus be generalised to the entire population of physics teachers in Singapore. The Ministry of Education does not permit surveying teacher samples beyond a certain percentage. Further research to refine the FIT-UP is recommended.

In Singapore, physics is taken by academically brighter students from the Express, Special, and Gifted streams. Students in the Normal stream are offered Combined Science, which entails the taking of any two subjects from physics, biology, and chemistry. These approaches are to ensure that attrition rates in physics are minimised whilst ensuring that school leavers have a reasonable grasp of the sciences. To what extent this contributes to the declining interest in physics among school students and, consequently on enrolment in physics at the university level, is not clear.

CONCLUSION

The work reported in this chapter uses the Rasch model to study the psychometric properties of a Likert scale relating to factors contributing to the declining interest in physics, as viewed from the lens of physics teachers. It is among the first few studies in the science education literature where the psychometric properties of a scale were examined comprehensively by using the Rasch framework. The scale can be used to explore factors influencing the take-up of physics among students, from the perspective of teachers. It also provides useful pointers for improving the physics learning environment in schools.

ACKNOWLEDGEMENTS

We gratefully thank Prof Trevor Bond for useful discussions. Grateful thanks are also due to Prof Trevor Bond and Prof Russell Waugh for their helpful comments on an earlier version of this chapter. We also thank the Nanyang Technological University for the award of a Research Scholarship to the first author and the Ministry of Education for permission to conduct this study in schools. (It is to be noted that the views and interpretations advanced in this chapter are those of the authors and do not necessarily represent those of any of the national agencies mentioned here).

REFERENCES

Andrich, D. (1978). Rating formulation for ordered response categories. *Psychometrika, 43*, 561–573.

Andrich, D. (1996). Category ordering and their utility. *Rasch Measurement Transactions, 9*, 465–466.

Angell, C., Guttersrud, Ø., & Henriksen, E. (2004). Physics: Frightful, but fun. *International Journal of Science of Education, 88*, 683–706.

Assessment and Qualifications Alliance. (2007). *The number of entries to A-level examination in sciences and mathematics 1985–2007*. Retrieved January 9, 2008, from http://www.iop.org/activity/policy/Statistic/file_25677.doc

Barmby, P., & Defty, N. (2006). Secondary school pupils' perceptions of physics. *Research in Science & Technological Education, 24*(2), 199–215.

Blenkinsop, S., McCrone, T., Wade, P., & Morris, M. (2006). *How do young people make choices at age 14 and age 16?* (Department for Education and Skills Rep. No. 773). London: National Foundation for Educational Research.

Bond, T. G., & Fox, C. M. (2007). *Applying the Rasch model: Fundamental measurement in the human sciences* (2nd ed.). New Jersey, NJ: Lawrence Erlbaum Associates.

Cervellione, K., Lee, Y. S., & Bonanno, G. R. (2008). Rasch modeling of the self deception scale of the balanced inventory of desirable responding. *Educational & Psychological Measurment, 69*(3), 438–458.

Chien, C. W., & Bond, T. G. (2009). Measurement properties of fine motor scale of Peabody developmental motor scales – second edition. *American Journal of Physical Medicine & Rehabilitation, 88*(5), 376–386.

Crawley, F. E., & Black, C. B. (1992). Causal modeling of secondary science students' intentions to enroll in physics. *Journal of Research in Science Teaching, 29*(6), 585–599.

Dobson, I. R. (2006). Science at the crossroads? The decline of science in Australian higher education. *Journal of Tertiary Education and Management, 12*(2), 183–195.

Embretson, S. E., & Reise, S. P. (2000). *Item response theory for psychologists*. New Jersey, NJ: Lawrence Erlbaum.

Fischer, A., Frewer, L., & Nauta, J. (2006). Towards improving food safety in the domestic environment: A multi-item Rasch scale for the measurement of the safety efficacy of domestic food handling practices. *Risk Analysis, 26*(5), 1323–1338.

Fisher, W. P., Jr. (1997). Is content validity valid? *Rasch Measurement Transactions, 11*, 548.

Gill, P. (1999). The physics/maths problem again. *Physics Education, 34*(2), 83–87.

Gustafson, J. E. (1980). Testing and obtaining fit of data to the Rasch model. *British Journal of Mathematical and Statistical Psychology, 33*, 220.

Higgins, G. (2007). Examining the original Grasmick scale: A Rasch model approach. *Criminal Justice and Behaviour, 34*, 157–178.

Institute of Physics. (2001). *Physics-Building a flourishing future: Report of the inquiry into undergraduate physics*. Retrieved January 8, 2009, from http://www.iop.org/activity/policy/Projects/Achieve/file_6418.pdf

Kessels, U., Rau, M., & Hannover, B. (2006). What goes well with physics? Measuring and altering the image of science. *British Journal of Educational Psychology, 76*, 761–780.

King, J. A., & Bond, T. G. (2003). Measuring client satisfaction with public education I: Meeting competing demands in establishing state-wide benchmarks. *Journal of Applied Measurement, 4*(2), 111–123.

Kyriakides, L., Kaloyirou, C., & Lindsay, G. (2006). An analysis of the revised olweus bully/victim questionnaire using the Rasch measurement model. *British Journal of Educational Psychology, 76*, 781–801.

Lee, N. P., & Fisher, W. P., Jr. (2005). Evaluation of the diabetes self-care scale. *Journal of Applied Measurement, 6*(4), 366–381.

Lee, Y. S., Grossman, J., & Krishnan, A. (2008). Cultural relevance of adult attachment: Rasch modeling of the revised experiences in close relationships in a Korean sample. *Educational and Psychological Measurement, 68*(5), 824–844.

Lim, S. M., Rodger, S., & Brown, T. (2009). Using Rasch analysis to establish the construct validity of rehabilitation assessment tools. *International Journal of Therapy and Rehabilitation, 16*(5), 251–260.

Linacre, J. M. (2002). Optimising rating scale category effectiveness. *Journal of Applied Measurement, 3*, 85–106.

Linacre, J. M. (2004). Optimal rating scale category effectiveness. In E. V. Smith, Jr. & R. M. Smith (Eds.), *Introduction to Rasch measurement* (pp. 258–278). Maple Grove, MN: JAM Press.

Linacre, J. M. (2009). *WINSTEPS (Version 3.68.1)* [Computer Software]. Chicago: Winsteps.com.

Liu, X., & Boone, W. J. (2006). Introduction to Rasch measurement in science education. In X. Liu & W. J. Boone (Eds.), *Application of Rasch measurement in science education* (pp. 1–22). Minnesota, MN: JAM Press.

Lyons, T. (2006). The puzzle of falling enrolments in physics and chemistry courses: Putting some pieces together. *Research in Science Education, 36*(3), 285–311.

Messick, S. (1981). Evidence and ethics in the evaluation of tests. *Educational Researcher, 10*(9), 9–20.

Messick, S. (1989). Validity. In R. L. Linn (Ed.), *Educational measurement* (3rd ed., pp. 13–103). New York: Macmillan Publishing.

Mok, M. C. M., Cheong, C. Y., Moore, P. J., & Kennedy, K. J. (2006). The development and validation of the self-directed learning scales (SLS). *Journal of Applied Measurement, 7*(4), 418–449.

National Science Foundation, Division of Science Resource Statistics. (2004). *Science and engineering degrees: 1966–2001.* Retrieved January 8, 2008, from http://www.nsf.gov/statistics/nsf04311/sectb.htm

Politis, Y., Killeavy, M., & Mitchell, P. I. (2007). Factors influencing the take-up of physics within second-level education in Ireland – the teachers' perspective. *Irish Educational Studies, 26*(1), 39–55.

Pomeranz, J. L., Byers, K. L., Moorhouse, M. D., Velozo, C. A., & Spitznagel, R. J. (2008). Rasch analysis as a technique to examine the psychometric properties of a career ability placement survey subtest. *Rehabilitation Counseling Bulletin, 51*(4), 251–259.

Rasch, G. (1960). *Probabilistic models for some intelligence and attainment tests.* Copenhagen, Denmark: Paedagogiske Institut.

Rasch, G. (1980). *Probabilistic models for some intelligence and attainment tests.* Chicago: The University of Chicago Press.

Reid, N. (2006). Thought on attitude measurement. *Research in Science & Technological Education, 24*(1), 3–27.

Roberts, G. (2002). *SET for success. The supply of people with science, technology, engineering and mathematics skills* (The Report of Sir Gareth Roberts's Review). Retrieved June 9, 2008, from http://www.hm-treasury.gov.uk/media/F/8/robertsreview_introch1.pdf

Siorenta, A., & Jimoyiannis, A. (2008). Physics instruction in secondary schools: An investigation of teachers' beliefs towards physics laboratory and ICT. *Research in Science & Technological Education, 26*(2), 185–202.

Smithers, A., & Robinson, P. (2006). *Physics in schools and universities: Patterns and policies.* Buckingham: Carmichael Press, University of Buckingham.

Smithers, A., & Robinson, P. (2008). What can be done to increase the take-up of A-level physics. *School Science Review, 89*(328), 49–59.

Spall, K., Barrett, S., Stanisstreet, M., Dickson, D., & Boyes, E. (2003). Undergraduates' views about biology and physics. *Research in Science & Technological Education, 21*(2), 193–208.

Spall, K., Stanisstreet, M., Dickson, D., & Boyes, E. (2004). Development of school students' constructions of biology and physics. *International Journal of Science Education, 26*(7), 787–803.

Stone, M., & Wright, B. D. (1994). Maximising rating scale information. *Rasch Measurement Transactions, 8*, 386.

Thomas, G., Anderson, D., Nashon, S. (2008). Development of an instrument designed to investigate elements of science students' metacognition, self-efficacy and learning processes: The SEMLI-S. *International Journal of Science Education, 30*(13), 1701–1724.

Tobias, S., & Birrer, F. A. J. (1999). Who will study physics, and why? *European Journal of Physics, 20*, 365–372.

Williams, C., Stanisstreet, M., Spall, K., Boyes, E., & Dickson, D. (2003). Why aren't secondary students interested in physics. *Physics Education, 38*(4), 324–329.

Wolfe, E. W., Ray, L. M., Harris, D. C. (2004). A Rasch analysis of three measures of teacher perception generated from the school and staffing survey. *Educational and Psychological Measurement, 64*(5), 842–860.

Wolfe, E. W., & Smith, E. V., Jr. (2007). Instrument development tools and activities for measure validation using Rasch models: Part I – Instrument development tools. *Journal of Applied Measurement, 8*(1), 97–123.

Woolnough, B. E. (1993). Teachers' perception of reasons students choose for, or against, science and engineering. *School Science Review, 75*, 270.

Woolnough, B. E. (1994). Why students choose physics, or reject it. *Physics Education, 29*, 368–374.

Wright, B. D. (1999). Fundamental measurement for psychology. In S. E. Embretson & S. L. Hershberger (Eds.), *The new rules of measurement: What every educator and psychologist should know* (pp. 65–104). Hillsdale, NJ: Lawrence Erlbaum.

Wright, B. D., & Master, G. N. (1982). *Rating scale analysis*. Chicago: Mesa Press.

Wright, B. D., & Mead, R. J. (1977). *The use of measurement models in the definition and application of social science variables*. (Army Research Institute Technical Rep. No. 17). Virginia, VA: U.S. Army Research Institute.

Pey-Tee Oon and R. Subramaniam
(National Institute of Education, Nanyang Technological University)

PAUL NEWHOUSE

7. COMPARATIVE PAIRS MARKING SUPPORTS AUTHENTIC ASSESSMENT OF PRACTICAL PERFORMANCE WITHIN CONSTRUCTIVIST LEARNING ENVIRONMENTS

ABSTRACT

This chapter reports on the first year of an applied research project that utilises new digital technologies to address the challenge of embedding authentic complex performance as an integral part of summative assessment in senior secondary courses. Specifically, it reports on the approaches to marking authentic assessment tasks to meet the requirements of external examination. On-line marking tools were developed utilising relational databases to support the use of the analytical rubric-based marking method and the paired comparisons method to generate scores based on Rasch modelling. The research is notable in seeking to simultaneously enhance assessment and marking practices in examination contexts and in so doing, also contribute to the advancement of pedagogical practices associated with constructivist learning environments. The chapter will be relevant to courses and subjects that incorporate a significant performance dimension.

BACKGROUND

The past three decades have seen the conspicuous emergence in education of support for theories of teaching and learning based on constructivist principles and for the use of Information and Communications Technology (ICT). However, in both cases the impact on classroom practice has not been as extensive as many had hoped. While there are many factors that may explain this situation, the connection to assessment practice is seen by many as a critical factor in both cases (Dede, 2003; McGaw, 2006; Pellegrino, Chudowsky, & Glaser, 2001). In a wide-ranging review of the literature on learning, the Committee on Developments in the Science of Learning (Bransford, Brown, & Cocking, 2000, p. 10) argued that, increasingly, commonly accepted understandings about learning are those bearing the label of constructivism. They argued that, "the contemporary view of learning is that people construct new knowledge and understandings based on what they already know and believe." Further, it is commonly accepted that learning occurs within a physical and psycho-social learning environment that determines the roles of the teacher and students and comprises a complex of relationships between entities

R.F. Cavanagh and R.F. Waugh (eds.), Applications of Rasch Measurement
in Learning Environments Research, 141–180.

such as learners, instructors, curriculum, and resources (Fraser, 1994). This has given rise to the notion of a constructivist learning environment (Jonassen, 2000) that for many educators is an ideal. Interactive technologies, such as ICT, involved in the delivery of the curriculum have a place within the psycho-social, not just the physical structures of a learning environment (e.g. Lynch, 1990). Thus there is a logical connection between the implementation of the use of ICT to support learning and the constructivist nature of the learning environments within which this occurs.

With the typically expressed intention of schooling being to provide students with the skills and knowledge foundational to successful living, it is increasingly argued that this requires students to deal with complex ill-structured problems where practical skills are linked with theoretical knowledge (Kozma, 2009). Kozma and others would argue that this is best achieved within a constructivist learning environment where students are supported in the development of complex performances that require cross-discipline knowledge, higher-order thinking and learning process skills along with practical skills. However, there is little doubt that such environments are still the exception rather than the rule for students in countries such as Australia.

It is perhaps self evident that what is taught should be assessed and what is taught should be determined by the needs of individuals and the society within which they exist. However, most often the reality is that what is taught is what is assessed and what is assessed bears little resemblance to what is needed (Lane, 2004; Ridgway, McCusker, & Pead, 2006). Rather, what is assessed, particularly for high-stakes purposes, is determined by what can readily be represented on paper using a pen in a short amount of time. Most often this is in stark contrast to the stated requirements of the curriculum and stated preferred pedagogy and does not match the rapidly changing requirements of future study, work or life activities associated with that curriculum. That is, assessment lacks alignment and authenticity but unfortunately drives education systems. This is a problem that, while not new, many would argue is growing in complexity and proportion (Dede, 2003; Lane, 2004; Lin & Dwyer, 2006; McGaw, 2006). Thus it is argued that the provision of constructivist learning environments is being constrained by serious shortcomings in common methods of summative assessment (i.e. it is principally designed to determine the achievement of a student at the end of a learning sequence rather than inform the planning of that sequence for the student).

It is still the case in most nations, Australia being a case in point, that high-stakes summative assessment for school students is conducted with little if any use of ICT. There is no doubt that the vast majority of teachers limit their use of ICT the closer students get to such assessment points and most often this is supported by parents and students (Whitefield, 2004). The rationale is that if the use of ICT is not permitted for completion of the assessment task then students need to practice such tasks without using the technology. For example, students are required to handwrite because word processing is not permitted in the 'exams'. Thus it is argued that the use of ICT to support learning in schools is being constrained by serious shortcomings in common methods of summative assessment.

Not only can it be argued that the implementation of constructivist learning environments and the use of ICT to support learning have been, and are currently, seriously constrained by summative assessment practices but also the limited implementation of each has impacted on the other. That is, there is evidence that ICT is more likely to be used in constructivist learning environments and such environments are more readily provided when ICT support is available (Jonassen, 2000). Learning environments are constructed by the participants and are thus dependent on their beliefs and actions, particularly the underlying pedagogical philosophy of the teacher. Therefore there is considerable variation in the ways ICT may be effectively incorporated within a learning environment, and there is no suggestion that a particular option is preferable. However, there has now been sufficient reported research to identify principles that may be applied to guide the inclusion of ICT support for effective learning environments. Many researchers, including educational bodies (e.g. Bransford et al., 2000), have elaborated the base principles critically built on theories of constructivism, including the concept of proximal learning, based on the work of Vygotsky (1978), that has led to the use of the term computer supported learning (DeCorte, 1990; Mevarech & Light, 1992). The hope is that with the support of ICT, a wider range of effective learning environments will be employed than has traditionally been the case (Glickman, 1991). However, both the use of ICT and the implementation of effective constructivist learning environments are constrained by a limited implementation of authentic performance summative assessment.

For decades students in schools in Western Australia (WA) wishing to enter universities have been required to undertake tertiary entrance examinations in a limited number of recognised courses considered to be 'academic'. Almost all of these examinations were conducted using paper and pen over a three-hour time period. From 2007, a large number of courses were implemented for tertiary entrance, with many of these including a major element of practical performance work that raised a range of issues concerning 'examinations'. The most notable challenge was that of authentic summative assessment – how to validly assess performance at a reasonable cost and in a manner that allows for reliable marking to generate a defensible score.

Developing a means of reliable authentic assessment consistent with pedagogical practices associated with constructivist learning environments is regarded as critical for courses with a significant performance dimension, since while students tend to focus on, and be motivated by practical performance, teachers will inevitably tend to 'teach to the test' (McGaw, 2006). Appeal from a student perspective and authenticity of assessment will be compromised if core performance components of courses are excluded from examinations. Furthermore, contemporary western societies increasingly expect that students will be able to demonstrate practical skills and the application of knowledge through performance in industry, professional and social settings (Australian Bureau of Statistics, 2002). In part, the difficulties presented from an 'examination' perspective by practical performance have contributed to an historical tendency for distinct separation of so called 'theory' and 'practice' components of many courses, with often the elimination of the practical component altogether. Finally, it is argued that students are more likely to experience deep learning through experiences that involve complex performance (Spector, 2006). Many educators (Grant, 2008) argue that there is a social justice imperative to the need to improve approaches to summative assessment and that the use of computer technology may assist in doing so.

ADDRESSING THE PROBLEMS OF AUTHENTIC ASSESSMENTS

The authentic assessment problem concerns more than assessing practical skills, it concerns assessing higher-order thinking and learning process skills demonstrated through complex performance and this, many educational researchers would argue, traditional paper-based assessment does very poorly (Lane, 2004; Lin & Dwyer, 2006). Concern centres around the validity of such assessment in terms of the intended learning outcomes, where there is a need to improve the criterion-related validity, construct validity and consequential validity of high-stakes assessment (McGaw, 2006). Kozma (2009) explains how tasks in the "outside world": require cross-discipline knowledge; relate to complex ill-structured problems; and are completed collaboratively using a wide range of technological tools to meet needs and standards. These characteristics are at odds with standardised pen-and-paper approaches to assessment and thus there is a need to consider alternative approaches with alternative technologies, in particular for the representation of student performance on complex tasks.

In general, alternatives to paper-based exams for high-stakes assessment have been considered to be too expensive and too unreliable to 'mark'. Recent advances in psychometric methods associated with Rasch modelling and improvements in digital technologies provide tools to consider alternative approaches to the assessment of a variety of performance relatively cost-effectively. Firstly, digital technologies may provide tools to collect evidence of performance including the use of video, audio, graphics and text representations. Secondly, digital technologies may be used to support marking processes through online repositories and marking interfaces and databases. Finally, digital technologies may be used to support the analysis of data generated by marking to provide reliable accurate scores. The paired comparisons method of marking that uses Rasch modelling is known to be highly reliable when human judgements are required but until recently was considered impractical for 'front-line' marking (Kimbell, Wheeler, Miller, & Pollitt, 2007). With the use of digital representation of student performance accessed by markers online and the use of Rasch modelling software this method becomes manageable. This chapter, in part, discusses the application of this method of marking within a larger study.

In 2008, a large collaboratively funded three-year study was commenced that addressed the performance assessment problem in four WA senior secondary courses. The aim was to successfully develop and implement a performance assessment task to create a single-scale score. This study was carried out by researchers from the School of Education at Edith Cowan University (ECU) and managed by the Centre for Schooling and Learning Technologies (CSaLT) in collaboration with the Curriculum Council of WA. The study built on concerns that the assessment of student achievement should, in many areas of the curriculum, include practical performance and that this will only occur in high-stakes context if the assessment can be shown to validly and reliably measure the performance and be manageable in terms of cost and school environment. Thus the assessment is summative in nature with reliability referring to the extent to which results are repeatable, and validity referring to the extent to which the results measure the targeted learning outcomes. There is a critical need for research into the use of digital forms of representation of student performance on complex tasks for the purposes of summative assessment that are feasible within the constraints of school contexts. This study investigated authentic digital forms of assessment with high levels of reliability, manageability, which were capable of being scaled-up for statewide implementation in a cost effective manner.

REVIEW OF THE LITERATURE

Every assessment, regardless of its purpose, rests on three pillars: a model of how students represent knowledge and develop competence in the subject domain, tasks or situations that allow one to observe students' performance, and an interpretation method for drawing inferences from the performances evidence thus obtained. (Pellegrino et al., 2001). The present study sought to improve summative assessment in courses requiring the application of theoretical knowledge to some form of practical performance through the use of digital technologies to support each of these three pillars. The focus of this chapter is on the third pillar. Pellegrino, Chudowsky and Glaser (2001) go on to argue that the nature of the latter two pillars "underlying most current assessments" (p. 2) are based on outdated conceptions of learning and are out of alignment with ideal classroom practices. They consider that "technology offers the possibility" (p. 6) of addressing this situation within the context of "formal measurement (psychometric) models" (p. 5). They particularly refer to the possibility of not being confined by paper formats and supporting assessors other than the teacher. They recommend that research is required into issues raised by such use of technology.

Many educational researchers argue that traditional assessment fails to assess learning processes and higher-order thinking skills, and go on to explain how digital technologies may address this problem (Lane, 2004; Lin & Dwyer, 2006). Further, in some courses students learn with technologies and this dictates that students should be assessed making use of those technologies. Dede (2003) suggests that traditionally educational assessment has been "based on mandating performance without providing appropriate resources, then using a 'drive by' summative test to determine achievement" (p. 6). He goes on to explain how digital technologies may address this problem and claims that "the fundamental barriers to employing these technologies effectively for learning are not technical or economic, but psychological, organisational, political and cultural" (p. 9). Lin and Dwyer (2006) argue that computer technology should be used to capture "more complex performances" (p. 29) that assess a learner's higher-order skills (decision-making, reflection, reasoning and problem solving) and cite examples but suggest that this is seldom done due to "technical complexity and logistical problems" (p. 28).

Apart from the lack of validity of traditional paper-based assessment methods another compelling rationale to consider the efficacy of performance assessment is that teachers tend to teach to the summative assessment (Lane, 2004; Ridgway et al., 2006). McGaw (2006) discussed this in the light of changes in the needs of the society, advances in psychometric methods, and improvements in digital technologies and believed that this was critical due to the influence of assessment on the judgements of teachers and students concerning the curriculum with "risk that excessive attention will be given to those aspects of the curriculum that are assessed" and that "risk-taking is likely to be suppressed" (p. 2). He goes as far as to argue that, "If tests designed to measure key learning in schools ignore some key areas because they are harder to measure, and attention to those areas by teachers and schools is then reduced, then those responsible for the tests bear some responsibility for that" (p. 3).

The committee of the American National Academy of Sciences presented a discussion of the arguments and concerns underpinning the use of computer-based assessment methods to replace traditional paper-and-pencil methods (Garmire & Pearson, 2006). They argue that assessing many performance dimensions is too difficult on paper and too expensive using "hands-on laboratory exercises" (p. 161) while computer-based assessment has the potential to increase "flexibility, authenticity, efficiency, and accuracy" but must be subject to "defensible standards" (p. 162). The committee raised a number of questions requiring research including that electronic portfolios, "appear to be excellent tools for documenting and exploring the process of technological design" (p. 170).

McGaw (2006) also believes that without change to the main high-stakes assessment strategies currently employed there is a reduced likelihood that productive use will be made of formative assessment. He is not alone in this concern, for example, Ridgway, McCusder and Pead (2006, p. 39) state that, "There is a danger that considerations of cost and ease of assessment will lead to the introduction of 'cheap' assessment systems which prove to be very expensive in terms of the damage they do to students' educational experiences." Therefore, from both a consideration of the need to improve the validity of the assessment of student practical performance, and the likely negative impact on teaching (through not adequately assessing this performance), there is a strong rationale for exploring alternative methods to paper-based examinations for performance assessment.

Assessment of Practical Performance

Research in, and the call to investigate "performance-and-product assessment" is not new as pointed out by Messick (1994, p. 14) who claims that mainstream schooling showed little interest in this until an "upsurge of renewed interest" in the 1990s with "positive consequences for teaching and learning" (p. 13). While Messick does not specifically address digital forms of performance assessment, his arguments for the need to address "issues of validity, reliability, comparability and fairness" apply, particularly to a range of validity criteria. He argues they are social values that require close attention to the intended and unintended consequences of the assessment through considerations of the purposes of the assessment, the nature of the assessed domain, and "construct theories of pertinent skills and knowledge" (p. 14). For example, he outlines situations under which product assessment should be considered rather than performance assessment. The issue is their relationship to replicability and generalisability requirements because these are important when performance is the "vehicle" of assessment. Lane (2004) outlines how a decline in the use of performance assessments in the USA led to a lack of alignment between assessment, curriculum standards, and instructional practices; particularly with regard to eliciting complex cognitive thinking. Globally, interest in performance assessment has increased with the increasing use of standards-referenced curricula. Standards-referenced curricula have evolved over the past 20 years particularly from the UK and more recently in Australian states since the early 1990s. The key concept in these curricula is that student achievement was defined in terms of statements describing what students understood, believed or could do. The term standards-referenced has been used recently to indicate that student achievement is measured against defined standards. However, a critical issue has been how to generate scores from these standards for high-stakes purposes.

Koretz (1998) analysed the outcomes of four large-scale portfolio-based performance assessment systems in the USA school systems, none being digital, and concluded that overall the programmes varied in reliability and validity and were resource intensive with "problematic" (p. 309) manageability. This body of literature clearly presents the assessment of student performance as critically important but fundamentally difficult with many unanswered questions requiring research. Findings such as this provide a rationale for considering digital solutions to performance assessment.

DIGITAL FORMS OF ASSESSMENT

There is a range of applications for digital technologies to support assessment from the use of computers to conduct the whole assessment process, such as with on-screen testing, to only assisting in one aspect of the task assessment process (e.g. recording performance or marking) (Bull & Sharp, 2000). The first area of the task assessment process that took advantage of computer-support was objective type assessments that automated the marking process (eliminating the marker) and allowed the results to be instantly available. Much of the published research in the field relates to higher education (e.g. Brewer, 2004), however, in the school sector assessment of student creative work in the arts has been addressed for some time with, for example, Madeja (2004) arguing the case for alternatives to paper-and-pencil testing for the arts. While there has been only limited empirical research there are many useful theoretical discussions of the issues such as Spector's (2006) outline of a method for assessing learning in "complex and ill-structured task domains". While providing useful ideas and rationales, these ideas remain largely untested in the reality of classrooms. What is known is that any use of ICT involves school change (Newhouse, Clarkson, & Trinidad, 2005) and will require training of teachers, changes in thinking, and pedagogical understandings that are difficult to accommodate (Newhouse, Williams, & Pearson, 2006).

In order to judge student performance, that performance needs to either be viewed or represented in some form. This may involve the assessor viewing a student performing, such as in a musical recital, or viewing the results of a student performing, such as in an art exhibition. Most often the latter occurs because this is either more appropriate or more cost-effective. In places such as Western Australia, the inclusion of either type of assessment for high-stakes purposes has been rare due to the costs and logistics involved. For example, student performance in conducting science experiments has not been included presumably due to the difficulty in supervising thousands of students and viewing their work, and production in design and technology, or home economics related areas, has been limited due to the products being bulky and therefore difficult to access by assessors. However, many forms of student performance can be recorded in digital representations using video, audio, photographic or scanned documents, and some student work is created in digital format using computer software. In these cases, the representations of student work can be made available to assessors relatively easily and cheaply using digital repositories and networked computer workstations.

A ground-breaking project aimed at assessing performance, titled E-scape, was conducted by the Technology Education Research Unit (TERU) at Goldsmiths College, University of London (Kimbell et al., 2007). This project built upon many years of work on improving assessment in the design and technology curriculum (Kimbell, 2004). E-scape combines three innovations in the assessment of practical performance by representing student work entirely in digital form, collating this work using an online repository, and marking it using a comparative pairs judgement technique. To some extent, the present study followed in the footsteps of E-scape.

For the purposes of the study, four particular forms of assessment were defined that employed digital technologies to represent the output of student performance. These forms were an *Extended Production Exam*, a *Focussed Performance Tasks Exam*, a *Reflective Digital Portfolio*, and an *interview* or *oral presentation*. These were not intended to provide an exhaustive list but rather define major forms that appeared to be relevant to the four courses involved in the study.

An *Extended Production Exam* was considered to be the completion, under 'exam conditions', of one practical assessment task that incorporated a full set of processes (e.g. design process, scientific investigation) and centred on one major scenario. Examples were found locally, nationally and internationally of performance on practical tasks being assessed through an extended production, or small project, under exam conditions. However, most did not involve the use of digital technologies. The most comprehensive example was that of Kimbell et al. (2007) in the UK where students spent two consecutive mornings of three hours duration each working on a structured design activity for the production of a pill dispenser. All student work output was collected digitally using a networked Personal Digital Assistant (PDA) device and local server.

A *Focussed Performance Tasks Exam* was considered to be the completion, under 'exam conditions', of a range of practical tasks that are not necessarily logically connected and typically focus on the demonstration of practical skills. Examples were found locally, nationally and internationally of performance on practical tasks being assessed through the completion of short tasks under exam conditions. However, many did not involve the use of digital technologies.

A *Reflective Process Digital Portfolio* was considered to be a collection of digital artefacts of work output with some reflective commentary (journaling) by the student, organised according to specified parameters such as form, structure, and a range of samples required. In a review of e-assessment, the digital portfolio is recommended as a "way forward" in the high-stakes assessment of "practical" work in that ICT "provides an opportunity to introduce manageable, high quality coursework as part of the summative assessment process (Ridgway et al., 2006). Three uses of portfolios are suggested, one of which is "to provide a stimulus for reflective activity". The use of portfolios is not new, particularly in areas such as the visual arts and design and technology but typically these have been paper-based (Garmire & Pearson, 2006). The exercise of assembling a portfolio is often seen as much as a "learning tool" as an "assessment tool" but the results are typically limited by physical storage space and methods of access (Garmire & Pearson, 2006).

An *audio or video interview or oral presentation* with a student is digitally recorded under controlled circumstances and following a pre-determined script of prompts and/or questions. Clearly the quality of the audio recording is critical so it is likely to require the use of a microphone attached to the student or directly in front of the student.

Methods of Marking

Task assessment is what is commonly referred to as 'marking'. Once students have completed the assessment task, the output needs to be judged by some method to determine a score, grade or ranking. Three methods of marking are considered here: 'traditional' true score marking, analytical judgements using standards-based frameworks, and comparative pairs judgements.

Traditionally, summative assessment has tended to involve students 'sitting' paper-based exams that are scored by allocating a number to items in the exam and then summing these numbers. This is sometimes called true score marking or cumulative marking. Pollitt (2004) argues that current methods of summative assessment that focus on summing scores on "micro-judgements" is "dangerous and that several harmful consequences are likely to follow" (p. 5). Further, he argues that it is unlikely that such a process will accurately measure a student's "performance or ability" (p. 5), and more holistic judgements of performance are required. He claims this has been tolerated because assessment validity has been overshadowed by reliability due to the difficulty and expense in addressing the former compared with the latter.

ANALYTICAL MARKING

Analytical marking using standards-reference frameworks and rubrics have been used for many years by teachers in Western Australia and other localities to mark student work but have less often been used for summative high-stakes marking. This involves the definition of standards of achievement against which to compare the work of students. Typically, this is operationalised for a particular assessment task through a rubric that describes these standards according to components of the task and through exemplars. The results may be represented as a set of levels of achievement or may be combined by converting these to numbers and adding them. However, using Rasch Modelling they may be combined to create an interval scale score.

In a report for the Curriculum Council of WA, Prof Jim Tognolini (2006) states that "one of the main advantages of a standards-referenced assessment system is that the results can indicate what it is students have achieved during the course" and that "at the same time, use the same scores for university entrance purposes". Further, he explains that this provides students with "a meaningful record of their achievements" and this will "facilitate smoother entry through different pathways into higher education and the workforce". He points out that all Australian states and many international systems including the Baccalaureate and PISA have a standards-referenced curriculum. He defines it as "where educational outcomes are clearly and unambiguously specified" and claims this has "significant power and appeal in more globalised contexts" providing a "mechanism for tracking and comparing outcomes over time and across jurisdictions". In Western Australia, this is now sometimes also referred to as 'analytical' marking.

The word 'rubric' is a derivative of the Latin word ruber meaning 'red' that in current usage is a guide listing criteria used for rating performance (Wiggins, 1998). The current research literature on marking keys promotes the use of criterion or rubric based marking keys to enhance transparency, reliability and, when the task is aligned with the learning outcomes, also validity (Andrade, 2005; Tierney & Marielle, 2004). Marking using a rubric base on a standards framework requires assessors to compare a student's work against what is theoretically possible. This is difficult and requires considerable depth of knowledge and experience and can still result in different assessors judging the same work differently because they have different standards in mind (Grant, 2008). This leads to a problem of reliability that is typically overcome by using more than one assessor for each piece of work and then having a consensus process. This may be costly and still somewhat unreliable. Hay and Macdonald (2008) investigated the validity and reliability shortcomings of performance assessment in Physical Education where teachers found it difficult to objectively apply a standards framework. However, in a study titled "Assessing Expressive Learning" that involved nearly 2000 art portfolios and the use of rubrics, it was found that "qualitative instructional outcomes can be assessed quantitatively, yielding score values that can be manipulated statistically, and that produce measures that are both valid and reliable estimates of student art performance" (Madeja, 2004).

COMPARATIVE PAIRS METHOD OF MARKING

Comparative pairs marking involves a number of assessors making judgements on achievement through comparing a student's work with that of other students, considering a pair of students at a time and indicating the better of the two. This is sometimes referred to as pairwise comparisons or cumulative comparisons. This method of marking requires Rasch Modelling and was used successfully by Kimbell, Wheeler, Miller and Pollitt (2007) in the E-scape project delivering high levels of reliability.

Pollitt (2004) describes the comparative pairs method of marking applied to performance assessment in his paper, "Let's stop marking exams". He claims the method he and his colleagues developed is "intrinsically more valid" and is "rooted in the psychophysics of the 1920s" (p. 2). He goes on to explain that while the system is better than the traditional system to this stage, it has not been feasible to apply, due to time and cost constraints, however, with the use of ICT to support this system these constraints are removed and "Thurstone's methods" that "have waited 80 years ... are at last ... feasible" (p. 21). He quotes Laming that there is "no absolute judgement. All judgements are comparisons of one thing with another" and explains that it is more reliable to compare performances or products between students than with "descriptions of standards" (p. 6). He claims that they have more than ten years experience in applying the method in a variety of contexts and that with expert application about 20 comparisons per student is required. However, he does suggest that the method should not be used with every type of assessment, with research required to determine the appropriateness and whether "sufficient precision can be achieved without excessive cost" (p. 16).

McGaw (2006) also believes that the comparative pairs method of marking provides an opportunity to improve the validity of high-stakes assessment in separating the "calibration of a scale and its use in the measurement of individuals" (p. 6). He claims that while the 'deficiency' of norm-referenced assessment has been understood for many years, it was seen that there was no alternative. Now he believes that with methods involving comparisons supported by digital technologies there is an alternative that should be explored. An important question is whether the advances in psychometrics that permit calibration of scales and measurement of individuals that allows interpretation of performance in terms of scales can be applied in public examination (McGaw, 2006, p. 7).

THE STUDY

In order to investigate the use of digital representations to deliver authentic and reliable assessments of performance, the present study brought together three key innovations:

1. The capture in digital files of the evidence of performance of students doing practical work.
2. The development of marking tools to access these digital files from an online repository and allow the evidence to be readily judged by experts.

3. The use of both analytical judgement and the comparative pairs judgement methods to assess these representations of performance to use Rasch modelling to generate reliable scores.

While each of these innovations is not new in themselves, their combination applied at the secondary level of education is new. Apart from Kimbell et al.'s (2007) work at the University of London, there has been no known precedent.

Fundamentally, the study investigated the use of digital forms of representation of student practical performance for summative assessment, whether the student created digital files or their performance was recorded in digital format by filming, photographing, audio recording or scanning. The digital representations of student performance were combined within an online repository. The use of online repositories for student work output is increasingly common, often referred to as online portfolios, with many products available to facilitate their creation and access (Richardson & Ward, 2005). The key feature is that the portfolios can be accessed from anywhere and thus markers from different jurisdictions can be involved, enhancing consistency of standards. Finally, the student work needed to accurately and reliably assess the outcomes without a huge increase in the cost of assessment. The study also engaged with a further long-standing dilemma in many courses; the design of assessment tasks to compare performance in varying curriculum contexts (e.g. soccer, volley-ball in Physical Education).

The main research question became:
How are digitally based representations of student work output on authentic tasks most effectively used to support highly reliable summative assessments of student performances for courses with a substantial practical component? Therefore, the specific aims of the research were:

1. To determine the feasibility of each digitally based form to support authentic summative assessment of student practical performance in different types of courses.
2. To establish ways of applying the comparative pairs marking procedure to digital forms of summative assessment to achieve high reliability in a cost-effective manner.
3. To extend existing conceptual models for digital forms of performance assessment.

The first year of the study was a 'proof of concept' project to explore the feasibility of particular digitally-based forms for external assessment for four courses: *Applied Information Technology; Engineering Studies; Italian;* and *Physical Education Studies*. The feasibility was investigated within a framework consisting of the four dimensions (Kimbell & Wheeler, 2005).
- Manageability: Concerning making a digital form of assessment do-able in typical classrooms with the normal range of students.
- Technical: Concerning the extent to which existing technologies can be adapted for assessment purposes within course requirements.
- Functional: Concerning reliability and validity, and the comparability of data with other forms of assessment.

- Pedagogic: Concerning the extent to which the use of a digital assessment forms can support and enrich the learning experience of students.

RESEARCH DESIGN AND METHOD

The study was evaluative in nature set within an ethnographic framework in that activity was considered to occur within learning environments where the characteristics of teachers and students and the culture created are critical to an understanding of all aspects of the curriculum and pedagogy, including assessment. Therefore, this study employed an ethnographic action research evaluation methodology using interpretive techniques involving the collection of both qualitative and quantitative data. That is, quantitative measures concerning achievement, costs and resource use were used but these needed to be interpreted within the context of the learning environment and in which the measures occurred. As such, this required an analysis of the perspectives of the key groups of participants (teachers, assessors, students) with data collected from each group. These data were compiled into case studies within a multi-case approach (Burns, 1996) in which each case is defined by one class for one course. This approach allowed for refinement and further development of findings based on multiple instances of the same phenomenon under different conditions (Willig, 2001).

The following groups of people were involved in the study.
- Teachers: Purposeful sampling was used to selected teachers for each of the courses who were both experienced in teaching the course and ICT literate.
- Students: One class of students for each selected teacher.
- Assessors: A panel of trained assessors for each of the four courses to include Curriculum Council moderators and researchers.
- Research Team: The investigators, consultants and research assistants.
- Working Parties: For each of the four courses there was a working party that comprised the three or four researchers, relevant Curriculum Council personnel, and teachers whose classes were involved.
- Advisory Group: An Advisory Group of representatives from the school systems and experts in assessment and/or technology education was assembled to work with the researchers to ensure a strong connection between schools, assessment theory and the study.

In the first year, the 2008 study involved a sample of 21 classes of senior secondary students currently enrolled in at least one of the four courses from 17 schools. For each course, a common assessment task was developed and implemented in between four and seven classes. Table 1 shows the number of classes and students involved in this year of the study and a description of the assessment task. Data from all sources on each class was combined to create a series of case studies structured to highlight design and implementation features. A range of types of quantitative and qualitative data were collected including observation in class, a survey of students, a survey of the teacher, interviews with the teacher and a group of students, student work output from the assessment task, and the assessment records of the teacher.

Table 1. Classes and students involved, and a description of the common assessment task for each course

Course	Classes	Students	Common assessment task
Applied Information Technology	7	115	A digital portfolio and a computer-based exam.
Engineering Studies	6	66	A production process exam.
Italian	4	35	A digital portfolio and an oral interview exam.
Physical Education Studies	4	39	A performance tasks exam with response questions.

COMMON ASSESSMENT TASKS

A common assessment task was developed and implemented for each of the four courses. For each course, the assessment task was developed by the working party, starting with a situation analysis.

It was important that assessment tasks constituted good professional practice, met the requirements of the course and were reasonably able to be implemented by a 'good' teacher in a real school. A situation analysis was required to consider what was possible within the requirements of the course and the constraints of the school environment and teacher and student capabilities. However, the aim was to move towards the 'cutting edge' of what is possible. For each course, the analysis considered the students, the course, the performance requirements, the potential technologies and the characteristics of teachers for the course. This was achieved through consideration of a set of questions by the working team for each course over one or two meetings. As a result of this process, there was an identification of content and outcomes conducive to digital forms of assessment for each course. This formed the basis for the development of the assessment tasks.

On the basis of the situation analysis, each working team decided on the nature of activity that would be involved in the assessment task(s) and then decided on an overall form for the assessment task. It was not intended that the task should be seen as the complete external assessment for the course. Each course team then set about defining the following parameters of the assessment task(s).

– A description of the overall task and any sub-tasks (including context for task).
– An explanation of how the task meets the assessment requirements of the course and the basis on which it will be assessed.
– The technology(s) used for digital capture of student performance.
– The constraints of technology use on the task or sub-tasks.
– The sequence of subtasks, types of response, forms of response, technology(s) used and time allowed.
– What students would produce, in what form(s) and any constraints such as file size, word counts, and viewing times.
– A detailed 'marking' schema or criteria for marking.
– An explanation of the authentication of student work.

At this point, teachers were recruited to the work teams on the basis that they would agree to implement the assessment task within a programme that accommodates the task. They were then involved in refining the assessment task(s) and completing the development of the marking criteria and marking key.

Marking criteria were developed from the assessment task and the course syllabus outcomes and content and presented in 'marking key' form or rubric form. For each criterion, a number of 'marks' were allocated and a description of the performance required to be allocated the number of 'marks'. Later, three criteria were distilled from these criteria for use with the comparative-pairs marking. Participating teachers were not required to use these marking keys but were permitted to do so if they wanted to for school-based assessment of the student work.

For the first year of the study, a hybrid assessment task structure was developed in order to compare the operation of a portfolio with a performance tasks exam. A multi-part reflective process portfolio was developed that included the development of a digital product, the collation of a process document associated with the digital product, and the presentation of two other digital artefacts. A performance tasks exam was developed that included a set of questions reflecting on the development of the digital product for the portfolio. The majority of the performance tasks exam involved students designing, producing and evaluating a logo and brochure associated with a design brief challenge. The exam was set for three hours using a desktop computer and standard office type software. Overall, the aim was to be as open-ended as possible to allow a variety of contexts, but structured to support valid and reliable marking. The components of the assessment task are described in Table 2 below.

APPLIED INFORMATION TECHNOLOGY

Table 2. Applied information technology assessment task

Component	Description
1 Portfolio Digital Product	Students created a prototype of an information solution in the form of a digital product. A default design brief was provided but teachers could replace this with any that was felt to be appropriate. The product must have been produced at school in no more than 15 hours work over a period of no more than four weeks.
2 Portfolio Process Document	Students were required to collate the document over a period of five hours with a maximum of nine pages as a single PDF file that comprised four sections: Research, Design, Production and Evaluation.
3 Portfolio Two Extra Artefacts	Students were required to present two digital artefacts that illustrated their skills in applying design principles in any two domains (e.g. graphics, databases). Students were required to complete a one-page document describing what hardware, software, techniques and skills were needed.

Component	Description
4 Exam Reflective Questions	Students respond to a set of reflective questions (on-screen) concerning the digital portfolio. Students could be permitted to view their portfolio product (not process document) while responding to the questions.
5 Exam Performance Tasks	A set of six tasks was provided as a scaffold to responding to a design brief. Task 1: Planning Logo and Brochure Students were given 15 minutes to develop two ideas for a logo and brochure. Task 2: Logo Students create a logo as a digital graphic. Task 3: Graphs Students create two different graphs using given data and spreadsheet software. Task 4: Brochure Students use some supplied digital images and data to create a tri-fold brochure. Task 5: Prepare Reflection Students prepare a 30 second reflection by listing headings or points. Task 6: Audio recording Students record a five-minute audio recording of their reflections.

Engineering Studies

The Engineering assessment task was a production exam which took students from a design brief to the construction of a model over a period of three hours using a series of specified activities. Each activity was timed, so students had a specific time frame in which to complete each activity. Each student had a mini computer (ASUS eeePC) on which they compiled their portfolio of output from the activities within a pre-formed template already loaded onto their computer. A researcher or the teacher coordinated the activity by showing a presentation that was projected onto a screen for all the class to see. This was the mechanism for managing the set time students had on each activity, prompting the students to move onto the next page of their portfolio at the appropriate time. This task involved the design and modelling of a solar water heater for a rural developing country context.

Italian

The Italian assessment task comprised a portfolio (folio) and a recorded oral presentation. The folio was a series of activities including map activity, retrieval chart and question answers, brainstorm, fact sheet, word processed reflection on practice talk and one minute voice recording evaluating final performance, to show the development of ideas and preparation for presentation. The oral presentation required the student to prepare and deliver a two-minute talk focussed on a local area/WA destination, providing information such as, features of the area, recreational activities and cultural events.

Physical Education Studies

The Physical Education Studies (PES) assessment task was a performance tasks exam including response questions. The task was completed in four sessions; two computer-based activities and two field-based activities connected with a tactical sporting challenge that generated two sets of typed responses and six video clips for each student. In the first session, students were set a tactical challenge situation for their sport and asked to analyse the challenge and propose solutions by typing responses to questions. In the second session, students undertook four different drills designed to enable them to demonstrate skills that were relevant to the challenge set in their sport. In the third session, each student had at least two opportunities to enact a response to the standard tactical problem (i.e the original challenge set) and an adapted tactical problem, featuring changed performance conditions. Each response in sessions two and three were video recorded. In the final session, students viewed videos of their performances from the previous two practical sessions and responded to reflective and evaluative questions about their performance and the challenge. A common task was adapted to fit the different physical activity contexts that respectively, the classes were utilising in under-taking the PES course (in this case Rugby, Volleyball, Swimming and Soccer). The two computer-based activities and two field-based activities generated two sets of typed responses and six video clips for each student. A single operator remote controlled multi-camera system was constructed that facilitated the capture of performance in a single digital file, requiring minimal post-production to deliver a digital video for student review and external marking.

EXTERNAL ASSESSORS AND MARKING TOOLS

For each course, two external assessors were recruited to mark each student's work using the analytical marking method, in *Physical Education Studies* (PES) this included one expert in the sport and one generalist while in all other courses the same two assessors marked each student's work. Five assessors were recruited for each course to using the comparative-pairs marking method. The two assessors recruited for the standards-referenced method were included in the five for the comparative-pairs method except for PES where only the generalist was included. For each course, the five assessors included at least two Curriculum Council officers and one ECU academic except for Italian where no ECU academics were involved in marking.

For each of the four courses, two marking tools were developed using the FileMaker relational database software: an analytical marking tool; and a comparative-pairs marking tool. These marking tools could be accessed through a web-browser using a simple user name and password on any computer workstation connected to the Internet. They could also be accessed from within the university's network using the FileMaker application. From the assessors perspective for each course, the analytical marking tool consisted of a 'Student Results List' screen and a series of 'Marking Key' screens, most typically one screen for each component of the assessment task. The 'Marking Key' screens provided the marking key on the left-hand side and the relevant student work displayed on the right-hand side. Judgements represented by numeric 'marks' were entered using the radio-buttons under each criterion. Assessors could navigate between screens using the buttons at the top of the marking key or by going back to the 'Student Results List' screen. Examples of these screens are shown in Figure 1 below.

FINDINGS FOR THE FIRST YEAR OF THE STUDY

This section discusses the findings of the first year of the study for each course separately, in a later section these findings are synthesised. Similar analysis of all the data was completed for each of the four courses, however, due to limitations of space, the analysis of marking the Engineering Studies, Italian and PES assessment task will not be as comprehensive as for Applied Information Technology.

Applied Information Technology Findings

All seven classes attempted the five components of the assessment task to varying degrees of completion. The three-hour examination, consisting of a one-hour theory paper and a two-hour practical test, was attempted by all students.

For the theory section consisting of several reflective questions, students' responses suggested that either the intention of the questions was unclear or that they did not know how to answer. One student commented, "the wording in the second part...a bit confusing. I had to guess at what it meant", and another, "it took me a while to work out what was meant by it". There was widespread confusion over the stages of the technology process and the distinction between these with many responses repeated. As one student noted, "it just seemed like you asked the same questions four times...I got four words out of a thesaurus and copied and pasted those in three or four times".

From observation, marking and comments made by students, the intention of the practical test was clearly understood by all participants namely to design and create a logo for a business and incorporate that into a tri-fold advertising brochure. The portfolio, consisting of a product, process document and two other digital artefacts, was intended to form part of the assessment structure for the course. However, there was widespread misunderstanding of this and five of the seven schools ran the portfolio in whole or in part as an additional task, not counting towards a students' final mark. It is therefore not surprising that students did not give the portfolio their best efforts and several portfolio submissions were incomplete.

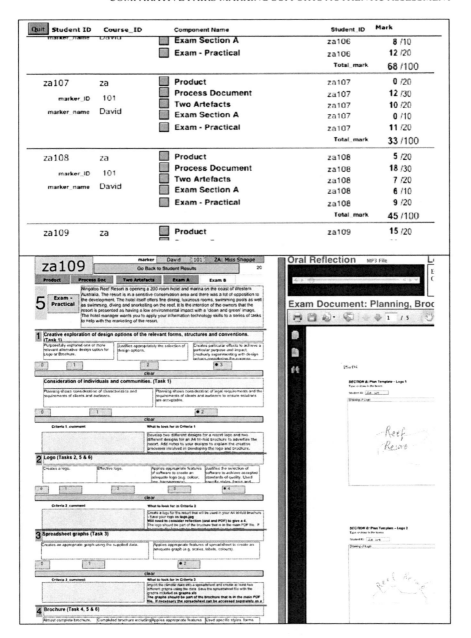

Figure 1. Analytical marking tool screens.

From the assessors perspective for each course, the comparative-pairs marking tool consisted of a 'Student Results List' screen and a 'Which is best' screen. The work from the pair of students to be compared is displayed on the left-hand and right-hand sides of the screen with judgements recorded using the green arrows with a holistic judgement and three criteria judgements. Examples of these screens are shown in Figure 2 below.

	Marker_ID	StudentA	StudentB	Holistic	Criteria1	Criteria2	Criteria3
Mark	115	ap105	ap101	B	B	A	B
Mark	115	ap105	ap103	A	A	A	A
Mark	115	ap106	ap104	A	A	A	A
Mark	115	ap106	ap105	A	B	A	A
Mark	115	ap107	ap104	A	B	A	A
Mark	115	ap107	ap105	B	B	B	B
Mark	115	ap110	ap105	A	A	A	A
Mark	115	bp104	ap108	B	B	B	B
Mark	115	bp105	ap105	B	B	A	B
Mark	115	bp105	ap106	B	B	A	B
Mark	115	bp105	ap107	A	A	A	B

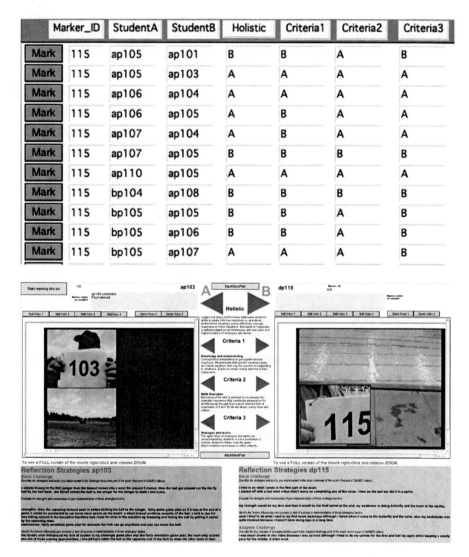

Figure 2. Comparative-pairs marking tool screens.

RESULTS OF MARKING

Student work from the portfolio and exam was uploaded to a server for online access by assessors. The portfolio and exam were assessed using the analytical marking method but only the performance tasks component of the exam (Component 5) was marked for 60 of the students using the comparative pairs marking methods. The reduced number of students involved was partly a budgetary constraint and also to ensure that for all students output from all tasks was available. Some of the results from analytical marking are shown in Tables 3 and 4. In general, there was little difference between the judgements of the two assessors with a difference in mean for the total of 0.3 on 37 (Table 3). There was a moderate to strong significant correlation ($p<0.01$) between the assessors' scores for all components of the assessment (Table 4).

Table 3. Descriptive statistics on marking for all students by external assessors (M1 and M2) using the analytical marking method and teachers

	N	Minimum (%)	Maximum (%)	Mean (%)	SD
M1_Total	115	7.0	83.0	36.7	17.0
M2_Total	115	4.0	80.0	37.0	18.3
Average M1 and M2	115	6.5	74.5	36.9	17.2
Teacher Total	26	28.1	91.8	57.9	17.1
Course	58	9.0	84.0	56.5	18.3

Five assessors used the comparative pairs marking tool to record judgements on their sets of pairs that were then combined and entered into the RUMMcc software package for each of the four criteria. Analysis through the software provided a summary of results that included scores for each exemplar ID (student). The exemplars were ranked from best (most number of times preferred) to worst (least number of times preferred). An 'Estimate' for the exemplar location in logits (logarithmic units of measurement) was provided that was the determinant of the rank order of the exemplars. In addition, a standard error of measurement and an 'Outfit' index value of whether the pattern was more or less Guttmann-like (expected to have a value of about 1.00) were also provided.

A Separation Index was calculated as an indicator of whether or not the exemplars were sufficiently diverse in quality to assure a broad enough range for the purposes of comparison. It is given as a number from 0 to 1. Values closer to 1.00 are more desirable. If the value is close to 0.00 (up to about 0.3 or 0.4) the range is too narrow. If it is above about 0.7, the separation is reasonable and if it is above 0.8, the separation is good. The Separation Index values for Applied Information Technology are given in Table 4 with all indicating a very good spread of quality in the exemplars (e.g. Holistic criterion was 0.958). Intra-rater reliability analysis was done in order to assess an individual judge's consistency with the judgements of the other judges in the group. The 'Outfit' statistic, in this instance, should be between 0.5 and 1.5. The group reliability is defined as the average of the individual rater reliability indices. For Holistic comparisons, the group reliability was 1.01. These intra-rater reliability coefficients are provided in Table 5.

Table 4. Descriptive statistics on marking for all students by external assessors (M1 and M2) using the analytical marking given by component (N=115)

Component		Range	Mean	SD	Correlation between M1 & M2 (r)
1-Portfolio Product	M1	0–18	6.8	5.7	
	M2	0–19	7.6	5.9	
	Average	0–17	7.2	5.6	0.84**
2-Portfolio Process	M1	0–28	8.8	7.9	
	M2	0–29	9.3	8.6	
	Average	0–28	9.0	8.0	0.89**
3-Portfolio Artefacts	M1	0–18	6.3	5.5	
	M2	0–19	5.8	5.0	
	Average	0–18	6.0	5.0	0.77**
4-Reflective Exam	M1	0–8	4.1	2.1	
	M2	0–10	4.8	2.2	
	Average	0–8.5	4.5	1.9	0.59**
5-Performance Exam	M1	0–20	10.7	3.8	
	M2	0–18	9.6	3.4	
	Average	0–16.5	10.1	3.2	0.61**

** Correlation is significant at the 0.01 level (2-tailed)

Table 5. Separation indices and intra-rater reliability coefficients for AIT in the first year

Type of judgement	Separation index	Intra-rater reliability coefficient					
		Rater 1	Rater 2	Rater 3	Rater 4	Rater 5	Overall
Criterion 1	0.940	1.057	0.800	1.259	1.145	1.007	1.050
Criterion 2	0.946	0.884	0.685	1.022	1.426	1.092	1.020
Criterion 3	0.951	1.342	0.831	0.903	2.517	0.972	1.310
Holistic	0.958	0.910	0.602	1.1016	1.016	1.367	1.010

The results from the comparative pairs marking method were compared with the results from the analytical marking method and the marks provided by teachers either for the assessment task or for overall achievement in the course. Table 6 shows the correlations between the results of comparative pairs marking (holistic –

Pairs_Holistic, and three specific criteria *Pairs_C1*, *Pairs_C2*, and *Pairs_C3*), analytical marking (average of the two markers), and marking provided by the teacher for the exam (*Teacher*) and course (*Course*). There were strong and significant correlations between the scores generated by the four comparative pairs marking criteria ($r=0.84$, 0.92 and 0.97 respectively, $p<0.01$), and between these scores and the score determined by analytical marking ($r=0.73$, 0.62, 0.73 and 0.70 respectively, $p<0.01$). There was little correlation between the score generated by the marking of the teacher (*Teacher*) and those by the external assessors by either method of marking except for a moderate significant correlation with the second specific criterion for the comparative pairs marking (*Pairs_C3*) ($r=0.461$, $p<0.05$). This lack of correlation was not unexpected as teachers were not required to use a particular marking key. The second specific criteria concerned the demonstration of "capability and facility with the range of required software" which may indicate that teachers tended to assess the student work in terms of their technical skill in using the software. However, the teacher's course mark for the semester (*Course*) appears to be weakly correlated with all criteria in the pairs marking ($r=0.47$, 0.42, 0.43, 0.46, $p<0.05$ and 0.36, $p<0.01$ respectively). A similar analysis with the ranking of performance yielded similar results (refer to Table 7).

Table 6. *Correlations for scores from marking of performance tasks exam (N=60)*

	Pairs_ Holistic	Pairs_C1	Pairs_C2	Pairs_C3	Teacher	Course	Analytical
Pairs_ Holistic	1	0.84**	0.92**	0.97**	0.33	0.47*	0.73**
Pairs_C1		1	0.74**	0.85**	0.18	0.42*	0.62**
Pairs_C2			1	0.90**	0.46*	0.43*	0.73**
Pairs_C3				1	0.33	0.46*	0.70**
Teacher					1	0.10	0.16
Course						1	0.36**
Analytical							1

** Correlation is significant at the 0.01 level (2-tailed) * Correlation is significant at the 0.05 level (2-tailed).

Table 7. *Correlations for rankings from marking of performance tasks exam (N=60)*

	Pairs_Holistic	Pairs_C1	Pairs_C2	Pairs_C3	Teacher	Course
Pairs_Holistic	1	0.84**	0.93**	0.97**	0.32	0.53**
Pairs_C1		1	0.75**	0.85**	0.14	0.43*
Pairs_C2			1	0.90**	0.43*	0.48*
Pairs_C3				1	0.33	0.48*
Teacher					1	0.18
Course						1

** Correlation is significant at the 0.01 level (2-tailed) * Correlation is significant at the 0.05 level (2-tailed).

CONCLUSIONS ABOUT MARKING

The assessors were asked for feedback on the suitability of the assessment tasks, the marking process of and the quality of student work. The examination and the portfolio tasks were acknowledged to be faithful to the course outline. The assessors considered that although the results were generally of a low standard, this was not due to unsuitability of the tasks and that students well versed in the course were able to perform well. The marking process was simplified by the fact that all submissions were in digital form, allowing anytime anywhere access, and by the use of the online marking tool. Some drawbacks of the marking system were the inevitable delays in opening large files and scrolling between the mark key and work sample. Changing a mark already entered was a little clumsy, requiring a post back of the marking form. The running score of the mark also didn't update until the marking form was submitted and this was confusing at first.

The amount of time taken by the expert assessors in the analytical marking varied from an average of about five to 25 minutes per student. The shorter times corresponded to students whose submissions of the five components were incomplete. The longer times were associated with student work which comprised large files (for example some animations were several MB) and these took time to download to the assessor's computer prior to marking particularly where this marking was done outside Australia. Apart from delays in downloading, longer time was spent on higher quality work, particularly where evidence of performance had to be gathered from several parts of the submission.

The comparative pairs marking focussed only on one part of the students' work, the performance tasks examination, so the time per student was correspondingly reduced. The time required to make a comparison was initially several minutes, mainly where the samples were of similar quality. However, as familiarity with the criteria increased, the time per pair became less. Because the comparisons were pre-determined and not dynamically generated, several were very one-sided and for these, the marking time was seconds rather than minutes. For the comparative pairs marking assessors took about three minutes per comparison.

The collation of student work in digital form had several obvious advantages for assessment such as ease of storage, backup, transmission, access and sharing. The database marking tools that facilitated online access to student work were responsive and easy to use provided that adequate Internet bandwidth was available to the assessor. However, there were difficulties accessing some files if the marker was within the networks of particular organisations and also the marking tools operated slowly and sometimes crashed or logged out. Marking was possible, and indeed took place, from countries outside Australia though the opening of large files presented delays. With regard to the analytic marking, the ability to view both the work sample with the marking rubric alongside it was convenient and ensured focus was maintained. Switching rapidly between different aspects of student work was easy. The database recorded and summed the scores and this was obviously quick and accurate. The analysis of the marking, with the strong correlations between assessors, indicates that the method was reliable.

APPLYING A RASCH MODEL TO THE RESULTS OF ANALYTICAL MARKING

A Rasch model was applied to the analytical marks using the responses of both assessors to generate a combined score for each student for each of the three components of the portfolio (Product, Process Document and Extra Artefacts analysed separately) and for the performance tasks exam (Component 5). For each component, if a student did not submit work they were removed and thus not all the 115 students were included in the analysis. The analysis gave a reliable set of scores for all three portfolio components (SI=0.96, 0.96 and 0.94 respectively) and for the exam (SI=0.85).

There were a few extreme outliers particularly for the first component, the product. These tended to be students scoring 0 on all, or almost all, of the criteria. The frequency distributions tended to be well spread, with high standard deviations and not very 'normal' in structure. Unless otherwise stated, the thresholds on all items worked adequately.

For each component correlations were calculated between location scores and the raw scores from each of the assessors and the mean of their scores. The results for the first component (Portfolio Product) are shown in Table 8. In each case, the analysis indicated strong significant correlations. For example, the correlations between location scores and mean raw scores were 0.96, 0.98, 0.99 and 0.99 respectively (p<0.01). The correlation coefficients between the location scores for the exam and raw marks were high for both markers and for the mean of their marks.

Table 8. Correlations between the location scores and raw marks from the two markers for the product component of the portfolio (N=83)

	Location	M1	M2	Mean
Location	1	0.86^{**}	0.88^{**}	0.96^{**}
M1		1	0.67^{**}	0.92^{**}
M2			1	0.91^{**}
Mean				1

** Correlation is significant at the 0.01 level (2-tailed) * Correlation is significant at the 0.05 level (2-tailed).

Component 1 – Product

Rasch modelling analysis using RUMM2020 realised a level of reliability with the Cronbach Alpha coefficient of 0.94 and the SI at 0.96. An analysis of individual items indicated that all operated satisfactorily. The Person-Item location distribution from this analysis is shown in Figure 3. There was a relatively large standard deviation of 2.9 although all items were well within the range of person locations but only spread between locations of -1 and 1. There were a large number of persons at a location below -10 representing students who completed little if any of this component of the portfolio. Scoring for the portfolio would have been improved with a reconsideration of the difficulty of some of the criteria.

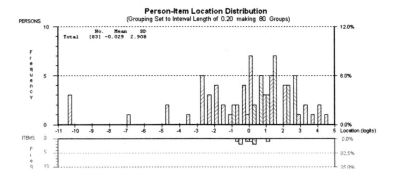

Figure 3. Person-item location distribution from the Rasch analysis of the scores allocated by the two assessors on the product component of the portfolio in.

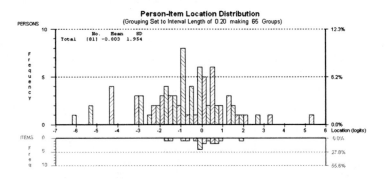

Figure 4. Some output from RUMM2020 from the Rasch analysis of the marks allocated by the two markers on the process document component of the portfolio.

Component 2 – Process Document

Rasch modelling analysis realised a level of reliability with both the Cronbach Alpha coefficient and the SI at 0.96. An analysis of individual items indicated that all operated satisfactorily. The Person-Item location distribution from this analysis is shown in Figure 3. There was a relatively large standard deviation of 2.0 although all items were well within the range of the majority of person locations. There were a large number of persons at a location, see Figure 4, representing students who completed little if any of this component of the portfolio.

Component 3 – Extra Artefacts

Rasch modelling analysis realised a level of reliability with the Cronbach Alpha coefficient of 0.94 and the SI at 0.92. An analysis of individual items indicated that all operated satisfactorily. The Person-Item location distribution from this analysis is shown in Figure 5. There was a relatively large standard deviation of 2.0 although all items were well within the range of person locations but only spread between locations of -1 and 1. There were a large spread of persons across locations representing the variations in the extent of completion by students of this component of the portfolio. Scoring for the portfolio would have been improved with a reconsideration of the difficulty of some of the criteria.

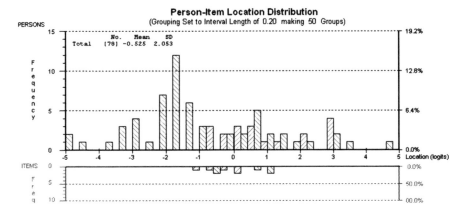

Figure 5. Some output from RUMM2020 from the Rasch analysis of the marks allocated by the two markers on the extra artefacts component of the portfolio.

No modifications were required although the thresholds for three of the criteria did not work very well (Criterion 1 – c1 and d1 – the response 2 was rarely used, Criterion 3 – c3 and d3 - the responses of 1, 2 and 3 and Criterion 4 the response 2 for one marker – d4).

Component 5 – Performance Tasks Examination

Rasch modelling analysis realised a level of reliability with both the Cronbach Alpha coefficient and the SI at 0.85. The reversed threshold on c2a was between a response of 3 and 4. As a result, the analysis was repeated with these responses (3 and 4) for c2a and d2a both scored as 3. This increased the SI marginally and removed the reversed threshold. The analysis gave a mean person location of 0.230, fit residual of -0.349 and standard deviation of 1.219. An analysis of individual items indicated that all operated satisfactorily. The Person-Item location distribution from this analysis is shown in Figure 6. There was a typical standard deviation of 1.3 with all items well within the range of person locations. Scoring for the exam would have been improved with a reconsideration of the scoring of criteria 5A and 5B where values of 2 and 1 were used for most students.

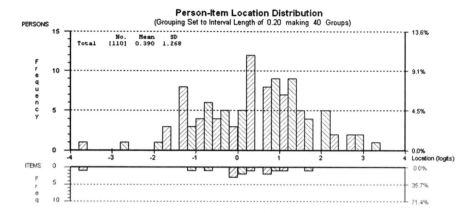

Figure 6. Some output from RUMM2020 from the Rasch analysis of the marks allocated by the two markers on the exam (component 5 only).

ENGINEERING STUDIES FINDINGS FOR FIRST YEAR

As the assessment task for engineering consisted of one discrete three-hour task supervised by a researcher and the class teacher, all students completed the task. They were paced through a series of activities, each with a time limit, and were forced to move onto the next task after a specific time. Some students felt they did not have enough time on some activities, mainly the modelling. The students quickly felt comfortable with the technology, though some felt the size of the keyboard made typing awkward. For many students, the external web-cam was difficult to manipulate to get clear images of their sketches, but the integrated web-cam worked well for their presentations. There was little ambiguity in the assessment task, although many students failed to recognise the implications of the remote design context and to carry that through into their presentations. One teacher felt that a different design task may have provided more opportunity for student scope.

All student work was marked by the classroom teacher, two external assessors using an analytic method of marking and five external assessors using a comparative pairs method of marking. Both the comparative pairs method of marking and the analytic standards-referenced method of marking using rubrics were successfully implemented with the support of online digital marking tools. The results of the analytical marking and the scores provided by the teacher are provided in Table 9. There was a moderate significant correlation between the scores generated by the two assessors ($r=0.43$, $p<0.01$) but this was much weaker than for the other courses. However, there was a big difference in the mean scores generated by both (63.8 and 49.3) that was also seen in the minimum and maximum scores. Clearly assessor M1 scored more 'leniently' than assessor M2.

Table 9. Descriptive statistics for scores from analytical marking for all students

	N	Minimum	Maximum	Mean	Std. Deviation
M1_Total	66	21	83	63.8	12.5
M2_Total	66	11	74	49.3	11.5
Average M1 & M2	66	16.5	72.0	56.5	10.1
Teacher	53	17	88	58.7	15.1
Course	29	41	92	63.9	12.9

Table 10. Correlation coefficients from the marking of the student work

	Pairs_ Holistic	Pairs_C1	Pairs_C2	Pairs_C3	Teacher	Course	Analytical
Pairs_ Holistic	1	0.94**	0.96**	0.91**	0.60**	0.57**	0.78**
Pairs_C1		1	0.95**	0.90**	0.59**	0.57**	0.76**
Pairs_C2			1	0.96**	0.62**	0.54*	0.84**
Pairs_C3				1	0.54**	0.53*	0.85**
Teacher					1	0.68**	0.54**
Course						1	0.30
Analytical							1

** Correlation is significant at the 0.01 level (2-tailed). * Correlation is significant at the 0.05 level (2-tailed).

The comparative pairs method of marking was used with five assessors each making 276 comparisons using a digital marking tool. Three assessors were teachers of Engineering, two of whom were involved in the standards-referenced marking. Two assessors were teacher trainers and in the research team. One holistic and three specific assessment criteria were developed for the comparative pairs marking from the criteria previously developed for the task. Analysis using the RUMMcc software package indicated a reliable set of scores (separation indexes of between 0.906 to 0.927) and acceptable intra-rater reliability coefficients for all raters on all criteria.

Table 10 shows the correlations between the scores generated by the comparative pairs marking, the analytical marking by the two markers (M1 and M2), and the scores provided by the teachers. There were strong and significant correlations between the scores generated by the four comparative pairs marking criteria (r=0.94, 0.96 and 0.91 respectively, p<0.01), and between these scores and the score determined by analytical marking (r=0.78, 0.76, 0.84 and 0.85 respectively, p<0.01). There was a moderate significant correlation between scores generated by the marking of the teacher (*Teacher*) and those by the external assessors by either method of marking (0.60, 0.59, 0.62, 0.54 and 0.54 respectively, p<0.01). A similar analysis with the ranking of performance yielded similar results.

Rasch modelling analysis was conducted on the analytical marking of the Engineering Studies exams using the judgements of both assessors to generate a combined score for each student. This analysis realised a level of reliability with both the Cronbach Alpha coefficient and the SI at 0.89. However, an analysis of individual items revealed 11 of 18 had reversed thresholds and with all items having a range of 10 or 15 values and with only 66 students, it was not surprising that few scoring categories were used. The Person-Item location distribution from this analysis is shown in Figure 7. There was a small standard deviation of 0.5 and two items were well above the range of person locations (criteria 3C for both assessors). Scoring for the exam would have been improved with a much reduced range of scoring categories and a reconsideration of the difficulty of criteria 3C.

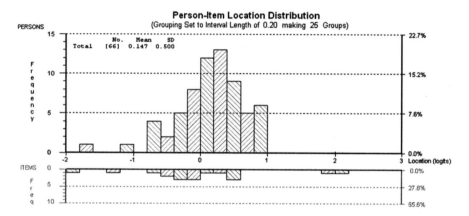

Figure 7. Person-item location distribution output from RUMM2020 from the Rasch analysis of the scores allocated by the two assessors on the engineering studies exam.

ITALIAN FINDINGS FOR FIRST YEAR

The portfolio tasks were only fully completed by students at one school. Part of the reason for this may be that assessment in Italian usually only includes items related to final performance and not items that measure process. Additionally, both the teachers and the students felt that the portfolio tasks could have been more clearly defined and this may also have been a contributing factor. Technology was not a contributing issue as all of the schools had the technical capacity to carry out the assessment tasks and store them in a digital form. The oral presentation was made by all students from all of the schools and was video recorded. However, there were some variations including talking for five minutes instead of two minutes and the use of presentation software during the presentations. Due to the lack of portfolio items for most students, a full set of assessment scores was collected only the oral exam. The videos of the oral exam for all students was marked by the classroom teacher, by two external assessors using an analytic method of marking and by five external assessors using a comparative pairs method of marking. Both the comparative pairs method of marking and the analytic standards-referenced method of marking using rubrics were successfully implemented with the support of online digital marking tools.

The results of the analytical marking and the scores provided by the teacher are provided in Table 11. There was a strong significant correlation between the scores generated by the two assessors (r=0.93, p<0.01). Both had similar means, standard deviations and ranges of scores. Clearly, both assessors had similar standards and understanding of the marking criteria.

Table 11. Descriptive statistics for scores from analytical marking for all students in the Italian course sample

	N	Minimum	Maximum	Mean	Std. Deviation
M1_Total	35	4.8	62.2	36.0	11.4
M2_Total	35	4.8	57.8	34.0	11.6
Average M1 & M2	35	4.8	60	35	11.3
Teacher	19	36	80	61.4	12.4
Course	19	49	84	65.0	11.2

Rasch analysis of the data from the comparative pairs method of marking realised a reliable set of scores for each specific criterion and the holistic judgments (separation indexes of between 0.926 to 0.953) indicating a high level of accuracy in the scores. The intra-rater reliabilities identified that only one rater on one criteria was outside acceptable boundaries. Overall, the intra-rater reliability was worst for criteria 1. This is not surprising as this criteria consisted of a number of components.

Table 12 shows the correlations between the scores generated by the comparative pairs marking, the analytical marking by the two markers (M1 and M2), and the scores provided by the teachers. For Italian, the correlations between the pairs marking and the analytical marking were high and statistically significant for all criteria including the holistic judgement (p<0.01). The teachers' marks for the assessment item were moderately but significantly correlated with the holistic pairs result (p<0.05). This was also true for the rankings where the rankings of the teachers' marks were correlated with the pairs marking rankings (statistically significant, p<0.05).

The main difficulties encountered by the assessors with both methods of marking were technical and largely concerning access to the videos. Because the videos were not in a streaming format, they had to wait for a video to download before viewing, this increased the time to mark. For the pairs marking, the markers appreciated being able to make a comment on a given student's performance which could be viewed again later when the student came up again for another comparison.

Table 12. Correlation coefficients from the marking of the student work for the Italian case studies (N=35)

	Pairs_Holistic	Pairs_C1	Pairs_C2	Pairs_C3	Teacher	Course	Analytical
Pairs_Holistic	1	0.97**	0.97**	0.98**	0.48*	0.19	0.70**
Pairs_C1		1	0.92**	0.95**	0.44	0.18	0.75**
Pairs_C2			1	0.95**	0.42	0.18	0.66**
Pairs_C3				1	0.43	0.11	0.70**
Teacher					1	0.82**	0.20
Course						1	-0.17
Analytical							1

** Correlation is significant at the 0.01 level (2-tailed). * Correlation is significant at the 0.05 level (2-tailed).

Rasch modelling analysis was conducted on the analytical marking of the Italian oral exams using the judgements of both assessors to generate a combined score for each student. This analysis realised a level of reliability with the Cronbach Alpha coefficient at 0.92 and the SI at 0.99. An analysis of individual items revealed that for the first criteria scores of 7 to 10 were rarely used, not surprising given that only 35 students were involved. The Person-Item location distribution from this analysis is shown in Figure 8. There was a large standard deviation of 6.5 and items were spread well within the range of person locations.

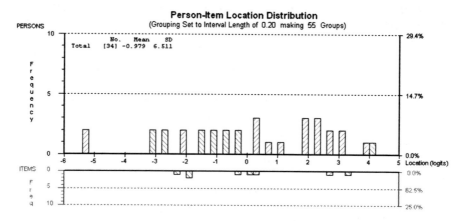

Figure 8. Person-item location distribution output from RUMM2020 from the Rasch analysis of the scores allocated by the two assessors on the Italian oral exam.

PHYSICAL EDUCATION STUDIES FINDINGS FOR FIRST YEAR

Overall, the examination task was regarded by the teachers and students involved as an appropriate means of assessment for the PES course. The task effectively encompassed conceptual, practical and reflective aspects and was able to be adapted for application and implementation in the varied activity contexts. The researchers identified a number of improvements that could be made to both task design and marking tools to enhance the reliability and validity of the assessment. Findings from the first year are informing practice in the second year of the project.

Students' responses to the assessment task (featuring text and video clips) were accessed online by markers located throughout Australia, and marked analytically using rubrics and by the paired comparisons method. The online marking tools facilitated both methods of assessment well using a simple computer server and an online database system. The paired comparisons method delivered a single scale with high reliability whereas the results of analytical marking were less reliable but still significantly correlated to the paired comparisons scores.

Students generally appeared to consider the task an appropriate means of assessment for the course. The task effectively encompassed conceptual, practical and reflective aspects and was able to be adapted for application and implementation in varied sporting contexts. Both students and teachers identified the scope for refinement of the conceptual/reflective parts of the task, specifically to avoid repetition in questions and enhance clarity for students. Students also identified that a sole reliance on text as a means of response to questions was limiting and recognised that it would be advantageous to also be able to use graphics/drawing tools.

The practical components of the task were implemented effectively. The practical components were designed to enable all students to have the opportunity to demonstrate their performance abilities. The researchers identified a number of improvements that could be made to enhance the validity of the task, such as, to provide a choice of skills to enable specialisation by position, the use of 'standard' feeder players in skill-drills, and extensions to the game-play contexts. Further, it was seen to be beneficial from a student perspective, to undertake the initial computer-based session and two practical components in a single day.

All student work was marked by the classroom teacher, by two external assessors using an analytic standards-referenced method of marking and by five external assessors using a comparative pairs method of marking. Both the comparative pairs method of marking and the analytic standards-referenced method of marking using rubrics were successfully implemented with the support of online digital marking tools.

The results of the analytical marking and the scores provided by the teacher are provided in Table 13. There was a strong significant correlation between the scores generated by the two assessors ($r=0.87$, $p<0.01$). Both had similar means, standard deviations and ranges of scores. Clearly, both assessors had similar standards and understanding of the marking criteria.

The comparative pairs method of marking provided a reliable set of scores for each specific criterion and the holistic judgments (separation indexes of 0.905 to

0.929) indicating a high level of accuracy in the scores. The intra-rater reliabilities identified one rater as lacking consistency for the first two criteria and holistic judgements and one rater highly inconsistent for Criterion 1 but not for the other judgements. Overall consistency was around 1.0 that represents a reasonable outcome.

Table 13. Descriptive statistics for scores from analytical marking for all students

	N	Minimum	Maximum	Mean	Std. Deviation
M1_Total	39	2.0	73.0	41.1	17.6
M2_Total	39	6.0	73.0	37.5	17.4
Average M1 & M2	39	8.5	73.0	39.3	16.9
Teacher	38	51.0	85.0	65.5	8.4
Course	38	36.0	81.0	60.0	13.3

Table 14 show the correlations between the pairs-comparison marking and the analytical standards-referenced marking (two assessors: M1 and M2). The second table refers to the rankings produced by each of the marking methods. The correlations between the pairs marking and the standards-referenced marking (Average) were high and statistically significant for all criteria including the holistic judgement (p<0.01). The teachers' marks for the assessment item were significantly moderately correlated with the results from the comparative pairs marking (p<0.01). Analysis based on rankings yielded similar results.

Table 14. Correlation coefficients from the marking of the student work for physical education studies

	Pairs Holistic	PairsC1	PairsC2	PairsC3	Teacher	Course	Analytical
Pairs Holistic	1	0.80**	0.78**	0.97**	0.42**	0.52**	0.89**
Pairs_C1		1	0.37*	0.80**	0.53**	0.69**	0.81**
Pairs_C2			1	0.72**	0.28	0.30	0.65**
Pairs_C3				1	0.38*	0.53*	0.88**
Teacher					1	0.46**	0.52**
Course						1	0.67**
Analytical							1

** Correlation is significant at the 0.01 level (2-tailed). * Correlation is significant at the 0.05 level (2-tailed).

The main difficulties encountered by the assessors with both methods of marking were technical and largely concerning access to the videos. Because the videos were not in a streaming format they had to wait for a video to download before viewing, this increased the time to mark. Also some assessors found particular videos difficult to see (e.g. dark images on overcast days) and had difficulty identifying the student being assessed (students did not wear distinctive uniforms or label bibs). Nevertheless, it is noted that marking was conducted effectively by assessors using an on-line medium and in a manner that allowed for input from assessors located throughout the state and inter-state. Assessors identified improvements that could be made to the interface specifically to reduce the content in some places. The comparative pairs interface was well received by assessors.

Rasch modelling analysis was conducted on the analytical marking data using the judgements of both assessors to generate a combined score for each student. This analysis realised a level of reliability with both the Cronbach Alpha coefficient and the SI at 0.96. However, an analysis of individual items revealed 11 of 38 had reversed thresholds and with most of these items having a range of eight or 11 values and with only 39 students it was not surprising that few scoring categories were used. The Person-Item location distribution from this analysis is shown in Figure 9. There was a typical standard deviation of 0.93 and two items were well outside the range of person locations (criteria 2A and 4C for only one of the assessors). Scoring for the exam would have been improved with a much reduced range of scoring categories and a reconsideration of the descriptions of criteria 2A and 4C.

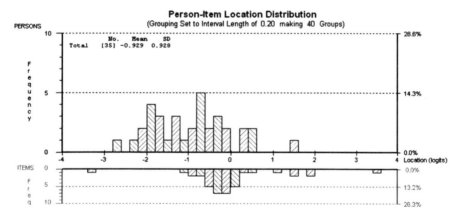

Figure 9. Person-item location distribution output from RUMM2020 from the Rasch analysis of the scores allocated by the two assessors on the engineering studies exam.

FEASIBILITY FRAMEWORK

Findings for all courses were analysed in terms of a feasibility framework. Two of the dimensions relate to the focus of this chapter: Functional and Pedagogic. The former refers to how well the assessment tasks functioned as measures of achievement, principally concerning questions of validity and reliability. The latter concerned how well the assessment tasks aligned with the preferred pedagogical practices for each course.

FUNCTIONAL DIMENSION

For all courses the students perceived the assessment tasks to be authentic and meaningful and, apart from in Italian, preferred the task to a written exam. In almost all cases the teacher perceived the assessment to be more authentic than a paper-based exam. In one AIT case and one Engineering Studies case the teacher did not perceive the overall assessment task to be adequately relevant. The Engineering teacher had focussed on systems and control technologies that did not align as well to the design focus of the assessment task. In general, the reflective questions exam in AIT was not perceived to be valuable and some PES students found the text-only response type limiting.

For all four courses the assessment task was structured permitting a good range of levels of achievement to be demonstrated. This was reflected in the wide range of scores from marking and the perceptions of teachers and students. In the AIT exam there may have been limitations to the opportunity to demonstrate higher-level achievement due to the nature of the tasks involved.

External assessors used an analytical marking rubric developed from a standards-based framework constructed specifically for the task that resulted in highly correlated marks and rankings except for in Engineering where they were only moderately correlated. In the AIT, Italian and Engineering cases there was little or no correlation between the teacher's marks and ranking and the external assessors' marks and rankings. Although teachers were provided with the analytical marking rubric there was no requirement to use it and most did not. There were no discussions between the teacher and markers in any cases about how to assess. It is likely that some of the discrepancy was due to teachers having greater knowledge of the students and past achievements. In PES there was overall a significant moderate correlation between scores resulting from teacher marking and external marking and in particular for two of the cases. Although teachers used their own marking keys there was evidence that this was done rigorously and all indicated strong support for the method of assessment and indicated alignment with typical pedagogical practices.

The comparative pairs method of marking was successfully implemented for all four courses with resulting highly reliable scores. In AIT it was only applied to the performance exam and in Italian only for the recorded oral presentation.

PEDAGOGIC DIMENSION

Typically in the AIT, Engineering Studies and PES courses students liked doing the practical work and disliked documenting work. They were happy to answer questions where they could type responses. In Italian many students did not like being recorded for the oral presentation. In almost all cases for AIT, Engineering and PES the assessment matched general pedagogy for the course and was viewed positively by teachers. This was not the case for one AIT teacher and one Engineering teacher. For almost all students, the portfolio component of Italian was not considered to be typical with many not used to using digital technologies in the course. In all four courses, the quality of work was highly dependent on the class the student was in, probably reflecting differences in capability of the students and pedagogical approaches by the teachers involved. In Engineering, in particular, students tended to feel that they need more time and more flexibility in what they did and the order in which components were completed.

CONCLUSIONS

In part, the study aimed to show that ICT could be used to support the provision of highly authentic reliable performance assessment in courses where the connection of practical skills to theoretical knowledge was critical. The contention was that in so doing, assessment practices would better align with the principles of constructivist learning environments and thus encourage their provision. It was recognised that a key component of the provision of such performance assessment would be reliable methods of marking that facilitated the use of human judgement. As such, the use of Rasch modelling was likely to assist in providing adequately reliable methods of marking. The study incorporated the use of both analytical marking and comparative pairs marking.

Detailed analytical marking criteria were developed for the assessors based on the task(s) itself and the standards framework for the course. This was represented as rubrics. The results of assessor marking tended to be highly correlated except for in Engineering where there was a significant but only moderate correlation between the external assessors. It may be that further consensus discussions between markers would improve this outcome. For all courses, the result of comparative pairs marking generated highly reliable sets of scores with Separation Indexes and Cronbach Alpha coefficients well in excess of 0.9. For all courses, the scores and rankings from analytical marking were significantly highly correlated with the scores and rankings from comparative pairs marking. The holistic and separate criteria scores and rankings were also highly correlated for the comparative pairs marking. In most cases there was little or no correlation between the results of marking by the teacher and the analytical marking and/or comparative pairs marking. This was likely due to a combination of teachers using different criteria, most classes being small samples and teachers taking into account background knowledge of the students or tasks. This may imply that teachers should not mark the work of their own students. At the least, it is recommended that to support highly reliable marking by teachers, considerable training is needed.

For all the courses, the students readily perceived the assessment task(s) to be authentic and meaningful. They preferred this to the alternative of a written exam. In almost all cases the teacher perceived the assessment to be more authentic than a paper-based exam. For all four courses the assessment task was structured permitting a good range of levels of achievement to be demonstrated. This was reflected in the wide range of scores from marking and the perceptions of teachers and students. In the AIT exam there may have been limitations in the opportunity to demonstrate higher-level achievement due to the nature of the tasks involved.

Assessment tasks worked best where the approach was familiar to students. This occurred for almost all cases in AIT and PES but not so for Italian where the portfolio component of Italian was not considered to be typical. In Engineering, although the method of collecting student work was somewhat unfamiliar to students, the task was relatively familiar and therefore most enjoyed the experience and successfully engaged. In Italian, many students did not like being recorded for the oral presentation. In almost all cases for AIT, Engineering and PES the assessment matched general pedagogy for the course and was viewed positively by teachers. This was not the case for one AIT teacher and one Engineering teacher. In all four courses, the quality of work was highly dependent on the class the student was in, probably reflecting differences in capability of the students and pedagogical approaches by the teachers involved.

Overall, the first year of the study found that the benefits outweighed the constraints. In particular, in three of the courses, student responses were overwhelmingly positive in all cases typically due to the practical nature of the work and relevance to their interests. Generally they preferred this to paper-based exams. In Italian, although students were not as positive they did indicate that it was valuable being able to reflect on their own performance by viewing the videos.

There were different benefits across the three general forms of digital assessment. Reflective portfolios generally permitted students to address a greater range of outcomes and demonstrate a greater range of knowledge and skills although this was not realised in Italian. Production exams generally permitted students to address a limited range of outcomes and demonstrate a reasonable depth of knowledge and skills dependent on the task and time. Performance task(s) exams generally permitted students to address a range of outcomes and demonstrate a limited depth of knowledge but a reasonable level of skill dependent on the task and time.

Overall it was demonstrated in all four courses that digital technologies could be used to provide highly authentic reliable performance assessment that better aligned with the principles of constructivist learning environments. The use of Rasch modelling along with either a well constructed analytical marking method of comparative pairs marking method overcame the limitation of the necessary dependence on human judgement in marking such assessments to deliver reliable scores suitable for high-stakes outcomes.

ACKNOWLEDGEMENTS

The theory discussed in this paper and the research upon which it is based are a result of the work of a research team organised by the Centre for Schooling and Learning Technologies at Edith Cowan University, and led by Paul Newhouse and John Williams. Significant work was contributed by researchers Dawn Penney (University of Tasmania), 'Chirp' Lim, Jeremy Pagram, Andrew Jones, Martin

Cooper, Alistair Campbell, doctoral student David Miller and a number of research assistants.

REFERENCES

Andrade, H. G. (2005). Teaching with rubrics: The good, the bad, and the ugly. *College Teaching, 53*(1), 27–30.

Australian Bureau of Statistics. (2002). *Measuring a knowledge based economy and society: An Australian framework* (Discussion Paper). Canberra: Australian Bureau of Statistics. (Document Number)

Bransford, J. D., Brown, A. L., & Cocking, R. R. (Eds.). (2000). *How people learn: Brain, mind, experience, and school.* Washington, DC: National Academy Press.

Brewer, C. A. (2004). Near real-time assessment of student learning and understanding in biology courses. *Bioscience, 54*(11), 1034.

Bull, J., & Sharp, D. (2000). *Developments in computer-assisted assessment in UK higher education.* Paper presented at the Learning to Choose: Choosing to Learn, Queensland, Australia.

Burns, R. B. (1996). *Introduction to research methods.* South Melbourne, Australia: Addison Wesley Longman Australia Pty. Limited.

DeCorte, E. (1990). Learning with new information technologies in schools: Perspectives from the psychology of learning and instruction. *Journal of Computer Assisted Learning, 6,* 69–87.

Dede, C. (2003). No cliche left behind: Why education policy is not like the movies. *Educational Technology, 43*(2), 5–10.

Fraser, B. J. (1994). Research on classroom and school climate. In D. Gabel (Ed.), *Handbook of research on science teaching and learning* (pp. 493–541). New York: Macmillan.

Garmire, E., & Pearson, G. (Eds.). (2006). *Tech tally: Approaches to assessing technological literacy.* Washington, DC: National Academy Press.

Glickman, C. (1991). Pretending not to know what we know. *Educational Leadership, 48*(8), 4–10.

Grant, L. (2008). *Assessment for social justice and the potential role of new technologies.* London: Futurelabo. (Document Number)

Hay, P. J., & Macdonald, D. (2008). (Mis)appropriations of criteria and standards-referenced assessment in a performance-based subject. *Assessment in Education: Principles, Policy & Practice, 15*(2), 153–168.

Jonassen, D. (2000). *Design of constructivist learning environments.* Retrieved March 9, 2007, from http://tiger.coe.missouri.edu/~jonassen/courses/CLE/

Kimbell, R. (2004). Design & technology. In J. White (Ed.), *Rethinking the school curriculum: Values, aims and purposes* (pp. 40–59). New York & London: Routledge Falmer.

Kimbell, R., & Wheeler, T. (2005). *Project e-scape: Phase 1 report.* London: Technology Education Research Unit, Goldsmiths Collegeo. (Document Number)

Kimbell, R., Wheeler, T., Miller, A., & Pollitt, A. (2007). *e-scape: e-solutions for creative assessment in portfolio environments.* London: Technology Education Research Unit, Goldsmiths College. (Document Number)

Koretz, D. (1998). Large-scale portfolio assessments in the US: Evidence pertaining to the quality of measurement. *Assessment in Education, 5*(3), 309–334.

Kozma, R. B. (2009). Transforming education: Assessing and teaching 21st century skills. In F. Scheuermann & J. Bojornsson (Eds.), *The transition to computer-based assessment* (pp. 13–23). Ispra, Italy: European Commission. Joint Research Centre.

Lane, S. (2004). Validity of high-stakes assessment: Are students engaged in complex thinking? *Educational Measurement, Issues and Practice, 23*(3), 6–14.

Lin, H., & Dwyer, F. (2006). The fingertip effects of computer-based assessment in education. *TechTrends, 50*(6), 27–31.

Lynch, W. (1990). Social aspects of human-computer interaction. *Educational Technology, 30*(4), 26–31.

Madeja, S. S. (2004). Alternative assessment strategies for schools. *Education Policy Review, 105*(5), 3–13.

McGaw, B. (2006). *Assessment to fit for purpose.* Paper presented at the 32nd annual conference of the International Association for Educational Assessment, Singapore.

Messick, S. (1994). The interplay of evidence and consequences in the validation of performance assessments. *Educational Researcher, 23*(2), 13–23.

Mevarech, A. R., & Light, P. H. (1992). Peer-based interaction at the computer: Looking backward, looking forward. *Learning and Instruction, 2,* 275–280.

Newhouse, C. P., Clarkson, B., & Trinidad, S. (2005). A framework for leading school change in using ICT. In S. Trinidad & J. Pearson. (Eds.), *Using information and communication technologies in education.* Singapore: Prentice-Hall, Pearson Education South Asia.

Newhouse, C. P., Williams, P. J., & Pearson, J. (2006). Supporting mobile education for pre-service teachers. *Australasian Journal of Educational Technology, 22*(3), 289–311.

Pellegrino, J. W., Chudowsky, N., & Glaser, R. (2001). *Knowing what students know: The science and design of educational assessment.* Washington, DC: National Academy Press.

Pollitt, A. (2004, June). *Let's stop marking exams.* Paper presented at the International Association for Educational Assessment conference, Philadelphia.

Richardson, H. C., & Ward, R. (2005). *Developing and implementing a methodology for reviewing e-portfolio products.* Wigan, UK: Joint Information Systems Committeeo. (Document Number)

Ridgway, J., McCusker, S., & Pead, D. (2006). *Report 10: Literature review of e-assessment.* Futurelab. (Document Number)

Spector, J. M. (2006). A methodology for assessing learning in complex and ill-structured task domains. *Innovations in Education and Teaching International, 43*(2), 109–120.

Tierney, R., & Marielle, S. (2004). What's still wrong with rubrics: Focusing on the consistency of performance criteria across scale levels. [Electronic Version]. *Practical Assessment, Research and Evaluation, 9*(2). Retrieved April 9, 2005, from http://PAREonline.net/getvn.asp?v=9&n=2

Tognolini, J. (2006). *Meeting the challenge of assessing in a standards based education system.* Perth, Australia: Curriculum Council of Western Australiao. (Document Number)

Vygotsky, L. S. (1978). *Mind in society: The development of higher psychological processes.* Cambridge: Harvard University Press.

Whitefield, A. (2004). *Laptop computers as a mediating tool between teacher beliefs and pedagogy.* Geelong: Deakin University.

Wiggins, G. (1998). *Educative assessment: Designing assessments to inform and improve student performance.* San Francisco: Jossey-Bass.

Willig, C. (2001). *Introducing qualitative research in psychology adventures in theory and method.* Buckingham: Open University Press.

Paul Newhouse
(Edith Cowan University)

REBECCA WALKER, SARAH HOPKINS
AND STEPHEN HOUGHTON

8. A RASCH MEASUREMENT OF DISORGANISATION

*Assessing a Commonly Mentioned but Rarely Examined Factor
Affecting School Performance*

ABSTRACT

Organisation is a key factor for successful everyday adaptive functioning in schools. Although it is widely recognised that the school environment requires students to be organised if they are to be successful, particularly at the secondary school level, there is currently a lack of instruments available for measuring this construct. To address this, a new teacher report measure of student disorganisation behaviours in the secondary school environment was developed. Following a review of the literature and currently available instrumentation, three phases were implemented: focus-group interviews with primary and secondary teachers; a pilot test of the newly developed instrument to check face validity and item functioning; and an analysis of data from a large scale administration based on the Rasch measurement model. The outcome was a 23-item teacher report scale entitled the Student Disorganisation Scale.

INTRODUCTION

Schools are complex learning environments that require students to be organised. Students are required to plan and manage their time and resources, and adequately adapt to changing situations if they are to achieve academic success (Abikoff, Nissley-Tsiopinis, Gallagher, Zambenedetti, Seyffert, Boorady, & McCarthy, 2009; Barkley, 1990). This is particularly so for secondary school students as their classes are organised into curriculum areas, set tasks are often more open-ended, and they are expected to organise time for study outside school hours (Gureasko-Moore, DuPaul & White, 2006).

Brown, Kerr, Zigmond and Harris (1984) surveyed nearly 4500 high school students and teachers (counsellors and administrators) to identify the key competencies that secondary school environments require from their students in order for them to manage their education successfully. Adults in the study ranked '*Meets due dates*' as the most important school survival behaviour, followed by '*Arrives at school on time*'. The school survival behaviour ranked top by students included '*Formulates plans for achieving goals*'. Across both adults and students, behaviours

*R.F. Cananagh and R.F. Waugh (eds.), Applications of Rasch Measurement
in Learning Environments Research, 181–206.*

associated with organisation were identified. In other studies, teachers have specifically identified good work habits as being important for academic success (Kerr & Zigmond, 1986) as well as being able to complete homework assignments (McMullen, Shippen & Dangel, 2007).

Many curriculum documents also identify the importance of behaviours and skills associated with organisation and highlight them as being a key outcome of education. For example, the National Declaration of Educational Goals for Young Australians (Ministerial Council on Education, Employment, Training and Youth Affairs, MCEETYA, 2008) states that:

> The curriculum will support young people to develop a range of generic and employability skills that have a particular application to the world of work and further education and training, such as planning and organising, the ability to think flexibly, to communicate well and to work in teams (p. 13).

The curriculum provided by the International Baccalaureate (IB), The Middle Years Program (MYP), also identifies *Organisation* as one of five key skill areas to be addressed. In this context, organisation encompasses outcomes specific to time management (including meeting deadlines and using time effectively) and self-management (including actions such as goal setting and the organisation of materials for learning). These outcomes are not directly assessed but are monitored, with the expectation that they are taught. A final year project completed by students provides an indirect assessment of these outcomes.

While it is widely acknowledged that students need to be organised, there only appears to be anecdotal evidence that many students are not organised. Moreover, this evidence also suggests these students are not receiving the help they need to become organised.

> Many educators and parents have learned to recognise deficiencies in reading, writing, and math, but not in organisation. Instead of being looked upon as a set of skills that needs to be taught, organisation is seen as something instinctive, something everyone should be capable of. While some students do have an innate ability to organise themselves, many don't. Because we don't attend to students who exhibit problems in this area as we do students who have trouble with math or reading, the disorganised student rarely gets the help [s/]he needs. The gap in his/her education continues to grow and has an increasingly negative impact on his/her academic career (Goldberg & Zweibel, 2005, p. 3)

This is not to say that it is a completely neglected area. For example, over a decade ago, Shore (1998) described the disorganised student as the one who is often unprepared for class, has a messy desk and school bag, loses school materials, has difficulty meeting work deadlines, has time management difficulties, has trouble starting work, is often confused about what to do in tasks, has a poor sense of time, produces written work that is difficult to follow, and has a hard time expressing themselves in a logical, sequential manner. Other researchers (such as Abikoff & Gallagher, 2008; Barkley, 1990; Heisler, 2009b) have also highlighted how disorganisation affects many aspects of a students' life at school and post school, and how disorganised behaviours and work habits can frustrate teachers, cause conflict in the home, and may transfer to the work place and social settings in adulthood. Indeed, disorganisation has been identified as a major problem in the American workforce (Williams & Eun Jung, 2000) and is known to be a particular hindrance in workplaces that deal with paper management (Sanders, 1994). Time management difficulties, specifically, have also been shown to negatively impact on individuals in the workplace (Macan, 1994).

Given the prominence assigned to organisation within the school curricula and the recognition of its importance for academic success in the school environment and beyond, it is not surprising to find it frequently discussed in educational circles. Numerous websites and unpublished articles aimed at helping students who have organisational problems (e.g., Boller, 2008; Lavoie, 2007; Heisler, 2009a, 2009b; National Study Group on Chronic Disorganisation, NSGCD, 2010) as well as a number of books on the topic (e.g., Goldberg & Zweibel, 2005; Shore, 1988) abound. What *is* surprising, however, is the limited body of research that has considered Organisation or Disorganisation as a specific construct to be investigated in the general student population. A limiting factor to date has been the lack of instruments available for measuring this construct.

Organisation, as it relates to a school environment, is defined by Zental, Harper and Stormont-Spurgin (1993) in terms of three specific abilities: (i) the ability to plan and manage activities within a time-frame, (ii) the ability to arrange objects and assignments in a systematic way that makes them easily retrievable, and (iii) the ability to structure an approach to a task. This definition was adopted in the current research along with the term *disorganisation*, to refer to students' lack of organisation. As such, students who are disorganised experience difficulty with establishing and maintaining an organised and structured approach to their studies (Elliot, McGregor, & Gable, 1999).

REVIEW OF RESEARCH INSTRUMENTS

The Study Skills literature is a large body of research that has investigated skills (or behaviours) associated with organisation among the general student population. Five common instruments used to assess students' Study Skills in the college educational environment, as reviewed by Crede and Kuncel (2008) and Entwistle and McCune (2004), are cited within this body: the Learning and Study Skills Inventory (LASSI), the Revised Version of the Inventory of Learning Processes (ILP-R), the Study Process Questionnaire (SPQ), the Approaches and Study Skills Inventory for Students (ASSIST) and the Motivated Strategies for Learning Questionnaire (MSLQ). These instruments were examined as part of this present research to identify items considered by the researchers to be related (at least in part) to organisation as defined by Zental, Harper and Stormont-Spurgin (1993). The findings from this examination are summarised in Appendix 1.

The Study Skills literature also cites instruments used to assess students' Study Skills in the secondary school environment, including the Learning and Study Skills Inventory – High School version (LASSI-HS), Middle School Learning Strategies (MSLS), Academic Competence Evaluation Scales (ACES), Learning Process Questionnaire (LPQ) and the School Motivation and Learning Strategies Inventory (SMALSI). These instruments were also examined to identify items that related to organisation (see Appendix 2).

Although a number of instruments have been cited above, it is important to note that organisation as a construct has been measured using only a small number of items, such as those from the subscale "Organised Studying", from the ASSIST. More commonly, items reflecting organised behaviours and skills have been combined with other items to measure different constructs. A good example of this is the subscale "Agentic Analytic" (on the ILP-R) or "Cognitive Strategies" (a subscale on the MSLS). It is apparent from the literature that instruments used in the Study Skills area have been designed to measure students' approaches to study rather than the degree of organisation that student's exhibit.

Some research has been undertaken to develop instruments that focus on time management (e.g., Barkley 1988; Houghton, Durkin, Ang, Taylor and Brandtman, in press) but few instruments have been developed to measure organisation more broadly. Zentall, Harper and Stormont-Spurgin (1993) did develop such an instrument to investigate the organisational problems experienced and exhibited by students with Attention-Deficit Hyperactivity Disorder (AD/HD). These researchers constructed the self-report Child Organisational Scale (COS) and the Child Organisation Parent Perception Scale (COPPS). The COS encompassed 11 items relating to organisation of time and 15 items relating to organisation of objects, while the COPPS included five items relating to the organisation of time and eight items to assess organisation of objects. This instrument was used by Grskovic, Zentall, and Stormont-Spurgin (1995) to study organisation problems among special education students, including those with AD/HD, learning disabilities or emotional handicaps. While normally achieving students were included in the study and assessed on organisation, this was for the purpose of comparison only. Furthermore, only a small sample of 51 students (aged eight–14 years old) was involved. In their initial work developing the instrument (Zentall, Harper & Stormont-Spurgin, 1993), only a small sample of 38 students (aged six–14 years old) was involved.

At the time of commencing this present research, there were, to our knowledge, no validated instruments specifically developed to measure the construct of Organisation apart from those developed by Zentall, Harper and Stormont-Spurgin (1993). However since this time, Abikoff and Gallagher (2008) have developed another instrument to investigate the organisational problems experienced by students with AD/HD. This new instrument comprises teacher, parent and child versions of the Child Organisation Skills Scale (COSS) to measure what they refer to as organisation, time management and planning skills or OTMP skills. The three COSS scale versions were developed through consultation with parents, teachers and clinicians who relayed the organisational difficulties children with AD/HD experience in their daily lives. From this, lists of these difficulties were composed for parents and teachers to evaluate, with adjustments being made accordingly. The lists were adapted into the organisational scales, with suitable reading ages for the child version. At this point in time, the three versions of the COSS have been revised and completed for a normative sample (see Abikoff & Gallagher, 2009). The revisions to COSS have resulted in a 42-item teacher version, a 66-item parent version COSS, and a 63-item child version COSS. Overall, the instrument is designed to measure OTMP behaviours in eight to 13 year olds. Each version takes approximately 20 minutes to complete and responses are recorded on a four-point Likert scale. The COSS produces a total score of OTMP behaviours, as well as three subscale scores for organisation, time management and planning.

While this work is important for furthering our understanding of organisation in young people, there are a number of issues relating to existing instruments for measuring organisation. Both the COS and COSS instruments were developed for special education populations and may therefore have limited applicability with the mainstream school population. The COS has been tested using only a small sample and the COSS takes approximately 20 minutes for teachers to complete, which given today's ever increasing demands on the teaching profession may not be suitable. Neither instrument has been evaluated using the Rasch measurement model. Therefore our goal was to develop a new scale to measure disorganisation in the everyday lives of young people in the secondary school environment.

AIMS

The aims of the research were linked to the three separate, yet inter-related phases. The aim of Phase 1, which involved focus-group interviews with primary and secondary teachers, was to identify key behaviours exhibited by students that teachers considered to be disorganised. These could then be used in items for the newly developed instrument to measure disorganisation. The instrument developed in Phase 1 was titled the Student Disorganisation Scale - Initial Version (SDS-IV). The aim of Phase 2, which comprised a pilot test of the SDS-IV with a small sample of students, was to refine the instrument. The face validity of the items was evaluated and statistical indicators of item functioning (appropriate for smaller samples) were explored. The refined instrument was titled the Student Disorganisation Scale - Piloted Version (SDS-PV). In Phase 3, the SDS-PV was completed by secondary school teachers for a larger sample of students in Years 8, 9 and 10 (ages 13 to 16 years). Analyses based on the Rasch measurement model were used to investigate overall item functioning, threshold ordering and differential item functioning. The aims of this phase were to (i) further refine the instrument, (ii) evaluate how well the final instrument targeted students in Years 8–10 and (iii) determine how well the instrument measured disorganisation (i.e., how well the responses fitted the Rasch Model). One final aim (iv) was to use the refined instrument, referred to as the Student Disorganisation Scale (SDS), to investigate differences in disorganisation between males and females, and differences between students grouped according to academic achievement.

Approval to conduct all phases of this research was obtained from the Human Research Ethics Committee of the administering institution. All principals of the participating schools and teachers were provided with an information sheet explaining the purposes of the research along with consent-to-participate forms. To preserve student anonymity, students' names were not written down at any stage.

PHASE 1: FOCUS GROUP INTERVIEWS

METHOD

Convenience sampling was used to select participants for the first phase of the research. A total of four focus groups were conducted. The first focus group comprised the Head of the Mathematics Department and three secondary school mathematics teachers from one independent senior high school located in a high Socio-Economic Status (SES) area of Perth (Western Australia). The second focus group consisted of the Head of the English Department, the Head of the Maths Department, the Head of Integrated Studies and two classroom teachers (Society and Environment teacher and a teacher of Integrated Studies) from one government senior high school located in a low SES area of Perth. The participants in the third focus group all attended one government senior high school located in a medium SES area of Perth and included the Year 12 Coordinator, a Vocational Studies teacher, a Society and Environment teacher and a maths teacher. The fourth focus group was conducted with three primary school teachers from three separate government primary schools located in low to middle SES areas.

All interviews were semi-structured with participants and researcher sitting in a circle to facilitate interaction. Eight guiding questions were prepared to generate discussion about students who exhibit organisational problems at school. During each of the interviews, the participants were asked to describe students who were experiencing organisational difficulties and detail the behaviours that they had observed both in and out of the classroom. They were encouraged to provide specific examples to the statements made. Interviews formally began with the researcher asking the initial guiding question "*Think about a student you have taught who you think was disorganised: What key behaviours did they exhibit?*" In some cases, when topics generated lengthy discussions, the researcher allowed the participant to elaborate on their responses as much as possible but then used the next guiding question to focus the discussion. When the topics being discussed reached saturation point, the next guiding question was asked. An audio-recording was taken of each of the focus groups and later transcribed. Using a qualitative approach, the interview data were reduced into categories using analytical procedures recommended by Miles and Huberman (1994) which were then annotated with representative quotes. Each interview lasted between 30 and 90 minutes.

RESULTS

Table 1. Categories developed from the focus group interviews and related items generated for the SDS-IV

Category	Item (This student ...)	Item no.
Homework	Does not hand homework in on time	1
	Leaves homework until the last minute before the due date	6
Class Work	Misses out key steps when working on a task in class	5
	Needs help from the teacher to explain each task to him/her step by step	9
	Is very focused on work related tasks in class *	21
	Is easily distracted from starting work in class	13
	Often writes work down then erases it	28
	Requires no teacher monitoring to stay on task *	26
	Needs teacher feedback to continue working on a task	36
	Rarely completes any work	20
	Appears reluctant to produce his/her best work	41
	Rushes to finish work	10
	Is not willing to read through his/her work and look for ways to improve it	32
	Does not form a plan for handing in work on time	31
	Has difficulty picking out important parts to a task	27
Prioritising	Does not make class work a priority	43
Communi-cation	Has difficulty expressing thoughts in a logical, sequential manner	38
	Produces written work that is hard to follow	24
	Has neat handwriting *	4
Open Ended Tasks and Group Work	Has trouble working on open ended tasks	7
	Does not work well with others in groups	44
	Interacts well with other students *	16
	Has difficulty seeing other people's point of view	22
Refocusing/ Task Switching	Has no trouble switching his/her focus when he/she is required to do so *	19
	Requires repeated prompting to shift his/her attention from one task to a new task	35
Routines	Does not appear to recognise school routines	39
	Needs constant reminding of lesson routines	18
	Does not appear to have developed personal routines	14
	Has difficulty adapting to changes in lesson routines	29
	Does not pack things away in an orderly manner	2
	Has difficulty functioning in structured situations	46
Managing Time	Does not have a good sense of time	23
	Has difficulty adhering to time schedules	42
	Has no trouble meeting set deadlines *	34
	Does not use a diary effectively	25
	Has difficulty estimating time needed to complete a task	33
	Is often on time to class *	12

Category	Item (This student ...)	Item no.
	Is one of the last students to leave class when the lesson ends	45
Belongings	Comes prepared to lessons *	8
	Loses or forgets equipment	11
	Requires the teacher to supply the equipment needed for the lesson	40
	Loses or misplaces personal items	30
	Loses or misplaces work	3
	Requires the teacher to look after his/her work	15
	Has an extremely messy school bag or no school bag	17
Other	Over estimates how well he/she performed on an assessment	37

Note: * Denotes items reverse-scored

Eight categories were identified from the focus-group data that were relevant to item development. A consultant panel comprising the current three authors selected a total of 46 items to be included in the SDS-IV. It was deemed important that the language used in the construction of the new items was commensurate with that used by the participants. Each item was written to follow the same stem: "This student ...". A 4-point Likert scale was used to record responses, which included the anchors Definitely Not True (scored 0), Not True (scored 1), True (scored 2) and Definitely True (scored 3). The majority of items were written to reflect disorganised behaviours so that a higher score indicated a higher degree of dis-organisation. Eight items were written in a way that necessitated reverse scoring. Items included in the SDS-IV are presented in Table 1 according to the category to which they relate.

The SDS-IV cover sheet included instructions for completing the questionnaire and a place for recording a teacher code and student code. Teachers were also required to indicate the gender of the student and the overall academic performance of the student, compared to other students in the same class, by ticking one of three boxes: in the bottom 25%, about average, in the top 25%.

PHASE 2: PILOT TESTING THE STUDENT DISORGANISATION SCALE (SDS)

METHOD

Convenience sampling was used to select three teachers to participate in Phase 2 of the research. These teachers were not part of the sample that was involved in Phase 1. All three teachers taught at the same senior high school located in a middle SES area in Perth: two were Society and Environment (S&E) teachers and one was a Maths teacher. In this phase of the research, the teachers completed the SDS-IV for one Year 9 class of students they were currently teaching and had taught for the previous three school terms (approximately nine months). The Maths teacher and one S&E teacher completed the SDS-IV for the same group of students (15 male and nine female students). The other S&E teacher completed the SDS-IV for a different class of students (seven male and 17 female students.) Each teacher also received a feedback sheet to complete that included questions relating to the face validity of the items, how easy the questionnaire was to complete, and how long it took to complete for each student.

The data from the two classes of different students (the maths and S&E classes) were used to examine item difficulty and internal consistency. These analyses endeavoured to identify items that were not functioning well.

To examine item difficulty, teachers' responses to each item, for each student, were first entered into an Excel spreadsheet. This resulted in a data matrix (m x n) that comprised m rows (corresponding to the number of students) and n columns (corresponding to number of items). Item difficulty was examined by summing the responses to each item (columns) and expressing this total as a proportion (p) of the maximum score attainable for that item (i.e., dividing by the highest score for the item x m). An associated q-value was then calculated for each of the items by finding the complement of the p-value (i.e., $q = 1 - p$), thus yielding complementary proportions that must also range from 0 to 1. Q-values represent the difficulty of the items, with high q-values indicative of items that participants do not often score highly on. Conversely, teachers are more likely to endorse items with low difficulty (i.e., a low q-value). In general, extreme values (very high or very low) have less discriminating power. Items with q-values below 0.20 and above 0.80 are generally considered not to be discriminating (Kline, 2000). Items with extreme q-values were considered for deletion. Within these boundaries it is desirable to have items ranging in difficulty to produce a discriminating measure.

To examine internal consistency, data were copied into a SPSS data file and Cronbach's Alpha was calculated. This statistic indicates the extent to which items are measuring the same underlying attribute (i.e., disorganisation) and the analysis highlights items where responses are not strongly correlated with the overall measure of disorganisation. These items were considered for removal. Nunnally (1978) recommended that an alpha value between 0.80 and 0.90 was ideal but a lower bound of 0.70 was acceptable.

Data from the Maths and S&E teachers based on the same class of students were used to examine inter-rater reliability. Inter-rater reliability of overall scores was assessed using Pearson's product-moment correlation coefficient. Inter-rater reliability of individual items was assessed using a percentage agreement.

RESULTS

On the feedback sheets, the three teacher participants reported that they found the SDS-IV straight forward and easy to complete; no clarifications were sought and no difficulties were expressed. Each individual questionnaire took approximately five minutes to complete. All were fully completed and so there was no missing data.

From data based on 48 students, q-values were calculated to examine item difficulty (see Table 2). As shown in Table 2, q-values were all in the suggested range (between 0.20 and 0.80). Item 26 (*Requires no teacher monitoring to stay on task*) was found to be the easiest item to endorse. Item 30 (*Loses or misplaces personal items*) and Item 40 (*Requires the teacher to supply equipment needed for the lesson*) were found to be the hardest items to endorse.

Table 2. Item difficulty for the SDS-IV

Item No.	q value	Item No.	q value
1	0.60	24	0.59
2	0.69	25	0.54
3	0.69	26	0.46
4	0.58	27	0.51
5	0.58	28	0.69
6	0.53	29	0.68
7	0.52	30	0.80
8	0.67	31	0.51
9	0.53	32	0.58
10	0.64	33	0.59
11	0.74	34	0.55
12	0.65	35	0.60
13	0.53	36	0.50
14	0.75	37	0.73
15	0.78	38	0.58
16	0.75	39	0.76
17	0.72	40	0.80
18	0.67	41	0.67
19	0.68	42	0.61
20	0.62	43	0.52
21	0.60	44	0.63
22	0.63	45	0.59
23	0.63	46	0.67

An analysis of internal consistency highlighted two problem items, where scores for the item were not significantly correlated with total scores: Item 45 (*This student is one of the last students to leave class when the lesson ends*) ($r =0.002$, p=n.s.) and Item 28 (*This student often writes down work then erases it*) ($r =0.15$, p=n.s.). A decision was made to delete Item 45 for this reason but to retain Item 28 at this stage because this behaviour was discussed at some length by the teachers in the focus group interviews. Thus, as a result of the pilot study, the 46-item SDS-IV was modified to become the 45-item SDS-PV. Cronbach's Alpha Coefficient calculated for the SPS-PV was 0.986. The ordering of items were the same for both instruments except Item 46 on the SPS-IV was relabelled as Item 45 on the SPS-PV.

Data from the Maths and S&E teachers based on the same class of students were used to examine inter-rater reliability. Based on summed (raw total) scores for each student, a strong correlation between the two teachers' responses was evident ($r = 0.964$, $p<.001$). By matching teachers' responses (scored 0, 1, 2, or 3) on each item for each student, a 68.1% agreement was found.

PHASE 3: RASCH ANALYSIS AND GROUP DIFFERENCES

METHOD

Cluster sampling was used to select three schools in the Perth metropolitan area that represented school communities of varying socio-economic status. These schools had not participated in Phase 1 of the research. Purposeful sampling was then used to select three teachers from within each school: a Maths, Society and Environment, and an English teacher currently teaching a Year 8, Year 9 or Year 10 class in their subject area. Teachers and classes were selected so that SDS-PV questionnaires were completed for students for each subject level, at each year level. In total, the instrument was completed for 242 students by the nine participating teachers from the three schools.

Data were copied into a SPSS data file and subsequently into a RUMM 2020 (Andrich, Sheridan, & Luo, 2009) data file. There were no missing data. The Rasch model of analysis was then used to investigate, interpret, and help modify the instrument. The RUMM 2020 program provides statistics for each item to identify items that are not functioning well and provides a global test of fit, the item-trait test of fit (a chi square). The item-trait test of fit indicates the degree to which item difficulties are consistent across the scale measured, independent of the person difficulties. An index of reliability, called the Person Separation Index (PSI), is also provided. The PSI indicates the degree of internal consistency and is analogous to Cronbach's alpha. Differential item functioning (DIF) techniques were also used to highlight bias in item responses across groups: two person factors were explored, Gender and Academic Performance. Items that show group bias are generally deleted from the developed instrument and so the DIF technique ensures that items are functioning equally for different groups within the population (Brodersen, Meads, Kreiner, Thorsen, Doward & McKenna, 2007). Based on the final SDS instrument, scaled scores measuring disorganisation were then used to explore group differences between males and females and across academic achievement levels using ANOVAs.

RESULTS

The SPS-PV was completed by nine teachers for 242 students. The composition of the student cohort is provided in Table 3.

The initial test-of-fit summary for the SDS-PV (see Table 4) indicates that there is not acceptable agreement about the difficulty of the items along the scale between all persons and that each person's response to an item cannot be predicted by a single measure. The Item-Trait Interaction Chi Square statistic provides an indication of the interaction between the person measures and the item responses along the scale. The Chi Square probability should ideally be greater than 0.05.

Table 3. Student numbers by gender and year level

Year Level	Male	Female	Combined
Year 8	44	40	84
Year 9	53	31	84
Year 10	28	46	74
TOTAL	125	117	242

The next stage in the analysis was to examine how each item was functioning using Individual Item Fit statistics. Ill-fitting items that were deleted were done so one at a time and item statistics were re-calculated each time. The extreme fit residual and probability value for Item 28 (*This student often writes down work then erases it*) indicated that this was the worst fitting item. The results of the pilot test also highlighted this as a problem item. The Item Characteristic Curve in Figure 1 shows the probability curve of expected responses for Item 28 and the points represent the actual responses. The person location indicates the degree of disorganisation displayed by students ranging from a low (-3) to a high (3) based on the instrument in its current version. The Characteristic Curve for Item 28 shows that students who were less disorganised scored higher than expected on this item and those who were more disorganised scored lower on this item than expected. As such, Item 28 was under discriminating and deleted from the instrument.

Table 4. Initial test-of-fit summary

	ITEM-PERSON INTERACTION			
	ITEMS		PERSONS	
	Location	Fit Residual	Location	Fit Residual
Mean	0.000	0.038	−0.684	−0.359
SD	0.480	3.713	1.825	2.394
Skewness		.825		−0.332
Kurtosis		−0.192		−0.238
Correlation		−0.022		0.019
ITEM-TRAIT INTERACTION		RELIABILITY INDICES		
Total Item Chi	749.738	Separation Index		0.97737
Square	135	Cronbach Alpha		0.98476
Degree of Freedom	0.000000			
Chi Square				
Probability				
POWER OF TEST-OF-FIT				
Power is EXCELLENT				

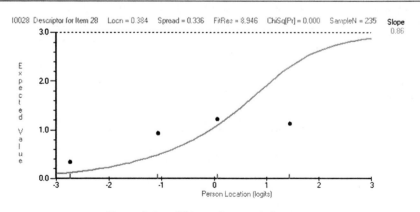

Figure 1. Item 28 item characteristic curve.

In order to review the remaining 44 items, a similar procedure was repeated. The Individual Item-Fit analysis was rerun and the item with the most extreme fit residual was identified. The Item Characteristic Curve for that item was then produced to examine further the functioning of the item and to explore the possibility of deleting the item. As a result of this procedure, Items 28, 10, 37, 19, 16, 4, 22, 26, 34, 38, 12, 9, 27, 25, 7, 44 and 24 were deleted in the order given. These deleted items are shown in Table 5.

Table 5. Deleted items from the item-fit analysis

Item no.	This student...
4	Has neat handwriting *
7	Has trouble working on open ended tasks
9	Needs help from the teacher to explain each task to him/her step by step
10	Rushes to finish work
12	Is often on time to class *
16	Interacts well with other students *
19	Has no trouble switching his/her focus when he/she is required to do so *
22	Has difficulty seeing other people's point of view
24	Produces written work that is hard to follow
25	Does not use a diary effectively
26	Requires no teacher monitoring to stay on task *
27	Has difficulty picking out important parts to a task
28	Often writes down work then erases it
34	Has no trouble meeting set deadlines *
37	Over estimates how well he/she performed on an assessment
38	Has difficulty expressing thoughts in a logical, sequential manner
44	Does not work well with others in groups

Note: * Denotes items reverse-scored

Item Thresholds were then examined to see how well the response categories for each item were working. Item Threshold testing highlighted that the response categories for Item 15 (*This student requires the teacher to look after his/her work*) were not appropriately ordered. Ideally, the Category Probability Curve should show each of the response category curves peak in sequence. The Category Probability Curve for Item 15 shown in Figure 2 illustrates that the curve relating to response category 2 (*True*) does not meet this expectation. Participants tended to respond to this item by ticking either response category 0 (*Definitely Not True*) or response category 3 (*Definitely True*). As the categories did not discriminate the responses well, Item 15 was removed from the instrument. The response category curves for all other items were found to be ordered correctly.

As an aim of this research was to develop an instrument that could be used to measure student disorganisation, it is important that items do not function differently for males and females, or for students characterised as being low, average or high achieving. A Gender DIF analysis highlighted only one item, Item 43 (*This student does not make class work a priority*), as showing differential functioning (class interval probability of 0.00366). The Characteristic Curve for Item 43 plotted separately for females and males is shown in Figure 3. This figure illustrates that females scored higher on this item than males who were deemed to be at the same location of around 0 logits. Item 43 was removed for this reason.

The Academic Performance DIF analysis highlighted that Item 5 and Item 41 were not functioning as expected. The Characteristic Curve for Item 5 (shown in Figure 4) revealed that this item (*This student misses out key steps when working on a task in class*) was under discriminating for both high-achieving students and low-achieving students.

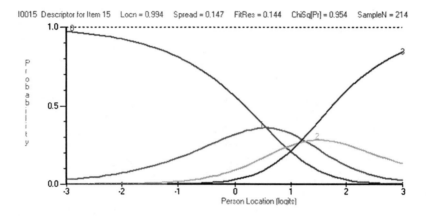

Figure 2. Category probability curve for item 15.

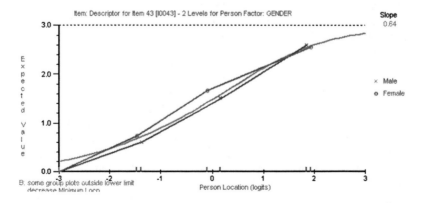

Figure 3. Item 43 item characteristic curve.

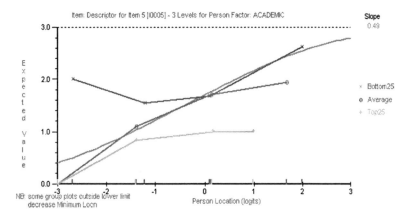

Figure 4. Item 5 item characteristic curve.

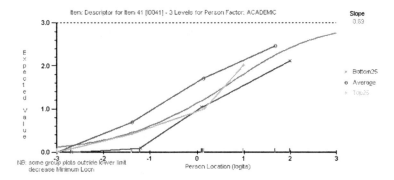

Figure 5. Item 41 item characteristic curve.

The Characteristic Curve for Item 41 (*This student appears reluctant to produce his/her best work*) plotted for each of the three achievement groups (shown in Figure 5) indicates a complicated pattern of results. This item appears to work as expected for high-achieving students but not for average-achieving or low-achieving students. Average-achieving students tended to score more highly on this item than expected; low achieving students tended to score lower on this item.

After the three items that produced differential functioning were removed, an item-fit analysis was repeated. Item 36 (*This student needs teacher feedback to continue working on a task*) was highlighted and removed. Items 17, 21, 29 and 35 were also highlighted as having extreme fit residuals but corresponding probability values were not highlighted as being extreme and each item's characteristic curve appeared acceptable. These items were retained. The final version of the instrument, henceforth referred to as the SDS, comprised 23 items. These are detailed in Table 6.

The final Test-of-Fit summary displayed in Table 7, indicates the SDS produced an excellent measure of disorganisation with an Item-Trait Interaction Chi Square of 0.091.

Table 6. Items in the SDS

Item No.	This student...
1	Does not hand homework in on time
2	Does not pack things away in an orderly manner
3	Loses or misplaces work
6	Leaves work until the last minute before the due date
8	Comes prepared to lessons *
11	Loses or forgets equipment
13	Is easily distracted from starting work in class
14	Does not appear to have developed personal routines
17	Has an extremely messy school bag or no school bag
18	Needs constant reminding of lesson routines
20	Rarely completes any task
21	Is very focused on work related tasks in class *
23	Does not have a good sense of time
29	Has difficulty adapting to changes in lesson routines
30	Loses or misplaces personal items
31	Does not form a plan for handing work in on time
32	Is not willing to read through his/her work and look for ways to improve it
33	Has difficulty estimating time needed to complete a task
35	Requires repeated prompting to shift his/her attention from one task to a new task
39	Does not appear to recognise school routines
40	Requires the teacher to supply equipment needed for the lesson
42	Has difficulty adhering to time schedules
45	Has difficulty functioning in structured situations

Table 7. Test-of-fit summary

	ITEM-PERSON INTERACTION			
	ITEMS		PERSONS	
	Location	Fit Residual	Location	Fit Residual
Mean	0.000	0.168	−0.873	−0.399
SD	0.617	1.945	2.624	1.634
Skewness		0.416		0.079
Kurtosis		−0.857		−0.198
Correlation		−0.029		−0.063

ITEM-TRAIT INTERACTION		RELIABILITY INDICES	
Total Item Chi Square	85.163	Separation Index	0.97734
Degree of Freedom	69	Cronbach Alpha	0.98313
Chi Square Probability	0.090554		
POWER OF TEST-OF-FIT			
Power is EXCELLENT			

The Person-Item Threshold Distribution for the final instrument shown in Figure 6 shows good item person targeting, except for those students at the extreme left and extreme right of the continuum. There are relatively few item thresholds at these locations. As the SDS provides a measure of disorganisation administered to a sample where the majority of students are not expected to be disorganised, the floor effect is understandable. It would be desirable, though, to have more items at the extreme right of the continuum to distinguish between very disorganised and extremely disorganised students.

RUMM 2020 was used to calculate a scaled score of disorganisation for each student, which was then copied into an SPSS data file along with person-factor data (gender and academic performance) to examine group differences.

The distribution of SDS scores for males and females was examined and indicators of skewness and kurtosis, and the probability plots showed no serious departures of normality. Levene's test showed no significant difference in the variability of group scores (F = 0.28, p = 0.60). The distribution of SDS scores for the three groups identified by academic achievement was also examined and no serious departures of normality were indicated. Levene's test showed no significant difference in the variability of group scores (F = 0.15, p =0.86).

Disorganisation (scaled) scores for male students and female students are displayed in Figure 6. A t-test confirmed that male students (M = -0.06, SD = 2.60, n = 125) scored significantly higher on the SDS than female students (M = −1.7, SD = 2.37, n = 117); t(240)=5.22, p <.001), Cohen's d = 0.70.

An ANOVA revealed a significant difference in the scaled total SDS scores across the three academic groups, F(2, 239) = 76.25, p < 0.001, η^2 = 0.39 (see Figure 8). The measure of effect size indicated that approximately 39% of variance in SDS scores could be explained by differences in students' academic performance (see Figure 9). Post-hoc comparisons with Bonferroni adjusted alpha levels (α = 0.017) confirmed that students in the Top 25% group (M = −3.07, SD = 1.93, n = 64) scored significantly lower on the SDS than students in the Average group (M = −1.18, SD = 1.98, n = 91); t(153) = 5.89, p <0.001, Cohen's d = 0.96. Students in

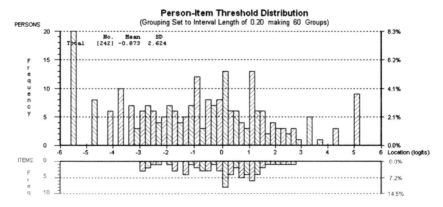

Figure 6. Person-item threshold distribution.

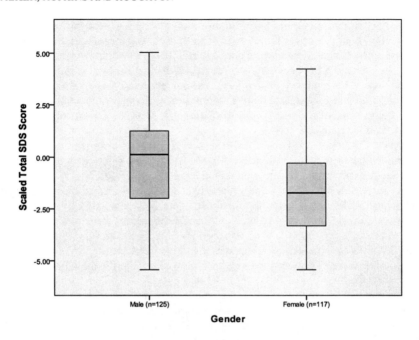

Figure 7. Boxplot of SDS scaled total scores according to gender.

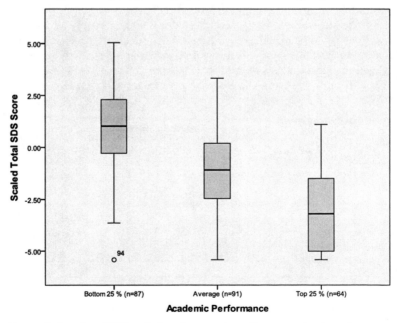

Figure 8. Boxplot of SDS scaled total scores according to academic performance.

the Top 25% group scored significantly lower on the SDS than students in the Bottom 25% group (M = 1.07, SD = 2.22, n = 87); $t(149)=11.96$, $p<.001$, Cohen's $d=1.98$. Also the Average group scored significantly lower on the SDS than students in the Bottom 25% group; $t(176) = 7.15$, $p<.001$, Cohen's $d = 1.07$.

The boxplot illustrating SDS scores for males and females within each performance group (Figure 8) indicates that males tend to be more disorganised than females regardless of their level of academic performance (based on teacher judgements) (see Figure 7).

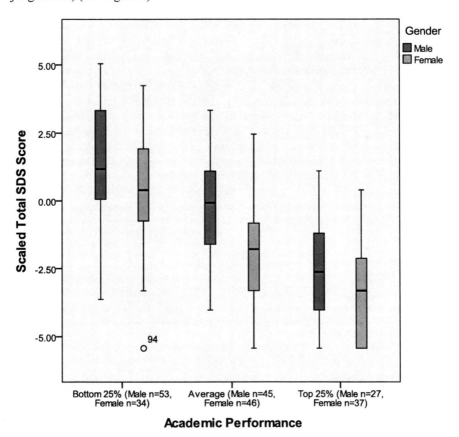

Figure 9. Boxplot of SDS scores for males and females across academic performance.

CONCLUSION

The present study provides educators and health related professionals (e.g. school psychologists) with a new, short, easy-to-administer instrument (available from the first author on request) with which to gauge teacher's perceptions of their student's organisational behaviours in everyday settings. Teachers have extensive opportunities to observe their students both in school and the classroom and are well placed to report on disorganisational behaviours. Given the important role teachers play in the assessment process, the Student Disorganisation Scale (SDS) can easily be utilised alongside existing questionnaires to determine aspects of a student's functioning that might be hindering his/her everyday performance. To develop the Student Disorganisation Scale, a rigorous sequential construction process was followed. In doing this, the SDS not only reflected the key concepts identified in the research literature but it was also representative of the realities of students' everyday functioning in the secondary school context. Thus, the present research has addressed an important element in secondary school educational contexts (i.e., student disorganisation), through the development of a psychometrically appropriate instrument.

It should be acknowledged that there was no demonstration of convergent and discriminant validity in the present study. This must be a strong focus of future research if the reliability and validity of the SDS is to be established. Finally, future research should attempt to replicate the present findings with ratings gathered from another source, such as parents, or the students themselves.

In conclusion, our findings contribute to a developing body of research showing the importance of organisational skills in everyday school settings. The new instrument presented here is not only an important development for evaluating student's disorganisational behaviour, but may also prove valuable for evaluating strategies implemented to improve such behaviour.

REFERENCES

Abikoff, H., & Gallagher, R. (2008). Assessment and remediation of organisational skills deficits in children with ADHD. In K. McBurnett & L. Pfiffner (Eds.), *Attention deficit hyperactivity disorder: Concepts, controversies and new directions* (pp. 137–152). New York: Informa Healthcare.

Abikoff, H., & Gallagher, R. (2009). *COSS: Children's organizational skills scales.* Retrieved June 1, 2009, from http://www.mhs.com

Abikoff, H., Nissley-Tsiopinis, J., Gallagher, R., Zambenedetti, M., Seyffert, M., Boorady, R., et al. (2009). Effects of MPH-OROS on the organisational, time management, and planning behaviours of children with ADHD. *Journal of the American Academy of Child and Adolescent Psychiatry, 48*(2), 166–175.

Andrich, D., Sheridan, B., & Luo, G. (2009). *RUMM 2020: A Windows interactive program for analysing data with Rasch unidimensional models for measurement.* Perth, Western Australia: RUMM Laboratory PTY Ltd.

Barkley, R. (1990). *Attention deficit hyperactivity disorder: A handbook for diagnosis and treatment.* New York: The Guildford Press.

Barkley, R. (1998). *It's about time.* Unpublished.

Biggs, J. (1987). *Student approaches to learning and studying.* Hawthorn, Australia: Australian Council for Educational Research Ltd.

Boller, B. (2008). Teaching organisational skills in middle school: Moving toward independence. *The Clearing House, 81*(4), 169–171.

Brown, G., Kerr, M., Zigmond, Z., & Harris, A. (1984). What's important for student success in high school? Successful and unsuccessful students discuss school survival skills. *The High School Journal, 68*(1), 10–17.

Crede, M., & Kuncel, N. (2008). Study habits, skills, and attitudes: The third pillar supporting collegiate academic performance. *Perspectives on Psychological Science, 3*(6), 425–453.

DiPerna, J., & Elliot, S. (1999). Development and validation of the academic competence evaluation scales. *Journal of Psychoeducational Assessment, 17*, 207–225.

Elliot, A., McGregor, H., & Gable, S. (1999). Achievement goals, study strategies, and exam performance: A meditational analysis. *Journal of Educational Psychology, 91*(3), 549–563.

Entwistle, N., & McCune, V. (2004). The conceptual bases of study strategy inventories. *Educational Psychology Review, 16*(4), 325–345.

Entwistle, N., Tait, H., & McCune, V. (2000). Patterns of response to an approaches to studying inventory across contrasting groups and contexts. *European Journal of Psychology of Education, 15*, 1, 33–48.

ETL Project. (2003). *Scoring key for the Approaches and Study Skills Inventory for Students* (ASSIST). Retrieved January 10, 2010, from http://www.etl.tla.ed.ac.uk/questionnaires/ASSIST.pdf

Goldberg, D., & Zweibel, J. (2005). *The organized student: Teaching children skills for success in school and beyond.* New York: Simon & Schuster.

Gureasko-Moore, S., DuPaul, G., & White, G. (2006). The effects of self-management in general education classrooms on the organisational skills of adolescents with ADHD. *Behaviour Modification, 30*(2), 159–183.

Heisler, M. (2009a). *Organisational training for teens is like a personal GPS for success.* Retrieved January 17, 2010, from http://www.anorganizedstudent.com/press.php

Heisler, M. (2009b). *An organised student offers organisational skills training for students: Peace of mind for parents.* Retrieved January 17, 2010, from http://www.anorganizedstudent.com/press.php

Houghton, S., Durkin, K., Ang, R., Taylor, M., & Brandtman, M. (in press). Measuring temporal self-regulation in children with and without attention deficit hyperactivity disorder: Sense of time in everyday contexts. *European Journal of Psychological Assessment.*

International Baccalaureate (IB). (2010). Retrieved January 10, 2010, from http://www.ibo.org

Kerr, M., & Zigmond, N. (1986). What do high school teachers want? A study of expectations and standards. *Education and Treatment of Children, 9*(3), 239–249.

Kline, P. (2000). *The handbook of psychological testing* (2nd ed.). London: Routledge.

Lavoie, R. (2007). *Organisational problems and the beginning of the school year.* Retrieved January 15, 2010 from http://www.ldonline.com

Liu, O. (2009). Evaluation of a learning strategies scale for middle school students. *Journal of Psychoeducational Assessment, 27*(4), 312–322.

Macan, T., (1994). Time management: Test of a process model. *Journal of Applied Psychology, 79*(3), 381–391.

McMullen, R., Shippen, M., & Dangel, H. (2007). Middle school teachers' expectations of organisational behaviours of students with learning disabilities. *Journal of Instructional Psychology, 34*(2), 75–80.

Miles, M., & Huberman, A. (1994). *Qualitative data: An expanded sourcebook* (2nd ed.). Thousand Oakes, CA: Sage Publications.

Ministerial Council on Education, Employment, Training and Youth Affairs (MCEETYA). (2008). *National declaration on educational goals for young Australians.* Retrieved March 1, 2010, from http://www.mceecdya.edu.au/mceecdya

National Study Group on Chronic Disorganisation (NSGCD). (2010). Retrieved January 16, 2010, from http://www.nsgcd.org

Nunnally, J. (1978). *Psychometric theory* (2nd ed.). New York: McGraw-Hill.

Pintrich, P., Smith, D., Garcia, T., & McKeachie, W. (1991). *A manual for the use of the Motivated Strategies for Learning Questionnaire (MSLQ).* Washington, DC: Office of Educational Research and Improvement.

Sanders, R. (1994). The corporate odd couple: The fastidious records manager vs. organisational messiness. *Records Management Quarterly, 28*, 2.

Schmeck, R., & Geisler-Brenstein, E. (1995). *The revised inventory of learning processes manual.* Carbondale, IL: Individuation Technologies.

Shore, K. (1998). The disorganised student. In K. Shore (Ed.), *Special kids problem solver: Ready to use interventions for helping students with academic, behavioural & physical problems* (pp. 171–181). New Jersey, NJ: Jossey-Bass.

Stroud, K., & Reynolds, C. (2006). *School motivation and learning strategies inventory.* Los Angeles: Western Psychological Services.

Weinstein, C., & Palmer, D. (2002). *Learning and study strategies inventory user's manual* (2nd ed.). Florida, FL: H & H Publishing Company Inc.

Weinstein, C., & Palmer, D. (1990). *Learning and study strategies inventory: High school version user's manual.* Florida, FL: H & H Publishing Company Inc.

Williams, R., & Eun Jung, O. (2000). *Student work habits: An educational imperative.* Education Resources Centre (ED 449446 Opinion Paper). Retrieved December 2, 2009, from http://www.eric.ed.gov

Zentall, S., Harper, G., & Stormont-Spurgin, M. (1993). Children with hyperactivity and their organisational abilities. *Journal of Educational Research, 87*(2), 112–117.

Rebecca Walker, Sarah Hopkins and Stephen Houghton
(Graduate School of Education, University of Western Australia)

APPENDIX 1A

INSTRUMENT	DETAILS	Subscales/Factors/Categories (NO. OF ITEMS IN THE SUBSCALE)
LASSI Weinstein & Palmer (2002)	Self-report 5-point Likert Scale 10 subscales 80 items in total	Study Aides (8 times) Time Management (8 items) Test Strategies (8 items)

ASSIST
ETL Project
(2003); Entwistle,
Tait & McCune
(2000)
	Self-Report
	5-point Likert Scale
	7 Sections
	Approaches to Study
	Skills Section:
	    4 subscales
	    60 items
		Strategic Approach (20 items)
		Including:
		    Organised Studying (4 items)
		    Time Management (4 items)
		    Monitoring Effectiveness (4 items)

ILP-R Schmeck & Geisler-Brenstein (1995)	Self-Report 6-point Likert Scale 19 subscales 90 items total	Methodical Study (5 items) Elaborative Self Actualisation (5 items) Agentic Serial (5 items) Agentic Analytic (5 items)
SPQ Biggs (1987)	Self-Report 5-point Likert Scale 6 subscales 42 items total	Achieving Motive (7 items) Achieving Strategy (7 items)
MSLQ Pintrich, Smith, Garcia & McKeachie, 1991)	Self-Report 7-point Likert Scale 15 subscales 81 items total	Time and Study Environment Management (8 items)

APPENDIX 1B

INSTRUMENT	NO. OF ITEMS RELATING TO ORGANISATION IN THE SUBSCALE AND AN EXAMPLE	
LASSI Weinstein & Palmer (2002)	1 item 6 items 1 item	• *I find it hard to stick to a study schedule.* • *When I decide to study, I set aside a specific length of time and stick to it.* • *I do poorly on tests because I find it hard to plan my work within a short period of time.*
ASSIST ETL Project (2003); Entwistle, Tait & McCune (2000)	9 items 3 items 4 items 2 items	• *I think I'm quite systematic and organised when it comes to revising for exams.* • *I'm pretty good at getting down to work whenever I need to.* • *Before starting work on an assignment or exam question, I think first how best to tackle it.*
ILP-R Schmeck & Geisler-Brenstein (1995)	1 item 1 item 1 item 3 items	• *I maintain a daily schedule of study hours.* • *I cram for exams.* • *I need to do things in a step-by-step orderly way.* • *Before I start a project, I get all my materials together.*
SPQ Biggs (1987)	1 item 1 item	• *I try to do all my assignments as soon as possible after they are given out.* • *I keep neat, well-organised notes for most subjects.*
MSLQ Pintrich, Smith, Garcia & McKeachie, 1991)	6 items	• *I rarely find time to review my notes or readings before an exam.*

APPENDIX 2

INSTRUMENT	INSTRUMENT DETAILS	SUBSCALES	NO. OF ITEMS RELATING TO ORGANISATION IN THE SUBSCALE AND AN EXAMPLE	
LASSI-HS Weinstein & Palmer (1990)	Self-Report 5-point Likert Scale 3 subscales 76 items in total	Time Management (7 items) Study Aids (8 items) Test Strategies (8 items)	4 items 2 items 1 item	• *When I decide to do schoolwork, I set aside a certain amount of time and stick with it.* • *I come to class unprepared.* • *I do poorly on tests because I find it hard to plan my work within a short period of time.*
MSLS (Liu, 2009)	Self-Report 4-point Likert Scale 3 subscales 52 items in total	Cognitive Strategies (26 items) Behavioural Strategies (14 items) Metacognitive Strategies (12 items)	6 items 3 items 2 items	• *Use a student planner.* • *School papers are disorganised.* • *Plan the steps before starting an assignment.*
ACES (DiPerna & Elliot, 1999)	Teacher completed 5-point Likert Scale 4 subscales 60 items in total	Study Skills (10 items)	7 items	• *Prepares for class.*
LPQ (Biggs, 1987)	Self-Report 5-point Likert Scale 6 subscales 36 items in total	Achieving Motive (6 items)	1 item	• *I always try to do all my assignments as soon as they are given to me.*
SMALSI (Stroud & Reynolds, 2006)	Self-Report 4-point Likert Scale 12 subscales	Test-Taking Strategies (15items) Organisational	1 item 10 items 7 items 1 item	• *I try to arrive early for tests so that I have time*

INSTRUMENT	INSTRUMENT DETAILS	SUBSCALES	NO. OF ITEMS RELATING TO ORGANISATION IN THE SUBSCALE AND AN EXAMPLE	
	170 items in total	Techniques (18 items) Time Management (17 items) Concentration /Attention Difficulties (17 items)		*to get ready.* • *I am often late getting to school.* • *I plan out the time I need for each school project.* • *It is hard for me to finish my homework.*

SECTION THREE: PERCEPTIONS OF THE LEARNING ENVIRONMENT

EMMA TOMKINSON AND STEPHEN HUMPHRY

9. THE GIFTED CLASSROOM SATISFACTION QUESTIONNAIRE

A Rasch Instrument

ABSTRACT

The primary purpose of this study was to create an instrument for collecting data from which valid inferences could be made for use in the context of a gifted and talented classroom. The data were analysed with a Rasch measurement model computer program (RUMM2020) and this showed there was a very good fit to the measurement model. The instrument produced and ranked lists of classroom satisfaction factors. Information from the literature was combined to inform the writing of the sample items and organisation of subtests. The content, language and structure were validated by teacher and student interviews. A pilot questionnaire was completed by 111 students from the academically selected year group who provided data by which the questionnaire could be further refined to form the two final instruments. This was done through a separate analysis of each item and subtest, with poorly functioning items deleted or rescored. Both products of this process, the 45 and 20 item versions of the *Gifted Student Classroom Satisfaction Questionnaire*, were shown to provide highly reliable information on the variation of satisfaction within a gifted and talented classroom and to substantiate that the questionnaire could be used to draw valid inferences.

INTRODUCTION

Gifted and talented education is an area in which interest and investment have increased dramatically in the past two decades. With the establishment of new selective programs, it is important that it is evaluated as part of a process of continual improvement (Barbe & Renzulli, 1981). Porath (2006a) stated, in regards to gifted students, "the inclusion of affect is critical; students' engagement, sense of belonging, and success as learners are integral to the (underpinning) philosophy of education" (p. 181). If the goals of an educational program are congruent with the perceived environment in which it is delivered, the assessment of students' perception of their learning environment will provide useful and meaningful information by which it can be improved (Griffin, Coates, McInnis & James, 2003). Evidence shows that student perceptions of a classroom are accurate (Gamoran, Nystrand & Berends, 1995). Walberg, Singh and Rasher's (1977) foundational work

R.F. Cavanagh and R.F. Waugh (eds.), Applications of Rasch Measurement in Learning Environments Research, 209–223.

in the area of student satisfaction showed that student perceptions of their instructional environment were an effective predictor of performance.

Previous attempts to measure student satisfaction have been based on traditional measurement approaches (Callahan, Tomlinson, Hunsaker, Bland & Moon, 1995). Modern test theory, the basis for the instrument constructed in this study, provides a number of advantages over traditional test theory (Embretson & Reise, 2000). Modern test theory uses a probabilistic model to relate response items to the traits of the person completing them, in contrast with traditional test theory, which uses the total score for the test. In the context of secondary school student satisfaction, modern test theory has only been applied once, in Bond and King's (2003) *School Opinion Survey*. This survey took a sample of over 40,000 students and nearly 36,000 parents from Queensland (Australia) public schools in order to establish benchmarks by which the achievements of the outcomes of the state education department could be mapped (Bond & King, 2003). It was, however, not written specifically for gifted and talented students. As Richardson (2004) stated, "content validity is situation-specific, and a questionnaire developed in one context may have low content validity in another context" (p. 352). The reliability of standardised test scores, developed for the mainstream, usually decreases for gifted students (Callahan et al., 1995).

This chapter will describe the process of producing an evaluation instrument that can produce reliable data that can be used validly in the context of a gifted and talented classroom. In order to construct an instrument for these purposes, the findings in the literature were utilised as a series of student activities which produced and ranked lists of classroom satisfaction factors. Information was combined to inform the writing of the sample items and organisation of sub-tests. The content, language and structure were validated by teacher and student interviews. A pilot questionnaire was completed by 111 students from the academically selected year group provided data by which the questionnaire could be further refined to form the two final instruments. This was done through a separate analysis of each item and subtest, with poorly functioning items deleted or rescored. Both products of this process, the 45 and 20 item versions of the *Gifted Student Classroom Satisfaction Questionnaire*, were shown to provide highly reliable information on the variation of satisfaction within a gifted and talented classroom, thus demonstrating validity.

THE CONTEXT

In 2007, academically selective secondary schooling was re-introduced into the Western Australian public education system by the Department of Education and Training, (DET). There had been a significant investment by DET to provide a successful program to cater for these students, currently referred to as *gifted and talented* in the Western Australian education system. The aim of this study was to construct an instrument that would enable teachers in this selective learning environment to evaluate the effectiveness of the adaptations they have made to their classroom environment, content and pedagogy from reliable and valid data. While much was done to prepare the school, staff and students for this new experience, the need for ongoing evaluation and subsequent improvements had been expressed by the school administrators. Evaluation has been recognised by researchers as a key requirement for the improvement of gifted and talented programs. Barbe and Renzulli (1981) considered the development of a plan of evaluation the fifth most important factor in establishing a school program for the gifted. The questionnaire developed through this research study provided a means for teachers to obtain information on the satisfaction of the gifted and talented students within their class-rooms. Satisfaction is measured in relation to factors which have been identified as essential for achievement within a gifted and talented classroom.

WHY USE RASCH MEASUREMENT?

The Rasch model was the first item response measurement model introduced that applied to intelligence and attainment tests. Rasch showed that the model satisfies the requirements of measurement (Andrich, 1988; Rasch, 1960). It was initially developed as a dichotomous model; that is, for tests where each item had only two responses. For the present survey, constructed with ordered responses for each item, the polytomous Rasch model, introduced by Andrich (1978), was used. While the model was initially developed for the use of Likert scales (Likert, 1932), it is applicable to ordered categories, with each category assigned a numerical score. It is not important that the difference between the categories on the referent scale is of consistent width, only that they are in order along that scale. The Rasch Measurement Model gives the probability of a person n, located on the latent trait β_n, choosing response category x which lies above the kth threshold location τ_{ki}, for an item i with maximum score m, as follows:

$$P\{X_{ni} = x\} = \frac{1}{\gamma_{ni}} \exp\left[\sum_{k=1}^{x} \tau_{ki} + x\left(\beta_n - \delta_i\right) \right]; \tag{1}$$

$$\gamma_{ni} = \sum_{x=0}^{m} \exp\left[\sum_{k=1}^{x} \tau_{ki} + x(\beta_n - \delta_i) \right]; \tag{1a}$$

X_{ni} is the score (rating) person n makes to item i;

x and k are positive integers which correspond to ordered categories of the rating scale;

m is a positive integer corresponding to the maximum possible score (rating);

'exp' represents the number e which is the base of the natural logarithms; and has an approximate value to three decimal places of 2.718;

τ_{ki} is the model parameter which represents the location of the "threshold of response category k on item i;

β_n is the model parameter which represents the location of person n on the latent trait;

δ_i is the model parameter which represents the location of the 'threshold' of response category k on item i;

γ_{ni} represents the 'normalisation constant' or sum of the numerators of Equation (1) and models from the zero score on the rating scale to m. This ensures the probabilities of person n responding to the ordered categories of item i sum to one.

Rasch modelling involves the measurement of a unidimensional trait, referred to as the latent trait, in this case, satisfaction in the gifted classroom. This implies that the responses to every item on the questionnaire are influenced by this one dominant trait, represented on a continuum or linear scale. Equation (1) models the probability of a response in each response category as a function of the person's location on the continuum, given the threshold locations. A student with a very high level of satisfaction has a high probability of responding in the most positive category for each item, with a lower probability of answering with the next most positive response and this continues with a lower probability for each subsequent response. Waugh and Chapman (2005) concluded that Rasch measurement is superior to classical test theory at constructing a linear scale of a latent trait, although there is some dispute in this area, with Fan (1998) failing to find that item response theory produced better tests. Rasch models do, however, provide a standard error of estimation for each item, rather than for the whole survey (Bond & King, 2003), enabling opportunity to increase reliability by adjusting items.

The present study applied item response theory to measure student satisfaction within a selective school classroom. In particular, the Rasch model was applied using the Rasch Unidimensional Measurement Model (RUMM2020) software (Andrich, Sheridan & Luo, 1997–2007). This program provides information that is clearly organised and presented in a variety of tabular and graphical forms.

A VALID CONSTRUCTION PROCESS

To establish the validity of data to be collected with the *Gifted Student Classroom Satisfaction Questionnaire*, it was not sufficient that it reflects the current international literature and best practice relating to both gifted and talented education and measurement. The legitimacy of the questions was also demonstrated when applied in the context for which it was designed. This was achieved in two stages. The first stage was a series of class activities and interviews with gifted and talented students and their staff. The second stage was a pilot of the questionnaire, with which the data were collected to analyse and refine the instrument.

The literature suggested that the use of sub-tests would enhance reliability, by allowing a test subject to focus on one issue at a time (Rea & Parker, 1997).

In order to prioritise issues for evaluation, interviews with a representative from the Department of Education and the school Principal were conducted to identify school and department priorities for an evaluation process. Informed by the literature review and interviews, five subtest headings were developed: physical environment; diversity; difficulty/speed of class; teacher's attitude and class atmosphere.

In order to validate the subtest headings and suggest items, brainstorming sessions were held with two classes of 20–25 students. The students were asked, "What affects your learning in a classroom?" and their responses were listed by the teacher. The two classes were then asked to do ranking exercises with the factors. Each student from the first class was asked to choose the single most important factor from the list and write it on a sticky note. They then formed groups of between four and six students to rank the choices of that group by sticking the notes in order on a piece of poster paper. The results of the groups combined to form a single ranked list for the class. The students in the second class were asked to work as a group to identify and rank the five most important factors under each of the subtest headings.

The pilot questionnaire was developed by combining the responses of these brainstorm sessions with the factors exposed in the literature review. The questionnaire was targeted at the schooling factors that classroom teachers and administrators may have the power to address. The subtest headings for the pilot questionnaire were refined to the following: physical environment/resources; difficulty/speed of program; type of work; teacher; class atmosphere. These changes were the result of problems experienced and suggestions made by students in the categorisation activity.

Individual interviews were conducted with students and staff to test the pilot questionnaire, with particular reference to the wording of the items. Two Year 8 students, not part of the original classes that participated in the brainstorm, completed and commented on the questionnaire. These students were chosen by their teachers for their communication skills, understanding of their peer group and the fact that they had returned a signed consent form. The same interview process was completed with one member of the school administration directing the program, and one Society and Environment teacher of the cohort. The teacher was selected as one who has read widely in the field of gifted and talented education, and has administered his own informal questionnaires to his classes.

In the interview, each participant was given the draft survey and a highlighter, and asked to fill out the questionnaire, imagining they were in one of their classes. They were asked to make a mark next to any ambiguous words or questions for later discussion. The interviewees all made suggestions about the first page of the survey and the example questions. These suggestions were noted and the survey adjusted accordingly.

The pilot survey was given to the students in seven mathematics classes. The 111 student participants were a subset of those enrolled in the Year 8 gifted and talented program in a selective school in 2007. The survey was administered during a normal maths class by the classroom teacher. An analysis of the data led to a process of refinement that produced the *Gifted Student Classroom Satisfaction Questionnaire* in both 45 item and 20 item versions.

The polytomous Rasch model (Rasch, 1960; Andrich, 1978) was used to analyse the response data for the questionnaire. The data were analysed in RUMM2020 (Andrich, Sheridan & Luo, 1997–2007). This package calculated the Person Separation Index, in addition to many other fit statistics, that is analogous to Cronbach's alpha when the Rasch model is applied (Andrich, 1982). The Rasch model estimates the location on the scale for each item, for each respondent, using their total score for the questionnaire. This total score is the sufficient statistic for the model, as it carries all the information available in the assessment of a student's satisfaction. Of the 111 questionnaires to be analysed, 24 of them had missing responses for one or more questions. This does not affect the reliability or functionality of the model for these students, or for others sitting the survey in the future that may omit to answer questions.

RELIABILITY OF THE DATA

The most basic of criteria for data collected through a questionnaire is that it is reliable: consistent results will be achieved if the data are completed repeatedly by the same students under the same conditions (Richardson, 2004). Reliability is a necessary condition of establishing the data from the questionnaire as a valid measure of student satisfaction. As the wording of the items in a questionnaire is crucial to obtaining valid measures, the questions were initially written in language intended for a Year 8 student, by a teacher who was currently teaching that age group. During interviews, students and teachers were asked to identify any language they thought would be unfamiliar, ambiguous or misleading. Changes were made to rectify any of these occurrences. For example, in the first question, the word 'aesthetic' was replaced with 'appearance and tone' after concern was raised in a teacher interview.

The Rasch model provides more detailed information than a single index of reliability, namely measurement error for each person estimate, based on Fisher information. The error in measurement is highest in the regions from which little information is gathered. For this reason, a good assessment is targeted at the respondents about whom the most information is desired. In Figure 1, a display of data from the full length final questionnaire, the horizontal axis represents the overall student satisfaction scale with the most satisfied being on the left. The bars below the axis represent the location of response options in relation to the satis-faction of the student, while the bars above the axis represent the location and frequency of student responses across the satisfaction scale. For this questionnaire, the most information is available at the higher end of the scale, representing those students who are most dissatisfied. This is the most useful information for schools to have in order for them to make positive change in their classrooms. Students with a high dissatisfaction rating may be at risk of underachieving, a major concern for selective schools.

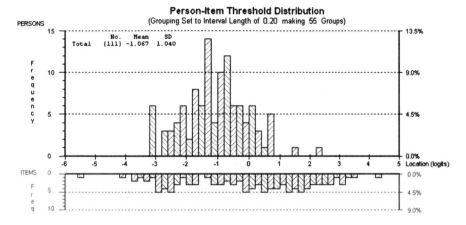

Figure 1. Person-item threshold distribution for the gifted student classroom satisfaction questionnaire (45 items).

Whilst traditionally, reliability has been calculated as a property of a test as a whole, the Rasch model allows for error to be calculated for each person and item location separately. The PSI provides a summary of the true error and measurement error for the whole questionnaire. The PSI ranges between 0 and 1, and it estimates the proportion of variance among ability attributable to the true variance in the trait measured. The PSI for the raw data is 0.911, which means that 9% of the variance in person estimates was due to factors other than those the survey was trying to measure. Through improvements and adjustments to the survey (in particular, by deleting items that did not perform) the PSI was improved to 0.928, an extremely strong reliability. Cronbach's alpha was also calculated, although from the subset of the data for which no responses were missing (sample size = 87). For this subset, the PSI was 0.888, while Cronbach's alpha was 0.892. These scores are similar, and both indicate that the data collected through the questionnaire reliably provide measures of satisfaction.

TESTS OF FIT TO THE RASCH MEASUREMENT MODEL

The fit of the data to the Rasch model is necessary, as it confirms the order within the data that is required to make inferences about that data. The RUMM2020 computer program reports a chi-square statistic and probability that indicates global fit of data to the model. It also reports the chi-square statistic for each item separately. Each item was analysed separately, with those that functioned poorly subsequently eliminated from the questionnaire. A useful tool in this analysis is the item characteristic curve, which maps the actual responses to each item to those expected, given the total data gathered through the questionnaire.

Table 1. Item 9

9	The textbooks we use in this subject are:	excellent.	good.	not very good.	terrible.

Item 9 is an example of a well functioning item. A copy of the question is given in Table 1.

For the item characteristic curve (Figure 2), the scaled student responses have been grouped into three class intervals, with their observed average locations marked by dots. The solid curve represents the expected values of the responses for each location, β, along the satisfaction continuum. The closeness of the dots to the curve for each item indicates a good fit. Item 9 is therefore functioning well within the questionnaire as a whole.

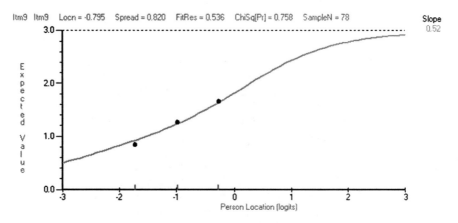

Itm9 Itm9   Locn = -0.795   Spread = 0.820   FitRes = 0.536   ChiSq[Pr] = 0.758   SampleN = 78   Slope 0.52

Figure 2. Item characteristic curve for item 9.

The advantage of using a smaller range in this Figure (and others in this chapter) is that it highlights the fit (or misfit) of data to the model in the range in which the means of persons in Class Intervals are shown. In addition, the item parameter estimates are more accurate in this range, and it is most relevant to the observed responses of the students.

Item 8 (Table 2) is, by comparison, not a good fit, as shown by the item characteristic curve (Figure 3). The three dots do not clearly indicate an increase in response category along the scale, and are not close to the expected value. That is, the observed means depart substantially from their expectation. This tells us that a very satisfied student is no more likely to think they learn better when the teacher uses technology, than a dissatisfied student. Conversely, the item is not a good indicator of classroom satisfaction, and therefore was deleted for further use of the survey. That is not to say that technology has no place in the gifted classroom, only that the evidence collected suggests it is not a factor in student satisfaction.

Table 2. Item 8

8 I learn much better when the teacher uses technology.	I can learn a bit more when the teacher uses technology.	It doesn't affect my learning when the teacher uses technology	I find it distracting when the teacher uses technology.

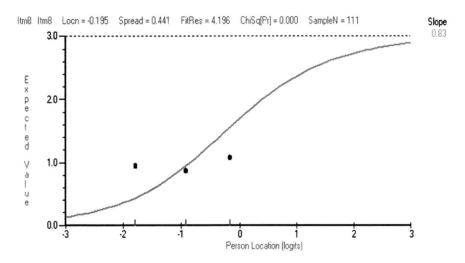

Figure 3. Item characteristic curve for item 8.

Some questions, for example Item 34 (Table 3), exhibited a high chi square and low probability statistics, because they discriminated between students of different satisfaction to a greater extent than expected. Note the steep increase in the dots as compared to the curve. This increases the PSI, thus serving the purpose for which the question was intended. If the four items with the highest chi square were removed from the final *Gifted Student Classroom Satisfaction Questionnaire*, the PSI would drop from 0.928 to 0.911. All four exhibited a similar item characteristic curve to Item 34 (Figure 4). These are therefore valid items for inclusion in the final questionnaire.

Table 3. Item 34

34 This class is:	highly stimulating	pretty interesting	not very interesting	boring

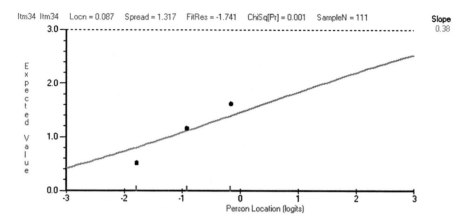

Figure 4. Item characteristic curve for item 34.

The process of elimination of questions from the survey was done no more than four at a time. This was due to the need to calculate the effect of removing the items on the expected probability curve, a function of the total scores. There was also a need to rescore some items due to disordered thresholds, resulting from ambiguous wording in the response categories. This was done using graphical analysis of the category probability curves. The curves show the probability, on the vertical axis, of a student at a point of satisfaction, on the horizontal axis, falling into a response category. When analysing these curves it is important that the response categories are in order (Andrich, 1978; 2005), and that each is the most likely choice at some point. An example of a good category probability curve, Item 12, is shown in Figure 5.

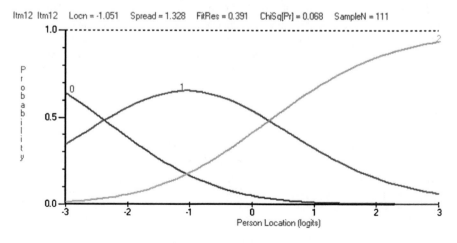

Figure 5. Category probability curve for item 12.

Table 4. Item 12

12 I always finish my homework well within the allocated time	I am given the right amount of time to complete homework tasks	I need longer to finish my homework tasks

In the curve displayed in Figure 5, it is evident that a person with a total satisfaction rating location of less than -2.38 on the scale would be most likely to choose the first response (scoring 0). Likewise, that a person with a total satisfaction above a location of 0.277, would most likely respond in the third category (scoring 2). In the context of the item itself, see Table 4, a person whose total response set indicated that they were highly satisfied, would be likely to consistently complete their homework within the given timeframe. In cases where the category probability curve reveals disordered thresholds (Figure 6), the item does not necessarily need to be deleted, but may be rescored, provided adequate fit after rescoring.

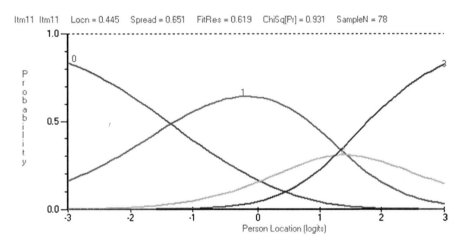

Itm11 Itm11   Locn = 0.445   Spread = 0.651   FitRes = 0.619   ChiSq[Pr] = 0.931   SampleN = 78

Figure 6. Characteristic probability curve for item 11 before rescoring.

Table 5. Item 11

The temperature in this room is:	perfect for working	bearable	quite uncomfortable	a major problem for my learning in this class

On analysis of the question (Table 5), it was decided that if a student had answered 'quite uncomfortable' (the category scored and labelled on the graph with a 2), then it would be 'a major problem for my learning in this class', so the two responses were both scored in the same category, with the resulting category probability curve shown below.

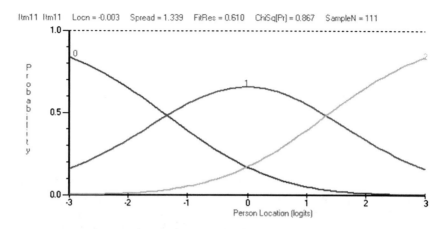

Figure 7. Characteristic probability curve for Item 11 after rescoring.

The process of elimination and rescoring ceased when there were no more items which produced the problems described above. At this point there were 45 items remaining. The *Gifted Student Classroom Satisfaction Questionnaire (45 items)* has excellent power of fit to the Rasch model and a very strong PSI (see Table 6). Graphical inspection of the category probability curves, with the consideration of the chi square and probability statistics for each item, indicated an overall fit to the Rasch model (see Figure 7 as an example).

Table 6. Test-of-fit statistics for the gifted student classroom satisfaction questionnaire (45 items)

ITEM-PERSON INTERACTION

| | ITEMS | | PERSONS | |
	Location	Fit Residual	Location	Fit Residual
Mean	0.000	-0.087	-1.067	-0.290
SD	0.675	1.014	1.040	1.459

ITEM-TRAIT INTERACTION   RELIABILITY INDICES

Total Item Chi Squ   129.56   Separation Index 0.93
Total Deg of Freedom 90.000   Cronbach Alpha   Not Applicable
Total Chi Squ Prob   0.0040

POWER OF TEST-OF-FIT

Power is EXCELLENT
[Based on SepIndex of 0.93]

VALIDITY

Borsboom, Mellenbergh, and van Heerden (2004) asserted that a questionnaire is more likely to produce valid measurements if the researcher places an emphasis on measurement design in the construction of a test, rather than analysing the validity post-data collection. In order to produce the *Gifted Student Classroom Satisfaction Questionnaire*, a rigorous construction process was followed that ensured the questionnaire reflected the literature on the subject, as well as the realities of students' perceptions of the classroom environment. It is important that the instrument measures what it is designed to (Loewenthal, 1996). For this reason, the design of the instrument began with the issues identified in the literature review. In addition, interviews, class activities and data analysis were employed to ensure the questionnaire was designed to match its intentions very closely. Further, by asking key stakeholders in the program, namely students, staff and administrators, what they perceived to be the important factors to assess, the instrument was written in the language and context of its intended audience. On the draft of the instrument, feedback was again sought from the key stakeholders, and the questionnaire was edited on their advice.

While Fraser used four independent judges to classify his items under subscale headings as they perceived fit (Fraser, Anderson & Walberg, 1982), the potential face validity for the subtests of the new instrument was established through classroom activities where the students were asked to categorise the items, given the subtests. Face validity is important as it indicates a subject's perception of the items, a factor which influences how seriously they take the test, and therefore how reliable their responses will be (Cohen & Swerdlik, 1999). In the case of this instrument, analysis of the PSI of the subtests separately was also a key factor in establishing reliability.

Validity is evidenced, not only through a rigorous construction process, but through tests of the data collected through the instrument in the measurement context. To establish the validity of the new data for measuring the attribute of satisfaction, two features had to be demonstrated "(a) the attribute exists and (b) variations in the attribute causally produce variation in the measurement outcomes," (Borsboom et al., 2004, p. 1061). Tests-of-fit of the data to the Rasch measurement model are integral to establishing validity of the results of the measurement process. The use of the Rasch model for analysis meant that the concept of satisfaction was able to be used as a basis for the writing and ordering of the responses. Each item was constructed as a set of responses which were ordered from highest to lowest satisfaction level, as described for example by Stone (2002). A refinement process, using the data package RUMM2020, was undertaken to ensure that the final survey was constructed only of items containing response options that were discriminatory and correctly ordered.

In addition, a pair-wise comparison of categories within each item was undertaken to avoid ambiguity between and establish valid ordering of the categories within each item. The ordering of the categories within each item was established through the inspection of the threshold locations for each item. If the thresholds between response categories are in order, from most to least satisfied on the satisfaction scale, then the students' interpretation of the responses are true to the intention of the survey. The order of the responses was established through the use of an item map.

The use of item response theory as a basis for the analysis of the data provided extensive information about the variations of responses in the questionnaire. This allowed for the construction of an instrument that provides reliable data because items which did not discriminate between students at different points on the satisfaction scale were deleted (Stone, 2003). The resulting set of items clearly separates students along a continuum of satisfaction with their classroom environment.

CONCLUSION

The environment in which an educational program is delivered should be congruent with its goals. Student perceptions of a classroom are highly accurate, and can thus provide useful and meaningful information to improve the learning environment. Learning environments include the students' relationship with their teacher and other students in the class, and also their perceptions of the subject, teaching pedagogy, physical environment and resources. All of these factors have specific implications for the gifted and talented classroom, an educational environment currently experiencing proliferation. While it is widely accepted that student satisfaction within a classroom is an effective predictor of success and achievement, the lack of suitable instruments has restricted measurement in this area.

The primary purpose of this study was to establish a data-based scale that showed data reliability and validity for use in the context of a gifted and talented classroom. In order to construct an instrument from which valid data could be organised on a linear scale, student activities from the literature, which produced and ranked lists of classroom satisfaction factors were used and Rasch analysed. Information was combined to inform the writing of the sample items and organisation of subtests. The content, language and structure were further validated by teacher and student interviews.

A pilot questionnaire was completed by 111 students from the academically selected year group provided data by which the questionnaire could be further refined to form the two final instruments. This was done through a separate analysis of each item and subtest using the RUMM2020 computer program which proved to be very efficient and useful, with poorly functioning items deleted or rescored. Both products of this process, the 45 and 20 item versions of the *Gifted Student Classroom Satisfaction Questionnaire*, were shown to produce data that provided reliable information on the variation of satisfaction within a gifted and talented classroom, thus demonstrating validity.

REFERENCES

Andrich, D. (1978). A rating formulation for ordered response categories. *Psychometrika, 43*, 357–374.
Andrich, D. (1982). An index of person separation in latent trait theory, the traditional KR.20 index, and the Guttman scale response pattern. *Education Research and Perspectives, 9*, 95–104.
Andrich, D. (1988). *Rasch models for measurement*. Beverly Hills, CA: Sage Publications.
Andrich, D., Sheridan, B., & Luo, G. (1997–2007). *RUMM2020*. Perth, Australia: RUMM Laboratory.

Barbe, W. B., & Renzulli, J. S. (1981). *Psychology and education of the gifted* (3rd ed.). New York: Irvington Publishers Inc.

Bond, T. G., & King, J. A. (2003). Measuring client satisfaction with public education II: Comparing schools with state benchmarks. *Journal of Applied Measurement, 4*, 258–268.

Borsboom, D., Mellenbergh, G. J., & van Heerden, J. (2004). The concept of validity. *Psychological Review, 111*(4), 1061–1071.

Callahan, M. C.,Tomlinson, C. A., Hunsaker, S. L., Bland, L. C., & Moon, T. (1995). *Instruments and evaluation designs used in gifted programs.* Research Monograph 95132 for the National Research Center on the Gifted and Talented, University of Connecticut.

Cohen, R. J., & Swerdlik, M. E. (1999). *Psychological testing and assessment* (4th ed.). California, CA: Mayfield Publishing Company.

Embretson, S. E., & Reise, S. P. (2000). *Item response theory for psychologists.* New Jersey, NJ: Lawrence Erlbaum Associates.

Fan, X. (1998). Item response theory and classical test theory: An empirical comparison of their item/person statistics. *Educational and Psychological Measurement, 58*, 357–381.

Fraser, B. J., Anderson, G. J., &Walberg, H. J. (1982). Assessment of learning environments: Manual for Learning Environment Inventory (LEI) and My Class Inventory (MCI) (Third Version). Australia & USA.

Gamoran, A., Nystrand, M., & Berends, M. (1995). An organisational analysis of the effects of ability grouping. *American Educational Research Journal, 32*, 687–715.

Griffin, P., Coates, H., McInnis, C., & James, R. (2003). The development of an extended course experience questionnaire. *Quality in Higher Education, 9*, 259–266.

Likert, R. (1932). A technique for the measurement of attitudes. *Archives of Psychology, 140*, 1–55.

Loewenthal, K. M. (1996.) *An introduction to psychological tests and scales.* London: University College London Press.

Porath, M. (2006a). Differentiation in practice. A resource guide for differentiating curriculum. *Roeper Review, 28*, 181.

Rasch, G. (1960/1980). *Probabilistic models for some intelligence and attainment tests.* (Copenhagen: Danish Institute for Educational Research), expanded edition (1980) with foreword and afterword by B.D. Wright. Chicago: The University of Chicago Press.

Rea, M. R., & Parker, R. A. (1997). *Designing and conducting survey research* (2nd ed.). San Francisco: Jossey-Bass Publishers.

Richardson, J. T. (2004). Methodological issues in questionnaire-based research on student learning in higher education. *Educational Psychology Review, 16*(4), 347–358.

Stone, M. (2002). Quality control in testing. *Popular Measurement, 4*, 15–23.

Stone, M. (2003). Substantive scale construction. *Journal of Applied Measurement, 4*, 282–297.

Walberg, H. J., Singh, R., & Rasher, S. P. (1977). Predictive validity of student perception: A cross-cultural replication. *American Educational Research Journal, 14*(1), 45–49.

Waugh, R. F., & Chapman, E. S. (2005) An analysis of dimensionality using factor analysis (True-score theory) and Rasch measurement: What is the difference? Which method is better? *Journal of Applied Measurement, 1*, 80–99.

Emma Tomkinson and Stephen Humphry
(Graduate School of Education, University of Western Australia)

ADRIAN YOUNG AND ROBERT F. CAVANAGH

10. AN INVESTIGATION OF DIFFERENTIAL NEED FOR PSYCHOLOGICAL SERVICES ACROSS LEARNING ENVIRONMENTS

ABSTRACT

The role of school psychologists in Western Australia has been reviewed a number of times since the establishment of services to schools. Current practice whereby school psychologist allocation to a range of schools is achieved, continues to rely on school student population figures, its socioeconomic index and an appraisal of the school's 'difficulty' level. Psychological services are then allocated accordingly, the decision-making mechanism based on an *ad hoc* conception of school need. The research reported in this paper concentrates on the issue of trying to establish what aspects or characteristics of learning environments constitute a greater or lesser level of need for services and then attempts to measure this need in an objective evidence-based manner. The various elements of school need for psychological services are posited to cluster around constructs extrapolated from the domains of service reported in the international professional literature. These are *characteristics of students, characteristics of schools* and *teacher expertise*. The three constructs constitute the preliminary conceptual framework for the study upon which the empirical investigation was based. The study was conducted in three phases: First, item development, theoretical framework refinement utilising data collected from a questionnaire; second, development of a pool of appropriate items, piloting and trialling; and third, utilising the refined linear scale to measure a sample of schools need for psychological services. Data were obtained from samples of principals, teachers and school psychologists working in two Department of Education and Training (DET) school districts. Data analysis employed the Rasch Rating Scale Model and Analyses of Variance. Data fitting the model confirmed that a uni-dimensional trait was measured. Data-to-model fit was estimated by item difficulty thresholds, individual item fit statistics, the person Separation Index and Principal Components Factors loadings of residuals. The results demonstrated that the linear scale instrument developed in the research provided an authentic measure of school need and that the measures of the phase three schools differed significantly from each other. The empirical findings of the study are discussed in the context of their application in informing decisions about the level of psychological services that should be provided to schools congruent with the psychological needs of their students.

R.F. Cavanagh and R.F. Waugh (eds.), Applications of Rasch Measurement
in Learning Environments Research, 225–241.

INTRODUCTION

The paper begins by examining the necessity for school psychology service delivery to adapt in response to the rapidly changing nature of schooling. Then the function of school psychology is examined from an international perspective which highlights the emergence of newer models of service delivery and the incumbent difficulties in their implementation. The absence of systemic attempts to document the functions of school psychologists in Western Australia and the absence of objective mechanisms to allocate psychologists to government schools is reported. The theoretical model upon which the study is based is presented next, together with the research questions, research methodology and empirical results. The findings are discussed in relation to the practical issue of providing psychological services to schools commensurate with an objective measure of school need.

School psychological services need to evolve to meet the changing needs of schools in the twenty first century. Political, social and economic factors have impacted significantly on the nature of schooling in the developed western economies with greater numbers of single-parent and low-income families, working parents, immigrant groups, violent incidents in schools and the community (Paisley & Borders, 1995; Swerdlik & French, 2000; Sheridan & Gutkin, 2000). The literature on school psychological services is replete with debate on changes in the role and functions of school psychologists (Bradley-Johnson & Dean, 2000; Denholm, Collis, Garton, Hudson, McFarland, MacKenzie and Owens, 1998). Despite these calls for reform they have yet to take hold at a grassroots level in North America (Sheridan & Gutkin, 2000) although in Australian schools, psychologists have become more engaged as evidenced by school-wide approaches to student health and well-being, welfare and discipline and aspects of curriculum development (Oakland, Faulkner & Annan (2002). This is also the case in New Zealand where the educational psychologists' role, in response to local reforms, is now described as an "idealised community psychology" because practitioners serve communities as well as schools, a movement away from an individual student focused model towards one of ecological contextualised practices (Oakland et al., 2002, p. 13).

The literature of psychological services provision in Australia, New Zealand and the United States demonstrates greater similarities than differences. This is due in part to the fact that all countries have immigrant populations, their economies and government school systems are flourishing, they have English as a first language and their respective psychology professions are grounded in the values of Western style psychology (Oakland et al., 2002). School psychological services in all countries are readily identified within the domains posited by Yesseldyke, Dawson, Lehr, Reschly, Reynolds, & Telzrow, (1997). Namely, service provision in Western Australia can be summarised as: behaviour management; psycho-educational assessment of students at educational risk and students eligible for special educational placement; student mental health and well-being; retention and participation of isolated, withdrawn, or truanting students; crisis and risk management; and evaluation of gifted and talented students (Area Manager Student Services personal communications, 2007; Swan Education District Student Services Plan, 2009–11).

However, the Australian context within which school psychologists operate has altered significantly in recent years (Denholm et al., 1998). Consequently, practitioners have needed to fully develop roles in: (a) psycho-educational evaluation and assessment interventions; (b) interventions to optimise educational services to students; (c) consultation and collaboration with parents and school staff; and (d) program development supervision. Nevertheless, there is a lack of information about what school psychologists actually do in providing services to schools and students, although general role descriptions are available. The following sections of this background to the study examine the development and nature of school psychological services internationally against a backdrop of external factors affecting society, government schools and the institution of schooling. It will be argued that it is timely to reconsider how school psychology services are allocated and provide services to those learning environments that are judged to be in greatest need.

THE NATURE OF SCHOOL PSYCHOLOGY

The school psychologist's role has been closely associated with assessing and diagnosing students who have been identified by teachers as not maintaining educational parity with their peers (Murray, 1996). School psychologists are routinely consulted for problem identification (Bardon, 1994; Murray, 1996). This assessment role is present in many services and it reflects the predominant training paradigm that existed from the 1950s to the present. It relies heavily on the medical model. A model which encourages professionals to concentrate on assessing, diagnosing and treating students referred for learning and or behaviour reasons (Sheridan & Gutkin, 2000). A commonly held view is that individual differences can only be understood by means of data obtained from diagnostic instruments whether of the standardised variety or criterion based. Some practitioners are therefore pre-occupied with finding a diagnosis and labelling students rather than obtaining data to be used in collaboration with teachers for the design of interventions. An emphasis on providing assessment-related services results in a cycle of reactive rather than pro-active responses. This in turn reinforces the perception that school psychologists are associated with problem identification rather than problem prevention. By focusing almost exclusively on student-related deficiencies or problems, the medical model leads school psychologists to both ask and answer the wrong questions (Conoley & Gutkin, 1995 cited in Sheridan & Gutkin, 2000). On the other hand, there are legitimate reasons for applying the medical model, viz. to establish eligibility for education support purposes as this is mandated by the legislative framework in Western Australia (The Education Act, 1999) and in the United States (Individuals with Disabilities Education Act amendments, IDEA, P.L. 105–117; U.S. Congress, 1997 cited in Sheridan & Gutkin, 2000).

School psychologists typically spend between 50 to 55 percent of their time on psycho-educational assessment. The remainder is allocated to direct intervention, problem-solving intervention, systems consultation, applied research and program evaluation (Reschly, 2000). Gilman & Gabriel, (2004) concluded that education professionals might well continue to consider school psychologists as largely assessment experts. So the school psychologist roles and functions have been a focus of continued debate with discussion repeatedly concentrating on how the profession can broaden its scope. For example, by moving towards designing and implementing academic and behavioural interventions and moving away from the present emphasis on assessment-related activities (Gresham, 2004; Roberts, Marshall, Nelson, & Albers, 2001 cited in Gilman & Gabriel, 2004). That is, a move towards consultation (Sterling-Turner, Watson, & Moore, 2002 cited in Gilman & Gabriel, 2004) and group and individual counselling (Prout, Alexander, Fletcher, Memis, & Miller, 1993 cited in Gilman & Gabriel, 2004).

The most relevant roles and functions of school psychologists have been the subject of discussion for many years (Passaro, Moon, Wiest, & Wong, 2004). Some have suggested that school psychology practice has not kept up with the debate and is now in need of a broad re-conceptualisation (Gutkin & Conoley, 1990; Sheridan & Gutkin, 2000). Others advocate expanded roles for school psychologists in teaching social and emotional intelligence (Quinn & McDougal, 1998 cited in Passaro et al., 2004) and teacher consultation and collaboration (Wiest & Kriel, 1995, 1997 cited in Passaro et al., 2004). Anticipating the need for a reappraisal of professional practice as school psychology moved into the 21st Century, Yesseldyke, Dawson, Lehr, Reschly, Reynolds, & Telzrow (1997), the National Association of School Psychologists (NASP) produced a blueprint for training and practice. This was intended to enable school psychologists and university departments to work together in developing the practice of school psychology. Blueprint II as it became known, advocated an expanded role for school psychologists in a proactive, preventive paradigm. Similarly, Yesseldyke et al. (1997) identified ten domains for enabling school psychologists to improve service to schools, students, families and agencies involved with children. The ten skills and competencies identified are:

1. data based decision making and accountability;
2. interpersonal communication, collaboration and consultation;
3. effective instruction and development of cognitive/academic skills;
4. socialisation and development of life competencies;
5. student diversity in development and learning;
6. school structure, organisation and climate;
7. prevention, wellness promotion and crisis intervention;
8. home/ school/ community collaboration;
9. research and program evaluation; and
10. legal, ethical practice and professional development.

These show the range of services school psychology can provide but these are not necessarily provided, although they may be provided in varying degrees. Oakland, Faulkner and Annan (2002) suggest the domains of school psychology services are identifiable through the following six delivery systems: (1) individual psycho-educational evaluations of students needing special consideration; (2) direct interventions to promote social, cognitive and emotional development; (3) indirect interventions for students through teachers or parents, for example; (4) research and evaluation to contribute to professional literature upon which practice is based; (5) supervision and administration services such as planning provision in schools and liaising with other agencies and; (6) prevention services in the social, personal and behavioural areas.

Specification of the domains and areas of service have helped to clarify the role of school psychology and reduce the confusion that has inhibited the further development of professional practice and its acceptance in the wider community. Some have suggested that if school psychologists fail to adapt to school reforms, societal and demographic changes in our communities and spend less time on assessment related activities, the profession may not survive (Bardon, 1994). Indeed, the literature over the past decade suggests this is the case and that the future direction of school psychology will be characterised by role expansion (Bradley-Johnson & Dean, 2000; Dwyer & Bernstein, 1998; Fagan, 2002 cited in Gilman & Gabriel, 2004; Gutkin, 1995; Swerdlik & French, 2000). As Gilman & Gabriel (2004) point out, the continuance of these calls for reform indicates that the desired reforms have not yet reached fruition, or more simply, that the profession has not moved quickly enough (Fagan, 2002 cited in Gilman & Gabriel, 2004; Yesseldyke, 2000). There may be a number of reasons for this tardiness including the practitioners' perceived lack of control over their role in schools (Nastasi, Vargas, Bernstein, & Plymert, 1998) or lack of training in assisting schools to tackle and solve large problems (Yesseldyke, 2000). Training is clearly necessary to equip school psychologists with the skills to manage system change (Bradley-Johnson & Dean, 2000).

In summary, there is confusion about the role of school psychologists although there is general agreement that it requires clarification. There is also consistent pressure for reform of practice and delivery of service. The following section exemplifies these issues.

SCHOOL PSYCHOLOGICAL SERVICES IN WESTERN AUSTRALIA

Written policy governing school psychology service provision is lacking in Western Australia, as is contemporary data about the functions of local practitioners and how they spend their time in schools. Overseas professional services are well documented (Gilman & Gabriel, 2004; Oakland et al., 2002). Although psychometric assessment of students' eligibility for education support placement and other specialist facilities is mandated by The Education Act (1999), and relevant legislative frameworks, the medical model orientation that is wide-spread in Western Australian contemporary practice perpetuates the problematic issues discussed by Sheridan & Gutkin (2000) and others (Swerdlik & French, 2000; Oakland et al., 2002). School psychologists elsewhere have shown a clear desire to reduce time spent on psycho-educational assessment (Gilman & Gabriel, 2004; Hosp & Reschly, 2002;

Oakland et al., 2002; Reschly, 2000). No corresponding data are available on Western Australian school psychologists' preferred roles and functions. This is even after the education reforms of the past decade and particularly in light of the Robson Report (2001) of the taskforce on structures, services and resources supporting Government schools. The report recommended that support services be closer to schools and allocated differentially to meet the diverse requirements of school leaders, teachers, students and their communities. These deficiencies in conjunction with more widespread concerns about psychological service provision to schools constitute the rationale for this study.

THEORETICAL FRAMEWORK

The various elements of school need for psychological services are posited to cluster around constructs extrapolated from the domains of service identified by Yesseldyke et al., (1997), the delivery systems described by Oakland et al., (2002) and services delivered in Western Australia (Area Manager Student Services personal communication, 2007; Swan Education District Student Services Plan, 2009–2011; West Coast Education District Student Services Plan 2008). These are characteristics of students, characteristics of schools and teacher expertise. These constituted the preliminary conceptual framework for the study upon which the empirical investigation was based. The operational definitions of the three elements were:

(1) characteristics of students - learning difficulties, disruptive behaviours, truancy, special needs, mental health issues, disabilities, suspension and exclusion data; (2) characteristics of schools - presence of agreed vision, goals, evidence of culture of improvement, staff morale, staff collaboration, willingness to consult with school psychologist, willingness to liaise with parents, inclusive practices, involvement of other agencies and; (3) teacher expertise - knowledge of pedagogy, behaviour management, rapport with students, presence of high expectations for student achievement, skill in identifying student difficulty early.

Research Objectives

The aim of the study was to make explicit those characteristics of schools, teachers and students that constitute concern and hence the need for school psychological services. Then to identify those characteristics of schools, teachers and students that differentiate the need for psychological services between schools. The research questions were: (1) What are school personnel perceptions of a school's need for psychological services? (2) Can a linear scale be constructed to measure teacher perceptions of school need for psychological services?

Methodology

The methodology chosen for this research is quantitative and applies the principles of authentic measurement. These are well documented in the literature on the history and philosophy of science (Hempel, 1966), and more recently in explication of objective measurement (Wright, 1999). However, this approach is not necessarily adhered to in human science research, particularly as in applied psychology and education. When Bond and Fox (2001) reviewed the development of psychological measurement, they concluded that in the absence of deliberate and scientific construction of measures, psycho-social research has made, and will continue to make limited progress. A narrow definition of measurement attributed to Stevens (1946 cited in Bond and Fox, 2001) has influenced the course of research in psychology and in turn on quantitative educational research. To overcome this deficiency, contemporary psychometricians have developed conjoint measurement and probabilistic models (Michell, 1990; Rasch, 1960; and Wright & Masters, 1982). These measurement models offer an alternative to inferential methods and most importantly, ensure development of objective (person-free) measures (Bond & Fox, 2001).

Psychological research has historically utilised Likert-type scales to measure a variety of behaviour traits and attitudes and the numerical scores from these scales are simplistically assigned to objects or events. This led to the practice of assigning numbers to objects in violation of the principles of measurement. That is, for a construct to be measurable, it must have an additive structure (Michell, 1990). Traditionally, ordinal data were obtained and these can only describe a trait in terms of the degree of its presence (e.g. greater than or less than). Alternatively, it is more desirable to have data stated in units to enable plotting on a scale with the distances between scale points being of equal magnitude. For traditional Likert scale instruments, the psychological distance between successive judgement points is not necessarily equal and particular items to a greater or lesser degree may influence this. In addition, the value of distances between the rating categories might differ for each item and for different respondents (Bond & Fox, 2001).

It is clear then, that reliance on the data derived from traditional use of a Likert type scale is insufficient of itself to measure the construct of interest in the present study – the school need for psychological services. Accordingly, the instrument development and refinement methods applied in this research will utilise the Rasch Model (Rasch, 1960) to produce data that are interval and measured in common units. The Rasch Model (Rasch, 1960) takes into account two parameters (i.e. the difficulty of the items and the ability of the persons to affirm the items). The probability of a respondent to affirm an item is considered a logarithmic function of the difference between the person's ability and the item's difficulty. The item difficulty and person ability parameters are both estimated in logits (logarithmic odds). The transformation of raw rating scale scores into these logits enables accurate comparison of data from different respondents and also valid comparison of data on different aspects of the need for school psychology services.

Research Design

The research was conducted in three phases with each phase building upon the preceding phase.

Phase One: A draft questionnaire was piloted with a randomly selected sample of four principals, three school psychologists and six teachers from two DET education districts. The results from this were used to inform the instrument development process in the next phases.

Phase Two: A 120-item pool of appropriate items was developed with multiple items written for each variable in the refined theoretical framework. A four category Likert type scale was used for responses (strongly agree, agree, disagree, and unable to judge). The items were tested in a small pilot study in which principals, school psychologists and teachers responded to the items and commented on clarity of wording and ease of response. Following revision, the instrument was trialled with a sample of 238 teachers in a random sample of twelve schools taken from the two education districts. To ease pressure on respondents, four versions of the instrument were administered with each containing a common set of items. The Rasch Unidimensional Measurement Model (RUMM) computer program (Andrich, Sheridan, Lyne & Luo, 2000) was used to test data-to-model fit. Then, a stepwise process using individual item fit-statistics was applied to construct a parsimonious scale of 35 items that complied with the requirements for objective measurement. The final set of items were chosen for good data-to-model fit, coverage of the construct domain and to have a range of difficulties commensurate with person scores. The decision to construct a scale comprised of 35 items was based on the possibility of multi-dimensionality in the data (the construct is comprised of three major sub-constructs) which might have required three separate scales; poor item-trait interaction leading to loss of items; lack of surety about item difficulties, and the targeting of items to persons.

Phase Three: The *Survey of Need for Psychological Services* (see Appendix A) is a 35-item instrument using a four category response scale (strongly agree, agree, disagree and cannot judge). The 35 items are hierarchically arranged in seven sub-scales with five items in each of the sub-scales. The instrument was administered to principals and teachers in a stratified random sample of 18 schools from two DET education districts. Characteristics such as type of school and school size were represented as far as possible in the sample in the same proportion as they occur in the population of schools in the two districts. Data were analysed using RUMM2020 and differences in teacher scores accounted for by membership of the staff of different schools were examined by an Analysis of Variance.

RESULTS

Phase One: The sample of principals, teachers and school psychologists critically examined the hierarchical arrangement of items within sub-constructs, ambiguity of item wording and content validity of written items within each of the seven sub-constructs. In addition, these respondents were asked to comment on the ease of understanding the survey and making judgements in accordance with the four response categories. This process resulted in changes to wording, some word deletions, some word substitutions and hierarchical re-ordering of some items within sub-constructs.

Phase Two: 238 survey forms were delivered to 12 primary, secondary and education support schools across two DET education districts. 153 completed data sets were collected, a return of 64.3%. Rasch Rating Scale Model analysis indicated that of the 120 items, 11 had elicited data with poor fit to the model (residuals $>\pm2.5$ and/or Chi Square probability statistics $\square 0.05$). These data were removed prior to further analysis. The summary test-of-fit statistics from the subsequent analysis of 109 items are presented in Table 1. In an ideal data-to-model fit, the mean of the fit residuals should be close to zero and the standard deviation close to 1.0. For item-trait interaction, the Chi Square probability value should be <0.05 with lower levels suggesting the data are not unidimensional. The total Chi Square probability for these data is considerably less than 0.05 suggesting multi-dimensionality in the data. The separation index is a measure of the degree to which teacher affirmation locations are distributed along a continuum. An ideal spread distribution of affirmation locations would result in an index approaching 1.0. The statistics presented in Table 1 show the data from the 109 items generally conforms to the requirements of the Rasch Rating Scale Model.

Table 1. RUMM summary test-of-fit statistics for need for psychological services scale

```
                    ITEM-PERSON INTERACTION
===========================================================
              ITEMS                        PERSONS
        Location  Fit Residual      Location  Fit Residual
-----------------------------------------------------------
Mean      0.00       -0.00            0.25       -0.24
SD        1.37        0.76            1.02        1.64
===========================================================
ITEM-TRAIT INTERACTION              RELIABILITY INDICES
-----------------------------------------------------------
Total Item Chi Squ       291.72   Separation Index 0.92
Total Deg of Freedom     218.00      Cronbach Alpha N/A
Total Chi Squ Prob         0.0006
===========================================================
POWER OF TEST-OF-FIT
-----------------------------------------------------------
Power is EXCELLENT
[Based on Separation Index of 0.92]
```

RUMM also produced a person-item location distribution (see Figure 1) displaying location of item thresholds and also location of teacher affirmativeness plotted on the same scale. The respective thresholds for the 109 items are distributed from 'easy' at the left to 'difficult' at the right. The distribution of the relative 'difficulty' of the items closely matches the affirmativeness distribution, indicating that the items present a range of difficulties that match the respondent's view of the need for psychological services in their particular school.

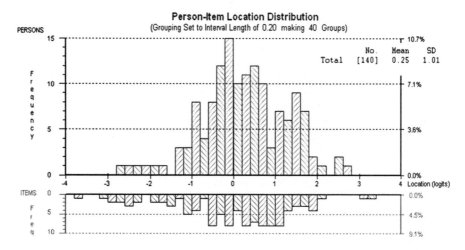

Figure 1. Person-item location distribution.

An Analysis of Variance (ANOVA) in person scores with the person factor of different schools was conducted using RUMM2020. A statistically significant difference between the data from different schools was found (F=3.08; p. < 0.05). This result suggests that the range of items can discriminate between the perceptions of teachers from different school environments of the school's need for psychological services. As indicated previously, a parsimonious scale of the best 35 items from the 109 item survey was constructed for the next phase to ensure precise targeting of items to persons and to reduce the possibility of multi-dimensionality in the Phase Three data.

Phase Three: The 35-item instrument was administered to 10 randomly selected staff in each of 18 target schools (primary, secondary and education support) across two DET school districts. 17 of the 18 schools completed the instrument and 148 data sets were collected out of a possible 180, a return of 82.2%. The summary test-of-fit statistics are presented in Table 2. The distribution of the fit residuals for items and persons are close to ideal and the Separation Index is high. However, the Chi Square probability value was <0.05 again suggesting multi-dimensionality in these data. In general, the data fit the Rasch Rating Scale model well, suggesting a measure of school need for psychological services was constructed.

RUMM also produced a person-item location distribution (see Figure 2) displaying location of item thresholds and also location of persons plotted on the

Table 2. RUMM summary test-of-fit statistics for need for psychological services scale

```
                    ITEM-PERSON INTERACTION
            ITEMS                               PERSONS
         Location  Fit Residual      Location  Fit Residual
------------------------------------------------------------
Mean       0.0000     0.15              0.47         -0.11
SD         1.46       1.06              0.84          1.17
ITEM-TRAIT INTERACTION                RELIABILITY INDICES
------------------------------------------------------------
Total Item Chi Squ    113.36     Separation Index    0.84
Total Deg of Freedom   70.00     Cronbach Alpha       N/A
Total Chi Squ Prob      0.0008
============================================================
POWER OF TEST-OF-FIT
------------------------------------------------------------
Power is GOOD
[Based on Separation Index of 0.84]
```

same scale. The respective thresholds for the 35 items are distributed from 'easy' at the left to 'difficult' at the right. The distribution of the relative 'difficulty' of the items closely matches the teacher distribution, indicating that the items present a range of difficulties that match teacher affirmativeness.

However, five of the items had either high residuals and/or low Chi Square probability values. In any future use of this scale, these items ought to be noted and treated with caution.

Finally, an Analysis of Variance (ANOVA) in person scores with the person factor of different schools was conducted for the 35-item data. A statistically

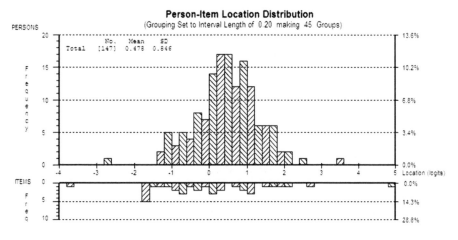

Figure 2. Person-item location distribution.

significant difference between the data from different schools was found ($F=2.00$; p. < 0.05). This result suggests that the final instrument can discriminate between the perceptions of teachers from different schools of the schools' need for psychological services. Comparison of the measured need for psychological services among the three learning environments revealed that, as a category, secondary schools had the greatest need. Primary schools in general had less need with the exception of one primary school with a low socio-economic index. Education support facilities, which might be expected to have a high need for psychological services, given they cater for students with special needs, were shown to be more self sufficient in managing student issues than some of the other schools.

CONCLUSION

Expressions of need for psychological services in the learning environments of primary, secondary and educational support schools were shown to be different. These expressions were the overt manifestations of their individual operational characteristics. The three kinds of learning settings are quite different in many respects. For example: (1) they cater for differing student populations in terms of age and learning needs; (2) the organisation and delivery of teaching programs are in part determined by structures unique to the type of school and; (3) there is an obvious size differential decreasing from secondary through to education support.

Differences such as these were reflected in the theoretical model underpinning the present study and the constituent items of the *Survey of Need for Psychological Services*. Rasch analysis of the data obtained from the *Survey of Need for Psychological Services* provided the means to quantify and measure the sub-constructs extrapolated from contemporary literature on school psychological services delivery. The resulting data fitted the Rasch Rating Scale Model making the instrument available for administration to a wider sample of schools thus adding to the database of quantified school need. As the research intentions were realised, informed decisions could be made about the level of psychological services that should be provided to schools, congruent with the psychological needs of their students.

REFERENCES

Andrich, D., Sheridan, B., Lyne, A., & Luo, G. (2000). *RUMM: A Windows-based item analysis program employing Rasch unidimensional measurement models*. Perth: Murdoch University.

Bardon, J. I. (1994). Will the real psychologist stand up: Is this past a prologue for the future of school psychology? *School Psychology Review, 23*(4), 584–588.

Bond, T. G., & Fox, C. M. (2001). *Applying the Rasch model: Fundamental measurement in the human sciences*. New Jersey, NJ: Lawrence Erlbaum Associates.

Bradley-Johnson, S., & Deans, V. (2000). Role change for school psychology: The challenge continues in the new millennium. *Psychology in the Schools, 37*, 1–5.

Denholm, C., Collis, K., Garton, A., Hudson, A., McFarland, M., MacKenzie, L. et al. (1998). Contemporary practices in a changing climate: Critical issues for Australian educational and developmental psychologists. *The Australian Educational and Developmental Psychologist, 15*(2), 74–93.

Dwyer, K. P., & Bernstein, R. (1998). Mental health in the schools: Linking islands of hope in a sea of despair. *School Psychology Review, 27*, 277–286.

Fraenkel, J. R., & Wallen, N. E. (2003). *How to design and evaluate research in education*. New York: McGraw Hill.

Gilman, R., & Gabriel, S. (2004). Perceptions of school psychological services by education professionals: Results from a Multi-State survey pilot study. *School Psychology Review, 33*(2), 271–286.

Gresham, F. M. (2004). Current status and future directions of school-based behavioural interventions. *School Psychology Review, 33*(3), 326–344.

Gutkin, T. B. (1995). School psychology and health care: Moving service delivery into the twenty-first century. *School Psychology Quarterly, 10*, 236–246.

Gutkin, T. B., & Conoley, J. C. (1990). Conceptualising school psychology from a service delivery perspective: Implications for practice, training and research. *Journal of School Psychology, 28*, 203–223.

Hempel, C. G. (1966). *Philosophy of natural science*. New Jersey, NJ: Prentice-Hall Inc.

Hosp, J. L., & Reschly, D. J., (2002). Regional differences in school psychology practice. *School Psychology Review, 31*(1), 11–24.

Michell, J. (1990). *An introduction to the logic of psychological measurement*. New Jersey, NJ: Lawrence Erlbaum Associates.

Murray, B. A. (1996). The principal and the school psychologist: Partners for students. *The School Psychology Bulletin, 1*, 95–99.

Nastasi, B., Vargas, K., Bernstein, R., & Plymert, K. (1998). Mental health programming and the role of the school psychologist. *School Psychology Review, 27*, 217–232.

Oakland, T., Faukner, M., & Annan, J. (2002). School psychology in four English-speaking countries: Australia, Canada, New Zealand and the United States. In C. Frisby & C. Reynolds (Eds.), *Comprehensive handbook of multicultural school psychology*. New York: Wiley and Sons.

Paisley, P., & Borders, L. D. School counselling: An evolving specialty. *Journal of Counselling and Development, 74*(2), 150–154.

Passaro, P. D., Moon, M., Weist, D. J., & Wong, E. H. (2004). A model for school psychology practice: Addressing the needs of students with emotional and behavioural challenges through the use of an in-school support room and reality therapy. *Adolescence, 39*(155), 503–513.

Rasch, G. (1960/1980). *Probabilistic models for some intelligence and attainment tests*. Copenhagen: Danish Institute for Educational Research, 1960. (Expanded edition. Chicago: The University of Chicago Press, 1980)

Reschly, D. J., (2000). The present and future status of school psychology in the United States. *School Psychology Review, 29*(4), 507–522.

Robson, A. (2001). *Investing in Government schools: Putting children first*. Report of the taskforce on structures, services and resources supporting Government schools. W.A. Department of Education.

Sheridan, S. M., & Gutkin, T. B. (2000). The ecology of school psychology: Examining and changing our paradigm for the 21st century. *School Psychology Review, 29*(4), 485–502.

Swan Education District Student Services Plan. (2004). *Optimising student services in schools*. Perth: Department of Education and Training.

Swerdlik, M. E., & French, J. L. (2000). *School psychology training for the 21st century: Challenges and opportunities. School Psychology Review, 29*(4), 577–587.

West Coast Education District Student Services Plan. (2007–2008). Perth: Department of Education and Training.

Wright, B. D. (1999). Fundamental measurement in psychology. In S. E. Embretson & S. L. Hershberger (Eds.), *The new rules of measurement: What every psychologist and educator should know* (pp. 65–104). New Jersey, NJ: Lawrence Erlbaum Associates.

Wright, B. D., & Masters, G. N. (1982). *Rating scale analysis: Rasch measurement*. Chicago: MESA.
Yesseldyke, J. (2000). Commentary déjà vu all over again: What will it take to solve big instructional problems? *School Psychology Review, 29*, 575–576.
Yesseldyke, J., Dawson, P., Lehr, C., Reschly, D. J., Reynolds, M., & Telzrow, C., (1997). *School psychology: A blueprint for training and practice II*. Bethesda, MD: National Association of School Psychologists.

Adrian Young and Robert F. Cavanagh
(Curtin University of Technology, Western Australia)

APPENDIX A

SURVEY OF NEED FOR PSYCHOLOGICAL SERVICES

Your school is:

INSTRUCTIONS:

Please do NOT write your name just remember the number in the top right corner.

If you strongly agree with the statement, please circle 4.

If you agree with the statement, circle 3.

If you disagree with the statement, circle 2.

If you can't judge, circle 1.

Teaching	Strongly agree	Agree	Disagree	Can't Judge
1.Teachers cater for individual differences	4	3	2	1
2.Student progress is documented regularly	4	3	2	1
3.Teachers know what each student needs	4	3	2	1
4.Teaching and learning produces high achievement	4	3	2	1
5.Test results are excellent	4	3	2	1

Development of academic skills	Strongly agree	Agree	Disagree	Can't Judge
6.Students need extra help	4	3	2	1
7.Students like to learn	4	3	2	1
8.Students respond well	4	3	2	1
9.Students are attentive	4	3	2	1
10.Students access study skills training	4	3	2	1

School development of socialisation and life skills	Strongly agree	Agree	Disagree	Can't Judge
11.Student attitudes are important	4	3	2	1
12.The school rewards appropriate behaviour	4	3	2	1
13.Behavioural issues are well managed	4	3	2	1
14.There are few discipline problems	4	3	2	1
15.Students quickly resolve conflict	4	3	2	1

Inclusivity in learning and development	Strongly agree	Agree	Disagree	Can't Judge
16.All classes have students with learning difficulties	4	3	2	1
17.We welcome students from diverse backgrounds	4	3	2	1
18.Teachers celebrate the school's diversity	4	3	2	1
19.New students can be seen by the psychologist	4	3	2	1
20.We use the psychologist's ideas for our programs	4	3	2	1

Prevention services and wellness promotion	Strongly agree	Agree	Disagree	Can't Judge
21.There is a need for child protection training	4	3	2	1
22.Programs have improved student well-being	4	3	2	1
23.The school has suicide prevention strategies	4	3	2	1
24.Parents utilise healthy eating programs	4	3	2	1
25.The school coordinates mental health services	4	3	2	1

Home/school/community collaboration	Strongly agree	Agree	Disagree	Can't Judge
26.Parents are welcomed into the school	4	3	2	1
27.The school keeps the community informed	4	3	2	1
28.The community helped develop the school ethos	4	3	2	1
29.Parents are active in the School Council	4	3	2	1
30.Teachers find parents easy to engage	4	3	2	1

School climate	Strongly agree	Agree	Disagree	Can't Judge
31.Teachers strive for school improvement	4	3	2	1
32.Teachers provide agenda items for staff meetings	4	3	2	1
33.Leadership is shared among teachers	4	3	2	1
34.Teacher/psychologist consultation is in place	4	3	2	1
35.Psychological services improve school climate	4	3	2	1

SIVANES PHILLIPSON

11. EVALUATING TERTIARY STUDENTS' PERCEPTIONS OF THE ENGLISH TEACHING ASSISTANTS' ROLE IN TEACHING AND LEARNING

A Rasch Analysis

ABSTRACT

This chapter describes the development, piloting and validation of an instrument that evaluates students' perceptions of English Teaching Assistant's (ETA) role in teaching and learning situations in a teacher-education institution in Hong Kong. The chapter consists of two parts: a pilot study and the validation study of the *Student Evaluation of English Teaching Assistant Role Scale* (SETARS). Participants in the pilot study were 153 pre-service student-teachers who were asked to rate their agreement to 20 statements related to two ETAs' role in and out of classroom situations on a 4-point category; from 1 (Strongly Disagree) to 4 (Strongly Agree), with an additional category of "Not-Applicable". The scale fitted the Rasch model well with the exception of two items. These items were removed from the scale for the validation study. The "Not Applicable" category was found to cause high missing values, and hence, removed from the scale. The validation study was carried out on 294 pre-service student-teachers' perceptions of eight ETAs across courses. Although the overall item and person fit and reliability of the tool was acceptable, the infit and outfit t values for a number of the items were larger than desired ($-2.00 < t < +2.00$). It was suspected that this anomaly existed because the scale was meant to measure students' perceptions of one or at the most two ETA(s) in a teaching and learning situation. Accordingly, the individual items spread and reliability improved when data were separately analysed for individual ETAs; with overall item spread reliability ranging from .90 to .94, and individual item's mean square ranged between .20 to 1.7, and standardised t generally being within the acceptable range. This shows that the SETARS is a valid and reliable unidimensional measure of students' perceptions of specific English Teaching Assistants' (ETAs) role in teaching and learning situations in Hong Kong. The chapter concludes with a discussion of how the SETARS can help educators to optimise students' learning environment by evaluating the perceived teaching and learning assistance given by English Teaching Assistants.

R.F. Cavanagh and R.F. Waugh (eds.), Applications of Rasch Measurement in Learning Environments Research, 243–258.

INTRODUCTION

Recent waves of Fullbright and other charity foundations' sponsored American English Teaching Assistants' (ETAs) integration into tertiary module teaching and learning in Asian countries, has raised concerns whether the ETAs are welcomed by local students. This movement is in line with increasing numbers of teaching assistants (TAs) in schools and tertiary institutions as part of the changes for a constructive teaching and learning environment in the UK and other developed countries around the world. In the UK for example, the key objective of recruiting teaching assistants is to remodel the teaching workforce in order to reduce the heavy workload of the teachers (Wilson & Bedford, 2008). Added value to student learning has also been the motive for integration of teaching assistance into teaching and learning (Minondo, Meyer, & Xin, 2001; Wilson & Bedford, 2008).

The TAs' role in teaching and learning has been a key issue. Previous studies have indicated that TAs have performed a variety of educational support roles. Minondo et al. (2001) identified five major role components for TAs in inclusive education: (a) instructional; (b) school support; (c) liaison; (d) personal support; and (e) one-to-one in-class support. A review of research on TAs showed that there has been a tendency to focus on investigation of TAs' impact on teachers' work and their perception of it (Bedford, Jackson, & Wilson, 2008; Wilson & Bedford, 2008). Research work has also concentrated on the TAs' role at a classroom level rather than both in class and out of class (Alaie, 2008; Blatchford, Russell, Bassett, Brown, & Martin, 2007; Downer, 2007; O'Neal, Wright, Cook, Perorazio, & Purkiss, 2007).

Furthermore, a number of studies on the TAs' role have found no evidence that the presence of TAs in subject teaching and learning have a measurable effect on student attainment and outcomes (Blatchford et al., 2007; Muijs & Reynolds, 2003). The Blatchford study, however, concluded that a TAs' presence in the classroom increased pupils' interaction with the teacher by focusing attention to teachers' teaching or tasks at hand. On the other hand, studies have found that students' performance in specific language skills improved with TAs' help. For example, students were found to make progress in English word recognition (Downer, 2007) and in early phonic reading (Savage & Carless, 2008). Teaching assistants' role in terms of language skills seemed to be important and effective especially in an early primary setting.

Although there is a widespread acceptance of the central role that TAs play in teachers' and students' needs, little has been explored about students' perceptions of a TAs' role in the overall subject teaching and learning, and in particular with help through English language, whether it is in or out of class support. Hence, this study aimed to fill the existing gap in research by developing an appropriate tool to investigate students' perception of ETAs' role in a tertiary context.

ENGLISH TEACHING ASSISTANT (ETA) PROGRAMME

Each year, sixteen graduates of universities across the U.S.A. are selected and sponsored through the Fullbright programme and other numerous private and

244

university grants funding as ETAs in a teacher-education institution in Hong Kong. The ETAs role is to assist with English language and cross cultural enhancement in teaching and learning activities across the institution. The role that the ETAs play, whether in formal teaching and learning situations or in the informal extra-curricula activities, has been considered as one that is important to student-teachers' excellence in their own educational programmes. Such presumption is yet to be ascertained at the student level. Hence, the purpose of this study to examine students' perception of ETAs' role in their tertiary learning situations, in relation to the broad aim of the ETA placement in the higher education setting, is important for further fine tuning of ETAs' role in students' learning.

METHOD

This study was implemented in two phases: a pilot study and a validation study. The method and results for each study is described separately.

THE PILOT STUDY

Participants

A total of 153 students from course units that involved two of the 16 ETAs participated in this study. These students were first to third year students in four different course units in a four year Bachelor of Education programme at a teacher-education institution in Hong Kong. Among the 153 students, the number of students from four modules was 53, 22, 65, and 13, respectively.

Development of Measure and Analysis

A scale was developed to evaluate students' perceptions of the ETAs' role in teaching and learning situations in relation to the purpose of their placement in the institution. In order to determine the items in the tool, a set of group interviews were conducted of ETAs, students and professors involved in the course programmes. The ETAs were asked to describe their understanding of their prescribed role in teaching and learning, whilst the professors and students were asked to describe their expectations of the ETAs in their module of teaching and learning. A list of descriptions and expectations of the ETAs' role was generated, and from this list, the *Student Evaluation of English Teaching Assistant Role Scale* (SETARS) was developed. The scale was comprised of the ETAs' role both within and out of the classroom. In developing the questionnaire, several crucial elements were considered including lay out of questionnaire, length of questionnaire, and statements' design, with the main aim being simplicity and clarity.

The complete scale consisted of a 20-item Likert-scale questionnaire and four item open-ended qualitative response questionnaire. This paper concentrates only on the former part of the scale. The Likert-scale varied from 1 (Strongly Disagree) to 4 (Strongly Agree). A fifth response category of "Not Applicable" was included to allow some flexibility in response for the students, and this was scored as missing data. Two examples of the items in the questionnaire are: "I am encouraged to talk when the ETAs lead the discussions in class" and "I learn when the ETAs correct my English errors in class." The scale was group administered at the end of each individual module during the first semester of the academic year.

A descriptive analysis, using SPSS version 17.0, was obtained for a general overview of the results, and Rasch analysis (Bond & Fox, 2007; Rasch, 1960, 1980, 1993) using WINSTEP version 3.61.2, was used to determine the fit and reliability of the items and the general performance of the category structures of the scale. Linacre's (2004) eight guidelines for optimising rating scales were used as the benchmark by which the categories in the scales were evaluated for their performance. Linacre intended the guidelines as a useful "starting point" (p. 276) for the researcher in attempting to understand the functioning of the categories within the pilot and validation scale. The guidelines, however, are not to be used as the final judge of the effectiveness of the scales.

RESULTS

Rasch Analysis of Pilot Study

Rasch analysis results showed an overall item fit measure of 1.00 for infit mean square and .99 for outfit mean square, similar to Rasch modelled expectations of 1.00 (see Table 1). The infit and outfit t values were both -.10 with standard deviations of 1.60, also showing acceptable values. The item separation reliability was .92 indicative of less than desired item spread on the measurement scale. The person ability estimate mean of 1.45 showed that this sample of 153 students found the items relatively easy for them to respond to, fitting with the aim of the researchers to incite confidence in students to report on the ETAs' role in and outside the classroom. The person fit measure, with an infit mean square of 1.01 and outfit mean square of 1.00, were also similar to Rasch modelled expectations of 1.00. The t values of -.30 for both infit and outfit were also indicative of acceptable fit as was the person separation reliability of .87 (Bond & Fox, 2007).

A detailed look at each item performance on the scale (Table 2) showed that the items generally performed well together as indicated by the point measure correlation of more than .40, except for one item – Item 17. Item 17: "I consulted with the ETAs to discuss my individual written work" had large mean squares and t values. The semantics of this item seemed to emphasise students' own work rather than the ETAs' role. Another item – Item 18: "I think the ETAs should be more familiar with the module content" also had less than satisfactory fit values and did not seem to fit in with the aim of the tool in evaluating the ETAs' role in module teaching and learning. Rasch analysis was computed without these two items and results showed an improved scale, and hence, the final scale for validation was an 18-item questionnaire.

Table 1. Summary of item and person estimates for SETARS 20 measured items of pilot study

Measure summary	Item	Person
Mean (SD adjusted)	.00 (0.62)	1.45 (1.48)
Reliability of estimate	.92	.87
Fit statistics		
Infit Mean Square		
Mean (SD)	1.00 (.22)	1.01 (.72)
Infit *t* (SD)	−.10 (1.60)	−.30 (2.10)
Outfit Mean Square		
Mean (SD)	.99 (.23)	1.00 (.73)
Outfit *t* (SD)	−.10 (1.60)	−.30 (2.10)

Table 2. Fit and pm correlation statistics for SETARS 20 measured items of pilot study

Items	Difficulty estimate	Error estimate	Infit mean square	Infit t	Outfit mean square	Outfit t	Point measure correlation
Item1	−1.51	.17	.88	−1.15	.86	−1.05	.61
Item2	1.20	.15	1.08	.74	1.16	1.31	.59
Item3	−.59	.17	.77	−1.96	.74	−2.13	.65
Item4	.43	.16	1.04	.33	1.05	.41	.62
Item5	.06	.17	.76	−2.00	.72	−2.27	.64
Item6	.33	.17	0.82	−1.46	0.82	−1.37	.63
Item7	.14	.17	.90	−.73	0.89	−.81	.64
Item8	−.55	.17	1.16	1.26	1.20	1.42	.57
Item9	.56	.16	1.17	1.28	1.18	1.36	.61
Item10	.00	.17	.90	−.80	.89	−.77	.70
Item11	.11	.18	0.88	−.81	.91	−.56	.67
Item12	−.44	.17	0.88	−.98	.85	−1.13	.69
Item13	.08	.17	0.86	−1.08	.84	−1.19	.68
Item14	.03	.17	.90	−.79	.86	−1.05	.68
Item15	−.11	.17	0.78	−1.77	.77	−1.83	.73
Item16	.50	.17	.90	−.76	.86	−1.07	.69
Item17	.99	.17	1.49	3.42	1.54	3.61	.55
Item18	.09	.17	1.59	3.84	1.56	3.50	.38
Item19	−.24	.17	1.07	.57	1.03	.29	.58
Item 20	−1.08	.17	1.18	1.51	1.13	1.01	.52

Figure 1 shows the category probability curves of responses in the pilot scale. The structure of the four categories show a peak at category 3 (Agree). The calibration structure increased monotonically and orderly, and the infit and outfit measures for category structure showed acceptable values. This showed the category structure of the four point Likert scale generally fit the purpose of the scale. However, the fifth response of "Not Applicable" was found to be not useful as it resulted in a high count of missing values. The final scale prepared for validation thus, was an 18-item questionnaire with a 4-point Likert scale of 1 (Strongly Disagree) to 4 (Strongly Agree) only.

Pilot Data of SETARS - Category Probability Curves

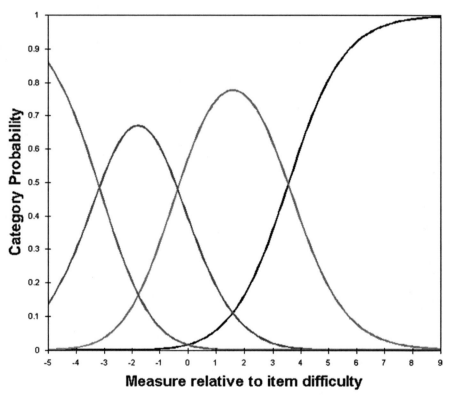

Figure 1. Category probability curves of 4 responses (with an extra non-applicable category) to item scale.

Descriptive Results of Pilot Study

Table 3 shows the mean and standard deviations of the student responses to the pilot questionnaire. There was generally a positive response from students in terms of the ETAs' role in and outside the classroom with mean responses ranging between

2.65 to 3.23. In particular, students were especially in favour of ETAs' participation more in class (M = 3.23, SD = .62), ETA's role in correcting their English errors in class (M = 3.10, SD = .66), and ETAs' role in sharing their cultural and educational experiences during class sessions (M = 3.23, SD = .62). Students also believed that ETAs had the same authority as their lecturer (M = 3.10, SD = .66), which showed the extent of importance students give to the ETAs role in module teaching and learning.

Table 3. Mean and standard deviation of responses to SETARS 20 measured items of pilot study

Items	Responses	Mean	SD
Item 1: I like the ETAs' participation in class sessions.	149	2.65	.69
Item 2: I believe the ETAs have the same authority as the lecturers.	150	3.11	.58
Item 3: I am encouraged to talk when the ETAs lead the discussions in class.	143	2.85	.66
Item 4: I pay more attention in class when the ETAs lead the discussions.	143	2.95	.57
Item 5: I pay more attention in class when the ETAs are co-teaching.	136	2.87	.59
Item 6: I learn when the ETAs correct my English errors in class.	134	2.92	.63
Item 7: I am encouraged when the ETAs correct my English errors in class.	148	3.10	.66
Item 8: I feel comfortable having study discussions with the ETAs out of the class.	141	2.82	.70
Item 9: I meet more often in my study groups when an ETA participates in our discussion.	144	2.97	.68
Item 10: I learn from the study discussions with the ETAs out of the class.	124	2.93	.65
Item 11: I learn when the ETAs correct my written work.	147	3.07	.65
Item 12: I think the ETAs are very helpful out of class.	144	2.95	.64
Item 13: I think the ETAs are easily reachable out of class.	145	2.96	.66
Item 14: I found that the ETAs are able to answer my questions about the module content.	145	2.99	.66
Item 15: I am able to more easily understand the module work in English because of the ETAs' assistance.	137	2.84	.68
Item 16: I am able to easily complete the module work in English because of the ETAs' assistance.	124	2.69	.77
Item 17: I consulted with the ETAs to discuss my individual written work.	138	2.93	.67
Item 18: I think the ETAs should be more familiar with the module content.	148	3.02	.63
Item 19: I want the ETAs to participate more in class.	150	3.23	.63
Item 20: I want the ETAs to participate more in class through sharing their life experience/American culture.	150	3.23	.63

THE VALIDATION STUDY

Participants

A total of 294 pre-service student-teachers from course units that involved eight of the 16 ETAs participated in this study. These students were of first to fourth year students from ten course units in a 4-year Bachelor of Education programme, and of a second semester course unit in one-year Postgraduate Diploma in Education programme at the same teacher-education institution in Hong Kong. Some of these students had responded to the pilot version of this study's scale.

RESULTS

Rasch Analysis of Validation Study

Rasch analysis results showed overall item fit measures of 1.00 for infit mean square and 1.01 for outfit mean square, very close to Rasch modelled expectations of 1.00 (see Table 4). The infit and outfit *t* values were -.10 and zero respectively with standard deviations of 2.00, also showing acceptable values. The item separation reliability was .97 indicative of a good spread of items on the measurement scale. The person ability estimate mean of .73 showed that this sample of 294 students found the items quite easy to respond to, fitting with the aim of the researchers to incite confidence in students to report on the ETAs' role in and outside the classroom. The person fit measures, with infit and outfit mean square of 1.01, were also similar to Rasch modelled expectations of 1.00. The *t* values of -.20 for both infit and outfit were also indicative of acceptable fit as was the person separation reliability of .92.

Table 4. Summary of item and person estimates for SETARS 18 measured items of validation study

Measure summary	Item	Person
Mean (SD adjusted)	.00 (0.60)	.73 (1.65)
Reliability of estimate	.97	.92
Fit statistics		
Infit Mean Square		
Mean (SD)	1.00 (.18)	1.01 (.60)
Infit *t* (SD)	−.10 (2.00)	−.20 (1.80)
Outfit Mean Square		
Mean (SD)	1.01 (.21)	1.01 (.60)
Outfit *t* (SD)	.00 (2.00)	−.20 (1.80)

A detailed look at each item performance on the scale (Table 5) showed that the items generally performed well together as indicated by the point measure correlation of more than .40. All items had acceptable mean square values (.50 <

MSQ <1.50). However, the infit and outfit t values for a number of the items were larger than desired (-2.00 < t <+2.00). Items 2, 15, 16 and 18, in particular, had quite large t values. Rasch analysis was computed without these items, one at a time, to see whether removal of any of these items improved the scale at all. It was found that the removal of an item only worsened the fit of the other items and did not improve the overall fit of the scale. The decision was hence made to leave the items as they were in the scale. Furthermore, the multidimensionality diagnosis showed that the scale with 18 items showed a highly unidimensional content with 71% of the variance explained by the existing items.

Table 5. Fit and correlation statistics for SETARS 18 measured items of validation study

Items	Difficulty estimate	Error estimate	Infit mean square	Infit t	Outfit mean square	Outfit t	Point measure correlation
Item1	−1.02	.10	.90	−1.31	.90	−.95	.70
Item2	1.17	.10	1.31	3.53	1.30	3.11	.60
Item3	−.54	.10	1.04	.57	1.08	.88	.66
Item4	.19	.10	.93	−.84	.90	−1.17	.72
Item5	.12	.10	.86	−1.79	.85	−1.85	.74
Item6	.37	.10	1.04	.52	1.04	.52	.69
Item7	.29	.10	.92	−.94	1.00	.08	.72
Item8	−.06	.09	.82	−2.31	.81	−2.22	.75
Item9	.61	.09	1.07	.89	1.08	.86	.68
Item10	.72	.09	1.05	.64	1.10	1.04	.69
Item11	.51	.09	1.05	.61	1.03	.35	.70
Item12	−.12	.09	.90	−1.24	.96	−.44	.72
Item13	.12	.10	1.17	2.00	1.21	2.23	.65
Item14	−.23	.10	.80	−2.68	.78	−2.76	.76
Item15	−.11	.10	.72	−3.83	.71	−3.71	.78
Item16	.05	.10	.75	−3.34	.73	−3.48	.77
Item17	−.80	.10	1.24	2.85	1.32	3.17	.60
Item18	−1.27	.10	1.38	4.33	1.47	4.26	.54

Table 6 shows the category structure of the responses in the validation scale, judged using Linacre's (2004) eight guidelines for optimising rating scales. There were more than ten observation counts for each category with a distribution peak in the middle at category 3 (Agree). The average measures increased monotonically and orderly, and the outfit measures for category structure showed acceptable values. This showed that the category structure of the four-point Likert scale generally fit the purpose of the scale (Figure 2).

Table 6. Rating scale category effectiveness for 4-point response category in the SETARS using eight guidelines set out by Linacre(2004)

No.	Guidelines	SETARS (18 items)*
1	At least 10 observation of each category	Category 1 = 390 (7%) Category 2 = 1652 (32%) Category 3 = 2068 (40%) Category 4 = 1079 (21%)
2	Regular observation distribution	Observation distribution triangular peaked at category 3
3	Average measures advance monotonically with category	Category 1 = -1.75 Category 2= -.29 Category 3 = .95 Category 4 = 2.47
4	OUTFIT mean-square less than 2.0	Category 1 = 1.12 Category 2 = 1.04 Category 3 = .91 Category 4 = 1.00
5	Step calibrations advance	Category 1 = NONE Category 2 = -2.42 Category 3= .13 Category 4 = 2.29
6	Ratings imply measures, and measures imply ratings	Coherence M->C C->M Category 1 = 73% 23% Category 2 = 60% 60% Category 3 = 56% 75% Category 4 = 76% 45%
7&8	Step difficulties advance by at least 1.4 logits and by less than 5.0 logits	Category 1 = -3.58 Category 2 = -1.18 Category 3 = 1.24 Category 4 = 3.47

*Categories: 1.Strongly Disagree, 2. Disagree, 3. Agree, 4. Strongly Agree.

SETARS 18-item Scale

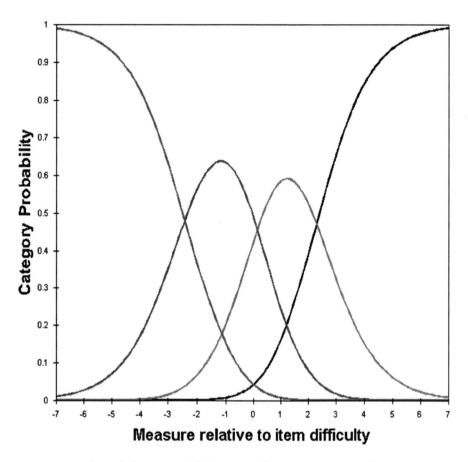

Figure 2. Category probability curves of four responses to item scale.

Descriptive Results of Validation Study

Table 7 shows the mean and standard deviations of the student responses to the validation questionnaire. There was generally a positive response from students in terms of the ETAs' role in and outside the classroom, with mean responses ranging between 2.34 to 3.11. In particular, students were especially in favour of ETAs' participation in class ($M = 3.10$, $SD = .84$) and ETAs' role in sharing their cultural and educational experiences during class sessions ($M = 3.11$, $SD = .77$). Item 2, where students agreed whether the ETAs had the same authority as the lecturers had the lowest mean, far below the pilot response.

Table 7. Mean and standard deviation of responses to SETARS 18 measured items of validation study

	Responses	Mean	SD
Item 1: I like the ETAs' participation in class sessions.	293	3.10	.84
Item 2: I believe the ETAs have the same authority as the lecturers.	293	2.34	.84
Item 3: I am encouraged to talk when the ETAs lead the discussions in class.	294	2.86	.78
Item 4: I pay more attention in class when the ETAs lead the discussions.	290	2.67	.85
Item 5: I pay more attention in class when the ETAs are co-teaching.	292	2.69	.83
Item 6: I learn when the ETAs correct my English errors in class.	292	2.64	.88
Item 7: I am encouraged when the ETAs correct my English errors in class.	288	2.67	.83
Item 8: I feel comfortable having study discussions with the ETAs out of the class.	294	2.84	.90
Item 9: I meet more often in my study groups when an ETA participates in our discussion.	293	2.56	.91
Item 10: I learn from the study discussions with the ETAs out of the class.	293	2.55	.93
Item 11: I learn when the ETAs correct my written work.	292	2.61	1.04
Item 12: I think the ETAs are very helpful out of class.	293	2.81	.90
Item 13: I think the ETAs are easily reachable out of class.	289	2.72	.89
Item 14: I found that the ETAs are able to answer my questions about the module content.	293	2.81	.81
Item 15: I am able to more easily understand the module work in English because of the ETAs' assistance.	292	2.78	.84
Item 16: I am able to easily complete the module work in English because of the ETAs' assistance.	292	2.71	.84
Item 17: I want the ETAs to participate more in class.	293	2.99	.80
Item 18: I want the ETAs to participate more in class through sharing their life experience/American culture.	294	3.11	.77

Upon closer scrutiny of the frequency of responses, it was found that 50.2% of the students did not agree that ETAs had the same authority as the lecturers. The standard deviations for the means were also larger than the pilot study – indicative of differences in student responses, probably according to the eight different ETAs in this study. Figure 3 shows the distribution of student responses across the eight ETAs. There was a similar pattern of student responses for most of the ETAs except for one ETA (ETA E) in six items that had to do with in-class teaching and out of class study discussions. This observation highlighted the fact that the

SETARS was meant to measure students' perceptions of one particular, or at the most two, ETAs in relation to a teaching and learning situation. The pilot study was based on only two ETAs, and therefore, it makes sense that, in view of the validation study, the SETARS's data must be analysed for individual or co-assisting ETAs, in relation to the purpose of their placement within a teaching and learning situation.

Rasch analysis generated for each ETA group showed improved individual item fit and spread indicating that the SETARS should be used and analysed for specific ETAs as students are responding to those ETA's teaching and learning competency. For example, Figure 4 and 5 show the bubble charts of good fitting items for ETA C and ETA F. Similar spreads were found for all of the eight ETAs, with overall item spread reliability ranging from .90 to .94, and individual items' mean square ranged between .20 to 1.70, and standardised t generally being within the acceptable range. It is worth noting that many of the same students in the sample evaluated across ETAs and courses, highlighting the robustness of invariance of the items in the scale.

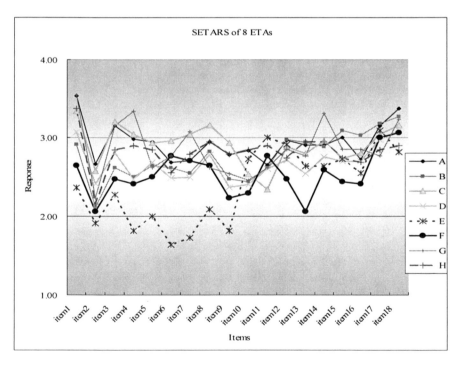

Figure 3. Distribution of student responses across the eight ETAs in the validation study.

items

t Infit Zstd

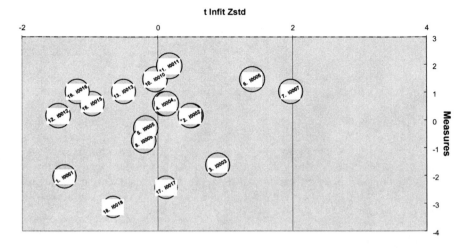

Figure 4. Bubble chart of SETARS' items for ETA C in the validation study.

items

t Infit Zstd

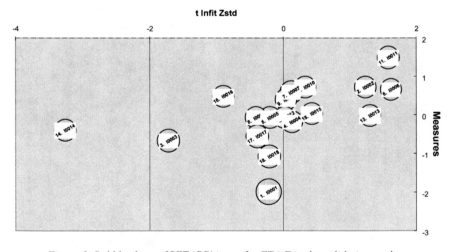

Figure 5. Bubble chart of SETARS' items for ETA F in the validation study.

DISCUSSION AND CONCLUSIONS

The purpose of this study was to examine students' perception of specific ETAs' role in their tertiary learning situations, in relation to the broad aim of the ETA placement in the higher education setting. This was done in order to further define an ETAs' role in a teaching and learning situation. The 18-item SETARs was found to be a valid and reliable unidimensional measure of students' perceptions of specific English Teaching Assistants' (ETAs) role in teaching and learning situations in Hong Kong. With this finding, the information obtained from the scale could safely be used to fine tune the ETAs' role within the teaching and learning of the tertiary courses in Hong Kong.

Generally, the ETAs' role in sharing their American cultural knowledge, and their participation in class and help in a broader context were favoured by the students. This general perception showed that the ETAs' role in assisting students' learning was found to be useful by the students themselves. The ETAs who were considered successful by students in responding to their in class and out of class teaching and learning needs, were encouraged to maintain and better their collaboration with students and teachers across the courses. Such a move was important since studies have found TAs' presence in the classroom increased pupils' interaction with the teacher by focusing attention to the teachers' teaching or tasks at hand (Blatchford et al., 2007) and that students' performance in specific language skills improved with the TAs' help (Downer, 2007; Savage & Carless, 2008). The student responses on the SETARS showed that ETA E was incompetent in engaging students in class and helping students out with their study discussions. This information facilitated the coordinator of the ETAs to debrief and counsel the ETA concerned for further improvement of her role in her assigned teaching and learning situation, hence, in turn improving the students' learning environment.

The SETARS also provided information for students' out of class learning activities. Such information was valuable as it allowed the teachers and the ETAs to organise coordinated and cohesive support for the students in the preceding sessions. This characteristic of the SETARS is distinctively important for the learning environment as prior research work mainly concentrated on TAs' role at classroom level rather than both in class and out of class (Alaie, 2008; Blatchford et al., 2007; Downer, 2007; O'Neal et al., 2007).

The SETARS, hence, could play an important role in helping higher education educators optimise their students' learning environment by evaluating the perceived teaching and learning assistance given by ETAs. The SETARS could also be adapted to evaluate other educational situations where TAs play a role in students' learning.

Future research could include the main teacher's evaluation of the ETAs or TAs into the collaborative nature of their relationships in order to provide an optimum learning environment for students in the higher education sector. This is especially important because previous research on TAs has shown that TAs' generally have some impact on main teachers' work and their perception of it (Bedford et al., 2008; Wilson & Bedford, 2008). Such impact might perhaps alter or affect the students' learning environment, which should ultimately be conducive for optimal and favourable learning outcomes.

ACKNOWLEDGEMENTS

This research was kindly supported by the Hong Kong Institute of Education Additional Departmental Research Fund.

REFERENCES

Alaie, A. (2008). High-Achieving post baccalaureate-student teaching assistants: Effective instruction in introductory laboratory classrooms. *Journal of College Science Teaching, 37*(4), 60–64.

Bedford, D., Jackson, C. R., & Wilson, E. (2008). New partnerships for learning: Teachers' perspectives on their developing professional relationships with teaching assistants in England. *Journal of In-service Education, 34*(1), 7–25.

Blatchford, P., Russell, A., Bassett, P., Brown, P., & Martin, C. (2007). The role and effects of teaching assistants in English Primary Schools (Years 4 to 6) 2000–2003. Results from the Class Size and Pupil-Adult Ratios (CSPAR) KS2 Project. *British Educational Research Journal, 33*(1), 5–26.

Bond, T. G., & Fox, C. M. (2007). *Applying the Rasch model: Fundamental measurement in the human sciences* (2nd ed.). Mahwah, NJ: Lawrence Erlbaum Associates.

Downer, A. C. (2007). The national literacy strategy sight recognition programme implemented by teaching assistants: A precision teaching approach. *Educational Psychology in Practice, 23*(2), 129–143.

Linacre, J. M. (2004). Optimising rating scale category effectiveness. In E. V. Smith & R. M. Smith (Eds.), *Introduction to Rasch measurement: Theory, models and application* (pp. 258–278). Maple Grove, MN: JAM Press.

Minondo, S., Meyer, L. H., & Xin, J. F. (2001). The role and responsibilities of teaching assistants in inclusive education: What's appropriate? *Journal of the Association for Persons with Severe Handicaps (JASH), 26*(2), 114–119.

Muijs, D., & Reynolds, D. (2003). Student background and teacher effects on achievement and attainment in mathematics: A longitudinal study. *Educational Research and Evaluation, 9*(3), 289–314.

O'Neal, C., Wright, M., Cook, C., Perorazio, T., & Purkiss, J. (2007). The impact of teaching assistants on student retention in the sciences: Lessons for TA training. *Journal of College Science Teaching, 36*(5), 24–29.

Rasch, G. (1960). *Probabilistic models for some intelligence and attainment tests.* Copenhagen: Danmarks Paedagogiske Institut.

Rasch, G. (1980). *Probabilistic models for some intelligence and attainment tests* (Expanded ed.). Chicago: University of Chicago Press.

Rasch, G. (1993). *Probabilistic models for some intelligence and attainment tests* (Reprint ed.). Chicago: MESA Press.

Savage, R., & Carless, S. (2008). The impact of early reading interventions delivered by classroom assistants on attainment at the end of year 2. *British Educational Research Journal, 34*(3), 363–385.

Wilson, E., & Bedford, D. (2008). "New partnerships for learning": Teachers and teaching assistants working together in Schools–The way forward. *Journal of Education for Teaching: International Research and Pedagogy, 34*(2), 137–150.

Sivanes Phillipson
(Shaw Campus, Kowloon Tong, Hong Kong Baptist University)

SECTION FOUR: COGNITION AND DEVELOPMENT IN THE LEARNING ENVIRONMENT

YUKO ASANO-CAVANAGH AND ROBERT F. CAVANAGH

12. SECONDARY SCHOOL STUDENTS' ENGAGEMENT IN LEARNING JAPANESE AS A SECOND LANGUAGE

ABSTRACT

The learning of Asian languages is a significant feature of national and state education policies. For example, the multi-million dollar *National Asian Languages and Studies in Schools Program* which was designed to increase participation and engagement in learning Asian languages. While much of the impetus for this press is due to international trade and economic priorities, the curriculum area of languages other than English is also important for educative and cultural reasons. Of the four Asian languages typically taught in local schools (Indonesian, Japanese Korean and Mandarin), Japanese has the highest enrolment. The research reported in this paper focussed on the engagement of Western Australian secondary school students in their classroom learning of Japanese. While the study of second language instruction and teaching is situated within the field of second language acquisition, it also applies conventional educational theory. For example, cognitive, meta-cognitive and socio-affective constructs. This similarity is reflected in the model of student engagement that informed instrumentation decisions in the investigation of local Japanese classroom learning. Engagement was conceptualised as a function of student *capability* for learning and the *expectations* placed on this learning. *Capability* was defined in terms of *self-esteem, self-concept, resilience, self-regulation* and *self-efficacy*. *Expectations* were defined as facets of learning for understanding – expectations of *explanation, interpretation, application* and having *perspective, empathy* and *self-knowledge*. A self-report instrument was administered to 278 Year 8 to twelve students. The instrument comprised 50 statements about attributes of students and their learning. Students responded on a four-category response scale. The data were tested against the Rasch rating Scale Model. Data fitting the model shows a unidimensional trait was measured and the measure was invariant. Data-to-model fit was assessed by estimation of item difficulty thresholds, individual item fit statistics, the Person Separation Index and Principal Components Factor loadings of residuals. The difficulty students had in affirming individual statements and groups of statements were also estimated to indicate common and less common perceptions of Japanese classroom learning. The results showed a balance between student views of their *capability* for learning and the *expectations* of this learning. Engagement was characterised by *resilience,*

R.F. Cavanagh and R.F. Waugh (eds.), Applications of Rasch Measurement
in Learning Environments Research, 261–280.

self-regulation and *self-efficacy*. The students affirmed expectations of *explanation, interpretation, application* and having *perspective, empathy* and *self-knowledge*. The *perspective* and *empathy* items were more highly affirmed. The empirical findings are discussed in consideration of second language instruction and learning theory. The paper concludes with some recommendations for instrument improvement and future studies.

Note: The research was conducted as part of an Australian Research Council funded Linkage Project between Curtin University of Technology and the Participation Directorate of the Western Australian Department of Education and Training.

INTRODUCTION

This paper commences by examining the importance of learning a second language in Australia. Then, theories of language acquisition and methods of L2 learning and instruction are discussed. A model of student engagement in classroom learning is then proffered as a suitable theoretical model upon which to base an investigation of engagement in learning Japanese as a second language. The research questions are presented next, followed by an account of the methodology and results. Finally, the results are discussed in relation to theoretical issues in L2 learning.

Significance of Studying Languages Other than English (LOTE)

One of the eight key learning areas specified in the Australian *National Goals for Schooling in the Twenty-First Century* and endorsed by the Ministerial Council on Education, Employment, Training and Youth Affairs (MCEETYA, 1999) is LOTE - Languages other than English. A significant factor in LOTE policy and practice in Australia has been national government support for Asian languages and Asian studies in all school systems. The rationale for this priority was economic, with the intention of improving Australia's capacity and preparedness to interact with Asian economies (DEEWR, 2002). In recent times, this has been shown by the Australian Government committing funding of $62.4 million over 2008/09 to 2010/11 for the National Asian Languages and Studies in Schools Program (NALSSP) (DEEWR, 2008). Prior to this national policy development, there were the beginnings of regional consciousness in the mid-1960s to mid-1970s, multi-cultural and Asia-literacy policies mid-1970s to late-1980s, and the *Tsunami* in the 1990s (Lo Bianco, 2000). The *Tsunami* period was a time of extensive interest and growth in learning the Japanese language. This was characterised by: "vast and rapid enrolment increases in Japanese language study - all levels, all states"; "Japanese becomes language of mass education; "Japanese taught at every university"; and "Japanese emerging as a community language as well" (Lo Bianco, 2000, p. 16). The impetus for these cultural shifts can be explained by the development of the Japanese economy and the expansion of trade with Australia that commenced in the 1970s.

In Western Australia, of the four languages targeted for national support (Chinese [Mandarin], Indonesian, Japanese and Korean), Japanese has the highest enrolment

(Curriculum Council, 2008). This is notwithstanding a recent upsurge in Chinese enrolments that has likely been stimulated by local reactions to the growth in the Chinese economy and the state's trade with China. Another important reason for LOTE instruction being nationally prominent centres on students' cultural learning as well as complementing other areas of the curriculum. For example, the Queensland Department of Education, Training and the Arts (2006) states that "learning a language other than English: introduces students to other languages as a means of accessing other peoples, ideas and ways of thinking; inspires interest in and respect for other cultures; intersects with a range of communication technologies; and develops an array of transferable skills that support other areas of the curriculum" (p. 1).

As a result of Australia's international economic relationships and the importance of LOTE as a curriculum area, it is likely that the study of the Japanese language in local schools will continue to be a significant component of schooling as will be the study of Asian languages in general. Consequently, aspects of Japanese subject instruction and learning, the outcomes of studying Japanese, and in general, the engagement of students in Japanese subject classrooms are important areas of educational research.

Theories of Language Acquisition

Larsen-Freeman and Long (1991) grouped theories of second language (L2) acquisition into three types - *nativist, environmentalist* and *interactionist*. In very broad terms, the *nativist* view assumes: that learners have "... knowledge that does not appear to derive from experience" Hawkins, 2008, 476); that "language acquisition is largely the result of children's innate, biological endowment" (Stromswold, 2006, p. 341); and that "genetic mechanisms ...account for specific brain structures (Quartz, 1993, p. 224). The innate knowledge that enables language acquisition was termed Universal Grammar by Chomsky (1972) - universal language specific knowledge.

Environmentalist theories challenge the *nativist* view by holding that an organism's experiences shape its development. The *environmentalist* view is typified by behaviourist and neo-behaviourist learning theories. These underpin stimulus-response instructional strategies that largely rely on "... imitation and discrimination drills, reading aloud and contrastive analysis of Ll and L2 sound systems" (Jones, 1997, p. 103). This view is also consistent with *connectionist* models of language learning in which the connection of neural networks and indeed brain functioning are considered to require the input of stimuli (see Nakagama and Tanaka, 2004).

Interactionist theories "... invoke both innate and environmental factors to explain language acquisition" (Larsen-Freeman and Long, 1991, p. 266). For example, "social interactionists believe that children acquire the ability to express their intentions or meanings in language through a process of negotiation with their mothers or principal caregivers" (Matychuk, 2005, p. 304). Another interactionist perspective is *functionalism*. "The functionalist viewpoint in linguistics can take different forms. A caricature of functionalist thinking is the notion that the structure of language is optimised, or nearly so, for its function as a means of human communication" (Pierrehumbert, 2002, p. 459). From this perspective, *functionalism* is also about the pragmatic function of language - *communication*.

This brief overview of language acquisition theories has revealed a complex, and at times, contradictory body of knowledge about learning and processes of learning. Pragmatically, if instructional methods are grounded in multiple models of learning then this theoretical diversity could well be reflected in the use of multiple ways of teaching second languages. The following section presents constructs, strategies and processes that exemplify how language acquisition theories in conjunction with more general pedagogical theories have been applied in the design and delivery of L2 learning.

L2 Learning and Instruction

When reporting on a meta-analysis of the effectiveness of L2 instruction, Norris and Ortega (2000. p. 420) proposed three types of instructional options based on the focus required of the learner - "focus on *meaning, forms*, or an *integration* of both meaning and forms". First, focus on meaning "leads to incidental acquisition of the L2 system from exposure, to rich input and meaningful use of the L2 (p. 420). Second, "focus on forms in isolation (FonFS instruction) assumes the target L2 forms can and need to be taught one by one in a sequence externally orchestrated according to linguistic complexity" (p. 420). Third, "focus on forms integrated in meaning (FonF instruction) capitalises on brief reactive interventions ... [that] draw learners' attention to formal properties of a linguistic feature which appears to cause trouble on that occasion [and], is learnable" (p. 420). The meta-analysis revealed that "both FonF and FonFS instructional categories had large average effect sizes" (p. 482), but also found there were "no differences in effectiveness between FonF and FonFS instruction" (p. 482).

L2 instruction can be also classified as *explicit* or *implicit* depending on the degree of explanation and the attention given to the second language structures. Explicit instruction involves explanation of rules and giving attention to the "rule-governed nature of L2 structures" (Norris and Ortega, 2000, p. 482). Alternatively, rule explanation is not emphasised in implicit instruction. The meta-analysis by Norris and Ortega (2000) showed a significant difference between the effectiveness of these treatments - "treatments involving an explicit focus on the rule-governed nature of L2 structures are more effective than treatments that do not include such a focus" (p. 483).

It is possible to better understand L2 instruction by considering the particular strategies that are taught to students and/or used by students to achieve L2 learning outcomes. Early classifications utilised a dichotomy and distinguished between *direct* and *indirect* strategies. This depended on whether a strategy "contributed directly to L2 learning" or was "indirectly involved with language learning" (Hsiao and Oxford, 2002, p. 370). More recently, polytomous classifications have been developed. For example classifying strategies as: meta-cognitive, cognitive or socio-affective; or in a similar but more detailed way, as meta-cognitive, cognitive, memory, compensation, social, or affective (Hsiao and Oxford, 2002, p. 371).

Meta-cognitive strategies include advance organisers, self-management, functional planning, self-monitoring, and self evaluation; *cognitive strategies* include repetition, translation, grouping, note-taking, deduction, keyword, contextualisation, transfer, and inferencing; and *socio-affective* strategies include cooperation, question for clarification, and self-talk (Hsiao and Oxford, 2002, p. 371).

Other constructs commonly associated with academic motivation and academic success have also been the subject of L2 learning research. For example, self-regulation, self-concept and self-efficacy (see Mills, Pajares and Herron, 2007; Vandergrift, Goh, Mareschal and Tafaghodtari, 2006). These constructs are contextually dependent so care needs to be exercised in their application for explaining L2 learning since "... L2 learning is different from the learning of other subject matters" (Hsiao and Oxford, 2002, p. 378). For example, when studying the self-efficacy of college Intermediate level French students, Mills, Pajares and Herron (2007, p. 423) operationally defined constructs such as 'self-concept' in terms of the language being learnt – 'French learning self-concept'.

While constructs such as meta-cognition and cognition can be used to categorise strategies that have respectively similar characteristics, these constructs are more complex than simply a conglomeration of strategies. For example, in the case of meta-cognition, Vandergrift, Goh, Mareschal and Tafaghodtari (2006, p. 433) point out that it comprises both assessment of knowledge or ability and also "... orchestrate[ing] different mental processes during problem solving". This conception of meta-cognition has elements of both knowledge and action.

Since instruction involves action, explicit/implicit *knowledge* is different from explicit/implicit *instruction*. Having made a distinction between knowledge and instruction, the nature of L2 knowledge is another important aspect of L2 learning. Ellis (2004) differentiated between *explicit* and *implicit* knowledge. Explicit knowledge is "knowledge about language and about the uses to which language can be [not is] put" (p. 229). Implicit knowledge can be explained as "basic linguistic competence", the kind of knowledge that underlies everyday language use", and does not involve "meta-linguistic awareness" (Ellis, 2004, p. 232). Ellis (2004, pp. 243 – 244) identified the following examples of explicit L2 knowledge: pronunciation; vocabulary; grammar; pragmatic aspects (e.g. "whether a message contains sufficient information for its comprehension by an addressee"); and socio-critical features (e.g. "to assert one's right to something on the basis of one's class, gender or ethnicity").

Explicit L2 knowledge about socio-critical features of learning is reflected in the *socio-affective* dimension of L2 instruction. This dimension concerns the management of emotions, feelings and emotional states (affect) and the techniques used when interacting with others (social interaction). This is reflected in formal instructional goals (e.g. curriculum outcomes) which emphasise the cultural relevance of studying a second language. From the perspective of learning processes in contrast to learning outcomes, socio-affective instructional strategies and procedures strongly influence motivation, decision-making and performance (Csizer and Dornyei, 2005; Masgoret and Gardner, 2003). For example, Masgoret and Gardner (2003, p. 205) found that "... attitudes towards the learning situation, integrativeness, motivation, integrative orientation, and instrumental orientation, are all positively related to achievement in a second language". Of these five variables, motivation had the strongest relation with L2 achievement. Socio-affective outcomes are a significant component of L2 curricula and in conjunction with associated instructional methods, help characterise L2 teaching and learning.

Notwithstanding motivation being a proven predictor of success in SLA, aptitude for L2 learning is also commonly accepted as a strong predictor in both formal settings and natural circumstances (Ellis, 2004). Ellis (2004, p. 494) viewed aptitude for learning a second language as a "special propensity for learning L2". Kiss and Nikolov (2005, p. 101) elucidated:

"Language learning aptitude has generally been regarded as a cognitively based learner characteristic that is responsible for a considerable portion of the variance in language learning achievement, viewed in terms of the amount of time needed by the individual to learn the material or develop the skill".

Two of the assumptions underlying the notion of 'aptitude' are that it is relatively stable and is either innate or fixed at an early age (Kiss and Nikolov, 2005). This conception of aptitude reflects some of the *nativist* theories of SLA.

In summary, this section of the paper has presented a range of epistemological and methodological perspectives on L2 instruction and learning. It canvassed the nature and types of knowledge that are taught and learnt in SLA with knowledge being differentiated from instruction. The strategies typically applied by teachers and learned by students to enable development of L2 proficiency were identified. The notion that strategies can be classified in accordance with theories of intellectual development and learning was explored (e.g. the study of meta-cognition requires an understanding of how children monitor and evaluate their learning). The connection between student motivation and L2 performance was examined from an attitudinal perspective. Finally, it was noted that variance in L2 aptitude, in conjunction with variance in motivation, significantly accounts for variation in L2 achievement.

In recent times, the notion of student engagement has been used to describe positive attitudes towards learning and the learning environment. It is proposed that investigating L2 learning in terms of student engagement will provide a view that is conceptually aligned with the theories and methods of L2 learning and instruction. This assertion is examined in the following section.

THE NOTION OF STUDENT ENGAGEMENT

The engagement of students can be viewed from several perspectives. For example, from a research perspective, Fredricks, Blumenfeld and Paris (2004) classified the research on engagement in three ways: (1) Behavioural - positive conduct, involvement in academic, social or school activities, and in extra-curricular activities; (2) Emotional - positive and negative reactions to teachers, classmates, academics and school; and (3) Cognitive - motivation to comprehend complex ideas and master difficult skills. From a teacher perspective, the results of phenomenographic investigation conducted by Harris (2008) suggested that teacher conceptions of student engagement could be categorised as follows:

"Participating in classroom activities and following school rules" [behaving];

"Being interested in and enjoying participation in what happens at school" [Enjoying];

"Being motivated and confident in participation in what happens at school" [Being motivated];

"Being involved in thinking" [Thinking];

"Purposefully learning to reach life goals" [Seeing purpose]; and

"Owning and valuing learning" [Owning]" (p. 65).

Significantly, the categorisation by Harris (2008) is similar to the Fredricks, Blumenfeld and Paris (2004) classification. The similarities centre on three constructs: student compliance with classroom and school expectations of conduct/behaviour; positive attitude towards the psycho-social environment; and motivation towards learning. Generally, other conceptions of engagement are consistent with one or more of these three constructs. For example, Glanville and Wildhagen (2007, p. 1021) explained engagement at school as "... a student's behavioural and psychological involvement in the school curriculum". Hughes and Zhang (2006, p. 406) defined classroom engagement to be indicated by "... student effort, attention, persistence, and cooperative participation in learning". Kenny, Blustein, Haase, Jackson and Perry (2006, p. 272) portrayed school engagement as "... positive attitudes toward school, teachers, classmates, and academic learning". Janosz, Archambault, Morizot and Pagani (2008, p. 22) saw school engagement as characterising "... both academic (achievement, motivation, involvement in learning activities) and social integration within the school (social isolation/rejection, quality of student-teacher relationships, participation in extracurricular activities)".

Cavanagh, Kennish and Sturgess (2008) proposed a model of student engagement in learning in which engagement at a given time and in a particular context was seen as a balance between a student's *capability to learn* and the *expectations of learning*. The construct of *learning capabilities* was operationally defined to comprise two broad attributes of students - the *expressive self* as typified in studies of *self-esteem* and *self-concept* and the *managerial self* as typified in studies of *self-regulation* and *self-efficacy* (see Martin, 2007). Additionally, *resilience* was included in the definition due to the prevalence of this notion in the research on school engagement and the conceptual similarity with the other attributes. This construct concerns a student's attitudes towards self and own learning. Alternatively, *expectations of student learning* was viewed as a student's perceptions of external expectations from the teacher, peers or other influences within the psycho-social learning environment. A framework developed by Wiggins and McTighe (2001) to explain learning for understanding was used to operationally define this construct. Wiggins and McTighe (2001) identified six facets of understanding. These are: can *explain*; can *interpret*; can *apply*; has *perspective*; can *empathise*; and has *self-knowledge*. A framework depicting a student's *capability to learn* and the *expectations of learning* constructs and the respective sub-constructs is presented in Appendix 1. This also shows indicator statements written to define each sub-construct.

Finally, in advancing the proposition that studying engagement in learning will illuminate learning and instructional aspects of the L2 classroom, it needs to be recognised that this will entail focus on the socio-psychological environment and the processes of learning. The knowledge and skills that need to be learned for proficiency in the second language and also the innate linguistic aptitude of the learner will therefore not be directly considered in this study.

RESEARCH OBJECTIVES

The aim of the study was to investigate the engagement in learning of secondary school students studying Japanese as a second language. The specific research questions were:
– How do secondary school students view their engagement in classroom learning of Japanese?
– How do they perceive their *capabilities* for classroom learning of Japanese?
– How do they perceive the *expectations* placed on their classroom learning of Japanese?

PROCEDURE

Instrumentation

The *Survey of Engagement in Learning Japanese* (see Appendix 2) is a self-report instrument utilising a four-category response scale (strongly agree, agree, disagree, and strongly disagree). It comprises two 25-item sub-scales. There are 25 items on *learning capabilities* and 25 items on *expectations of learning*. Since self-knowledge is more about 'self' than external expectations, this sixth facet was not included as a sub-construct within *expectations of learning*. There are five items for each of the sub-constructs, and these items were written in order of difficulty with the first item in the group expected to be easier to affirm than the subsequent items.

Sample

The sample comprised 279 students from two Perth metropolitan senior high schools. Participation was voluntary. The characteristics of the sample are presented in Table 1 below.

Scores from one to four were entered into the computer package RUMM2020 (Andrich, Sheridan, Lyne & Luo, 2003) with missing data coded as nine. Data were then analysed using the Rasch Rating Scale Model (Andrich, 1978a & 1978b) to test the measurement properties of the data. The following six criteria are met when the data fit the Model:

Table 1. Sample characteristics

YEAR EIGHT	161
YEAR NINE	75
YEAR TEN	18
YEAR ELEVEN	10
YEAR TWELVE	15
TOTAL	279
GIRLS	152
BOYS	127
TOTAL	279

- The items are measuring a single continuous latent variable – the scale is uni-dimensional; and
- The item responses are independent of one another – local independence. The only relation between items is explained by the conditional relationship with the latent variable;
- Specific objectivity - comparison of two items' difficulty parameters are assumed independent of any group of subjects studied, and comparison of two subjects' trait level does not depend on any subset of items being administered;

Relation between subject ability and item difficulty (the Rasch Model) - The probability of endorsing an item is a function of the difference between a person's level on the underlying trait and the difficulty of the item;

- Calibration - both person ability estimates and item difficulty estimates are measured in logits – for example in the case of person affirmativeness in attitude scales, the logarithmic odds of a person affirming certain statements of attitudes; and
- Intervality - raw scores are tested against the Rasch Model and when the data fit the model, interval person ability estimates and interval item difficulty estimates are produced.

Two analyses were performed. The first was of the complete data-set to identify items that had a good fit to the model. In the second analysis, data from items which did not fit the model well were deleted and the remaining data were re-analysed. More information on the analytic procedures is presented in the following section on the results of the RUMM2020 analyses.

RESULTS

The 50-Item Scale

Item thresholds were estimated to show the person ability estimate at which there is an equal probability of the persons selecting two adjacent response categories. For a particular item, the probability of selecting response categories should be ordered according to the overall ability of the persons. This is illustrated for Item 17 in

Figure 1 - Category probability curve for Item 17. Persons with more engagement are located to the right of the horizontal axis and those with less to the left. The vertical axis is the probability of selecting a response category. Curve 0 (strongly disagree) shows the probability of a person located four logits below the mean is 0.8 and this decreases to zero as person ability increases. For Curve 1 (disagree), the probability increases from 0.2 for a person located four logits below the mean to a maximum value of 0.6 for a person located 1.4 logits below the mean, and then decreases for higher person locations. The intersection of Curve 0 and Curve 1, –2.4 logits is the threshold for the strongly disagree and disagree categories. The other two thresholds are respectively -0.34 logits and 2.01 logits. The ranking of the threshold values is ordered in line with increasing student engagement.

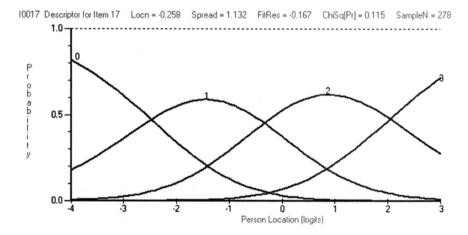

Figure 1. Category probability curve for item 17.

When thresholds were estimated for the 50-item data, Items 2, 12, 21, 22, 36, and 44 had a disordering of thresholds. For Item 12, *In this class and in this subject I know I can overcome small problems*, the respective thresholds were -0.78, -2.13, and 2.24 logits as shown in Figure 2 - Category probability curve for Item 12. The first two thresholds are not in order of increasing student engagement mainly due to the selection of the second (Curve 1) and third (Curve 2) response categories. The wording of the item might have confounded students and this could have caused illogical choosing of the categories. Irrespective of the reason for the choice, the data for this item has limited use as a measure of engagement.

The fit of data to the Model for each of the 50 items was also estimated. When the data fit the model well, the fit residual, the difference between the actual score and that predicted by the Model should be low (RUMM2020 sets a default value of <±2.5). RUMM2020 also estimates a Chi Square with Bonferroni adjusted probability values indicating data to model fit. Poor data to model fit is illustrated in Figure 3 - Item characteristic curve for Item 5.

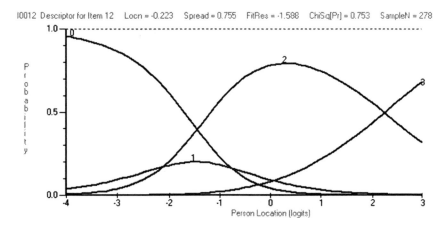

Figure 2. Category probability curve for item 12.

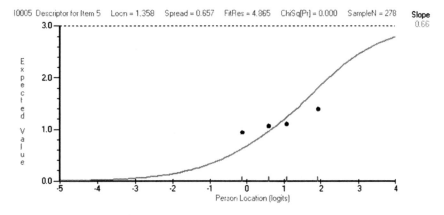

Figure 3. Item characteristic curve for item 5.

The ogive shows the theoretical relation between the expected value and person location for Item 5. The four class interval observed scores do not fit the ogive due to the Class Interval 1 observed score being higher than expected and the Class Interval 4 observed score being lower than expected. The RUMM analysis revealed eight items had fit residuals greater than ±2.5 and/or Chi Square probability values less than the Bonferroni adjusted value. These were Items 3, 5-9, 24 and 26.

The 36-Item Scale

The RUMM2020 analysis of the remaining data (14 items deleted) showed the data fitted the model well. For example, thresholds were ordered, fit residuals were <±2.5, and with the exception of Items 4 and 43, the Chi Square probability values were more than the Bonferroni adjusted value. Additionally, the Person Separation Index (the proportion of transformed scores considered true) was 0.94 indicating high reliability and the Item-Trait Interaction Chi Square probability value was 0.05 suggesting unidimensionality. This was confirmed by a Principal Components Factor Analysis of residuals. After the linear Rasch measure was extracted from the data set, there was minimal evidence of common variance in the remaining residuals. A further consideration was the possibility of items functioning differently for certain groups of persons – e.g. girls and boys, different age groups. When differential Item Functioning due to gender and year of schooling was examined by RUMM2020, analysis of variance did not reveal any item bias.

In order to better describe the meaning of the scale and the data, the difficulty the students had in affirming each of the 36 items was estimated in logits. Table 2 contains the items and their difficulties. Lower logits show an item was relatively easy to affirm and higher logits show an item was relatively difficult to affirm. For example, Item 1 (logit -0.23) was easier to affirm than Item 4 (logit 0.14).

DISCUSSION

The Rasch Rating Scale Model is designed for data that are unidimensional and measuring a latent trait that is not multidimensional. The trait of interest in this study was student perceptions of their engagement in classroom learning of Japanese. In order for the data to fit the model, the two major constructs (*learning capabilities* and *expectations of learning*), the ten sub-constructs and the instrument items were all required to indicate the latent trait. The first salient issue arising from results of the study was the nature of the eight items eliciting data not fitting the model – Items 3, 5–9, 24 and 26 in Table 3.

The majority of these items elicited data on the students' view of themselves, particularly *self-concept*. The misfit as illustrated in the item characteristic curves (e.g. Figure 3) showed the observed values for the class intervals were similar and did not vary as the person engagement locations changed. From a measurement perspective, the items might not be sufficiently sensitive to aspects of these attributes leading to the level of the attribute not varying with engagement. Theoretically, it is possible that the sub-constructs of *self-esteem* and *self-concept* are not indicators of classroom engagement in learning Japanese as theorised. This is notwithstanding *socio-affective* strategies being recognised in the literature on the learning strategies taught to second language students (Hsiao and Oxford, 2002). Similarly, the effect of 'context' (e.g. the particular language being learned) on academic motivation constructs (Hsiao and Oxford, 2002) could explain why *self-esteem* and *self-concept* were not found to characterise engagement in the classrooms examined (see Mills, Pajares and Herron, 2007).

Data on *resilience, self-regulation* and to a more limited extent *self-efficacy*, did fit the model well. *Self-regulation* and *self-efficacy* are referred to as meta-cognitive strategies in the literature on L2 learning strategies and attainment of learning outcomes (Hsiao and Oxford, 2002; Vandergrift, Goh, Mareschal and Tafaghodtari, 2006).

The second salient issue emerging from the results are the trends in the item difficulties presented in Table 2. First, in general, the levels and distributions of the

Table 2. Item difficulties

In this class and in this subject			Logit
1	SE1	I am OK	−0.23
4	SE4	I am confident to make choices and decisions	0.14
10	SC5	I am one of the best students but still want to improve	1.52
11	R1	A little difficulty is OK for me	−0.03
13	R3	I expect to succeed in the end	−0.37
14	R4	I bounce back after having difficulties	0.27
15	R5	Anything that goes wrong can be fixed	−0.01
16	SR1	I think about my achievement	0.00
17	SR2	I am clear about my strengths and weaknesses	−0.20
18	SR3	I know how to learn better	−0.03
19	SR4	I make an effort to improve my learning	0.09
20	SR5	I am in control of my learning	0.08
23	SEF3	I can easily identify what will give me difficulty	−0.12
25	SEF5	I never give up	0.35
In this class and in this subject, I am expected to			
27	EXP2	Explain what I've learnt by using *some* of my own ideas	0.15
28	EXP3	Use *many* of my own ideas to explain what I've learnt	0.07
29	EXP4	Connect different ideas together	−0.16
30	EXP5	Explain the work differently from how it was taught	0.69
31	INT1	Repeat what I have been told	−0.46
32	INT2	Show I know the work	−0.75
33	INT3	Explain to other students how the work can be done	0.17
34	INT4	Compare different ways of understanding the work	0.29
35	INT5	Have a deep understanding of the work	0.13
37	APP2	Use what I've learnt previously to help me complete new tasks	−0.93
38	APP3	Use what I've learnt to do things outside of the class	0.28
39	APP4	Use what I've learnt in *many* ways outside of the class	0.69
40	APP5	Find *new* ways to use what I've learnt outside of the class	0.46
41	PERS1	Think about what others believe after listening to them	0.11
42	PERS2	Not ignore opinions different from my own	−0.68
43	PERS3	Understand why others see things the way they do	−0.18
45	PERS5	Be very careful about how I react to the views of others	−0.37
46	EMP1	Try to understand the views of others	−0.49
47	EMP2	Try to be unbiased in understanding the views of others	−0.27
48	EMP3	Show how I know others feel differently from me	−0.14
49	EMP4	Show sensitivity and concern for the views of others	−0.23
50	EMP5	Be willing to change my own views to show respect to others	0.15

learning capabilities item difficulties and the *expectations of learning* item difficulties were similar. This suggests a balance between the students' capabilities and what is expected of their learning. This balance is consistent with the theory of engagement informing the investigation (see Cavanagh, Kennish and Sturgess, 2008).

Table 3. Eight items not fitting model

3	SE3	I am proud of what I have achieved
5	SE5	There is very little in me that needs to improve
6	SC1	I check how well I'm doing by looking at what others do
7	SC2	How I feel about myself comes from looking at others
8	SC3	I compare myself with others when I need to
9	SC4	Comparing myself to others changes what I do
24	SEF4	Even when problems are big, I feel I must succeed
26	EXP1	Use the words of others when explaining things

Second, across the *learning capabilities* sub-constructs there is little variation in the item difficulties with many of the difficulties being within 0.5 logits of the zero point. The majority of the fitting items concern what Martin (2007) described as the 'managerial-self' conception of selfhoods that is found in studies of *self-regulation* and *self-efficacy*. The similarity in item difficulties could also be due to a lack of variation in these attributes in Japanese L2 students.

Third, in contrast, there are larger differences within the *expectations of learning* item difficulties. The *explanation, interpretation* and *application* items were generally more difficult to affirm than the *perspective* and *empathy* items. Thus it might be concluded that expectations of *explaining, interpreting* and *applying* were not as characteristic of the Japanese L2 learning environments investigated as were expectations of *perspective* and *empathy*.

Fourth, the *cognitive strategies* of repetition, translation, grouping, note-taking, deduction, keyword, contextualisation, transfer and inferencing (see Hsiao and Oxford, 2002), are conceptually similar to the *explanation* and *interpretation* facets of learning for understanding. However, the expectations as operationally defined by the instrument items are likely more demanding of students than the L2 learning *cognitive strategies*. Since *explanation* and *interpretation* are identified as requisites for deep learning (Wiggins and McTighe, 2001), perhaps more attention should be given to the higher levels of these facets when *cognitive strategies* are used in secondary school Japanese L2 learning.

Fifth, the *perspective* and *empathy* sub-constructs are conceptually similar to the *socio-affective* dimension of L2 instruction comprising management of emotions, feelings and emotional states in social interaction. These are associated with L2 curriculum outcomes about cultural relevance, respect and sensitivity; and also motivation, decision-making and performance (Csizer and Dornyei, 2005). The majority of the item difficulty logits for the *perspective* and *empathy* items were relatively low due to students easily affirming these qualities were expected of them in their Japanese L2 classroom. This suggests there was an emphasis on *socio-affective* outcomes and learning strategies in the classrooms investigated.

CONCLUSION

Analysis of data from the Survey of Engagement in Learning Japanese enabled a quantification of constructs found in the extant literature on second language instruction and learning. The students affirmed their *resilience, self-regulation* and *self-efficacy* as learners of Japanese and also that this learning required them to *explain, interpret, apply,* have *perspective* and have *empathy.* The misfitting of data from *self-esteem* and *self-concept* items does not necessarily negate these attributes being characteristic of Japanese L2 learners. Rather than modifying the theory of engagement by removing these sub-constructs, more information should be collected on the performance of the items with a view to item re-writing.

Since the data fitted the Rasch rating Scale Model, the instrument and constituent items should be invariant when administered to other groups of Japanese L2 learners. However, increasing the sample might enable improvement of the metric through consideration of richer data.

Finally, the nationally recognised importance of studying languages other than English, requires a better understanding of the instructional, learning and indeed engagement processes in the second language classroom. The construction and testing of appropriate measures is key to learning more about second language acquisition.

REFERENCES

Andrich, D., Sheridan, B., Lyne, A., & Luo, G. (2003). *RUMM: A Windows-based item analysis program employing Rasch unidimensional measurement models.* Perth: Murdoch University.

Andrich, D. (1978a). Application of a psychometric rating model to ordered categories which are scored with successive integers. *Applied Psychological Measurement, 2*(4), 581–594.

Andrich, D. (1978b). Rating formulation for ordered response categories. *Psychometrika, 43*(4), 561–573.

Bond, T. G., & Fox, C. M. (2001). *Applying the Rasch model: Fundamental measurement in the human sciences.* Mahwah, NJ: Lawrence Erlbaum Associates, Publishers.

Cavanagh, R. F., Kennish, P., & Sturgess, K. (2008, November 30–December 4). *Development of theoretical frameworks to inform measurement of secondary school student engagement with learning.* Paper presented at the 2008 annual conference of the Australian Association for Research in Education, Brisbane.

Chamot, A. U., & El-Dinary, P. B. (1999). Children's learning strategies in immersion classrooms. *The Modern Language Journal, 83*(3), 319–338.

Csizer, K., & Dornyei, Z. (2005). Language learners' motivational profiles and their motivated learning behaviour. *Language Learning, 55,* 613–659.

Curriculum Council. (2008). *2007 Secondary education statistics (Years 10, 11 and 12).* Osborne Park, Western Australia: Curriculum Council.

DEEWR. (2002). *Review of the Australian government languages other than English programme (LOTE).* Canberra, ACT: Department of Education, Employment and Workplace Relations.

DEEWR. (2008). *National Asian Languages and Studies in Schools Program (NALSSP).* Canberra, ACT: Department of Education, Employment and Workplace Relations.

Department of Education, Training and the Arts. (2006). *Curriculum: Learning, teaching and assessment.* City East, Brisbane: The State of Queensland. Retrieved July 10, 2008, from http://education.qld. gov.au/curriculum/area/lote/index.html

Ellis, R. (2004). *The study of second language acquisition.* Oxford, England: Oxford University Press.

Fredricks, J. A., Blumenfeld, P. C., & Paris, A. H. (2004). *Review of Educational Research, 74*(1), 51–109.

Glanville, J. L., & Wildhagen, T. (2007). The measurement of school engagement: Assessing dimensionality and measurement invariance across race and ethnicity. *Educational and Psychological Measurement, 67*(6), 1019–1041.

Harris, L. R. (2008). A phenomenographic investigation of teacher conceptions of student engagement. *The Australian Educational Researcher, 35*(1), 57–79.

Himizu, H., & Green, K. (2007). Japanese language educators' strategies for and attitudes toward teaching Kanji. *Language Learning*, 57(1), 57–85.

Hsiao, T. Y., & Oxford, R. L. (2002). Comparing theories of language learning strategies: A confirmatory factor analysis. *Modern Language Journal*, 86(3), 368–383.

Hughes. J. N., & Duan Zhang, D. (2006). Effects of the structure of classmates' perceptions of peers' academic abilities on children's perceived cognitive competence, peer acceptance, and engagement. *Contemporary Educational Psychology*, 32, 400–419.

Janosz, M., Archambault, I., Morizot, J., & Pagani, L. S. (2008). School engagement trajectories and their differential predictive relations to dropout. *Journal of Social Issues*, 64(1), 21–40.

Kenny, M. E., Blustein, D. L, Haase, R., Jackson, J., & Perry, J. C. (2006). Setting the stage: Career development and the student engagement process. *Journal of Counselling Psychology*, 53(2), 272–279.

Kiss, C., & Nikolov, M. (2005). Developing, piloting, and validating an instrument to measure young learners' aptitude. *Language Learning*, 55, 99–150.

Larsen-Freeman, D. (2007). Reflecting on the cognitive-social debate in second language acquisition. *Modern Language Journal*, 91(5), 773–787.

Lo Bianco, J. (2000). *After the Tsunami, some dilemmas: Japanese language studies in multi-cultural Australia*. Melbourne, Victoria: Language Australia.

Macaro, E. (2006). Strategies for language learning and for language use: Revising the theoretical framework. *The Modern Language Journal*, 90, 320–337.

Masgoret, A. M., & Gardner, R. C. (2002). Attitudes, motivation, and second language learning: A meta-analysis of studies conducted by Gardner and Associates. *Language Learning*, 53(1), 123–164.

Martin, J. (2007). The selves of educational psychology: Conceptions, contexts, and critical considerations. *Educational Psychologist*, 42(2), 79–89.

Mills, N., Pajares, F., & Herron, C. (2007). Self-efficacy of college intermediate French students: Relation to achievement and motivation. *Language Learning*, 57(3), 417–422.

Ministerial Council on Education, Employment, Training and Youth Affairs. (1999). *The Adelaide declaration on national goals for schooling in the twenty-first century*. Carlton, South Victoria, Australia: MCEETYA.

Mori, Y. (1999). Beliefs about language learning and their relationship to the ability to integrate information from word parts and context in interpreting novel Kanji words. *The Modern Language Journal*, 83, 534–547.

Mullock, B. (2006). The pedagogical knowledge base of four TESOL teachers. *The Modern Language Journal*, 90, 48–66.

Norris, J. M., & Ortega, L. (2000). Effectiveness of L2 instruction: A research synthesis and quantitative meta-analysis. *Language Learning*, 50, 417–528.

Shimizu, H., & Green, K. (2002). Japanese language educators' strategies for and attitudes towards teaching Kanji. *The Modern Language Journal*, 86, 227–241.

Tang, Y. (2006). Beyond behaviour: Goals of cultural learning in the second language classroom. *Modern Language Journal*, 90(1), 86–99.

Vandergrift, L., Goh, C., Mareschal, C., & Tafaghodatari, M. H. (2006). The Metacognitive Awareness Listening Questionnaire (MALQ): Development and validation. *Language Learning*, 56, 431–462.

Vygotsky, L. S. (1978). *Mind and society: The development of higher psychological processes*. Cambridge, MA: Harvard University Press.

Vibert, A., & Shields, C. (2003). Approaches to student engagement: Does ideology matter? *McGill Journal of Education*, 38(2), 221–240.

Wiggins, G, & McTighe, J. (2001). *Understanding by design: A brief introduction*. New Jersey, NJ: Prentice Hall Inc.

Yuko Asano-Cavanagh and Robert F. Cavanagh
(Curtin University of Technology, Perth, Western Australia)

APPENDIX 1

THEORETICAL FRAMEWORK

LEARNING CAPABILITIES

	SELF-ESTEEM	SELF-CONCEPT	RESILIENCE	SELF-REGULATION	SELF-EFFICACY
MORE CAPABILITY	has positive self image	strives to be perfect	unqualified expectations of coping	responsible for learning	perseveres in the face of adversity
	confident to make decisions	motivated by self reflection	can deal with failure	improves own learning	has determination
	has pride in self	self reflecting	expects success	understands own learning	recognises contextual influences
	trusts self to act	at ease comparing self with others	overcomes small setbacks	assesses own learning	has expectations of self
LESS CAPABILITY	sees worth in self	compares self with others	is aware of problems	aware of learning	makes effort

Expectations of learning for understanding

	EXPLANATION	INTERPRE-TATION	APPLI-CATION	PERSPEC-TIVE	EMPATHY
MORE DEMANDING	sophisticated	profound	masterful	insightful	mature
	in-depth	revealing	skilled	thorough	sensitive
	developed	perceptive	able	considered	aware
	intuitive	interpreted	apprentice	aware	developing
LESS DEMANDING	naive	literal	novice	uncritical	egocentric

277

APPENDIX 2

SURVEY OF ENGAGEMENT IN LEARNING JAPANESE

Office use only
  Year   ....

  Gender (male or female)   ....

INSTRUCTIONS
  If you **strongly agree** with the statement, please tick 4   1   2   3   4
  If you **agree** with the statement, please tick 3   1   2   3   4
  If you **disagree** with the statement, please tick 2   1   2   3   4
  If you **strongly disagree** with the statement, please tick 1   1   2   3   4

PART A: How I see myself in this class

In this class and in this subject		Strongly Disagree	Disagree	Agree	Strongly Agree
SE1	I am OK	1	2	3	4
SE2	I feel good in myself	1	2	3	4
SE3	I am proud of what I have achieved	1	2	3	4
SE4	I am confident to make choices and decisions	1	2	3	4
SE5	There is very little in me that needs to improve	1	2	3	4
In this class and in this subject		Strongly Disagree	Disagree	Agree	Strongly Agree
SC1	I check how well I'm doing by looking at what others do	1	2	3	4
SC2	How I feel about myself comes from looking at others	1	2	3	4
SC3	I compare myself with others when I need to	1	2	3	4
SC4	Comparing myself to others changes what I do	1	2	3	4
SC5	I am one of the best students but still want to improve	1	2	3	4
In this class and in this subject		Strongly Disagree	Disagree	Agree	Strongly Agree
R1	A little difficulty is OK for me	1	2	3	4

R2	I know I can overcome small problems	1	2	3	4
R3	I expect to succeed in the end	1	2	3	4
R4	I bounce back after having difficulties	1	2	3	4
R5	Anything that goes wrong can be fixed	1	2	3	4

In this class and in this subject		Strongly Disagree	Disagree	Agree	Strongly Agree
SR1	I think about my achievement	1	2	3	4
SR2	I am clear about my strengths and weaknesses	1	2	3	4
SR3	I know how to learn better	1	2	3	4
SR4	I make an effort to improve my learning	1	2	3	4
SR5	I am in control of my learning	1	2	3	4

In this class and in this subject		Strongly Disagree	Disagree	Agree	Strongly Agree
SEF1	I try when I need to	1	2	3	4
SEF2	I want to be successful	1	2	3	4
SEF3	I can easily identify what will give me difficulty	1	2	3	4
SEF4	Even when problems are big, I feel I must succeed	1	2	3	4
SEF5	I never give up	1	2	3	4

PART B: What is expected of me

In this class and in this subject, I am expected to		Strongly Disagree	Disagree	Agree	Strongly Agree
EX1	Use the words of others when explaining things	1	2	3	4
EX2	Explain what I've learnt by using *some* of my own ideas	1	2	3	4
EX3	Use *many* of my own ideas to explain what I've learnt	1	2	3	4
EX4	Connect different ideas together	1	2	3	4
EX5	Explain the work differently from how it was taught	1	2	3	4

In this class and in this subject, I am expected to		Strongly Disagree	Disagree	Agree	Strongly Agree
INT1	Repeat what I have been told	1	2	3	4
INT2	Show I know the work	1	2	3	4
INT3	Explain to other students how the work can be done	1	2	3	4
INT4	Compare different ways of	1	2	3	4

	understanding the work				
INT5	Have a deep understanding of the work	1	2	3	4

In this class and in this subject, I am expected to		Strongly Disagree	Disagree	Agree	Strongly Agree
AP1	Follow instructions to complete tasks	1	2	3	4
AP2	Use what I've learnt previously to help me complete new tasks	1	2	3	4
AP3	Use what I've learnt to do things outside of the class	1	2	3	4
AP4	Use what I've learnt in *many* ways outside of the class	1	2	3	4
AP5	Find *new* ways to use what I've learnt outside of the class	1	2	3	4

In this class and in this subject, I am expected to		Strongly Disagree	Disagree	Agree	Strongly Agree
PS1	Think about what others believe after listening to them	1	2	3	4
PS2	Not ignore opinions different from my own	1	2	3	4
PS3	Understand why others see things the way they do	1	2	3	4
PS4	Be fair in making judgements about how others see things	1	2	3	4
PS5	Be very careful about how I react to the views of others	1	2	3	4

In this class and in this subject, I am expected to		Strongly Disagree	Disagree	Agree	Strongly Agree
EM1	Try to understand the views of others	1	2	3	4
EM2	Try to be unbiased in under standing the views of others	1	2	3	4
EM3	Show how I know others feel differently from me	1	2	3	4
EM4	Show sensitivity and concern for the views of others	1	2	3	4
EM5	Be willing to change my own views to show respect to others	1	2	3	4

THANK YOU VERY MUCH FOR TAKING THE TIME
TO COMPLETE THIS SURVEY

PENELOPE KENNISH AND ROBERT F. CAVANAGH

13. THE ENGAGEMENT IN CLASSROOM LEARNING OF YEAR 10 AND 11 WESTERN AUSTRALIAN STUDENTS

ABSTRACT

The consideration of issues related to student engagement in classroom learning has taken on increasing importance in Western Australia since the passing of legislation to raise the school leaving age to 17 years, which came into effect in 2008. There are now more students retained at schools in Years 11 and 12 than previously. Engaging these students in learning is of the upmost importance for secondary schools.

This paper presents a hypothesised model of student engagement in classroom learning that is based on the principles of Flow Theory (i.e. a person achieves a state of flow when there is a match in high skills and high challenges). The hypothesised model proposes that student engagement occurs when there is a balance between student *learning capabilities* (skills) and the *expectations of student learning* (challenges). Each of these comprised sub-constructs, of which there were 11 in total. The research sought to determine which of the 11 sub-constructs that comprise the student engagement in classroom learning were the most difficult and which were easier to identify in Year 10 and 11 students. It also sought to determine whether membership of different groups of students accounted for variance in the calibrated scores (these groups being gender; school year; subject; and whether it was a favourite or least favourite subject). The sample comprised 112 Year 10 and 11 students from metropolitan and rural government schools in Western Australia. Each student was assigned a rating from zero to five by two researchers on each of the 11 sub-constructs. The Rasch Rating Scale Model was used for analysis of the quantitative data. Firstly, the raters experienced differing levels of difficulty in identifying the respective sub-constructs in the students. That is, the 11 items in the instrument presented varying levels of difficulty of affirmation. Secondly, the engagement scores differed by gender (boys displaying lower levels of engagement) and whether favourite or least favourite subject was reported (favourite subjects displaying higher levels of engagement). The year of schooling of the student and the subject area (e.g. English, Mathematics, Science, and Society and Environment) did not account for variance in engagement scores. The implications of these findings are discussed.

R.F. Cavanagh and R.F. Waugh (eds.), Applications of Rasch Measurement
in Learning Environments Research, 281–300.

INTRODUCTION

This paper starts by outlining the importance of student engagement in classroom learning in Australia and then presents a theoretical model of student engagement in classroom learning. The research questions are followed by the methodology used and the results. The paper finishes with a discussion of the results in relation to classroom learning. The Western Australian parliament passed legislation in 2005 to raise the school leaving age to 16 years in 2006 and 17 years in 2008, which means that all young people in their 16th and 17th year must be in education, training or employment in Western Australia. As a result, there are more students enrolled at school in Years 11 and 12 than were previously. This change does not just apply to Western Australia, but is a national trend. In May 2009, the Council of Australian Governments (COAG) agreed on a new Jobs and Training Compact for young Australians. Anyone under the age of 17 must be 'earning or learning' (i.e. they must be in full-time school, training or work, or a combination thereof). The compact is to be implemented by 2015. Indeed, some states and territories have raised the leaving age already (Queensland, Tasmania and South Australia to 17 years and Victoria to 16 years), whilst New South Wales have stated they will raise their leaving age to 17 years by 2010.

National research (Marks and Fleming, 1999) found that in the 1995 Year 9 cohort, 9% of students left school before the beginning of Year 11, and also that students who have low levels of achievement (literacy and numeracy) were more likely to leave school early. These findings indicate that a significant proportion of students retained in Western Australian schools as a result of the change in legislation will have low levels of achievement.

With regard to academic performance, several studies have found that relationships exist between engagement and academic achievement and student attributes. For example, self-concept and aspirations (Finn and Rock, 1997; Marsh, 1992; National Centre for Education Statistics, 1995). Furthermore, Wellborn (1991), cited in Reeve, Jang, Carrell, Jeon, and Barch, (2004, p. 148), stated "... in school settings, engagement is important because it functions as a behavioural pathway by which students' motivational processes contribute to their subsequent learning and development". These findings suggest that student engagement may be associated with educational outcomes.

Since more students with low levels of achievement and possible lower engagement will remain in the WA education system, there is a need to more fully understand the nature and influences on student engagement in classroom learning. The starting point for gaining this understanding is the development of a theory about the engagement phenomenon.

This paper reports on part of the second phase in a large scale ARC Linkage project into *student engagement in classroom learning*. The first phase focused on defining a theoretical model of *student engagement in classroom learning*. The second phase was to conduct face-to-face interviews from a representative sample of Western Australian secondary school students. The third phase is to administer a self-report rating scale instrument to a large number of students to enable instrument refinement and analysis of interactions between engagement variables.

One of the aims of the project is to develop an instrument that can measure *student engagement in classroom learning* so that the impact of pedagogical changes and improvement in curriculum design can be quantified. This is of importance to administrators and teachers of engagement programs throughout Western Australia which have been set up in response to the raising of the leaving age.

THEORETICAL FRAMEWORK

Flow Theory emerged from descriptions of optimal experiences (see Csikszentmihalyi 1990a & 1990b; Hekter, Schmidt and Csikszentmihalyi, 2007; Massimini, Csikszentmihalyi and Carli, 1987). Schweinle, Meyer and Turner (2006, p. 272.) explained that *"Optimal experience, or flow, occurs when a person perceives the challenges in a certain situation and his or her skills are balanced and above average"*.

Cavanagh, Kennish and Sturgess (2008) proposed that the concept of engagement in classroom learning could be explained by applying the basic tenets of Flow Theory. Cavanagh, et al. (2008, p. 7) applied this model to the notion of engagement and proposed that:

> "... students who are engaged within a particular situation will have a balance between the perceived level of the challenge being faced and their perceived capability (or skill) to meet the incumbent requirements".

In the classroom learning environment, students skills were defined as *learning capabilities* and the classroom challenges were defined as *expectations of learning*. Figure 1 presents the hypothesised model of student engagement in classroom learning.

(a) Learning Capabilities

The learning capabilities that students bring to the classroom were operationally defined as *self-esteem, self-concept, resilience, self-regulation* and *self-efficacy*. Martin, in 2007, described self-esteem and self-concept as the "expressive self". He argued that the reason why high levels of self-esteem and self-concept are viewed as worthy educational goals is as a consequence of the mediating effect they have on human behaviour. Resilience was found to be often identified in research on student engagement and participation. Howard and Johnson (1998) commented that the literature consistently characterised resilient children as having "...social competence, problem solving skills, mastery, autonomy and a sense of purpose and a future" (p. 1). Self-regulation and self-efficacy can be thought of in terms of the tools students use to learn, "building meta-cognitive knowledge of oneself as a learner contributes to viewing oneself as an able learner, which influences not only success in learning, but also motivation to learn" (White and Frederiksen, 2005, p. 212).

Sets of hierarchically ordered descriptors were written for each of the five sub-constructs, to indicate how 'more' of the sub-construct would be seen in a student and also how 'less' of the sub-construct would be seen. Two indicator statements were also written in behavioural terms for each descriptor. Table 1 presents the five descriptors and behavioural statements for *resilience*.

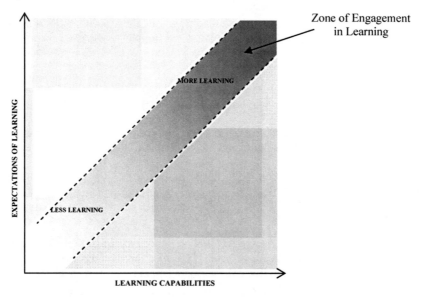

Figure 1. Hypothesised model of student engagement in classroom learning.

Table 1. Hierarchical descriptors and behavioural statements for 'resilience'

Level of Sub-construct	Descriptors	Behavioural statements
More resilience	Has unqualified expectations of coping	Expects he/she will always be OK . Doesn't face any unfixable problems.
	Can deal with failure	Things going wrong is not an issue for him/her . Believes things will eventually work out well.
	Expects success	Expects if he/she works at problems they will be solved . Expects to eventually succeed.
	Overcomes small setbacks	Considers overcoming small problems is possible . Can deal with small hassles.
Less resilience	Is aware of problems	Accepts that a little difficulty is OK. Is aware that things go wrong sometimes.

The five sub-constructs, descriptors and behavioural statements for *learning capabilities* are presented in Appendix A.

(b) Expectations of Student Learning

Expectations of student learning was viewed in terms of expectations in learning for understanding. The framework used was the six facets of understanding proposed by Wiggins and McTighe in 2001. These are:
- Can explain
- Can interpret
- Can apply
- Has perspective
- Can empathise
- Has self-knowledge

The six facets were postulated to be sub-constructs of the general construct of *expectations of learning*. The Wiggins and McTighe (2001) framework contains five hierarchically ordered descriptors for each facet. Table 2 presents the descriptors for *expectations of 'application'*.

Table 2. Descriptors and behavioural expectations statements for 'application'

Level of Sub-construct	Descriptors	Behavioural statements
Higher 'application'	*Masterful*	The student is expected to find new ways to use his/her knowledge and skills. The student is expected to be flexible in how he/she uses knowledge and skills.
↑	*Skilled*	The student is expected to use knowledge and skills to perform well in a range of situations. The student is expected to use knowledge and skills to perform well in different situations.
	Able	The student is expected to use skills to perform well in some situations. The student is expected to use knowledge to perform well in some situations.
	Apprentice	The student is expected to use the same ways of doing things in different situations. The student is expected to use routines that help get jobs done.
Lower 'application'	*Novice*	The student is expected to use what has been learnt with help from others. The student is expected to follow instructions to complete tasks.

Two indicator statements were written in terms of student behaviour for each of the descriptors. The six sub-constructs, descriptors and behavioural statements for *expectations of learning* are presented in Appendix B.

RESEARCH OBJECTIVES

The research investigated the engagement in classroom learning of Year 10 and 11 students in Western Australia. The research questions were:

1. Which aspects of student engagement in classroom learning were the most difficult to identify in the Year 10 and 11 students, and which were the easiest to identify?
2. Is variance in the student engagement scores accounted for by membership of particular groups of students, (e.g. male or female, year of schooling, subject area studied and whether or not the subject was a favourite)?

METHODOLOGY

Sample

The data were collected as part of a larger study on secondary school student engagement in classroom learning. The sample was 112 Year 10 and 11 secondary students from government schools in metropolitan and rural areas of Western Australia. The sample characteristics are presented in Table 3 below.

Table 3. Sample characteristics

		Total Sample	Females	Males
All Respondents		*n=112*	*n=59*	*n=53*
Gender		%	%	%
	Females	53	–	100
	Males	47	100	–
School year				
	Yr 10	48	54	42
	Yr 11	52	46	58
Subject				
	English	27	27	26
	Maths	30	20	40
	S&E	20	22	17
	Science	24	31	17
Favourite subject				
	Most	62	58	68
	Least	38	42	32

DATA COLLECTION

The instruments of data collection were developed from the theoretical framework outlined above. One instrument was a researcher-completed rating scale instrument in which ratings were assigned using the framework presented in Appendices One and Two. The second instrument was a traditional; interview schedule which required students to provide qualitative information on their engagement.

Students were also asked to indicate which of the four core subjects (Mathematics, English, Society and the Environment and Science) were their most or least favourite. The researchers then selected one of these subjects as the focus of their interview. The students were asked to consider their responses only in relation to the nominated subject.

The two researchers assigned a rating for each of the 11 sub-constructs in the frameworks provided in Appendices One and Two. At the end of the interview, the raters compared their ratings, reviewing and resolving any differences in scores. Each of the sub-constructs was scored from 0 to 5, where 0 indicated minimal evidence of the sub-construct and 5 indicated a very high level of evidence of the sub-construct.

In addition to the rating process, the interviews were recorded to provide qualitative data to supplement the quantitative data.

DATA ANALYSIS

The data were entered into Excel and then imported into RUMM2020 (Andrich, Sheridan, Lyne & Luo, 2003). RUMM2020 applies the Rasch Rating Scale Model for data analysis (Andrich, 1978). A number of statistics were estimated. First, summary test-fit-statistics were estimated to show the item-person interaction, item-trait interaction and reliability indices. Second an item map was generated to show how well the distribution of student scores matched the distribution of item difficulties. Third, individual item-fit statistics to ascertain how well individual item data fitted the model:

- Location - the degree to which students provided affirmation of the sub-construct measured in logits (logarithmic odds of answering positively).
- SE - the standard error of the location measured in logits.
- Residual - the difference between the actual response and the expected response according to the model. The closer to zero the residual, the better the fit to the model. Residuals less than ± 2.5 (a default value used by RUMM2020) indicate the data fit the model.
- The Chi square test shows item-trait interaction. Probability values should be above the Bonferroni adjusted level.

Fourth, analysis of variance (ANOVA) was conducted to test whether variance in student scores accounted for by membership of particular groups (e.g. females and males). The F-Statistic and its level of significance were estimated ($p < 0.05$).

The qualitative data comprised students' statements about 11 aspects of their engagement. Since a record was also made of the rating assigned to each of these aspects, it was possible to reconcile statements with ratings. These statements were then used to qualify the quantitative results.

RESEARCH RESULTS

The results are presented in three sections. Firstly, the summary fit statistics and an item map. Secondly, the individual item fit statistics. Thirdly, the results of the ANOVA.

Overall Fit of Data to the Rasch Rating Scale Model

The summary test-of-fit statistics were calculated by RUMM2020 (Andrich, Sheridan, Lyne & Luo, 2000) to examine the psychometric properties of the data. These are presented in Table 4. Firstly, the item-person interaction measures the extent to which the students have been rated in a logical and consistent manner. The fit residuals for both items and persons are within acceptable ranges for the mean scores and standard deviation (means should be close to zero and standard deviation should be close to 1), indicating a good overall data to model fit. Secondly, the item-trait interaction indicates the consistency of the item 'difficulties' across the range of different student engagement measures (the 11 sub-constructs) on the scale. The Chi Square probability value >0.05 suggests the data represents a unidimensional trait, thus the data fit the model well. Thirdly, the Separation Index indicates the degree to which locations of students spread across a continuum, (i.e. students with higher locations were attracted higher scores on the items and those with lower locations attracted lower scores on the items). Ideally, this index will be close to 1.0; in this case a separation index of 0.87 indicates that the power of the test-of-fit was excellent.

Table 4. RUMM summary test-of-fit statistics – student engagement scale

ITEM-PERSON INTERACTION

| | ITEMS | | PERSONS | |
	Location	Fit Residual	Location	Fit Residual
Mean	0.00	0.44	0.61	-0.17
SD	0.39	0.80	1.06	1.19

ITEM-TRAIT INTERACTION		RELIABILITY INDICES	
Total Item Chi-Square	21.11	Separation Index	0.87
Total Deg of Freedom	22.00	Cronbach Alpha	N/A
Total Chi-Square Probability	0.51		

POWER OF TEST-OF-FIT

Power is EXCELLENT
Based on Separation Index of 0.87

RUMM also produced an item map (see Figure 2) displaying location of item thresholds and also location of students plotted on the same scale. The plot on the left of the vertical line shows the distribution of the relative locations of students in logits and the plot on the right shows the distribution of item thresholds (uncentralised). In the item plot, the first two digits are the item number and the third digit after the decimal point is the threshold. The respective thresholds for the 11 items are distributed from 'easy' at the bottom to 'hard' at the top. The distribution of the relative 'difficulty' of the items closely matches the student distribution, indicating that the items present a range of difficulties that match the students' differing abilities.

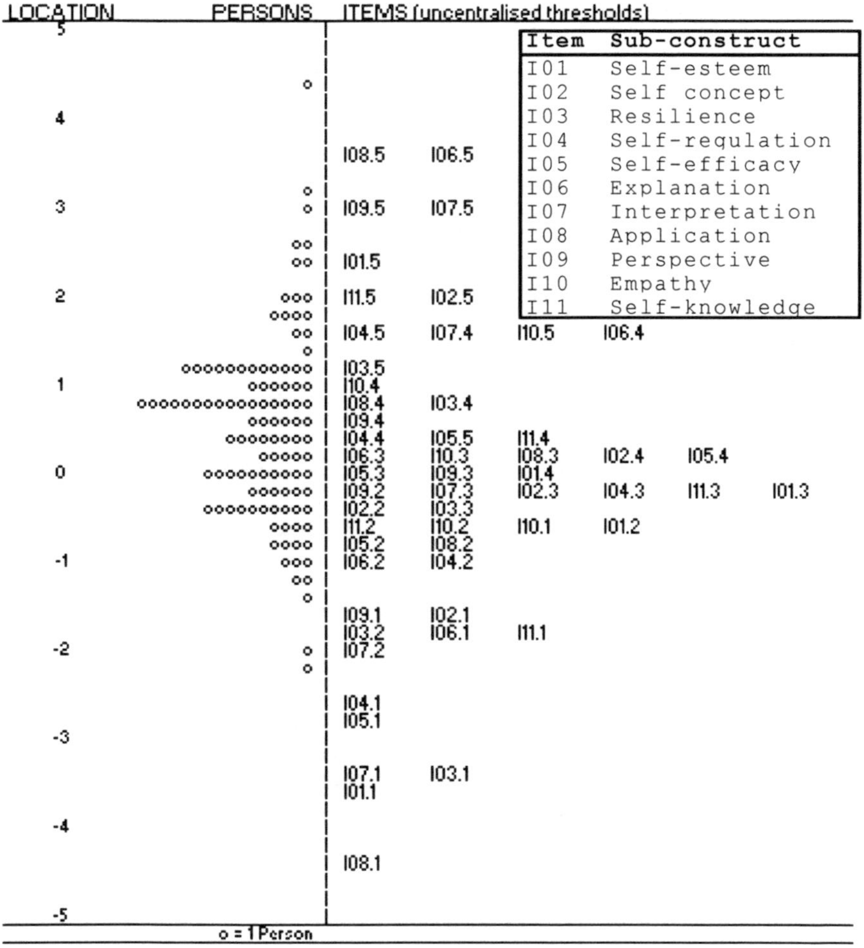

LOCATION	PERSONS	ITEMS (uncentralised thresholds)			
			Item	**Sub-construct**	
5			I01	Self-esteem	
	o		I02	Self concept	
4			I03	Resilience	
		I08.5 I06.5	I04	Self-regulation	
			I05	Self-efficacy	
	o		I06	Explanation	
3	o	I09.5 I07.5	I07	Interpretation	
	oo		I08	Application	
	oo	I01.5	I09	Perspective	
	ooo	I11.5 I02.5	I10	Empathy	
2	oooo		I11	Self-knowledge	
	oo	I04.5 I07.4 I10.5 I06.4			
	o				
	ooooooooooo	I03.5			
1	ooooooo	I10.4			
	ooooooooooooooooo	I08.4 I03.4			
	ooooooo	I09.4			
	oooooooo	I04.4 I05.5 I11.4			
	ooooo	I06.3 I10.3 I08.3 I02.4 I05.4			
0	ooooooooo	I05.3 I09.3 I01.4			
	ooooooo	I09.2 I07.3 I02.3 I04.3 I11.3 I01.3			
	oooooooooo	I02.2 I03.3			
	oooo	I11.2 I10.2 I10.1 I01.2			
	oooo	I05.2 I08.2			
-1	ooo	I06.2 I04.2			
	oo				
	o				
		I09.1 I02.1			
		I03.2 I06.1 I11.1			
-2	o	I07.2			
	o				
		I04.1			
		I05.1			
-3					
		I07.1 I03.1			
		I01.1			
-4					
		I08.1			
-5					

o = 1 Person

Figure 2. RUMM item map.

Examination of the item map shows how the individual items or sub-constructs were rated. Item I08 (Application) has the largest spread, with I08.1 placed at the lowest location of -4.5 and I08.5 placed at the highest location of 3.5. Off all 11 items, item I10 (Empathy) is placed higher up, with I10.1 at a location of -0.6. This indicates that of the lowest level expectations, empathy in learning was the most difficult for which to find evidence.

Difficulty of Affirming Student Attributes

Individual item fit statistics were calculated and these are presented in Table 5.

Table 5. *Individual item (sub-construct) fit statistics - in order of location*

Item	Sub-construct	Location	SE	Residual	DF	Chi Sq	Prob
I03	Resilience	−0.60	0.10	−0.30	95.34	1.89	0.38
I05	Self–efficacy	−0.50	0.09	−0.50	95.34	2.18	0.33
I04	Self–regulation	−0.27	0.10	−0.70	95.34	1.80	0.40
I01	Self–esteem	−0.25	0.10	1.21	95.34	1.28	0.52
I07	Interpretation	−0.09	0.15	0.40	59.59	1.40	0.49
I08	Application	−0.02	0.11	1.32	93.64	4.43	0.10
I11	Self–knowledge	0.09	0.09	1.00	94.49	3.46	0.17
I02	Self concept	0.12	0.09	0.09	95.34	0.05	0.97
I10	Empathy	0.44	0.12	1.42	53.63	1.88	0.39
I09	Perspective	0.45	0.13	1.14	48.52	1.34	0.51
I06	Explanation	0.62	0.14	−0.10	60.44	1.36	0.50

The item difficulties were located within a range from -0.60 to +0.62 logits. This shows that the raters identified differing levels of the 11 sub-constructs in the students. The residuals were within the acceptable boundaries of +/- 2.5 (a default set by RUMM2020). All of the Chi-square probability values (Bonferroni adjusted) were acceptable, indicating that the items measure *student engagement in classroom learning* very well.

The sub-construct (I03 Resilience) had the lowest location (-0.60), indicating that finding evidence of resilience in the students was easier for the raters than for the other sub-constructs. Evidence of resilience was gathered by asking students *"how do you cope, manage or get on when problems arise in class?"* The students offered problem solving solutions, such as asking the teacher or a fellow student for help, re-reading their notes, or putting in extra study time to help with comprehension. Most students were positive about their ability to face problems and weren't too worried about not being able to deal with small setbacks, or even larger ones.

In the middle, close to zero was the sub-construct I08 Application, with a location of -0.02. Evidence of expectations of application in student learning was elicited by asking *"Are you expected to use what you have learnt? For example to solve new problems or fix something."* Most students felt that they were expected to be able to repeat what had been taught in a lesson and some thought they would be expected to apply the learning in other situations. Very few students could demonstrate higher levels of application were expected of them, unless what was taught was vocational, such as writing job applications or mathematics for trades people.

The sub-construct (I06 Explanation) was the hardest to confirm, (Location of 0.62). Evidence of expectations of explanation in student learning was gathered by asking "*Are you expected to talk or write about what you have learnt?*" For evidence of low levels of explanation, students could demonstrate that they were expected to use the words of others to explain things, however this was not often true, in many instances students stated they were not expected to talk or write about what they had learnt, "we just copy out of the books, there is no discussion". Some students provided further evidence by saying they were expected to add some or lots of their own ideas to the things taught, "we have to go away and do research on the computers". However, at the top end, very few students stated they were expected to show in-depth or sophisticated levels of explanation in the chosen subject. This appeared to be especially true when mathematics was discussed.

Examination of the locations showed that the sub-constructs of student learning capabilities (I01 to I05) were easier to affirm than the sub-constructs of expectations of student learning (I06 to I11). It is hypothesised that this is because it is harder for a student to conceptualise the expectations that are put upon them than the capabilities they can demonstrate. Whilst conducting the interviews, students were guided to not think about whether they did talk or write about what they learnt, but rather whether they were expected to talk or write about what they learnt.

Variance in Engagement Scores Due to Group Memberships

School Year: When the data is examined by the person factor of school year, the relative mean scores for Year 10 and Year 11 students are 0.716 and 0.508 respectively, as shown along with the frequency distribution for each of the school years in Figure 3. An analysis of variance (ANOVA) was conducted by RUMM2020, ($F= 1.07$; $p>0.05$) which found no evidence of a statistically significant difference between the ratings of the students' school year.

Gender: Figure 4 shows the Person Frequency Distribution by gender. The mean score for females is 0.89 and 0.28 for males. An ANOVA was conducted and the effect of gender was found to be statistically significant, ($F= 9.92$; $p<0.05$). Thus males were rated lower than females on the *Student Engagement in Classroom Learning* scale.

Subject: Figure 5 shows the frequency distributions for students by subject. The mean scores for three of the subjects, English, Science and S&E are close, (0.747, 0.763 and 0.791 respectively), whilst Maths has a much lower mean score of 0.204. The ANOVA conducted found that the difference was not statistically significant ($F =2.12$; $p>0.05$).

On consideration, the lower score for mathematics was understandable when the comments the students made were reviewed. Mathematics did prove more difficult to affirm for some of the sub-constructs; perspective, empathy and explanation in particular. These are three aspects of learning that are not often associated with the teaching and learning of mathematics.

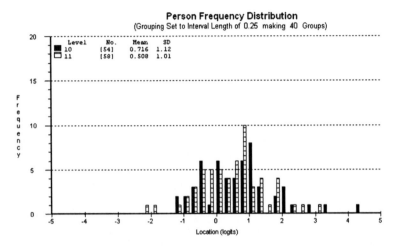

Figure 3. Person frequency distribution by school year.

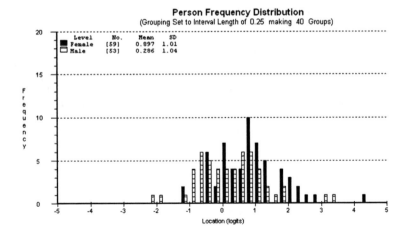

Figure 4. Person frequency distribution by gender.

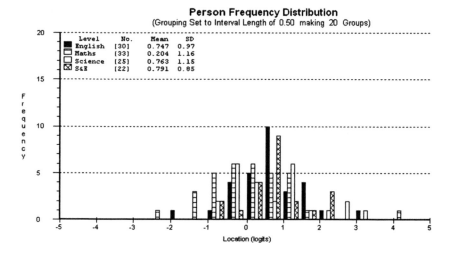

Figure 5. Person frequency distribution by subject.

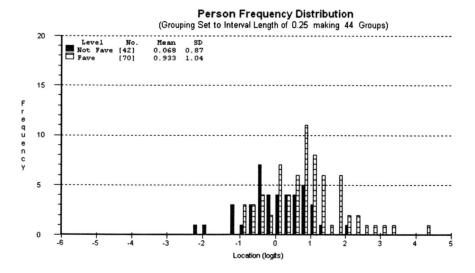

Figure 6. Person frequency distribution by favourite subject.

Favourite subject: The mean score of students who were asked about their favourite subjects was 0.93 and 0.06 for those who were asked about their least favourite subject. The ANOVA was again conducted by RUMM2020 and it was found to be statistically significant ($F = 20.33$; $p < 0.05$). This difference is clearly shown in Figure 6, with the distribution of scores for non-favourite subjects lower than the distribution of scores for favourite subjects. This difference between the scores of those discussing their favourite subject and those discussing their least favourite subject was expected, with much higher scores on the engagement scale for those rating their favourite subject.

DISCUSSION

Firstly, all 11 sub-constructs were measured – the data on each sub-construct fitted the Model. Thus measures were obtained for all 11 aspects of engagement which could be taken as evidence of construct validity.

Secondly, the construct of student engagement was theorised as a balance between learning capabilities (five sub-constructs) and expectations of student learning (six sub-constructs). However when the difficulties of identifying the constituent sub-constructs in these two dimensions were estimated, the locations of the expectations of learning sub-constructs were higher than those for the learning capabilities sub-constructs. It might be concluded that the expectations of student learning were less than commensurate with the students' capability. This is a significant finding. Vygotsky (1978) proposed that the Zone of Proximal Development is the gap between the level at which the subject is being taught and the students' current development. "If the gap is too large, the teaching will not be effective, if the gap is too small, the learner will not be stretched enough to learn adequately" (Mooney, 2000, p. X).

Thirdly, within the two dimensions, no particular ordering of sub-constructs was postulated. Indeed Wiggins and McTighe (2001) were careful to point out that the facets were in no particular order. This is reflected in the order of sub-construct difficulties which does not match that in either of the theoretical frameworks in Appendices A and B. Thus, a developmental learning sequence across the subconstruct should not be assumed. For example, explanation does not necessarily precede interpretation.

Fourth, the finding on gender is significant. Males showed less evidence of engagement than females. This finding is supported by the literature, providing evidence of the validity of the model. Fullerton (2002, p. 31) studied 11,150 students in the *Longitudinal Surveys of Australian Youth* and found:

> "...gender was found to be a strong influence on student's engagement, with females showing significantly higher levels of engagement than males; in all school sectors, in coeducational as well as single-sex schools, and at all achievement levels".

Fifth, the notion of favourite subjects being more engaging than least favourite subjects was also examined. Subjects that were the student's favourite attracted higher levels of engagement than subjects that were the student's least favourite. Glanville and Wildhagen (2007) also found a relationship between student engagement and what they called 'academic interest'. "...Academic interest is measured with the student's agreement that his or her classes are interesting and challenging, whether the student gets a feeling of satisfaction from doing what he or she is supposed to do in class and how often the student tries as hard as he or she can".

The age of students is closely related to their year of schooling. It appears that the engagement of students did not vary with age.

Differences between the four subject areas studied did not account for variance in the student engagement scores. Interestingly, Shernoff (2003) found that the type of instructional practices used (e.g. lecture, examination, coursework, group work) had more of an impact on engagement levels of students than the subject studied (when looking only at core subjects). The effect of instructional practices on engagement as defined in this study need further investigation.

CONCLUSION

This paper determined which of the 11 sub-constructs that comprise the student engagement in classroom learning scale were the most difficult and which were the easiest to identify in Year 10 and 11 students. It also determined whether membership of different groups of students accounted for variance in calibrated scores.

Further research using alternative instruments could be conducted to triangulate these findings, for example, the use of a student-self-report instrument.

The research has shown the utility of the Rasch Rating Scale Model for calibrating the 11 sub-constructs of the student engagement in classroom learning and also the identification of the significant variances between different student types.

REFERENCES

Andrich, D. (1978). Application of a psychometric rating model to ordered categories which are scored with successive integers. *Applied Psychological Measurement, 2*(4), 581–594.

Andrich, D., Sheridan, B., Lyne, A., & Luo, G. (2003). *RUMM2020: a Windows-based item analysis program employing Rasch unidimensional measurement models.* Perth: Murdoch University.

Cavanagh, R. F., Kennish, P., & Sturgess, K. (2008). *Development of theoretical frameworks to inform measurement of secondary school student engagement with learning.* Paper presented at the 2008 annual conference of the Australian Association for Research in Education, Brisbane.

Csikszentmihalyi, M. (1990a). *Flow: The psychology of optimal experience.* New York: Harper & Row.

Csikszentmihalyi, M. (1990b). Literacy and intrinsic motivation. *Daedalus, 119*(2), 115–140.

Finn, D. F., & Rock, D. A. (1997). Academic success for students at risk for school failure. *Journal of Applied Psychology, 82*(2), 221–234.

Fullarton, S. (2002). Student engagement with school: Individual and school-level influences. Camberwell, Victoria: ACER.

Glanville, J. L., & Wildhagen, T. (2007). The measurement of school engagement: Assessing dimensionality and measurement invariance across race and ethnicity. Educational and Psychological Measurement, 67(6), 1019–1041.

Hektner, J. M., Schmidt, J. A., & Csikszentmihalyi, M. (2007). *Experience sampling method: Measuring the quality of everyday life.* Thousand Oaks, CA: Sage Publications.

Howard, S., & Johnson, B. (1999). Tracking student resilience. *Children Australia, 24*(3), 14–23.

Marks, G. N., & Fleming, N. (1999). *Early school leaving in Australia: Findings from the 1995 Year 9 LSAY cohort.* Camberwell, Victoria: ACER.

Martin, J. (2007). The selves of educational psychology: Conceptions, contexts, and critical considerations. *Educational Psychologist, 42*(2), 79–89.

Marsh, H. W. (1992). Extracurricular activities: Beneficial extension of the traditional curriculum or subversion of academic goals? *Journal of Educational Psychology, 84*(4), 553–562.

Massimini, F., Csikszentmihalyi, M., & Carli, M. (1987). The monitoring of optimal experience. A tool for psychiatric rehabilitation. *Journal of Nervous and Mental Disease, 175*(9), 545–549.

Mooney, C. G. (2000). *Theories of childhood.* St. Paul, MN: Redleaf Press.

National Centre for Education Statistics. (1995). Extracurricular participation and student engagement, Retrieved February 19, 2008, from http://nces.ed.gov/pubs95/95741.pdf

Reeve, R., Jang, H., Carrell, D., Jeon, S., & Barch, J. (2004). Enhancing students' engagement by increasing teachers' autonomy support. *Motivation and Emotion, 28*(2), 147–169.

Schweinle, A., Meyer, D. K., & Turner, J. C. (2006). Striking the right balance: Students' motivation and affect in elementary mathematics. *Journal of Educational Research, 95*(5), 271–293.

Shernoff, D. J., Csikszentmihalyi, M., Schneider, B., & Shernoff, E. S. (2003). Student engagement in high school classrooms from the perspective of flow theory. *School Psychology Quarterly, 18*(2), 158–176.

Vygotsky, L. S. (1978). *Mind and society: The development of higher psychological processes.* Cambridge, MA: Harvard University Press.

White, B., & Frederiksen, J. (2005). A theoretical framework and approach for fostering metacognitive development. *Educational Psychologist, 40*(4), 211–223.

Wiggins, G., & McTighe, J. (1998). *Understanding by design.* Alexandra, VA: Association for Supervision and Curriculum Development.

Penelope Kennish and Robert F. Cavanagh
(Curtin University of Technology, Western Australia)

APPENDIX A

FRAMEWORK OF LEANING CAPABILITIES

Learning capabilities	Self-esteem	Self-concept	Resilience
MORE	*Has positive self image* Sees very little in self that needs to improve. Is highly confident.	*Strives to be perfect.* Even though he/she knows he/she does very well, still looks for ways to improve. Knows self very well.	*Has unqualified expectations of coping.* Expects he/she will always be OK. Doesn't face any unfixable problem.s
	Has confidence to make decisions. Is confident to make choices about how to do things. Is confident to make choices about what to do.	*Motivated by self reflection.* Thinking about self makes he/she feel good. Thinking about self helps he/she do better.	*Can deal with failure.* Things going wrong is not an issue for him/her. Believes things will eventually work out well.
	Has pride in self. Is proud of his/her achievements. Thinks he/she is good compared to others.	*Self reflecting.* What he/she does shapes his/her view of myself. Thinks about self when necessary.	*Expects success.* Expects if he/she works at problems they will be solved. Expects to eventually succeed.
	Trusts self to act. Trusts self to do what is right for self. Has faith in own ability.	*At ease comparing self with others.* How he/she feels about self comes from how others see him/her. Is comfortable comparing self with others.	*Overcomes small setbacks.* Considers overcoming small problems is possible. Can deal with small hassles.
LESS	*Sees worth in self.* Is happy with self. Sees some good qualities in self.	*Compares self with others.* Compares self with others. Checks own progress against that of others.	*Is aware of problems.* Accepts that a little difficulty is OK. Is aware that things go wrong sometimes.

APPENDIX B

FRAMEWORK OF LEANING CAPABILITIES

Learning capabilities	Self-regulation	Self-efficacy
MORE	*Takes responsibility for learning.* Is in total control of own learning. Is in charge of own learning.	*Has perseverance in the face of adversity.* Keeps trying when things go seriously wrong. Never gives up.
	Makes improvement in own learning Builds on what he/she can do well. Improves how he/she learns.	*Has determination.* Wants to overcome most difficulties. Wants to succeed when things become hard.
	Understands own learning. Knows how to learn better. Knows how he/she learns best.	*Recognises contextual influences.* Knows some situations present more difficulty than others. Knows when and where he/she can succeed.
	Assesses own learning. Thinks about mistakes. Thinks about achievements.	*Has expectations of self.* Would like to succeed. Believes success is a possibility.
LESS	*Awareness of learning.* Is aware of mistakes. Is aware of achievements.	*Makes effort.* Tries when necessary. Makes an effort when required.

APPENDIX C

FRAMEWORK OF EXPECTATIONS OF LEARNING
FOR UNDERSTANDING

Expectations	Explanation	Interpretation	Application
MORE The student is expected to:	*Sophisticated* Bring together many ideas to explain something in a new way. Develop original (new) explanations of what was taught.	*Profound* Show a deep and very clear understanding of the work. Find simple explanations for complicated things.	*Masterful* Find new ways to use his/her knowledge and skills. Be flexible in how he/she uses knowledge and skills.
The student is expected to:	*In-depth* Understand the work in a way that is different from what was taught. Find connections between different parts of what was learnt.	*Revealing* Compare different ways of understanding the work. Explain the differences between ways of understanding the work.	*Skilled* Uses knowledge and skills to perform well in a range of situations. Use knowledge and skills to perform well in different situations.
The student is expected to:	*Developed* Include a range of own ideas when explaining what was learnt. Explain what was learnt using own words.	*Perceptive* Correctly explain to others how work should be done. Help others understand why what the class are learning is important.	*Able* Use skills to perform well in some situations. Uses knowledge to perform well in some situations.
The student is expected to:	*Intuitive* Explain what was learnt by including extra information. Include some of own ideas when explaining what was learnt.	*Interpreted* Show that he/she correctly understands the work. Explain why what he/she has learnt is important.	*Apprentice* Use the same ways of doing things in different situations. Use routines that help get jobs done.
LESS The student is expected to:	*Naive* Use the words of others when explaining things. Use the ideas of others when explaining things.	*Literal* Repeat what has been told. Repeat what has been read.	*Novice* Use what has been learnt with help from others. Follow instructions to complete tasks.

APPENDIX D

FRAMEWORK OF EXPECTATIONS OF LEARNING
FOR UNDERSTANDING

Expectations	Perspective	Empathy	Self-knowledge
MORE The student is expected to:	*Insightful* Make sure own feelings don't cloud judgements. Carefully and fairly evaluate the views of others.	*Mature* Be willing to see things the way others do. Seek out views highly different from my own.	*Wise* Make serious decisions based on knowing what has been learnt. Make serious decisions based on knowing what he/she has understood.
The student is expected to:	*Thorough* Be critical of the views of others in a fair way. Balance own views against the views of others.	*Sensitive* Sees things in ways similar to others. Develop attitudes similar to others.	*Circumspect* Has a clear understanding of both his/her strengths and weaknesses. Clearly sees the strengths and weaknesses of others.
The student is expected to:	*Considered* Understand the views of others. Think carefully about the views of others.	*Aware* Know that others feel differently from self. Be aware that others see things differently from self.	*Innocent* Think about what he/she knows. Be aware of things he/she should know.
The student is expected to:	*Aware* Show awareness of differences in what others value. Reconsider own point of view after listening to others.	*Developing* Force self to make sense of ideas that seem strange to me. Discipline self to understand attitudes different to my own.	*Thoughtful* Identify what he/she doesn't understand. Spend time thinking about what he/she can and can't do.
LESS The student is expected to:	*Uncritical* Not ignore points of view different from own. Use own views to be critical of things or people.	*Egocentric* Try to make sense of ideas that seem strange. Try to understand attitudes different to own.	*Unreflective* Accept that others can help him/her see what I need to know. Let others tell him/her what he/she needs to know.

CLAIRE MALEY AND TREVOR G. BOND

14. MEASURING COGNITIVE DEVELOPMENT IN EARLY CHILDHOOD LEARNING ENVIRONMENTS

ABSTRACT

Discussions of the transition from prior-to-school settings to more formal year one learning environments often involve the concept of children's school readiness. A Piagetian perspective suggests the presence and use of particular operatory structures indicative of the concrete operational stage of cognitive development are requisite for a child to achieve successful learning outcomes in the new formal learning environment of primary school. In any case, the non-standardised skills-based checklists used by many early childhood educators to infer children's levels of readiness for year one seem inadequate, as the debate surrounding 'unready' children and under-achievement persists. This paper presents the findings of a study in which forty-two children in a preschool learning environment were administered a Piagetian conservation of number task using the Genevan *méthode clinique* as outlined in *The Child's Conception of Number* (Piaget & Szeminska, 1941/1952). Participants were also assessed routinely by their teachers using the teacher-developed Key Indicators of Readiness for Year One (KIRYO) Checklist, and then judged qualitatively on their preschool and early year one achievement by their respective teachers. Children's performances on each of the above-mentioned indicators were scored quantitatively using comprehensive performance criteria derived from each item's source. Analysis using the Rasch Partial Credit Model indicated that concrete operational thinking, rather than mastery of the KIRYO checklist indicators, was more closely aligned with teachers' perceptions of success in the year one learning environment. The implications for professional discussion and decision-making, as well as insights for teachers of early childhood sectors are canvassed.

BACKGROUND

Inspired by the impressive work of other researchers in the field (Bond, 2001, 2003; Drake, 1998; Bunting, 1993), this study was undertaken to determine if the attribute termed cognitive development could be helpful in inferring those children ready for success in the formal learning environment of year one. In particular, the aim was to verify which, out of a more conventional school readiness checklist, or the measurement of cognitive developmental levels, was more closely aligned with

R.F. Cavanagh and R.F. Waugh (eds.), Applications of Rasch Measurement
in Learning Environments Research, 301–324.

successful learning outcomes in year one of primary school - as judged by year one teachers.

Most prior-to-school setting teachers make readiness judgements based on a child's level of achievement on teacher-developed readiness checklists (Clift, Stagnitti & DeMello, 2000). Such checklists usually include a number of indicators derived from the reading of key texts in the early childhood field which focus on mastery of a range of fine motor, gross motor and social skills. Children able to demonstrate all (or most) of the indicators are deemed 'ready' to proceed to year one to undertake more formal learning experiences. Whilst children's levels of physical/motor/social development are the primary focii of most teachers' readiness judgements, children's levels of cognitive development, generally, are not assessed (Maley, 2005).

Despite the recently renewed interest in cognitive development (Boardman, 2006), it appears as though most teachers still adhere to the, perhaps misinterpreted yet common, idea that a delay in motor development would signify the possibility of a delay in cognitive development. Some bodies of knowledge would assert that motor development does not always indicate corresponding cognitive development, suggesting that current readiness checklists could be misleading and inaccurate. Baldwin (1980) describes cognitive development as, "a series of qualitative changes in cognitive functioning rather than merely as the quantitative increase in certain skills" (p. 86).

The most influential theory in the field of cognitive development is that developed by Jean Piaget. At the turn of the millennium, TIME magazine named him as one of the 100 most influential thinkers of the previous century. He is credited with having discovered that young children are intellectually quite different from adults; they do not think in the same ways (Baldwin, 1980; Elkind, 1989; Ginsburg & Opper, 1988; Gruber & Vonèche, 1977; Wallach, 1969; Wood, 1998). Specifically, the research of Piaget and his Genevan team focused on "children's gradual attainment of intellectual structures which allow for increasingly effective interactions with the environment" (Ginsburg & Opper, 1988, p. 13). Given that a successful transition from prior-to-school settings to primary school learning environments involves children 'interacting effectively with the environment' of formal schooling, Piaget's theory provided a perspective still worthy of investigation.

Piagetian theory describes children's intellectual development as progressing through an invariant sequence of age-related (not age-dependent) stages of thinking: sensorimotor (birth to approximately 2 years), preoperational (approximately 2 to 7 years), concrete operational (approximately 7 to 11 years), and formal operational (approximately 11 years onwards) (Ginsburg & Opper, 1988). Each cognitive developmental stage is characterised by the construction of different psychological structures, each new one of which enables a distinct and more effective type of interaction between the child and the environment (Ginsburg & Opper, 1988; Elkind, 1981, 1986).

Of particular relevance to educators in early childhood learning environments is the transition from Piaget's second, preoperational, stage, to the third, concrete operational stage. Children's thinking in Piaget's preoperational stage of cognitive development is described as ego-centric; children experience difficulty taking into account others points of view, and use language in qualitatively different ways from those of adults (Elkind, 1981; Smidt, 1998). Piagetian theory claims that when a child attains concrete operational structures, s/he is then able to de-centre intellectually, take others points of view into account, use more stable, systematic and logical thought processes, and achieve a more stable equilibrium between self and the learning environment (Ginsburg & Opper, 1988; Baldwin, 1980; Piaget, 1970; Smidt, 1998; Vernon, 1976; Wood, 1998).

The concept of equilibrium – the progressive balancing of an organism with its environment – is considered significant, especially to the issue of children's school readiness. Adherents to Piagetian theory would view children's transition to year one as a "specific form of biological adaptation of a complex organism to a [new] complex environment" (Flavell, Miller & Miller, 2002, p. 5). As a result, the focus of this study was the premise that children thinking in the concrete operational stage of cognitive development would be more able to achieve equilibrium effectively with the demands of a formal year one learning environment – and thus, achieve more successful learning outcomes – than those children inferred to be thinking in the preoperational stage.

THE STUDY

The Key Indicators of Readiness for Year One (KIRYO) Checklist used in this study was developed by the experienced teachers of the preschool hosting the study. It included 29 indicators drawn from key texts in the early childhood education field, with a strong focus on the development of fine and gross motor skills (such as threading, cutting, running, jumping, hopping, etc.) The checklist had been used annually and reflectively for a number of years by the teachers in that pre-school as the basis on which they would make their professional judgements about the readiness (or otherwise) of each of their young students for 'promotion' to year one, often described as 'going up to the big school!'

To assess the cognitive developmental levels of the children in this study, a Piagetian conservation of number task was administered using the *méthode clinique* procedures as described by Piaget (1961, 1970) and scored using the Rasch-based procedures implemented earlier by Drake (1998). Children's performances on both the KIRYO checklist and the conservation task were recorded, together with qualitative judgements from both the preschool and successive year one teachers on the participant's actual levels of achievement in both learning environments.

Position 1

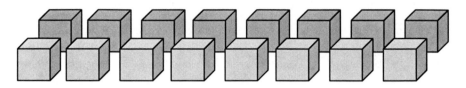

Position 2

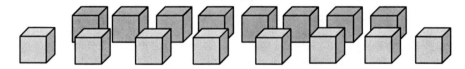

Position 3

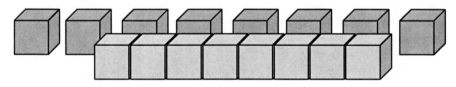

Position 4

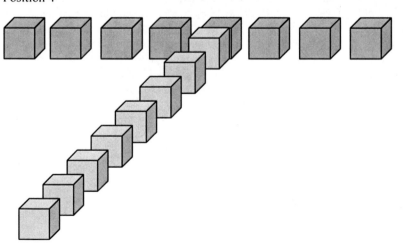

Figure 1. Conservation of number task.

PIAGET'S CONSERVATION OF NUMBER TASK

The conservation of number task, extracted directly from *The Child's Conception of Number* (Piaget & Szeminska, 1941/1952), was used specifically to infer the presence and use of concrete operational developmental structures. This conservation task is particularly apt for the study as number is the first concept a child conserves; and, additionally, it relates directly to early concepts taught in the formal year one mathematics curriculum.

Concrete operational thinking is demonstrated when a child comprehends that the equality of a number of two sets of objects is independent of the appearance of the two sets when either is perceptually transformed (Baldwin, 1980; Ginsburg & Opper, 1988; Wallach, 1969). For example, a child constructs a second set (B) of objects based on the first (A) using one-to-one correspondence, and then can conserve that equality (A=B) although one set has been manipulated to appear longer or shorter than the other (see Figure 1). Both the child's conservation judgement and its operational justification are important, jointly, as the latter helps to reveal the qualitative nature of thought processes that determine whether the child demonstrates conservation.

METHOD

Sample

This study was conducted at a medium-sized state school in Queensland, Australia. Forty-two preschool children with informed parental consent, from a total eligible student cohort of 100, compiled the sample. Although comparatively small, the sample size was sufficient to reflect the basic relationships in the data for this exploratory investigation. At the time of data collection, the 18 girls' and 24 boys' ages ranged from four years and 11 months to five years and 11 months.

DATA COLLECTION

During the last three weeks of the preschool year, each of the participants were individually interviewed and administered the conservation of number task using the *méthode clinique* qualitative interview procedures as explicated by Piaget (1961, 1970). Each interview lasted between 10 and 15 minutes approximately, and was video-taped for later selective transcription and detailed analysis.

As part of the preschool end-of-year assessment routine, each participant was assessed by the preschool teacher according to the KIRYO Checklist. Children's levels of development of the various items in the checklist were categorised dichotomously as either 'needs help' or 'satisfactory'. Children who achieved all, or almost all criteria in the 'satisfactory' category were deemed by their preschool teachers ready for year one. Each applicable checklist was photocopied, de-identified, and then coded to maintain children's anonymity. No form of screening for children's cognitive development levels was used by the preschool teachers.

On the last day of the preschool year, the preschool teachers were asked to provide qualitative judgements about each participant's overall level of readiness for year one. Using their professional knowledge, teachers selected the most appropriate of the following polytomous categories for each participant: either, 'not yet ready', 'nearly ready', or 'ready' for probable success in the year one learning environment. These judgements were recorded on a separate checklist for use by the researcher. In the last week of semester one in the following school year (i.e., about six months later), the successive year one teachers were asked to provide two qualitative judgements concerning participants' year one achievements to that point. The first of these two qualitative judgements was based on a question similar to that asked of the preschool teachers about six months earlier; it concerned each participant's level of readiness for success in year one at the *beginning* of the school year. The year one teachers judged each of the participants to have been either, 'not yet ready', 'nearly ready', or 'ready' for probable success in the year one learning environment. The second judgement concerned each participant's *actual* level of successful learning as at the *end* of semester one (at that current point in time). Participants were judged qualitatively to be either, 'not yet at level', 'almost at level', or 'at level' in their achievement of Key Learning Area (KLA) outcomes based on the year one curriculum. The year one teachers had no knowledge of the preschool teachers' qualitative judgements. These year one teachers' judgements were also recorded on a separate checklist for use by the researcher.

These two teachers' professional judgements were used, in conjunction with the three above-mentioned sources of data, to help verify the relative effectiveness of the KIRYO Checklist and conservation task as indicators of school readiness.

Scoring

The Rasch Partial Credit Model was applied to co-calibrate – for the first time ever – the three key sets of items (child's performance on the readiness checklist, preschool and year one teachers qualitative judgements, and the child's level of cognitive development) during the child's progression from informal learning experiences of preschool to the formal learning environment of year one. Specifically, these items were used to help to investigate the relative effectiveness of both the preschool's KIRYO Checklist and Piaget's conservation of number task as potential indicators of school readiness. Partial Credit scoring of the data required the construction of four sets of performance criteria: one each for the conservation task; KIRYO checklist; the preschool teachers' qualitative judgements; and the year one teachers' qualitative judgements (see Appendix A). Item responses were divided into hierarchically ordered levels of ability to which partial credit, for partial success, could be assigned. Items for this project were either dichotomous (two criteria: i.e., needs help/satisfactory) or polytomous (three criteria: i.e., not yet ready/nearly ready/ready). Thus, scoring was completed using a progressive two-step $(0, 1)$ or three-step $(0, 1, 2)$ system as required by Rasch analysis and espoused in Bond and Fox (2001; 2007). Partial credit scoring can help produce more precise estimates of person ability than a mere fail/pass, or dichotomous scoring (e.g. Bond & Parkinson, 2010).

Participants' scores were recorded as individual student data lines within a larger data file inclusive of all children's performances. Each data line consisted of the following: the participant's identifying code (2 digits); the participant's score on the conservation of number items (13 digits); the participant's score on the KIRYO Checklist indicators (29 digits); the score applicable to preschool teachers' qualitative judgement (1 digit); and lastly, the scores applicable to the year one teachers' two qualitative judgements (2 digits) (see example below).

05 0001101210010 11111111111111111111111111111 2 22

Each data line represents the transformation of qualitative data to quantitative data, which were then subjected to Rasch analysis. Items for which there was no response were regarded as missing data, and the data line left blank at the applicable point. In such cases, the Rasch model estimates ability and difficulty based on the available data.

RESULTS

It is well-known that the Rasch model is effective in the assessment of aspects of child and cognitive development (e.g. Bond & Fox, 2001, 2007; Bond & Parkinson, 2010). The data in this study were subjected to analysis using Quest software (Adams & Khoo, 1993).

Rasch Analysis of All Data Combined

Whilst co-calibration of tests/data is often completed for more pragmatic reasons (Bond & Parkinson, 2010), in this study, the data from all four sources were Rasch analysed together to help establish whether they could be considered to be measuring the same underlying latent trait of school readiness. Determining whether the items actually investigated the single construct of school readiness was necessary, of course, before attempting to suggest *which* of the indicators more closely aligned with successful achievement in the year one learning environment.

Unidimensionality

Routinely accepted values for the transformed t statistic of the infit and outfit mean square residuals range from -2 to +2, and are held to indicate data unidimensionality (Bond & Fox, 2001; Drake, 1998) especially for such low-stakes, investigatory purposes. Rasch analysis of the combined data revealed marginally misfitting items K20 (infit t =1.5, outfit t = 2.0), and K14 (infit t = .7, outfit t = 2.2). Despite the presence of the borderline outfit statistics, given that the highest misfit estimate for item K14 (one of the KIRYO checklist items) sits just slightly outside the generally accepted fit statistic range, this was taken as indicating sufficient test unidimensionality for these exploratory purposes.

Person-Item Map

Figure 2 is, of course, the person-item map produced from the Rasch analysis of the combined data set. Whilst Quest routinely represents each person ability location by an X, participant reference codes, instead, were inserted on the left hand side of the variable map to assist a more meaningful interpretation. The combined test items are located on the right-hand side of the figure, with K, N, P and O representing KIRYO checklist items, conservation of Number items, Preschool teachers' judgements, and year one teachers' judgements, loosely grouped left to right, respectively.

Evidently, items K2, K3, K4, K13, K14, K15, K16, K21, K23, K26, and K28, plotted at -2.46 logits, presented as the criteria least difficult to satisfy (e.g. checklist items such as running, jumping, etc.); whilst item N9.2 (use of logical reasoning to consistently justify the invariance of the two sets in the conservation of number task), plotted at +5.30 logits, presented as the criterion most difficult to satisfy. Case 7, located at +5.84 logits, displays as the most successful participant, whilst case 2, located at -1.93 logits, appears as the least successful on this suite of combined items.

```
     Most Successful              Most Difficult
 6.0
             7


                                N9.2

 5.0                            N2.2 N11.2 N13

                                N12.2


            11
 4.0        10                  N11.1
                                N3.2
            37                  N10.2
            17  34           |
            23               |
            16  39  42       |  N4 N6.2
 3.0        35               |  N7.2
            6                |
            8  14  21  24    |
            26               |  One2.2
            40  22  5  38  41|  One1.2
            12  30  28  29   |  N6.1 N8.2 N10.1
 2.0        4  3  19          |  N7.1
            1  32  31         |  N12.1
                             |    K12
            9  13  27        |
            15  20              N8.1    One2.1
```

```
        36                |
  1.0                     |              N5
        18                |
                          |              Pre1.2
                          |
                          |              One1.1
                          |              N1
                          |
                          |              K6  K9  K20   N9.1
   .0                     |              N3.1
                          |              K19
        25                |
                          |              K7  K18   N2.1
                          |
                          |
  -1.0   33               |              K5  K8  K10  K24
                          |
                          |
                          |              K1  K11  K17  K25
                          |
         2                |
  -2.0                    |    |         Pre1.1
                          |
                          |
                          |              K2  K3  K4  K13  K14  K15
                          |              K16  K21  K23  K26  K28
                          |
  -3.0              KIRYO Cons Number Teacher Judgement
```

Note. Case colours indicate Preschool teachers' judgements of children as: 'not yet ready', 'nearly ready', and 'ready' for success in year one.

Figure 2. Item difficulty and person ability estimates for all 45 items.

The case colours indicate the preschool teachers judgements of 'Not Yet Ready (red)' (1 child, approximately 2% of cohort), 'Nearly Ready (blue)' (7 children, approximately 17%), and 'Ready (green)' (34 children, approximately 81%) for success in the more formal learning environment of year one. The substantial (almost) three logits difference between item P1.1 (preschool teachers' qualitative judgement of 'Nearly Ready') and item O1.1 (year one teachers' qualitative judgement of 'Nearly Ready'), as well as the two logit difference between items P1.2 (preschool teachers qualitative judgement of 'Ready') and O1.2 (year one teachers qualitative judgement of 'Ready') indicates an apparently sig-nificant (i.e. professionally meaningful) disparity between these teachers' understandings of what it means to be ready for success in year one early formal learning environments.

Output Tables

As Rasch analysis Wright-maps present the relations between person ability and item difficulty only (Bond & Fox, 2001; 2007), error estimates, fit statistics and the reliabilities of these estimates are reported in the following tables: Table 1 – item fit statistics (for all 45 items); Table 2 – case fit statistics.

Transformed t statistics for cases 12, 15, and 32 indicate that their response patterns over-fitted the Rasch model's expectations, *i.e.,* were more Guttman-like than stochastic: Case 12, plotted at +2.19 logits (infit t -3.46; outfit t -1.22); case 15, ability +1.37 logits (infit t -2.23; outfit t -1.50); case 32, ability +1.86 logits (infit t -3.44; outfit t -1.42). The above-mentioned cases were considered very predictable under the Rasch model as the "expectation ... that there will be a zone of uncertainty or unpredictability around the person's level of ability" (Bond & Fox, 2001, p. 178) was not apparent in these cases.

Conversely, with an estimated ability of +3.33 logits (infit t +3.17; outfit t +0.63), case 23 presents as more haphazard than predicted by the Rasch model. The data presents case 23 as a high performer in the conservation of number task data and one of 15 perfect-status achievers in the KIRYO Checklist data (see Figure 1). However, review of the Qualitative Judgements Chart reveals that he was judged, by his year one teacher, to be 'not yet ready' for probable success in the year one learning environment (as opposed to 'ready' as judged by the preschool teacher), and still 'not yet at level' at the end of semester one. Despite making judgements that conflict with case 23's evident high abilities, the year one teacher seems to have shown quite important insight in her professional judgement.

Review of this participant's conservation task and KIRYO Checklist performances presented him in the top 3% of the cohort. However, closer inspection of the Rasch model fit statistics produced for this student (see Table 4) revealed results in support of the year one teacher's judgements. The fit statistics for case 23 (infit mn sq +2.79; oufit mn sq +1.08; infit t +3.17; outfit t +0.63) indicates a performance detected as erratic under Rasch model expectations. The misfit indicators suggest that whilst case 23 achieved a high overall score, he failed to satisfy the criterion of some of the *least* difficult items on the test. The data file revealed that he failed (unexpectedly) on items N4, N12, O1 and O2. Although the overall score of the child implied readiness, the misfit suggested that this score should not be taken at face value.

Indeed, this child had moved to Australia (from a culturally-different country of birth) only a few months prior to the testing, and spoke English as a second language. Additionally, case 23 was the only participant to have 'missing data' in his data line as his response to item N13 was incomprehensible to the researcher – largely because of case 23's unfamiliarity with, and lack of the required vocabulary in the English language. Thus, it seems that the year one teacher had a qualitatively sensitive view of the child's readiness (i.e. language readiness problem) that was detected quantitatively by Rasch analysis.

Table 1. Rasch analysis results for all 45 items

Item	Score		Threshold/s/Error				Infit	Outfit	Infit	Outfit
#	Max Score		1		2		Mnsq	Mnsq	t	t
N1	34	42	0.49	−0.46			0.94	1.11	−0.10	0.40
N2	42	84	−0.56	−1.06	4.99	−0.96	1.25	0.13	0.80	0.90
N3	46	84	−0.13	−0.88	3.84	0.76	1.15	1.15	0.70	0.60
N4	14	41	3.16	0.36			1.20	1.24	1.30	0.70
N5	32	42	0.86	0.42			1.02	0.81	0.20	−0.20
N6	33	84	2.25	0.63	3.28	0.63	0.77	0.70	−1.20	−0.60
N7	37	84	2.06	0.63	3.08	0.60	0.80	0.69	−1.10	−0.70
N8	53	84	1.38	0.63	2.20	0.62	0.81	0.76	−1.00	−0.40
N9	39	84	0.06	0.94	5.30	1.06	1.11	1.11	0.40	0.40
N10	30	84	2.25	0.63	3.73	0.70	0.80	1.11	−1.00	0.40
N11	9	84	4.00	0.94	5.00	1.13	1.02	1.46	0.20	0.70
N12	29	84	1.88	0.66	4.75	0.86	1.26	1.19	1.30	0.70
N13	4	41	4.95	0.57			1.20	0.63	0.60	0.10
K1	40	42	−1.58	0.83			0.46	0.09	−0.90	−0.40
K2	41	42	−2.46	1.11			1.00	0.13	0.30	0.30
K3	41	42	−2.46	1.11			1.00	0.13	0.30	0.30
K4	41	42	−2.46	1.11			1.00	0.13	0.30	0.30
K5	39	42	−1.01	0.70			0.61	0.22	−0.70	−0.50
K6	36	42	0.04	0.52			1.05	1.27	0.30	0.60
K7	38	42	−0.58	0.62			0.80	0.75	−0.30	0.10
K8	39	42	−1.01	0.70			0.61	0.22	−0.70	−0.50
K9	36	42	0.04	0.52			0.81	0.70	−0.40	−0.20
K10	39	42	−1.01	0.70			0.71	0.52	−0.40	0.00
K11	40	42	−1.58	0.83			0.90	0.63	0.00	0.30
K12	26	42	1.72	0.36			0.99	0.89	0.00	−0.20
K13	41	42	−2.46	1.11			0.56	0.06	−0.40	0.20
K14	41	42	−2.46	1.11			1.45	10.60	0.70	2.20
K15	41	42	−2.46	1.11			1.18	0.22	0.50	0.50
K16	41	42	−2.46	1.11			1.00	0.13	0.30	0.30
K17	40	42	−1.58	0.83			1.39	0.71	0.80	0.40
K18	38	42	−0.58	0.62			1.89	2.81	1.70	1.50
K19	37	42	−0.25	0.56			1.56	1.44	1.30	0.70
K20	36	42	0.04	0.52			1.57	2.95	1.50	2.00
K21	41	42	−2.46	1.11			0.56	0.06	−0.40	0.20
K22	Item has perfect score									
K23	41	42	−2.46	1.11			0.56	0.06	−0.40	0.20
K24	39	42	−1.01	0.70			0.84	0.43	−0.20	−0.20
K25	40	42	−1.58	0.83			0.46	0.09	−0.90	−0.40
K26	41	42	−2.46	1.11			1.18	0.22	0.50	0.50
K27	Item has perfect score									
K28	41	42	−2.46	1.11			1.18	0.22	0.50	0.50
K29	Item has perfect score									
P1	75	84	−1.97	1.56	0.52	0.97	0.95	0.74	0.00	−0.30
O1	55	84	0.36	0.75	2.41	0.62	0.86	0.99	−0.70	0.10
O2	49	84	1.47	0.63	2.49	0.62	0.85	0.82	−0.80	−0.40
Mean			0.00				0.98	0.99	0.10	0.30
SD			2.21				0.31	1.65	0.80	0.60
r			0.86							

Note. The prefixes in the Item column represent items relating to the following: N = conservation of number task; K = KIRYO Checklist; P = Preschool teachers' qualitative judgement; and O = Year One teachers' qualitative judgement.

Table 2. Rasch analysis results for all 42 cases

ID #	Score Max Score		Threshold / Error		Infit Mnsq	Outfit Mnsq	Infit t	Outfit t
01	36	54	1.86	0.41	0.69	0.34	−1.03	−0.80
02	12	53	−1.93	0.40	0.99	0.83	0.00	0.26
03	37	54	2.02	0.41	0.62	0.27	−1.37	−0.88
04	37	54	2.02	0.41	1.24	0.86	0.82	0.14
05	39	54	2.36	0.41	1.07	0.73	0.31	0.07
06	42	54	2.89	0.44	0.94	0.51	−0.60	0.03
07	52	54	5.84	0.78	0.71	0.13	−0.32	1.83
08	41	54	2.71	0.43	0.51	0.22	−1.71	−0.52
09	34	54	1.53	0.40	0.83	0.98	−0.49	0.22
10	47	54	4.00	0.51	0.66	0.20	−0.77	0.31
11	48	54	4.28	0.54	1.10	2.17	0.37	1.25
12	38	54	2.19	0.41	0.26	0.12	−3.46	−1.22
13	34	54	1.53	0.40	1.00	0.60	0.11	−0.41
14	41	54	2.71	0.43	0.81	1.19	−0.49	0.56
15	33	54	1.37	0.41	0.43	0.23	−2.23	−1.50
16	44	54	3.29	0.46	0.62	0.37	−1.01	0.07
17	45	54	3.51	0.48	1.09	0.45	0.35	0.27
18	29	54	0.71	0.40	1.03	1.00	0.19	0.18
19	37	54	2.02	0.41	0.64	0.28	−1.26	−0.84
20	33	54	1.37	0.41	0.81	0.96	−0.55	0.17
21	41	54	2.71	0.43	0.76	0.23	−0.68	−0.50
22	39	54	2.36	0.41	0.97	0.36	0.02	−0.45
23	44	53	3.33	0.47	2.79	1.08	3.17	0.63
24	41	54	2.71	0.43	0.84	0.43	−0.40	−0.16
25	22	54	−0.40	0.39	1.25	1.63	1.10	1.07
26	40	54	2.53	0.42	1.16	1.32	0.58	0.64
27	34	54	1.53	0.40	1.20	1.77	0.71	1.11
28	38	54	2.19	0.41	0.89	0.75	−0.28	0.05
29	38	54	2.19	0.41	0.91	0.68	−0.20	−0.05
30	38	54	2.19	0.41	1.18	0.55	0.65	−0.23
31	36	54	1.86	0.41	1.18	0.97	0.67	0.24
32	36	54	1.86	0.41	0.26	0.15	−3.44	−1.42
33	18	54	−1.00	0.39	1.47	1.21	2.07	0.52
34	45	54	3.51	0.48	1.68	13.08	1.51	2.77
35	43	54	3.09	0.45	1.48	1.00	1.27	0.51
36	32	54	1.20	0.41	1.09	0.68	0.39	−0.37
37	46	54	3.75	0.49	0.92	0.32	−0.05	0.27
38	39	54	2.36	0.41	0.59	0.42	−1.43	−0.36
39	44	54	3.29	0.46	0.56	0.19	−1.20	−0.17
40	39	54	2.36	0.41	0.54	0.19	−1.68	−0.85
41	39	54	2.36	0.41	1.70	1.72	1.92	0.91
42	44	54	3.29	0.46	0.86	0.34	−0.25	0.03

Mean	2.27	0.96	0.99	–0.19	0.08
SD	1.35	0.44	1.98	1.31	0.82
r	0.89				

Targeting

Whilst the data under investigation here were found to measure the single latent trait of school readiness for these purposes, Rasch measurement requires that tests also be suitably *targeted* to the sample to ensure that the relative difficulty of the items informs the construct under investigation. Thus, for this part of the study, the conservation of number task data and the KIRYO Checklist data were Rasch analysed *separately* to help infer which of the two was more suitably targeted for this sample of young children.

The conservation of number task was found to be the more closely targeted indicator of children's school readiness (see Figure 3). With a mean person ability estimate of –.25 (SD=1.14) (i.e., close to the item mean of 0), it stands as the better-matched test over the KIRYO Checklist (person mean +3.08; SD=1.26), or the three sources of data analysed together (person mean 2.27; SD=1.35). Where only one child was completely unsuccessful on the conservation of number task (achieving a 0 score all on items), 15 children "topped out" with perfect scores on the KIRYO Checklist. This demonstrates clearly that the children found the readiness checklist very easy in comparison to the conservation task. Whilst some would argue that this could be expected of the two criterion-referenced – rather than norm-referenced – testing devices, the results from the year one teachers' readiness judgements suggest that the readiness criteria adopted in the KIRYO Checklist are as inappropriately easy for this sample as evidenced by the foregoing comparison of its measurement properties compared to those of the conservation of number task.

The results reveal that the conservation task is not only well targeted at the sample in order to inform the construct it investigates, but that it is the better targeted of the sample of readiness indicators. As the KIRYO Checklist was far too easy for the sample it was, as a result, less well-matched to enlighten effectively the construct under investigation. Given the evidence, Piaget's conservation of number task stands as the indicator more closely aligned with success in early formal learning environments as judged qualitatively by the year one teachers.

Inter-Relationships

The use of the Rasch Partial Credit model revealed quite remarkable inter-relationships in the data. In particular, it highlighted the close alignment between the year one teachers' qualitative judgements of readiness and some key items in the conservation of number task. Apparently, the Piagetian perspective corresponds nicely with the year one teachers' judgement of 'ready' for year one learning environments (see Figure 4). The consistent conservation judgements (items N6.2, 7.2, and 8.2 – which are used in the conservation of number task to detect the presence and use of concrete operatory structures in a child's thinking) are located at this same 'ready'

313

cut-off zone indicated by the shading in Figure 4. This empirical evidence suggests that an understanding of logical systems is, at least potentially, a likely contributor to the successful achievement of learning outcomes in the formal learning environment of year one. Less equivocally, it seems Piaget's theory of knowledge is relevant to understanding more completely the nature of readiness for a successful transition from preschool to primary school learning environments.

Children's Consistent Conservation Judgements.

Not surprisingly, the empirical evidence in this small-scale study indicated that the preschool teachers' and the year one teachers' understandings of what it means for children to be 'ready' for year one formal learning environments did not concur. The substantial two logit difference between the preschool teachers' and year one teachers' judgements of 'ready' – not to mention the apparent link between the year one teachers' professional judgements and Piagetian theory-driven criteria – is indication of the need for reconsideration of the understanding of 'readiness for formal learning environments' that is held by these preschool teachers, in particular.

```
Conservation of Number Task        KIRYO Checklist Indicators
───────────────────────────────────────────────────────────────────
   4.0                   |          4.0   XXXXXXXXXXXXX |
                         |                              |
                         |                              |
                         |                              |             12
                         |                              |
                         |                              |
                       X |                  XXXXXXX     |
   3.0                   |          3.0                 |
                         |                              |
                         |    9.2                       |
                         |   11.2                 XX    |
                         |    2.2                       |
                       X | 13                           |
                         |   12.2                  X    |
   2.0                   |          2.0                 |
                         |                              |
                         |                         X    |
                       X |                              |
                         |                              |
                         |   11.1                       |  6  9   20
                      XX |    3.2                       |
                         |   10.2                       |       19
   1.0                   |          1.0                 |
                      XX |                              |
                         |    6.2                       |       7 18
                    XXXX |                         X    |
───────────────────────────────────────────────────────────────────
```

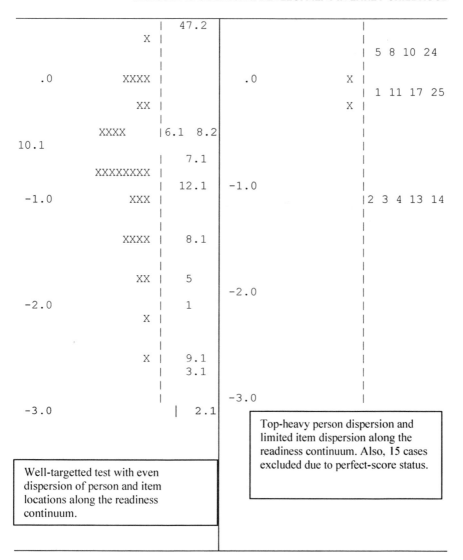

```
                        |  47.2                              |
                  X |                                        |
                    |                                        |  5  8  10  24
     .0       XXXX |              .0                  X   |
                    |                                        |  1  11  17  25
                  XX |                            X   |
                    |                                        |
                XXXX     |6.1  8.2                        |
  10.1                                                       |
                    |   7.1                              |
          XXXXXXXX  |                                        |
                    |  12.1      -1.0                    |
  -1.0          XXX  |                                        |2  3  4  13  14
                    |                                        |
                    |                                        |
                XXXX  |   8.1                              |
                    |                                        |
                    |                                        |
                  XX  |   5                                |
                    |          -2.0                      |
  -2.0              |   1                                |
                  X  |                                        |
                    |                                        |
                    |                                        |
                  X  |   9.1                              |
                    |   3.1                              |
                    |                                        |
                    |          -3.0                      |
  -3.0              |   2.1
```

Top-heavy person dispersion and limited item dispersion along the readiness continuum. Also, 15 cases excluded due to perfect-score status.

Well-targetted test with even dispersion of person and item locations along the readiness continuum.

Figure 3. Targeting of conservation of number task in comparison to the KIRYO checklist indicators.

Caveat Emptor

It should be noted that the co-calibration presented here is the first Rasch-estimated 'look' at exploring the potential relationships between teachers' professional judgements, and children's performances on both a routinely used school readiness checklist and Piaget's conservation of number task. Whilst no previous statistical indicators for the reliability and validity of the KIRYO Readiness Checklist and teacher's readiness judgements are available for comparison, the item characteristics for the conservation of number task (as revealed in Figure 2 and Table 1) were found to be consistent with those first established by Drake (1998). As all conservation task interviews were administered, examined and scored by the researcher, inter-rater reliability for the number task is not an issue in this study. With regards to the teachers' qualitative judgements and readiness checklist assessments, it was the usual professional practice for these teachers to crosscheck and engage in professional reflective discussion regarding these items; however, this was not completed in any formal way. Indeed, the feedback of the quantitative results of this investigation stimulated ongoing professional discussion – at least amongst the pre-school teachers themselves.

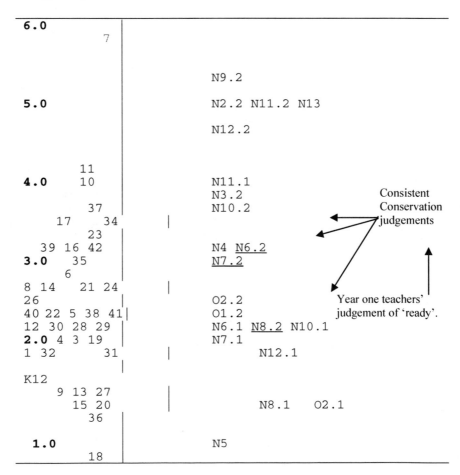

```
              |       P1.2    O1.1
              |       N1
              |
              |       K6 K9 K20    N9.1
  0.0         |       N3.1
              |       K19
        25    |
              |       K7 K18       N2.1
              |
              |
 -1.0   33    |       K5 K8 K10 K24
              |
              |
              |       K1 K11 K17 K25
              |
        2     |
 -2.0         |   |        P1.1
              |   |
              |   |
              |       K2 K3 K4 K13 K14 K15 K16 K21
              |   |       K23 K26 K28
              |   |
 -3.0         | KIRYO   Cons Number    Teacher Judgement
```

Note. Year one teachers' qualitative judgement of 'ready'.

Figure 4. Conservation of number task and year one teachers'
qualitative readiness judgements.

Whilst the use of the above-mentioned items should be implemented in a large-scale, cross-sectional replication of this investigation, this small-scale study was exploratory and completed in one site by one researcher with the teachers and students who volunteered and cooperated. Thus, the larger than preferred person and item errors and the lack of a specific Rasch modelling of inter-rater variability are considered to be relevant caveats underlying interpretation, rather than dis-qualifying features of this exploratory investigation. The aim was to apply the Rasch model to illuminate the issue of school readiness and the possibility of its relationships with Piagetian cognitive development – it's not the high-stakes rigour of the illuminant that's important here, rather it's the nature of what is potentially illuminated, and noted for ongoing, more demanding investigation.

IMPLICATIONS

The 29 skills-based items that make up the KIRYO checklist apparently do not stand as appropriate indicators of readiness for successful outcomes in the year one learning environment. The empirical evidence herein suggests that a more com-prehensive preschool readiness checklist would benefit from the inclusion of some cognitive developmental indicators in the Piagetian tradition, not just the more rudimentary functional and mechanical skills such as K11 'gluing' and K13 'mouse control on computer'. As asserted earlier in this paper, and commonly argued, cognitive development is not necessarily dependent on an increase in psychomotor skills.

There is no doubt that being able to glue neatly and use a computer mouse steadfastly are useful for both children and their year one teachers. However, on the current evidence, it seems far more important for children to be ready cognitively, rather than merely physically, for successful learning outcomes if they aim to avoid progression and achievement problems in later schooling. It is now widely accepted that success in early learning is a strong predictor of future successful schooling. Thus, the transition from preschool to year one learning environments is a crucial time for all young learners and they deserve the most appropriate of all tools on which judgements about their futures can be confidently made. The strong empirical evidence of a continuum of readiness presented in this small-scale exploratory investigation provides another example of the functionality of the Piagetian framework for the school education sector.

As indicated by these results, preschool teachers should reflect upon possibly extending their ideas about what it means to be ready for successful learning outcomes in the formal year one learning environment. Children's actual levels of successful achievement, as recorded by their year one teachers half-way through that year, indicate that half the children were not ready in spite of the preschool teachers' earlier professional judgement of 'ready'. Conversely, the case might also have been that the year one teachers were so concerned with syllabus content they continued to teach regardless of the apparent lack of readiness of the children in their classes for those learning experiences. In either case, the lack of a shared professional understanding of the concept of readiness for the year one learning environment amongst teachers at this crucial transition point seems, on the surface, indefensible. At best, it presents as a potentially serious discontinuity in children's learning experiences and their teachers' expectations of them at an important transitional period.

The results of this exploratory study have highlighted several key areas where advances can be made. Foremost, teachers' judgements about children's progression to year one should be more developmentally sensitive and include an understanding of the Piagetian framework. In addition, the inclusion of several indicators based on children's understandings of logical systems, especially conservation of number concepts, on preschool readiness checklists could assist in inferring those children not yet ready for year one. Finally, all of these teachers could endeavour to be more responsive to the varying levels of cognitive development in children of similar age ranges in their class.

Indeed, the results for the persons and items under investigation in this small-scale study indicate that Piagetian theory and school readiness, together, are worthy of continued more rigorous investigation. This small study capitalises on the capacity of the Rasch model to deal meaningfully with small data sets, to resolve in the face of missing data and, most importantly, to align persons and items on the same interval-level measurement scale. Future studies could benefit from more sophisticated Rasch analysis to examine further the interactions between items and persons and their judges, as well as the internal structure and validity of the school readiness variable.

REFERENCES

Adams, R. J., & Khoo, S. T. (1993). *Quest: The interactive test analysis system.* Hawthorn: ACER.

Baldwin, A. L. (1980). *Theories of child development* (2nd ed.). New York: John Wiley & Sons.

Boardman, M. (2006). The impact of age and gender on prep children's academic achievements. *Australian Journal of Early Childhood, 31*(4), 1–6.

Bond, T. G. (2001). Ready for school? Ready for learning? An empirical contribution to a perennial debate. *The Australian Educational and Developmental Psychologist, 18*(1), 77–80.

Bond, T. G. (2003). Relationships between cognitive development and school achievement: A Rasch measurement approach. In R. F. Waugh (Ed.), *On the forefront of educational psychology* (pp. 37–46). New York: Nova Science Publishers.

Bond, T. G., & Fox, C. M. (2001). *Applying the Rasch model: Fundamental measurement in the human sciences.* Mahwah, NJ: Lawrence Erlbaum Associates.

Bond, T. G., & Fox, C. M. (2007). *Applying the Rasch model: Fundamental measurement in the human sciences* (2nd ed.). Mahwah, NJ: Lawrence Erlbaum Associates.

Bond, T. G., & Parkinson, K. (2010). Children's understanding of area concepts: Development, curriculum and educational achievement. In M. Wilson, G. Engelhard & M. Garner (Eds.), *Advances in Rasch measurement* (Vol. I, pp. 529–552). Maple Grove, MN: JAM Press.

Bunting, E. (1993). *A qualitative and quantitative analysis of Piaget's control of variables scheme.* Unpublished Honours Thesis. Townsville: James Cook University of North Queensland.

Clift, S., Stagnitti, K., & DeMello, L. (2000). A developmentally appropriate test of kinder/school readiness. *Australian Journal of Early Childhood, 25*(4), 22–26.

Drake, C. (1998). *Judgements versus justifications in Piaget's control of variables scheme.* Unpublished Thesis. Townsville: James Cook University of North Queensland.

Elkind, D. (1981). *The hurried child: Growing up too fast, too soon.* Canada: Addison-Wesley Publishing Company.

Elkind, D. (1986, May). Formal education and early childhood education: An essential difference. *Phi Delta Kappan,* 631–636.

Elkind, D. (1989, October). Developmentally appropriate practice: Philosophical and practical implications. *Phi Delta Kappan,* 113–117.

Flavell, J. H., Miller, P. H., & Miller, S. A. (2002). *Cognitive development* (4th ed.). Upper Saddle River, NJ: Prentice Hall.

Ginsburg, H., & Opper, S. (1988). *Piaget's theory of intellectual development* (3rd ed.). New Jersey, NJ: Prentice Hall.

Gruber, H. E., & Vonèche, J. J. (1977). *The essential Piaget.* London: Routledge & Kegan Paul, Ltd.

Maley, C. R. (2005). *Examining the role of cognitive development as an indicator of school readiness: An empirical contribution to a perennial debate.* Unpublished Honours Thesis. Townsville: James Cook University.

Piaget, J. (1961). *The child's conception of number* (2nd ed.). London: Routledge and Kegan Paul Ltd.

Piaget, J. (1970). *The origin of intelligence in the child* (3rd ed.). London: Routledge and Kegan Paul Ltd.

Piaget, J., & Szeminska, A. (1941/1952). *The child's conception of number.* London: Routledge & Kegan Paul.

Smidt, S. (1998). *A guide to early years practice.* New York: Routlege.

Vernon, P. E. (1976). Environment and intelligence. In V. P. Varma & P. Williams (Eds.), *Piaget, psychology and education: Papers in honour of Jean Piaget.* London: Hodder and Stoughton.

Wallach, L. (1969). On the bases of conservation. In D. Elkind & J. H. Flavell (Eds.), *Studies in cognitive development: Essays in honour of Jean Piaget.* New York: Oxford University Press.

Wood, D. (1998). *How children think and learn* (2nd ed.). Oxford: Blackwell.

Claire Maley and Trevor Bond
(School of Education, James Cook University, Queensland)

APPENDIX A

Conservation of Number Performance Criteria Derived from *The Child's Conception of Number* (Piaget, 1961) by Drake (1998, p. 45–46)

Item	Stage I: Absence of conservation	Stage II: Intermediary reactions	Stage III: Necessary conservation
N1	1.0 Incorrectly identifies the number of counters in the first set constructed.	1.1 Correctly identifies the number of counters in the first set constructed.	
N2	2.0 Global comparison: Does not construct equivalent second set. Reliance on perceptual cues.	2.1 Intuitive correspondence: Constructs equivalent second set using one to one correspondence: set constructed is identical to first.	2.2 Operational correspondence: Constructs equivalent sets using one to one correspondences, without making both sets look identical.
N3	3.0 Constructs equivalent sets only with assistance.	3.1 Carefully constructs sets, checking to ensure equivalence.	3.2 Constructs equivalent sets easily and quickly with confidence.
N4	4.0 Counts the second array to determine the number of counters within it.	4.1 Infers that the second array must be composed of the same number of counters as the first.	
N5	5.0 Does not infer the equivalence of the two arrays or infers the equivalence with assistance.	5.1 Infers the equivalence of the two arrays independently.	
N6	6.0 Judges that the equivalence of the two sets is changed if the appearance of one set is lengthened.	6.1 Sometimes correctly judges that the equivalence of the two sets remains the same if the appearance of one set is lengthened.	6.2 Consistently judges that the equivalence of the two sets remains the same if the appearance of one set is lengthened.

N7	7.0 Judges that the equivalence of the two sets is changed if the appearance of one set is condensed.	7.1 Sometimes correctly judges that the equivalence of the two sets remains the same if the appearance of one set is condensed.	7.2 Consistently judges that the equivalence of the two sets remains the same if the appearance of one set is condensed.
N8	8.0 Judges that the equivalence of the two sets is changed when faced with the Müller-Lyer effect.	8.1 Sometimes correctly judges that the equivalence of the two sets remains the same when faced with the Müller-Lyer effect.	8.2 Consistently judges that the equivalence of the two sets remains the same when faced with the Müller-Lyer effect.
N9	9.0 Makes no justifications, limited to judgements.	9.1 Uses illogical, inconsistent reasoning or counting to justify the variance or invariance of the two sets.	9.2 Uses logical reasoning to consistently justify the invariance of the two sets.
N10	10.0 Does not use identity argument to justify belief.	10.1 Uses identity argument illogically or inconsistently to justify the variance or invariance of the two sets.	10.2 Justifies true belief referring to the identity argument.
N11	11.0 Does not use reversibility argument to justify belief.	11.1 Uses reversibility argument illogically or inconsistently to justify the variance or invariance of the two sets.	11.2 Justifies true belief referring to the reversibility by inversion argument.
N12	12.0 Does not use compensation argument to justify belief.	12.1 Uses compensation argument illogically or inconsistently to justify the variance or invariance of the two sets.	12.2 Justifies true belief referring to the compensation argument.
N13		13.0 Does not refer to the necessary nature of conservation.	13.1 Refers to the necessary nature of conservation.

The Key Indicators of Readiness for Year One (KIRYO) Checklist

Item		score 0	1	Item		score 0	1
K1	Balancing			K16	Makes independent choices		
K2	Running			K17	Persists with tasks, copes with failure		
K3	Jumping			K18	Mixes well with other children		
K4	Climbing (scramble net)			K19	Understands the purpose of group rules and complies		
K5	Hopping			K20	Shares, takes, turns, negotiates roles and resolves conflicts		
K6	Skipping			K21	Sorts and matches objects by colour		
K7	Kicking a ball			K22	Names and matches basic colours		
K8	Throwing / catching a ball			K23	Copies basic pattern e.g. two colour patterns		
K9	Cutting			K24	Drawing ability		
K10	Threading			K25	Completes a nine piece puzzle using a variety of strategies		
K11	Gluing			K26	Gives simple descriptions of past events		
K12	Pencil grip			K27	Uses own grammar style, which is approximation of adult grammar		
K13	Mouse control on computer			K28	Is beginning to develop awareness of listener needs and provides feedback on information when introducing a new topic		
K14	Expresses needs, feelings & ideas						
K15	Comprehends spoken or visual messages			K29	Shows an interest in explanations of how and why		

Preschool Teachers' Qualitative Judgements about Student Progression to Year One

Item	Score		
	0	1	2
P1	30.0 "Not yet ready" for probable success in year one	30.1 "Nearly ready" for probable success in year one	30.2 "Ready" for probable success in year one

Year One Teachers' Qualitative Judgements about Student Progression to Year One

Item	Score		
	0	1	2
O1	31.0 "Not yet ready" for probable success in year one	31.1 "Nearly ready" for probable success in year one	31.2 "Ready" for probable success in year one
O2	32.0 "Not yet at level" in achievement of year one KLA outcomes	32.1 "Nearly at level" in achievement of year one KLA outcomes	32.2 "At level" in achievement of year one KLA outcomes

INDEX

CPSIA information can be obtained at www.ICGtesting.com
Printed in the USA

269993BV00004B/27/P

9 789460 914911